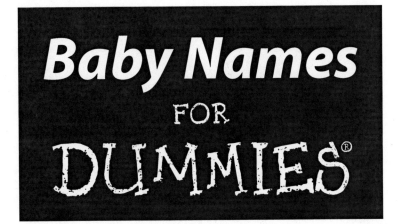

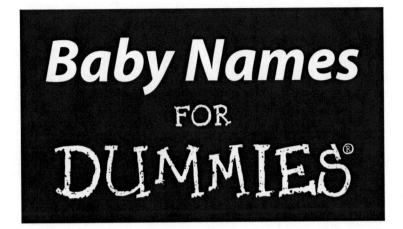

Baby Names FOR DUMMIES®

by Margaret Rose

WILEY

Wiley Publishing, Inc.

Baby Names For Dummies®

Published by
Wiley Publishing, Inc.
111 River St.
Hoboken, NJ 07030-5774
www.wiley.com

WILEY

About the Author

Margaret Rose has a PhD in linguistics and has been researching historic names and naming practices for the last twenty years. In addition to the academic research, she has had the unusual experience of helping hundreds of people choose names — not for their children but for characters they play in historic re-creation groups. She has also been a consultant on historic names for novels and movies (unproduced, alas).

Dedication

For Seth, because when I was seventeen I promised him my first book — although neither of us would have predicted it would be this one!

Author's Acknowledgments

The best research is done in the context of a community of researchers who, even if they don't contribute directly to a work, encourage the interest, sharpen the skills, and keep one honest. In this spirit, I want to give thanks to a long line of "name geeks" in whose company my research has been done, and especially to Sharon, Judy, and Brian. I also want to acknowledge the invaluable data on name popularity provided by the Social Security Administration at: `http://www.socialsecurity.gov/OACT/babynames/`.

Publisher's Acknowledgments

We're proud of this book; please send us your comments through our Dummies online registration form located at www.dummies.com/register/.

Some of the people who helped bring this book to market include the following:

Acquisitions, Editorial, and Media Development

Project Editor: Jennifer Connolly

Acquisitions Editor: Tracy Boggier

Copy Editor: Jennifer Connolly

Technical Editor: Sharon Krossa

Editorial Manager: Michelle Hacker

Editorial Supervisor: Carmen Krikorian

Editorial Assistant: Hanna Scott

Cover Photos: © Hank Morgan/AGE Fotostock

Cartoons: Rich Tennant www.the5thwave.com

Composition Services

Project Coordinator: Adrienne Martinez

Layout and Graphics: Carl Byers, Andrea Dahl, Joyce Haughey, Stephanie D. Jumper, Heather Ryan, Mary Gillot Virgin

Proofreaders: Leeann Harney, Jessica Kramer, TECHBOOKS Production Services

Indexer: Sherry Massey

Publishing and Editorial for Consumer Dummies

> **Diane Graves Steele,** Vice President and Publisher, Consumer Dummies
>
> **Joyce Pepple,** Acquisitions Director, Consumer Dummies
>
> **Kristin A. Cocks,** Product Development Director, Consumer Dummies
>
> **Michael Spring,** Vice President and Publisher, Travel
>
> **Kelly Regan,** Editorial Director, Travel

Publishing for Technology Dummies

> **Andy Cummings,** Vice President and Publisher, Dummies Technology/General User

Composition Services

> **Gerry Fahey,** Vice President of Production Services
>
> **Debbie Stailey,** Director of Composition Services

Contents at a Glance

Table of Contents

Introduction

⬤ ⬤

*N*ames are a passion of mine: understanding what they mean, where they come from, and how they're used. Ordinarily this may seem like a rather dry, academic pursuit, but everyone has a name and it seems that everyone is fascinated to find out more about the subject. I have had the good fortune to find many opportunities to share my passion with others, or to use it to guide them in their name choices. This book is yet another chance to do so, and I'm grateful for the opportunity.

About This Book

With all the registering for baby items, buying baby clothes, trying to figure out why it takes an entire afternoon to install the car seat, figuring out how that stroller actually breaks down with one hand (that has to be a myth), deciding between seven shades of what you really think are the same color for the nursery, attending baby showers, opening baby gifts, writing thank-you notes (who said life would be tiring *after* the baby?), and picking out all the toys and books that promise to make your child the next Nobel prize winner, who has time to sift through an entire phone books' worth of entries in a baby-names book?

I understand that your time is valuable, so this book gives you the cream of the crop: the best tips on choosing a name, the greatest ways to find inspiration, and the pick of the litter of names that are actually in common use.

If you feel daunted by the whole process, use this book to lead you through a few beginning exercises to get you limbered up. If you already have decided ideas about choosing names, use this book to find some other angles to consider to focus and test those ideas. If you simply want to devour all the possible information on the topic, use this book to find a smorgasbord of ideas and facts to digest.

Conventions Used in This Book

Luckily, you don't have to read the book cover to cover, if you don't want to, but you can if you feel so inclined (there are, however, no bonus points or potential for extra-good karma for doing so). Just check out the table of contents in the front of this book to find the section or sections that interest you and read them. Or, if you're feeling whimsical, just open the book to any section that strikes your fancy and start reading!

To make getting to the information easier, I not only use icons to direct you to particular tips and great pieces of advice (see "Icons Used in This Book," later in this chapter), I also use the following conventions:

- **Language:** When discussing the history and usage of names, unless otherwise noted, this book refers to usage generally in Europe, more narrowly in the English-speaking world, and most specifically in the United States.

- **Name popularity:** Information on name popularity prior to the 20th century is drawn from many sources, but for information as of 1900, I use the name statistics generously provided by the U.S. Social Security administration, based on the names on applications for Social Security identification numbers. This information covers the 1,000 most popular names for each gender in each decade, or in each year for the last decade. When the discussion of a name mentions it being "on the (popularity) charts," these lists are what is meant.

- **All caps:** Although all caps usually means that someone is "yelling" at you, I use all caps for each name entry. Plus, if you see an all-caps name within an entry, that's a signal that you can find an entry for that particular name elsewhere in the book (a handy cross-reference accompanies each all-caps name to make finding the entry even easier).

- **Index:** The index is your friend! I arrange the entries of names by topic (each chapter covers a different topic) and then alphabetically in each chapter. So, if you're looking for particular names, or if you want to quickly browse through the names listed in this book, flip back to the index.

- **Gender:** After each name listed in the book, you see an **(f)**, indicating a name primarily used for girls, an **(m)**, indicating a name primarily used for boys, or **(f, m)**, indicating a name used for both genders.

- **Boldface:** When reading through a name's entry, any name that you see in boldface represents a shortened version or variant of the name being discussed.

- **Name origin:** Many people are looking for an Irish, Arabic, Latin, or some other specific origin when choosing a name for their children. If this describes you, you simply have to look at the very beginning of the name entry (okay, after the name itself and gender symbol) to see from what origin the name derives. Sometimes you may just see a "?" which means the origin is unknown; however, if you see a question mark following the origin (as in "Gaelic?"), this means that the origin may be as listed but is uncertain.

How This Book Is Organized

This book is organized in parts, with several chapters in each part, exploring some particular theme. Here is a brief tour of the contents.

Part 1: Getting Ready to Name Your Baby!

While this book, as a whole, is about *what* to name your baby, Part I covers *how* to name your baby. There is a whole range of factors to consider, and while you may not consider all of them important, trying them on for size can help you find the preferences and styles that fit your needs best. Read this section — more than anything else, it's what makes this book different from the next one on the shelf.

Part II: Finding Names from Religion and Literature

Whether I take names from the books of the great religions, or from novels, plays, and poetry, these names come with detailed and fascinating stories attached. One of the definitions of literature is that it endures across time, and for this reason literary names have been a way to bridge the centuries, reviving classic names again and again.

Part III: Naming through the Ages

If you hear the name Jennifer, Emily, or Heather, you'll immediately have an idea of when that person was born. And although you may be wrong in individual cases, the fact remains that naming fashions have changed over time, and that particular names are characteristic of particular eras. This section takes a brief tour through the centuries, examining names that were popular in various eras.

Part IV: Describing the World: Names of Quality, Character, and Location

At some point in life, everyone will ask, "What does my name mean?" With only a few exceptions, if you dig far enough back, every name means something. The chapters in this section explore some of the common types of meaning that have produced names, from virtues and descriptions, to locations and forces of nature. Meaning can also come from the associations a name brings, and this section covers names associated with particular cultures.

Part V: Seeking the Stars: Names from Popular Culture

Name fashions arise from the names we hear, and those names that more people hear are more likely to become fashionable. So it isn't surprising that TV and film stars, characters on the big or small screens, and nationally known sports heroes have had a disproportionate influence on which names become popular. Even popular songs have produced fashionable names.

Part VI: The Part of Tens

This section presents additional resources and reviews as well as some important considerations in choosing a name.

Icons Used in This Book

Throughout this book, you'll see icons that easily flag you toward particular facts or useful information that you need.

To quickly find great pieces of advice, look for this icon.

Although you can't possibly remember everything you read in this book, this icon points out particular paragraphs that you won't want to forget!

Whenever you see this icon, you can either skip the technical or historical info found in that paragraph, or you can just read right through it for some great enlightenment.

Part I
Getting Ready to Name Your Baby!

The 5th Wave   By Rich Tennant

"We're going to stick to a more traditional name for the baby—'Chuckles', 'Zippy', something like that."

In this part . . .

While this book, as a whole, is about *what* to name your baby, Part I covers *how* to name your baby. There is a whole range of factors to consider, and while you may not consider all of them important, trying them on for size can help you find the preferences and styles that fit your needs best. Read this section — more than anything else, it's what makes this book different from the next one on the shelf.

Chapter 1

What's in a Name?

So why do people make such a fuss about choosing the right name? After all, it's just a label. Life would be so much simpler if we were all assigned unique ID numbers at birth, right? Despite the occasional oddity who may legally change his name to "789223," we have a strong sense that names are more than just an arbitrary "handle" for identifying and addressing people. Across the scope of time and space, names have been used for description, to identify a person's place in society, to shape a person's life and character, even sometimes as a type of magic charm to bless or protect the bearer.

Okay, so you thought parenting was going to be tough, and now you may think choosing a name will be even tougher. Well, don't worry. I've broken down some general ideas on choosing names in this chapter so you can get warmed up for your quest for *the name*.

Making Sure You Understand the Process

When you distract yourself from the serious terrors of parenting with the less daunting task of choosing the exactly right name for your child, it can be useful to keep in mind two opposing principles:

✔ **You can't win:** No matter what name you pick, there's a 50-50 chance that your child will hate it at some point. The child given a dignified traditional name will bewail the cultural straitjacket you've imposed on him and declare that henceforth he will only answer to "Sablewolf." The child with the imaginative colorful name will be permanently scarred by having to constantly correct people's pronunciation and spelling. The name carefully chosen to have only positive associations will appear in next year's hit sitcom for the obnoxious buffoon. And your favorite nickname for your child will pop up in the next generation's slang with a really unfortunate meaning. You can't win. Don't sweat it.

✔ **This isn't about you:** As a friend of mine is fond of pointing out, children are named when they're very small and unable to defend themselves. You see your child's name as an opportunity for creative expression, but she's going to have to wear it. This isn't going to be a fancy holiday outfit that the kid only has to squirm through a few parties in — it's going to be her second skin. Pick the name the way you would a special gift: something the receiver can use and make their own, not something meant to look pretty on a shelf but totally impractical in everyday life.

Planning the Decision Process

Because you are reading this book, I assume that you're interested in putting some thought into the decision process. (Either that, or you simply enjoy reading name books.) The key factor is not to leave things until the last minute. Very few people have their greatest creativity under pressure — the rest of us do better when we have some breathing space for our brainstorming. When you think you've found *the name,* allow some time for it to grow on you or to grow stale. If you're tired of a name before the baby comes, then it probably wasn't the perfect name after all. Give yourself a chance to bounce your ideas off other people.

Knowing the Territory

Names don't exist in a vacuum. Much of your and your child's experience depends not simply on the choice of name, but on how that name fits into present and past naming cultures. As a foretaste, Figure 1-1 shows the top-ten most popular names for boys and girls for each decade of the last century. Notice that it isn't simply the individual names that change in position, but the overall nature of the popular names may change dramatically over time.

Figure 1-1: A chart showing the top-ten boys' and girls' names over the last century.

Boys (31 different names)

Rank	1900s	1910s	1920s	1930s	1940s	1950s	1960s	1970s	1980s	1990s	2000s
1	John	John	Robert	Robert	James	Michael	Michael	Michael	Michael	Michael	Jacob
2	William	William	John	James	Robert	James	David	Christopher	Christopher	Christopher	Michael
3	James	James	James	John	John	Robert	John	Jason	Matthew	Matthew	Joshua
4	George	Robert	William	William	William	John	James	David	Joshua	Joshua	Matthew
5	Joseph	Joseph	Charles	Richard	Richard	David	Robert	James	David	Jacob	Andrew
6	Charles	George	George	Charles	David	William	Mark	John	Daniel	Andrew	Joseph
7	Robert	Charles	Joseph	Donald	Charles	Richard	William	Robert	James	Daniel	Ethan
8	Frank	Edward	Richard	George	Thomas	Thomas	Richard	Brian	Robert	Nicholas	Daniel
9	Edward	Frank	Edward	Thomas	Michael	Mark	Thomas	William	John	Tyler	Christopher
10	Henry	Walter	Donald	Joseph	Ronald	Charles	Jeffrey	Matthew	Joseph	Joseph	Anthony

Girls (55 different names)

Rank	1900s	1910s	1920s	1930s	1940s	1950s	1960s	1970s	1980s	1990s	2000s
1	Mary	Mary	Mary	Mary	Mary	Mary	Lisa	Jennifer	Jessica	Ashley	Emily
2	Helen	Helen	Dorothy	Betty	Linda	Linda	Mary	Amy	Jennifer	Jessica	Emma
3	Margaret	Dorothy	Helen	Barbara	Barbara	Patricia	Karen	Melissa	Amanda	Emily	Madison
4	Anna	Margaret	Betty	Shirley	Patricia	Susan	Susan	Michelle	Ashley	Sarah	Hannah
5	Ruth	Ruth	Margaret	Patricia	Carol	Deborah	Kimberly	Kimberly	Sarah	Samantha	Olivia
6	Elizabeth	Mildred	Ruth	Dorothy	Sandra	Barbara	Patricia	Lisa	Stephanie	Britany	Abigail
7	Dorothy	Anna	Virginia	Joan	Nancy	Debra	Linda	Angela	Melissa	Amanda	Alexis
8	Marie	Elizabeth	Doris	Margaret	Judith	Karen	Donna	Heather	Nicole	Elizabeth	Ashley
9	Mildred	Frances	Mildred	Nancy	Sharon	Nancy	Michelle	Stephanie	Elizabeth	Tailor	Elizabeth
10	Alice	Marie	Elizabeth	Helen	Susan	Donna	Cynthia	Jessica	Heather	Megan	Samantha

Exploring ideas of naming

Across the ages, names have been chosen by many different methods. Your name may indicate your place in the family. It may give other circumstances of birth, such as the day of the week or some special holiday. There may be a traditional formula that assigns each child the name of a particular relative. Some cultures give you a "baby name" to start with and then an adult name when you grow into it. In other cultures you may change your name to commemorate a notable event in your life, or to change your luck. It's not uncommon in some cultures to have multiple names used for different purposes — we do this informally in America, but in other cultures the names may be very different from each other but all have legal status.

Sharing the Fun

Some of you may be looking forward to raising a child on your own, but most will be sharing the experience with a partner. And if you're fortunate, your child's life will also be full of relatives and friends who have a stake in seeing him grow up happy.

Remember to share the fun of choosing a name with the other key people in your child's life. This isn't to say that you need to try to please everyone, but try to show that you value their opinions. If it seems like one parent feels much more strongly about names, the other parent may bow out of the process to avoid conflict and feel left out. Always leave room for negotiation. If it's absolutely imperative that your first son be named after your father, suggest that your partner choose a diminutive of the name for everyday. If you're dead set against a particular type of name, try to explain why, rather than making it sound arbitrary.

Chapter 2

Considering the Factors in Picking Out a Name

In This Chapter

▶ Understanding your likes and dislikes in names

▶ Avoiding common pitfalls in naming

▶ Familiarizing yourself with name fashions

Chances are, you've given careful thought to some aspects of naming your child, but others may have never occurred to you yet. Some of the considerations in this chapter may seem obvious; others may seem irrelevant; others will provoke an "Aha!" or "Hmm!" moment. My idea isn't to overwhelm you with details and worries in this chapter, but to give you a chance to discover which aspects of names are important to you. (You can find more information on actually putting the name itself together in Chapter 3.)

Selecting a Name You Like and Your Child Can Live With

Right now, you're probably feeling very possessive about your child, which is only natural because you have all the control (and responsibility) over what your child's experiences will be, including the choice of a name. But while it would be silly to pick a name that you, yourself don't like, it's just as important to put yourself into your child's future shoes and try to make sure that he or she will like it as well.

Figuring out what kinds of names you like

If this is the first time you've thought about what sorts of names you like, you're a pretty unusual person. Most of us — even those who like our names — have fantasized about what name we wish we had. You may have picked names for pets or toys, or maybe you've written stories and chosen names for the characters. At the very least, you've probably heard names and thought, "How nice!" (Or, on occasion, "What were his parents thinking?") You may even have spent time thinking about what you'd like to name your own children. Now is the time to look at your likes and dislikes more deliberately and closely. In this section, I give you a couple of exercises to try to make sorting out your likes and dislikes a bit easier.

Here's a good exercise to start with:

1. **Make a list of names of people you don't know** (so you won't be prejudiced by how you feel about the individual). Good sources would be business directories, lists of students or the like, or lists of currently popular baby names.

2. **Rate how much you like the name,** say on a scale of one to five.

3. **Look for your "likes" by checking for the following in your rankings:**

   • Patterns that occur often, such as Biblical names

   • Certain sounds that show up a lot, such as the initial sounds of Carl, Kelly, and Cody

   • Names that share a particular length or rhythm, such as Angela, Melanie, and Emily.

   • Similar types of names, such as mostly traditional or mostly colorful

How we react to or feel about certain names is bound up with our experiences with the people bearing them, so it's important not only to consider whether you like a name esthetically — as a sound and on paper — but whether you like the people it reminds you of.

This exercise can give you a sense of whether you would be happier naming your child after a friend or relative, or whether you would really prefer a certain "look and feel."

Just follow these steps:

1. **Think about the names of people you know: relatives, friends, co-workers.**

2. **Make a list of the names you like from among them.**

3. **Add in the names of your favorite characters from books, movies, or TV.**

4. **Compare the two lists, asking yourself the following questions:**

   • Do you feel more strongly about names based on sound and appearance or based on who they remind you of?

   • Are there any names that show up on both lists?

Testing the name

When branding companies design new product names, they survey potential customers for their reactions to the names and what images they associate with them. It would be silly to test your name that thoroughly, but a little bit of outside feedback can save you a lot of trouble and regret. There are things you'll think are obvious about the names you like — how to say them, what they mean, what images they bring up — that may not be as universal as you think. Several aspects of a child's name can be worth testing on an audience before you find yourself too firmly attached to your choice. But make sure the people you survey understand that you're looking for reactions, *not* asking them to decide for you!

Because you're not asking people to decide on a name for you, you may find it's easier to go outside the immediate family for feedback. Your parents, especially, are likely to interpret "What do you think about these names?" as "Please pick something for me."

Asking a friend or neighbor

Particularly if you are considering an unusual name, or an unusual spelling of a name, you should try out the written form on a variety of people and ask how they would pronounce it. This can give you a sense of how much time your child is going to spend correcting (or just steaming about) people's pronunciations of the name.

If you're considering an unusual pronunciation of a familiar name, try it out on people to see if they have trouble understanding it. Or it may be that people will mis-hear the name as something more familiar.

Write the name out in different ways (printed, cursive, and typed) and see how people comment on it.

Asking a child

If you really want to know what sort of teasing your child may receive over a name, ask a child. Better yet, ask a group of children. If you're lucky enough to know a group of grade school children who are on familiar terms with you, tell them the name you're considering and ask what sorts of nicknames they would make from it. (You may need to get them loosened up and giggly first. Tell them about funny nicknames you had and ask about nicknames their friends call them.)

Asking the world

We currently have an excellent and easy way to find out what the world at large thinks about a name: the World Wide Web. Use your favorite Internet search engine and plug in the individual names you're considering (in all their spelling variants). Try various combinations as phrases by putting them in quotation marks (for example, "first + last," "first + middle + last"). Here's what such a search can reveal about your choice:

- ✔ Some well-known (or notorious) person may share the same full name that you're considering for your child.

- ✔ The number of "hits" a search finds can tell you how popular the name is, or if some bearer is particularly famous. (If you find a large number of people with the same full name you're planning to give your child, consider the possibilities for confusion of identity.)

- ✔ Some search engines will suggest a different spelling for the name if you're using a spelling that it doesn't consider standard. (This can be a clue that you've picked a spelling that people may consider a typo.)

- ✔ Your search may discover brand names, companies, or ordinary words identical to the names you're considering. Consider what sorts of associations they have.

Asking yourself

You'll be using this name every day for quite a long time. You should make sure that you'll like it as much in the future as you do on first glance. On the other hand, if a name doesn't tickle your fancy at first but there's a good reason to keep on considering it (for example, if your partner really, really likes it), give it a chance to grow on you. Use these ways to test the name for yourself:

- ✔ **Write the name out in several variations and post them somewhere that you'll look several times a day.** If you post the name somewhere like the bathroom mirror, the refrigerator door, or your computer desktop, you can see how you feel about the name after a couple of days or even a week.

✔ **Imagine various everyday contexts in which you will be addressing or talking to your child.** Play-act calling out to your child in a group of friends or announcing dinner time. Imagine yourself trying to get your child's attention across a crowded store. Practice saying goodnight as you tuck your child in. Say each of these out loud and see how it sounds. (There's no point in sternly scolding your child with his full formal name if you burst out giggling every time you say it.)

✔ **Imagine important milestones in your child's life — especially as an adult.** You're listening to a play-by-play announcement on the sports field. The announcer lists names over the loudspeaker at a graduation ceremony. You're opening a wedding invitation with your child's name embossed in gold. You spot your child's name on an office door. You turn on the radio and hear an announcement from the Nobel Prize committee. (Okay, maybe you need to scale the fantasies back a little.) Will the name you're considering hold its own in a wide range of contexts? Does it have the flexibility to be both formal and familiar? Can it play as well as preside over meetings?

Watching out for naming pitfalls

Just because you don't want to follow naming rules or patterns, doesn't mean that just anything goes. And just because you plan to follow the rules doesn't mean you won't make any mistakes. Luckily for you, I've compiled the following list of ways to avoid common mistakes parents make when picking a name for their children:

✔ **Start anywhere except the beginning of baby-name lists.** Have you ever wondered why there seem to be so many people with names beginning with "A"? Baby-name lists are usually organized alphabetically. Most people don't read through the entirety of "500,000 Baby Names" before starting to fall in love with a few choices. This means that, statistically, people who pick names this way are more likely to pick a name earlier in the alphabet. One reason this book is organized by topic rather than strictly alphabetically is to avoid this tendency.

✔ **Know where your name ideas come from.** If a name "just comes to you" and you can't remember where you got the idea for it, try to find out more about the name. Especially in the case of unusual or invented names, chances are you didn't simply come up with it off the top of your head. If you can't remember where it came from, how do you know it doesn't mean (or refer to) something embarrassing? Find out if it was a product name, or a small town in Eritrea, or the latest obscure espresso drink. If the name is at all questionable, you can be sure that at some point in your child's life, she will run into someone who recognizes it.

✔ **Check out the current popularity (if any) of a name you are considering.** You'd be surprised how many parents first discover that they've picked the current number-1 name when their child hits pre-school and then wish they had chosen something less common. Names move quickly up and down the charts these days, so you can't assume that you'd automatically know whether a name is in the top ten.

✔ **Discuss and consider names for both genders** even if you're absolutely sure what gender your child will be (even ultrasound has been known to be wrong). There's nothing quite like going through life named Adam solely because your parents thought you were going to be a girl and when push came to shove, the only source of inspiration they had at hand was a Gideon Bible. (Not that there's anything wrong with Adam as a name, of course!)

Discovering the Pygmalion Effect: How names may shape your child's experience

When considering possible negative consequences of particular names, you usually think in terms of childhood teasing. But there's a darker side to the first impressions of names. Scientific studies have shown that people respond very differently to certain names or certain types of names. You may have heard about experiments where different names were put on the same homework assignment and given to multiple teachers to grade. Names that were perceived as "old fashioned," like Bertha or Marmaduke, were given lower grades on the average. The problem is, "old fashioned" is a relative term. When those studies were first done, Emily and Ethan would have been considered old-fashioned names, now they're as current as can be.

Names with novelty spellings can also fare badly. Sindee may be considered inherently more frivolous than Cindy. Diminutives are seen as less formal and so less serious than the full forms of names. Jimmy Carter made a bit of a stir by using Jimmy rather than James in politics. (At least he had the choice — name your son "Jimmy" and it's harder to go in the other direction.)

You want to give your child every advantage . . . but there comes a point when you wonder whether maybe you ought to be challenging these attitudes instead. When it's a matter of someone considering a name "too old-fashioned," you can chalk it up to personal taste. But the same types of scientific studies show even stronger effects if a name looks "too African American" or "too Hispanic." If you're thinking twice about naming your daughter Shanika (whether you're African American or not) because you're worried that her resumes may end up in the second stack, or if you're really wavering between naming your son Jose after his grandfather, or going with Joseph instead because it'll make teachers think he's smarter, are you making a rational decision for your child's best interests or surrendering to prejudice?

There is no good answer to this problem because we can't make it disappear except in our own actions. Decide for yourself whether to make it a factor in your choice of names.

Checking Out Naming Trends

When tracking the effects of pop culture and tradition on naming, it can be easy to miss some of the other fashions that come into play. For instance when Brittany shot up to number 6 in the '90s, it wasn't simply a fixation on teenage pop singers, but a name whose time had clearly come. I doubt that if the pop princess had been named "Guatemala," the name would have caught on nearly as solidly (see the bullet below for more on the trend towards Brittany). Clearly, parents don't conspire to promote a particular name or trend, but checking out the following trends can show you if your favorite names follow the crowd or stray from the pack:

- **Spellings beginning with "C-" versus "K-":** On the average, spellings starting with "C-" were more common in the early and mid–20th century, while spellings with "K-" proliferated in the later century.

- **Spellings of "-ie" versus "-y":** In girls' diminutives like Cathy, spellings ending in "-ie" gave way to those ending in "-y" and were later supplemented by "-i" and even "-ee." Similarly in boys' diminutives, the earlier fashion for Tommie, Bobbie, and Johnnie shifted to a preference for Tommy, Bobby, and Johnny.

- **Names rhyming with Jayden:** You may also see fashions in the sound of names, independent of their origins. Currently there is a rash of boys' names rhyming with Jayden, including Aidan, Braden, and Caden. Parents aren't likely to be deliberately choosing these names to rhyme, but somehow a certain "sound" has become popular. There was a similar fad in the mid–20th century for short, one-syllable boys' names such as Brad, Don, Gene, Greg, Kirk, Mark, and Rick.

- **Names beginning with "Br-":** Around the '70s and continuing to the present day, you see an explosion of interest in all sorts of names beginning with "Br-" followed by a combination of the related sounds "d," "t," and/or "n." Of course, there are names like Brandon, Brent, Brian, Bryant, and Brenda that show up earlier. But suddenly there's a flood of names, such as Braden, Brandt, Branden, Brandyn, Brayden, Braydon, Brandan, Brannon, Brendan, Brenden, Brennan, Brennen, Brendon, and Brenton for the boys, and Brandy, Brianna, and Brittany for the girls.

- **Names ending in "-n":** The fad described above for names rhyming with Jayden is part of a larger fashion for two-syllable names ending in "n" for boys, such as Ashton, Bryson, Camden, Carson, Colton, Dawson, Dillon, Gavin, Justin, and Payton.

- **Two-syllable names ending in "-sey" or "-say":** Girls have their own current fashion in sound. Currently there are a number of popular names ending in "-say" or "-sey," regardless of the original meaning of the names: Casey, Chelsey, Kelsey, and Lindsay.

Following the Crowd — or Not

If you talk to people who have extremely popular names or extremely rare names, you'll find strong opinions on both sides. It's another one of those "can't-win" situations. Choose a popular name and your child may pine for something more exotic. Choose a unique and exotic name and your child may want to disown you in mortification. Store away the following thoughts for the day when you're asked to justify your choice.

Checking out common naming trends

Whether you want to follow or avoid the crowd in naming, you need to know what the crowd is doing. In names as in everything, trends are made up of large numbers of individual independent decisions. When Jennifer shot up from obscurity to number 1 in the '70s, the parents who chose it weren't getting together in conspiracies to promote the name. And many parents of young Emilys will tell you they had no idea the name was wildly popular — they just liked it.

When it comes to tradition in name fashions, we see a great divide between boys' names and girls' names. Whether you think it unfair or not, boys have always been given more traditional and conservative names, while girls' names are where the parents' imaginations have taken flight. (This was happening as early as the 12th century, so we don't have to take all the blame today.) Boys' names don't move in and out of fashion as quickly, and it's far less common for a name to come out of nowhere and shoot up to the top of the boys' charts than it is for girls. Sixteen male names stayed in the top 100 most popular names through the entire 20th century, while only three female names did. If you take any three-decade span across the century, you'll generally find at least five male names that stayed in the top ten throughout that period

(although there's a bit of a break in the '70s). If you try the same thing with female names, once you get past the middle of the century, there are no names that stay in the top ten for three decades at a time.

The top boys' names are all drawn from the "old standards" — either Biblical names or names established in popularity in the Middle Ages — and the most popular spellings are always the traditional ones: Michael, David, James, Robert, John. Girls' names start out the same way at the beginning of the 20th century, but then start adding less traditional names (Shirley, Linda, Sharon, Cynthia, Jennifer) or popularizing diminutives and variants of the traditional names (Karen, Nancy, Lisa).

When we look beyond the very popular names, one of the most notable trends over the century reflects patterns of immigration and attitudes among immigrants towards names and assimilation. Many of the names that drop out of use after the first couple decades of the 20th century are ones brought by immigrants from central and southern Europe, then abandoned by the next generation. (In the case of clearly German names, probably abandoned in response to anti-German attitudes during WWI.) In many cases, these families were simply substituting an American version of the older names: Frank instead of Franz or Francesco; Joan instead of Johanna or Giovanna. But names with no equivalent simply fell out of fashion for the most part.

While European immigration declined, the later part of the century has seen great increases in immigration from other parts of the Americas and from the countries of Asia and the Pacific. Here we get an interesting contrast. The growing Hispanic communities have tended to hold tight to traditional names, even when English equivalents are available (Juan, Jose, and Luis for boys, and Maria for girls, although once again girls' names are less traditional). Asian immigrants, in contrast, have tended to adopt "American" names, even in the first generation (although they will often have a traditional name to use within the community), and extremely few Asian names have spread into more general use. (India seems to be an exception to this, to some extent.)

In the earlier part of the century, names in the African-American community were largely distinguished by fashions for particular names or particular types of names (e.g., surnames of historic figures such as Washington or Jefferson). But with the general shift to more creative naming in the second half of the century, African American name fashions have become more distinct, including an interest in names from African languages or from Arabic, and for the distinctive sound pattern of invented names like Lakeish, Deshawn, and so on (see Chapter 11). These fashions in turn have spread into other communities.

We often think of the '60s as ushering in an era of Rainbows and Dakotas, but curiously, while there's a lot of talk about how creative and innovative naming has become, the names moving in and out of the top ten in recent decades have included many revivals of traditional names: for girls, Emily, Emma, Hannah, Olivia, Abigail, Elizabeth, Stephanie, and Melissa; for boys, Joshua, Matthew, Andrew, Ethan, and Anthony. The very colorful meanings and spellings have been given mostly to girls, while the creativity in boys' names comes more in reviving forgotten older names and seeking out interesting surnames to borrow.

Living with a very popular name

Here are some great reasons you can tell your child to enjoy having a popular name:

  ✔ **Endless exploration:** The very popular names tend to be names with a long and ancient history. You can spend your entire life exploring your name and discovering new things about it. You may have hundreds — even thousands — of famous namesakes, and you can pick and choose among them to decide who you want to identify with. And conversely, your name won't be so solidly identified with any one particular namesake that you get sick and tired of the association. If you're named WILLIAM, you have the entire scope of Western history since the Norman Conquest to mine for material.

✔ **Several choices:** Very popular names have usually accumulated a lot of variants and nicknames. This is particularly the case for names that belonged to popular early saints. You could populate an entire small town with people named versions of John and Mary and never repeat yourself. You not only have choices based on what different cultures have done with the name (Giovanni, Jean, Juan, Sean, Ian, Evan, Johan, Jan, Ivan; Maria, Marie, Moira, Maryam, Marija), but each one has spawned a variety of diminutives, pet forms, and just plain spelling variants (Jon, Jack, Jenkin, Johnny, Jacky; Marion, Mariot, Marissa, Molly, Polly, Malkin — just to cover the English ones). If you want to have the opportunity to try on a variety of short forms and nicknames, then you want to have a name that's been extremely popular for the last seven or eight centuries.

✔ **Instant connections:** Even without a long history, being part of a popular name-group gives you an instant connection with a large number of other people. Members of the Fred Society have fun with this — the only requirement for membership is that you are named Fred, in some form. A slightly more sinister twist on the idea is seen in the movie *Heathers,* but even there, the essence is a group of contemporaries who feel a bond in part because they share a name.

✔ **Personalized gear:** If your name uses a common spelling of a popular name, you have access to a lot more random "stuff" with your name on it. You can grow up seeing your name on souvenirs, stickers, and labels.

✔ **Often heard:** You're used to hearing people use your name and mean someone else. It doesn't distract you or freak you out.

✔ **Background noise:** With a popular name, your name becomes more "background." When introduced to people, they don't immediately comment on your name. When they walk away, they remember something about *you,* not that you had an odd name. You're less conspicuous. When a new teacher scans through the class roster, his eyes don't stop a moment on your name as he takes note of who you are. You can fly under the radar if you choose and when you become conspicuous, it's for something you do, not something you can't help.

✔ **No oddities:** People don't consider your name odd. No matter how interesting it may be in absolute terms, it has an inherent dignity lent by the validation of majority opinion. You haven't had to justify your name, explain it, or excuse it. You can point to important people, brilliant people, and talented people with your name and know that it's a name that can bear the weight.

Discovering the uniqueness of a name

Here are some great reasons you can give your child for loving a unique name:

- ✓ **Special meaning:** If you have an unusual — even unique — name, then you grow up automatically knowing you are special. Your name *means* something. Maybe it means something obvious or maybe there is a fascinating story behind how your parents came to choose that name. Maybe it was designed especially just for you and nobody else in the world has that name.

- ✓ **Almost famous:** In the race for fame and celebrity, you have an automatic head start. People meet you — or even just hear about you — and you instantly catch their attention. You stand out from the crowd. People can't easily get you confused with someone else. Your accomplishments can't accidentally get attributed to someone else of the same name.

- ✓ **Great expectations:** Simply by virtue of your name, you come across as innovative, creative, and cutting-edge. People expect interesting things from you. No matter what you do, you're less likely to shock people.

- ✓ **Grand uniqueness:** You aren't tied down by a vast history; you get to make your own reputation. You're unlikely to encounter someone who thinks you don't fit the stereotype of your name — there's no stereotype to fit. And if you do run into someone with the same name as you, it's like being in another country and running into someone from your small hometown. Why, you're almost automatic cousins or something!

- ✓ **Very personal:** When someone uses your name, you know they're talking to *you*. It's easy to get your attention in a crowd. And if you want to find mentions of yourself on the World Wide Web, you don't have to wade through mountains of irrelevancies.

Chapter 3

Putting the Name Together

In This Chapter

▶ Understanding the various parts of a name

▶ Identifying a name's gender (or avoiding the question entirely)

▶ Discovering a name's meaning

▶ Checking out how the name sounds

▶ Taking a good look at the name

▶ Using a name to make connections for your child

There are so many things to consider when deciding on a name that it's impossible to keep track of all of them at once. In this chapter, I narrow the topic down into a number of different considerations so you can avoid that overwhelmed feeling and easily decide which factors are most important to you and which ones don't really make that much difference. This chapter also leads you through some technical aspects of naming and touches on some topics in naming history to put the issues into perspective.

Think of this chapter as a toolbox. If you find it hard to pinpoint or articulate just why you like or don't like a name or a type of name, you may find a tool here that shows you how to put it in words. Especially if you find yourself negotiating name choices with a partner, it's better to be able to say something more than, "I just don't like it," or "It sounds funny to me." This chapter may also offer you ways of solving conflicts over names that hadn't occurred to you.

Building a Name

The overall structure of the name may seem like a pretty standard template in our American culture, but that doesn't mean you can't do something different. Use the following sections to discover your own unique name template, or just stick with the standard first-middle-last template with a splash of nickname thrown in.

Legal names: First and last names

To understand the variety of names available and some of their histories, it helps to know something about different types of names. In American culture, there are two basic types of "official" names: surnames and given names. Surnames are fixed names shared by a family and usually inherited from a parent. Given names are chosen for each individual (normally by a parent, although people sometimes choose their own later in life).

Whatever you call your child on everyday occasions, some version of the name will be your child's "legal name" — the one filled out on official forms. Given names and surnames may be treated somewhat differently on a legal basis. Surnames are expected to be fixed and stable: If you shorten your given name from Jonathan to Jon, it's less critical than if you shorten your surname from Johnson to Johns.

If you're a member of a couple that have both kept your original surnames, the birth of a child may be the point where you decide that something must be done. But whether you've already combined your surnames or plan to do it for your child's name only, a double-barreled surname brings its own issues. When you analyze how the name sounds, the surname will be the equivalent of that piece of enormous furniture that you have to arrange the rest of the room around. You will, in effect, be giving your child *four* names and will need to take them all into account when considering sound, rhythm, initials, and the rest. And yet there are practical reasons for having both parents referenced in the child's name. So, if the two of you are using different surnames and you don't want to saddle your child with a hyphen, this is one of those times when a middle name can come in handy.

Middle names

Middle names behave like given names in both legal and social terms: They are chosen for the individual rather than being shared automatically based on family ties. Historically, the middle name had a number of specific functions, but today you can think of it as a "second chance" in designing a name. If you can't make up your mind between two names . . . use both! If both parents have their hearts set on a particular name . . . use both! If you're torn between giving your child a cutting-edge, fashionable name and something more traditional and conservative . . . do both! The middle name can be a wonderful safety valve against putting all your naming eggs in one basket. But there are also some traditional uses for the middle name that you may want to consider.

Discovering the history of the middle name

The middle name is a bit of a historical oddity. The idea of something like a given name is pretty much universal. Family names, too, are extremely widespread. But the peculiar thing that we call a middle name is a lot less obvious a concept — it's a second "given" name that isn't a type of nickname describing something about the person.

The first roots of the middle name as we know it shows up in Medieval Italy where it was taken from the same pool as the first name and seems to have served as a religious purpose, as suggested by the occasional use of Maria as a middle name by men. By the 16th century, you can find a few examples in France and Spain, mostly among the very high nobility, which was also the class that took it up first in England in the 17th century. Name fashions have a tendency to roll downhill from the upper classes, and it wasn't long before more ordinary people were using middle names, too.

In addition to middle names with religious significance, you can find examples where a very common given name that is traditional in the family has been supplemented with a more unusual middle name (perhaps the name used for everyday?). For example, if the extended Taylor family insists on having a George in every generation, then the cousins George Kelly Taylor, George Aloysius Taylor, and George David Taylor may use their middle names to avoid confusion. We also see surnames being used as middle names, typically of a relative or godparent.

Despite the near universality of middle names today, there's no law that says you have to have one. I wouldn't advise skipping it for a Joseph Smith, but a middle name may simply get in the way for a Zachariah Montgomery. The lack may upset the bureaucrats: There are stories from World War II of soldiers enrolled with the middle name "Nmi" (for "No Middle Initial") because the enlistment forms weren't allowed to have the space blank. On the other hand, middle names are easy enough to add later in life, if your child gets tired of making explanations.

In some communities, one of two given names is reserved for a name with religious associations: the name of a saint, or a name indicating a particular devotion. When Catholics use a confirmation name as part of the legal name, it may become the middle name.

It's still the case that a child's surname is most commonly inherited from the father, so the middle name is sometimes used to bring in the mother's family name or some name traditionally used in the mother's family.

Socially, we usually distinguish between first names (the name a person is normally called by) and middle names (an additional name that may or may not be used in combination with the first name). At various times, there have been informal rules about what the middle name should be and how it should be used, but today it's pretty much a free-for-all. No one will think twice about someone going by the middle name instead of the first name.

Checking out the history of name categories

You may think nothing of turning a surname into a given name today, but in many times and places the two have been clearly distinct categories. If you go far enough back in Western history (say, to the early Middle Ages), people had only one fixed name — their given name. Anything else was just a matter of description, such as Alfred the Baker or Margaret from London. And the given names used during that period set the standard for acceptable given names for centuries. That is, names like Alfred and Margaret were considered acceptable as given names while names like Baker and London were not. This period also produced most of the saints whose names were later given to people as baptismal names. (In fact, traditionally, "baptismal name" has been nearly synonymous with "given name.") Names could be added to this pool of given names, but with nowhere near the volume and enthusiasm with which we create new given names today.

Because so many of those new given names these days come originally from family surnames, it can be fun to know something about where those names came from. Back before the rise of inherited surnames there were roughly four types of surnames that could be added to the given name to identify and distinguish people. You may have had a name that told your parentage (usually your father), such as Jackson, Mackenzie (son of Coinneach), or Rodriguez (son of Rodrigo). People may have identified you by where you lived, like Ashley, Brooke, or Devon. You may have been named for what you did for a living, like Smith, Tailor, or Hunter. Or you may have had a nickname that described something about your appearance, habits, or personality, like Cameron (bent-nose), Cole (black as coal), or Grant (tall, large).

Nicknames

Nicknames may be a diminutive form of a person's given name (so-called because they're either shorter than the original name or because they originated as affectionate childish forms of the name), for example, Tom for Thomas. Another type of nickname may be something unrelated to the legal name, such as Ronald Reagan's nickname Dutch.

Although you can't predict which nicknames of the second type may attach themselves to your child, you may find yourself considering what diminutive nicknames your name choice may lend itself to. If you definitely want your child to have a nickname, try the following naming ideas:

- ✔ **Pick a name that already has nicknames associated with it.** If the name already has nicknames associated with it, you can give your child a variety of options of what to be called.

- ✔ **Keep your eye on the "old standard" names.** Usually, the more popular a name has been and the longer it's been around, the more likely it is to have nicknames associated with it (and the more different ones there are likely to be). So old standards are a good choice if you want to offer your child an array of nickname potential.

Conversely, if you want to discourage the use of nicknames, try these naming strategies:

- ✔ **Pick a name that currently has *no* nicknames associated with it.** If you want the name you pick to be used as your child's name, this is one way to make sure it is.

- ✔ **Pick a relatively new name.** Newer names generally haven't had a chance to develop nicknames yet, or haven't been popular enough to need them yet.

- ✔ **Pick a single-syllable name.** This won't prevent nickname suffixes being added if people really want to. Jade could, in theory, be turned into Jadey. But one-syllable names are less likely to come with existing nicknames attached.

- ✔ **Pick a name that originated as a nickname for some other name.** Although people may mistakenly use the original form of the name instead, they aren't likely to substitute a different nickname for the one you choose.

If you do pick a nickname to be your child's first name, you eliminate options. A woman named Margaret has the option to go by Margie or Meg or Maggie or Peg. A woman named Margie or Meg or Maggie or Peg doesn't have the same social permission to go by Margaret or one of the other nicknames. A man named Thomas can be Tommy as a boy, Tom to his college friends, and return to Thomas if he has a profession where a little extra gravitas is an advantage. But a man named Tommy has to make it fit all occasions. Just as you can use middle names to expand your child's options, the careful choice of a formal given name rich in nickname potential can give you the best of both worlds.

Additional names

Particular communities or cultures in the U.S. may use other categories of names. Catholics may take the name of a particular saint as a "confirmation name," but it would not normally be used every day or become part of the legal name. Observant Jews will have a Hebrew name, which may be the original form of their everyday name, or may be unrelated to it. It's not at all uncommon for people of Chinese, Japanese, or Korean heritage to have a name in their ancestral language and an "American name" as well. Often the two are similar in sound, although unrelated. For example, a woman with *Hsiou-* as the first part of her Chinese name may use *Susan* as her American name.

Picking a Gender-Appropriate Name

Probably more fuss is made over choosing a gender-appropriate name than any other aspect of naming. Face it: For all the advances made in equality of the sexes, we're still a society with deep anxieties about gender roles and attributes. And yet, our ancestors a century ago, though much less enlightened about gender equality, seem to have been more relaxed about keeping strict distinctions between "men's names" and "women's names." Oh, the majority of names only show up for one or the other, of course. But in the Social Security name ranking statistics for 1900, the name Mary shows up at number 391 for men, a high enough ranking that it's hard to explain away as random data-entry errors. At the same date, both George and William ranked in the 600s for women. (Fictional detective Nancy Drew had a female friend named George — it seems to have been unremarkable at the time.) Don't go overboard onto the "boy named Sue" side, but keep in mind that name gender isn't a fixed law of the universe.

Giving a name gender

What makes a name a "boy's name" or a "girl's name" anyway? Name books give a lot of attention to the importance of choosing carefully, but spend little time looking at how you know or decide a name is in one category or the other. Cultures vary in how names are assigned to a gender — if they're specific at all — but there are three basic methods: by grammar, by meaning, or by custom.

Gender from grammar

In some languages, words can have a grammatical gender that changes how you say things. For instance, in Spanish, some words can end in either *a* or *o*, depending on whether the word refers to a feminine *(a)* or masculine *(o)* noun, such as "la casa blanca" (the white house) versus "el gato blanco" (the white cat). In such a language, there may be an obvious difference in sound and spelling between boys' names and girls' names. In Spanish, names ending in *o* will generally be boys' names, while names ending in *a* will generally be girls' names.

Sometimes the grammatical difference can look like entirely different words. The French word for "beautiful" is *belle* when describing a feminine noun (including women) and *beau* when describing a masculine noun (including men). So when these words get turned into names, we naturally expect to find Belle used for girls and not boys, and Beau used for boys and not girls. We see the same thing in the Welsh names Gwen and Gwyn. These are different grammatical forms of the same word, meaning "white, fair." So we expect the feminine form Gwen to be used for girls, and the masculine form Gwyn to be used for boys.

English long ago abandoned the idea of grammatical gender. There's nothing in the shape of a name that forces us to understand it as a man's name or a woman's name in English, although the grammar of the languages we borrow names from affects some of our unconscious rules.

Gender from meaning

When you look at the original meaning of names, some meanings look like they fit our ideas about boys better, or our ideas about girls better. The gender meaning may be obvious, as in "victorious warrior," or it may be based on cultural roles such as "gift of peace" if women are seen as peace-makers. As with grammatical gender, the farther we get from the name's origins, the less of an influence meaning will be on whether we consider something a boy's name or a girl's name. When people lose track of the fact that Mackenzie means "son of Coinneach," they feel comfortable giving it to girls without thinking that the name is unfeminine.

But when the meaning of a name is obvious to us, it can affect what gender we think it's appropriate for. Flower names are associated in our culture with girls, because we have a notion that girls ought to be pretty and delicate. So even if you pick a flower that's never been used as a child's name before — like pimpernel — people would be surprised if you gave it to a boy.

Gender from custom

In modern American culture, by far the strongest influence on whether a name is considered masculine or feminine is simple custom and habit. If you're used to seeing a name being used for boys, you consider it a boy's name, without thinking about its origins and history. If you're used to seeing a name being used for girls, you consider it a girl's name. The proof of this can be seen in names that have switched from one gender to the other, such as Ashley, Lauren, Sydney, or Madison. The last one shows the triumph of custom over meaning, because the word "son" is still recognizable in it, and yet today it's overwhelmingly used as a girl's name.

So if custom and habit are the most important influences on whether you consider a name a boy's name or a girl's name, you can see how hard it is to be absolutely sure in the matter, especially when you span the globe. Few American parents would think of naming a son Meredith, but when your daughter Meredith travels to England, people will wonder why she has a boy's name. And when she brings home her French boyfriend Jean, you'll try not to blurt out, "Why do you have a girl's name?"

Checking out some gender guidelines

You can divide names into three groups: names that are rarely if ever used for the other gender, for example, William, John, or Edward for boys, or Anne, Jennifer, or Katherine for girls; names that are strongly associated with one gender, but you wouldn't be surprised to see used for the other, for example, Michael, Jesse, or Adrian for boys, or Alexis, Courtney, or Kelly for girls; and names for which you don't have strong associations one way or another, for example, Taylor, Jordan, Casey, or Tracey.

If you want to minimize any possibility of confusion, you may want to choose names from the first group. In general, these will be older, established, traditional names — ones that may in some cases be thought of as a bit stodgy or old-fashioned. On the other end of the spectrum, if you want to encourage your children not to be bound by cultural stereotypes of gender, you may want to aim for the third group.

If you're not sure how a name will be perceived, here are some guidelines for what makes a name seem male or female:

- **Names ending in "-a" are feminine.** Because of the influence of Latin and the Romance languages on the name pool, the ending "-a" is strongly associated with female names. So even when names are borrowed from languages that don't have this rule, names ending in "-a" tend to be used as girls' names. Sasha started out as a Russian boy's nickname for Alexander, but it only makes the American charts as a girl's name. Andrea started out as a variant of male Andrew, but has turned into a female name.

- **Names ending in "-e" are feminine.** This isn't as strong a rule as the rule above and comes specifically from France, where it's common to find male and female pairs of names where the second adds an "-e": Jean/Jeanne, Gabriel/Gabrielle, Noel/Noelle.

- **Nicknames ending in y/i/ie/ey/ee form a sliding scale.** Fashions in these spellings have been shifting, but the innovations will tend to be used for girls first. The spellings "-ee" and "-ie" are more likely to be found for girls. Consider feminine Aubree, Bailee, and Beverlee versus unisex Aubrey, Bailey, Beverly. Billie, Bobbie and Bobbi are more popular for girls, versus unisex Billy, and predominately boys' Bobby. Cary and Carey are more common for boys while Carrie and Cari are found only for girls. Jodie shifted from male to female while Jody is used for both and Jodi only for girls. Randy was briefly used for both, but then women shifted to using Randi. Robb and Robby are mostly found for men only, but Robbie for both. Sandy is used for both and Sandi only for women. Terry is used for both but more commonly for men while Terri and Terrie are found for women only. Tracy and Tracey are in the process of shifting from men to women while Traci and Tracie are used by women only. So we can set up a sliding scale from masculine to feminine: -y ⇨ -ey ⇨ -ie ⇨ -i ⇨ -ee.

Switching gender

Many names have changed which gender they're associated with over the last century or more. In many cases, these are names taken from family surnames that don't have an established traditional gender. In the 19th century, it was more common for boys to be named after family surnames, so many names entered the name pool on that side and only later became applied to girls as well: such as Clyde, Leslie, SIdney, Dale, Lynn. In some cases, relatively rare names that started out as male names were given a spurt of popularity by a famous woman who happened to bear the name, and the resulting fad overshadowed the name's original use. Lauren is a good example of this in the U.S. The shift from rare male use to popular female use corresponds fairly well with the career of actress Lauren Bacall.

In almost all cases, one rule holds fast: Boy's names turn into girl's names, but not the other direction. Sad to say, it's as if once a name has "girl cooties" people decide it's not appropriate for boys any more. Even when names are still used for both boys and girls, the more popular the name becomes for girls, the more likely it is to fall out of use for boys. Some names where you can seen this has happened over the later part of the 20th century include: Shannon, Whitney, Lindsay, Dana, Stacy, Robin, Sandy, and Shirley. Pat is one case where the girls didn't win. With the rise in popularity of Patricia in the mid–20th century, female use of Pat overtook male use, but then it declined sharply, leaving the field to the boys.

There's one notable exception: Douglas started out in the late 16th century as a girl's name (among women connected with the Douglas family), but it gradually shifted over, perhaps because of the resemblance to the male name Dougal, and today it's considered unimpeachably masculine.

- ✔ **Arbitrary differences in spelling.** For some names, an arbitrary spelling distinction between a male form and a female form has developed. Leigh has become feminine (both alone, and in combination, for example, Ashleigh) while Lee stayed mostly masculine. Frances and Francis started out interchangeable for men and women, but around the mid–20th century, they split with Frances falling out of use for men and Francis becoming much less common for women. Both Leslie and Lesley have always been more popular with women than men, but Lesley fell out of use for men entirely midcentury. Sydney shifted from men to women, but Sidney is used primarily by men.

- ✔ **Differences in initial letters.** Overall, names starting with D or W are more commonly boys' names than girls' names. (This isn't a rule, just a statistical trend.) Similarly, names starting with K, L, M, S (especially Sh), or Y are more commonly girls' names. This means that if you pick an unfamiliar name starting with one of these letters, people will subconsciously be inclined to assume the corresponding gender.

Finding out What the Name Means

It sometimes seems that name books overemphasize the meaning of names. How often in his life is a Jeffrey going to meditate on the deep significance of whether his name means "peace of the land," "peaceful traveler," or "peace-hostage" (the literal meanings of the names that merged to become Jeffrey)? Random strangers will confide to you the original meaning of their names . . . and a good percentage of the time they'll be wrong, because the books they got the meaning from were wrong.

Name meanings can be the frosting on the cake when making your choice, but if you couldn't guess the meaning just by hearing the name, it's likely to have much less impact on your child than other considerations.

Mulling over literal meanings

In many cultures, the literal meaning of a name has been important in its choice. An ancient Roman father may name his daughter Tertia (third) for being born third. A Medieval mother may name her son Noel for being born on Christmas. Today, you may name a daughter Jasmine with the thought that she may be as sweet and beautiful as the flower, but you'd be less likely to name her Wisteria for a similar reason. The difference isn't in the meaning, for both of them describe flowers, but because one is established as a personal name and the other isn't yet.

Older names often have literal meanings that no longer make sense in our culture. No one today is likely to need "spear-strength" (Gertrude), and in a democratic society we have little need of a "folk-ruler" (Walter). You may wish generally for a child's life to be blessed (Benedict), but it's no longer considered high praise to call a woman a cow (Rebecca). The older a name is, the less you can be certain of its meaning at all. When the history of a name is well-documented, then you can trace back that Nils is a Swedish shortening of Nicholas, which comes from Greek Nikolaos and therefore means "victory of the people." But all that's known of the Scottish name Anabel is that it rather certainly does *not* come from the names Anna and Belle — even the original language is unclear.

In this book, every attempt has been made to trace the meanings of the names listed, but keep in mind that this is an imprecise science. Some names have multiple origins and those given here may not be exhaustive. The meaning of a name may be uncertain or lost in the mists of time. And in specific cases, a name may be chosen for a personal meaning that has nothing to do with the historic origins of the name.

Does the name have to mean something?

Given that many of the traditional names used today have obscure origins and meanings, is it important that a name have a meaning at all? When new names are created, they may be designed for a pleasant sound rather than being based on words at all. Or they may coincidentally be similar to existing names but can't be said to be that existing name. Here are some types of names for which a meaning is hard to assign:

- Names based on initials: Kaysee standing for K.C., Jaydi standing for J.D., and so on.

- Names deliberately created by cutting and pasting existing names: Romi created from Ruth + Naomi, Verilyn created from Vera + Marilyn (or, for that matter, Marilyn itself, from Mary + Lynn).

- Names created from anagrams: Myra from Mary, Vanessa as a partial anagram of Esther Vanhomrigh.

- Names created to match a sound pattern: Shamika, Tiana.

The greatest use of literal name meanings today comes in the coining of new names. Parents seeking a unique name will look for some quality (Harmony) or meaningful object (Crystal) or place of significance (Sierra) that they feel expresses something about what they desire for their child. But these meanings are generally poetic and allusive. You no longer bestow literal descriptions like "Long-hair" or express your practical hopes for life accomplishments, such as "Folk-lawyer."

Discovering apparent meanings and meaning shifts

Just as words have a "dictionary" meaning but also carry meanings of context and implication, names have not only a linguistic meaning and origin, but any number of associated meanings that they have picked up through use. The name John comes from a Hebrew name meaning "God has favored," but through much of its use this meaning has been less important than its reference to John the Baptist. The name Anastasia may come from a Greek word meaning "resurrection," but a parent may choose it instead for an air of foreign mystery.

Identifying the origin of a name may not always be straightforward. When Rose first started being used in the early Middle Ages, it came from a Germanic root meaning "horse," but it has long since come to be associated instead with the flower. The name Jesse is biblical, meaning "God exists," but track star Jesse Owens took his name from his initials, J.C., for James Cleveland, so in his case the name Jesse technically means "the supplanter from the land of cliffs." You just can't tell by looking at it. The name Mckayla looks like it comes from a Scottish or Irish surname, until you trace its origins from Michaela, a feminine form of Michael.

Listening to How the Name Sounds

Everyone has opinions about which names sound good and which sound awkward or unpleasant, but it isn't always easy to define why. This can be a problem if you're trying to convince a partner that you aren't simply being whimsical in disliking a name, or if you're trying to identify other pleasant-sounding names you may want to consider. You can talk about the sounds of names in much the same way you may talk about poetry. Don't let that scare you away if you never cared much for English classes. I make it easy to understand in the following sections.

Getting the pronunciation you want

The first question you need to ask is how you want the name to be pronounced and whether people will have a good idea of the right pronunciation when they see the name. For even mildly common names, you can expect that people will have seen and heard the name before and may already have their own ideas about how the name is pronounced. Plus, some names may have more than one possible pronunciation from the written form. Consider the case of Jean, which may be the English woman's name pronounced the same as Gene, or may be the French man's name pronounced something like "Zhahn." You can expect that if the name you choose looks like an English name (even an unfamiliar one), people will try giving it an English pronunciation first. For example, if you coin the name Rike, intending it as a creative spelling of Ricky, most people on seeing it will instead pronounce it similar to Mike.

If a name looks more foreign, people are less likely to assume that they know how it should be pronounced. Someone encountering the Spanish name Jimena for the first time may try to give it an English pronunciation (Gimeena?), but the same person seeing its variant spelling Ximena is more likely to ask how to say it. If you want people to use a non-English pronunciation, it may help to use a spelling variant that signals, "Don't make assumptions."

If the name is unusual, be open to the possibility that the pronunciation you have in mind isn't one that other people will consider "correct." The first time you ever encountered the name Sean, you may have assumed it would be pronounced like the word "seen." If you gave the name to your son and tried to insist on that pronunciation, you'd run into a lot of people who would stubbornly pronounce it the same as Shawn.

Whether the name you pick is unusual, of foreign origin, or simply spelled unusually, you can save yourself some frustration by writing the name and showing it to a variety of people and asking how they would pronounce it.

Hitting the tempo, rhyme, and rhythm

Among the tools for looking at the sound of a name are stress, the arrangement of stressed and unstressed syllables, and rhyme.

If you have good reasons to chose a name that breaks the rules, then break them. Sound rules are there to help you explain why a combination just doesn't sound right, or to help you figure out if there's a way to "tweak" the name to clear your objections.

Stress

Words and names are made up of syllables — the smallest pieces that are easy to say separately. For example, John has one syllable while Mary has two (Ma-ry), Amanda has three (A-man-da), and Anastasia has four (An-as-tas-ia). Any name will have at least one syllable that is stressed, or pronounced more strongly than the others. A long name may have more than one stress. If you aren't sure where the stress is, you can find it by emphasizing each syllable in turn and figuring out which one doesn't sound "wrong" (for example, *A*-man-da, a-*man*-da, a-man-*da*). Some languages have very firm rules about stress. In French, the main stress always falls on the last syllable, so names we've borrowed from the French language tend to follow this rule: ma-*rie*, jean-*nette*. Italian names are usually stressed on the next to last syllable: giu-*sep*-pe, ma-*ri*-a. English names tend to be stressed on the first syllable (*Will*-iam, *Su*-san), but longer names can be odd (e-*liz*-a-beth).

Why does this matter? When you put your first, middle, and last names together, the stresses in the different names can either work together in a pleasant way or fight with each other and sound awkward. When a last syllable stress is followed by a first syllable stress, the combination may limp a little: Desir*ée Will*iamson. Similarly, if you have too many unstressed syllables run together, it may sound like you're mumbling in the middle: *Brit*tany Antoin*ette* Parker. One of the reasons that a series of short (one-syllable) names can sound odd is because the resulting sound is all stress with no rest. Compare the flow of Greg Cliff Smith and Gregory Clifford Smith.

Although having all short names can sound choppy because the name is all stress, having all very long names can cause its own problems. If the stresses fall in different places in the different names, you can have the awkward clumping or long stressless sections discussed above. But if you have a series of multisyllable names with the same stress pattern, the name can sound too sing-song. Cynthia Beverly Calloway gets a rhythm rolling that overpowers the name itself.

So you should try combining names of variable length. If your surname is very long, combine it with given and middle names of one or two syllables: Lee Thomas Jefferson. Conversely, if your surname is short, then at least one of the other names should be longer: Heather Rose Jones.

On the other hand, breaking this rule on the short side can produce a name that sounds very muscular and powerful: Jack Reed, Ann Clark. Breaking the rule on the long side can make a name sound aristocratic: Gwendolyn Tracy Hamilton.

Rhyme and alliteration

Rhyme is when two words have exactly the same sounds in their last one or more syllables: Jack and Zack, Amanda and Miranda. The rhyme is less noticeable if the matching syllables are unstressed (Branden and Allen), but you can also get a rhymelike effect from stressed syllables even if they aren't at the end of the name (Jayden and Brady).

Generally, rhyme is bad. It distracts attention from the names and focuses it on the act of rhyming. (It's also a magnet for teasing.) Consider the experience of being introduced to Mr. Aidan Braden Haydon. What will you walk away remembering about him? (Notice that rhyme isn't about how things are spelled, it's about how they sound.)

A relative of rhyme is alliteration: a series of words all starting with the same consonant sound (remember that consonants are any letter except a, e, i, o, and u). The use of alliteration in names seems to set off fewer alarm bells in the listener. Whatever you may think of the name Herbert Hoover, you aren't likely to react, "How funny, both names start with an "H"!" So while you may want to be aware of whether the name you're designing has alliteration, it isn't necessarily something you should try to avoid.

Repetition

Back when names were descriptions of who you were, people wouldn't have been startled to meet a Carl Carlson of Carleton if Carl Jr. just happened to live in the aforementioned town. But now that you view name creation as a more controlled and deliberate process, you consider that much repetition of "Carl" to be a bit odd. A little oddity makes a name interesting; too much draws attention away from the person. James Jamison is interesting, James James sounds like a mistake or a joke.

You can get the same unfortunate effect if the end of one name echoes the beginning of the next. If you like the names Robert and Bertram, it may be better to order them as Bertram Robert instead. The same suggestion goes for individual sounds. If you end one name and start the next with the same sound, the names will run together in people's ears. Janet Tania Anderson will turn into Janetanianderson. Watch out for this possibility not only in the full name but when you drop the middle name. Carlos Salazar Martinez runs into the problem when he uses his middle name while Rachel Anne Lambert runs into it when she doesn't.

Matching first and middle names

When putting a name together, the surname is a given, but a judicious combination of first and middle names can give the name balance and harmony.

In terms of sound, use these tips when aiming for a pleasing variety:

- ✔ Avoid having the names rhyme.
- ✔ Avoid having your stresses come in clumps or all at the beginning and end of the names, if possible.
- ✔ Avoid having the same number of syllables in both first and middle names (although you can break this if the surname has a different number of syllables).
- ✔ Avoid repeating the same syllable in both names, especially right next to each other, such as Carl Carleton Brown.
- ✔ Avoid having the same sound at the end of the first name and the beginning of the middle name, such as Robert Bertram Connerly.

Here are some positive things you can do with the combination:

- ✔ If one name is very traditional, make the other one a bit unusual.
- ✔ If one name is very exotic, make the other a little more staid.
- ✔ If your surname is extremely common (like Smith or Jones), you not only can get away with being a little more creative in the first and middle names, but you have a moral obligation to do so.
- ✔ Consider making at least one of the names one that comes with nicknames.
- ✔ Think about giving at least one name with family connections.

Breaking the rules

Names that "work" are all around — when they work perfectly, you probably don't even notice. Hollywood screen names are often good examples of names designed to get the sound and flow right. Marilyn Monroe: mixed numbers of syllables, stress on alternating syllables (*Mar*-il-yn Mon-*roe*), no rhymes, and the alliteration, as I said, makes it interesting.

However, some names can break all the rules and still sound great. According to the "rules," singer Marion Anderson should have an "unsuccessful" name. Her first and last names both have three syllables, with the stress on the first one in both cases. And the names rhyme, although on an unstressed syllable. But instead of going "clunk," the name sounds like a song itself.

But look at some names that *do* clunk:

- **Engelbert Humperdinck:** Be honest. Haven't you always giggled inside when you heard this name? It has the same syllable and stress issues as Marion's name. No true rhyme here, but the near-rhyme repetition of "bert" and "perd" don't help things.

- **Franklin Delano Roosevelt:** Do you suppose there's a reason other than newspaper economics that he ended up being "FDR" on everyone's lips? The only "rule" the name really breaks is the one against all the names being polysyllabic, but that may be enough if you break it thoroughly.

- **Ronald McDonald:** It's a perfectly ordinary Scottish-sounding name, but the rhyming names make it sound a trifle absurd — perfect for the clown who represents the McDonald's restaurants.

You should use the sound rules to analyze names that already sound funny to you, not to eliminate names that sound perfectly fine.

Looking at the Name

Visual effects have been a major force in much of recent name creativity. Even when a popular or traditional name is used, efforts may be made to make it visually distinct. Some of these are more successful than others.

Adding spelling effects

When Anne Shirley of Green Gables insisted that her name was "Anne with an e," she was pointing out what we all know deep down: The spelling of your name is important and meaningful. A Kathy knows that she isn't a Cathy and most certainly not a Cathi!

This hasn't always been the case. In most languages (and in English through much of history), while there may be several possible ways to spell a name, they grew out of dialectal variations in how sounds were represented, or differences in how conservative the spelling was. One of the reasons that modern English spelling is so . . . challenging is that when you borrow words and names from other languages, you borrow their spellings at the same time. So something of the name's origins can stick to a particular spelling like mud on a shoe. Ann is more of a plain English girl, while Anne has a slightly sophisticated French air. Anna hints of Old Country grandmothers, but Annie is a fun-loving girl.

Of course, the first purpose of spelling is to tell the reader how to say the name. It would be absurd to write your name as *X*lp?T* and then insist that it be pronounced "William." On the other end of the scale, it wasn't so long ago that no one would blink if you wrote your name *Joan, Joanne,* or *Joanna* on alternate Tuesdays. In between these two extremes, different spellings can reflect different origins for similar-sounding names.

When you look at the whole range of current names that includes Devan, Devin, Devon, Devyn, Davin, Davon, Devan, and Deven, you may be excused for thinking that people are using whatever random vowels they like. But when you step back from the modern fad for this group, you find that the names in this group that appear earliest all have distinct origins reflected in their spellings.

Devon comes from the place name (a county in England), but Davin and Devin come from variants of the Irish surname Ó Damhín, from a name meaning "an ox." The other names may be considered spelling variants of one of these names, but then you come to the question of whether Deven ought to be considered a variant of Devon (and so English) or of Devin (and so Gaelic). This is the sort of thing that drives the compilers of baby name books crazy.

Chances are most parents who choose one of these names over another are working from personal preference, rather than caring about the origins of the name.

English can have various ways of spelling the same sound, so if encouraging a certain pronunciation is the key factor, then there's no reason not to choose among Lee, Lea, Leigh, and Li. But spelling charts the history and origins of a name, so if the goal is to emphasize a particular meaning or derivation, then the specific spelling may be more important. The spelling Li is strongly associated with Chinese names. Historically, the spellings Lee, Lea, and Leigh come from the same word (meaning "meadow"), but if you want to evoke a particular Civil War general, then you need to spell it Lee. When we encounter Lea as a common noun, it's generally in poetry (it's the thing lovers are traipsing o'er), so using that spelling as a name will have a slightly more romantic, poetic feel.

Suppose you don't care about what the spelling *says* about the name, but you want to make sure that in inventing your own unique spelling people will still understand how the name should be pronounced? With the caveat that some spellings are associated with a particular gender in some contexts (see "Checking out some gender guidelines," earlier in this chapter), here are some rules for relatively harmless spelling variations:

✔ You can generally interchange "-i," "-y," "-ee," "-ey," and "-ie." Not always, but generally.

✔ In an unstressed syllable, which vowel you use almost doesn't matter.

✔ The difference between single and double "m," "n," "l," "r," and "s" won't normally affect pronunciation — but some of the double letters may look odd at the end of a name.

✔ If a name begins with a "C-," you can substitute either *K* or *S* depending on the pronunciation, but if you substitute in the other direction (substituting a name beginning with "K-" or "S-" with *C*) you may have problems. Sierra spelled Cierra will probably still get the same pronunciation, but Kimberly spelled Cimberly won't.

Using initials and monograms

At some point, your child's name will be written using initials for one or more of the elements. The day when you start monogramming gym clothes should not be the first day you realize what you have done to little Patrick Ingram Goodman or Kathy Kimberly Kooper. Initials aren't just a negative consideration. They're also an opportunity to give your child a few more naming choices. There may be only a handful of people who are instantly recognizable from their initials alone. But it's probably no accident that we embrace a JFK but would tend to avoid referring to someone as WCH. Just as a sequence of names can either flow or go "clunk," a name using initials can either be an elegant option or something reserved for legal forms.

As usual, you can't paralyze yourself by trying to avoid any funny or unfortunate meaning in your child's initials. Between the multitude of three-letter words in English and our fondness for TLAs (three letter acronyms), the chances are that somewhere, to someone, any possible set of initials will mean something.

The best you can do is to follow a few simple principles:

✔ Avoid initials that spell out words that are, or that resemble, foul language. If you wouldn't want to hear it coming out of your child's mouth, don't design it into his name.

- ✔ Avoid initials that spell ordinary words with strong negative connotations, like "ass" or "fat."
- ✔ Avoid (well, try to anyway) names where a combination of a name plus initial will produce one of the above. Zachary Rowe may not be happy to be "Z. Rowe" (zero).

Making Social Ties

While you usually think of names as creating distinctions — identifying a child as a specific individual — another common use has always been to create connections between people. Family surnames are one obvious way of doing this, and the use of hyphenated or double surnames to connect both parents' families is an extension of this idea. But the choice of a given name or middle name can also be an opportunity to create a special connection between your child and some other individual.

Using namesakes and family names

The idea of creating or commemorating connections with the choice of first name started in Europe in the early Medieval period. Before that, there were a lot of different names, and you may have gone most of your life without meeting someone with the same name. Around about the 11th century, Europeans started picking up the idea of naming children after someone else. They may have used the name of a famous ancestor to say, "Look how important a family my child was born into." They may have used the name of a powerful ruler in the hopes that their child would find a similarly elevated place in life — or simply out of flattery or admiration. So dynasties of kings and queens gave rise to generations of copycat Williams, Edwards, Mathildas, and Eleanors.

Spiritual connections were another strong influence on names. Naming a child after a saint may have been done to place the child under that saint's protection. Or if the parents had prayed to a particular saint for a successful and healthy pregnancy, the child may have been named for that saint in thanks. Thus, you find an explosion of Johns, Margarets, and Katherines. Later on, godparents became another influence on names. In 16th-century England, the normal practice was for every baby to be appointed three godparents, two of the same sex and one of the opposite sex, and the baby would normally be named after one of them.

Survey says: How parents choose their children's names

An informal survey suggests ten ways that parents choose names. Your method may be the 15th or 32nd!

1. A name already used in your family.

2. The name was always a favorite, a name you would have wanted for yourself, perhaps.

3. You just saw the name somewhere — you don't quite remember where — and liked it.

4. You found it while looking through a baby name book and liked what the book said about it.

5. You saw it in a book or magazine (or on a name tag) in the hospital after the baby was born.

6. The name was chosen according to a particular tradition (for example, named for a grandparent or godparent).

7. The name appears in your favorite song or is a favorite fictional character in a book or TV show or movie.

8. It's the name of a close friend.

9. It's the name of a famous person you admire.

10. The name was pure inspiration: It just came to you.

Even when social customs don't prescribe this type of name choice, it is common for parents to include the name of a relative or friend in a child's name to commemorate (or encourage) a special bond between the two. Grandparents are probably the most popular choice for this purpose. Another, although less personal, family connection comes from the practice of giving the mother's maiden name to a child, either as a given name or a middle name. (This has been one of the routes by which surnames turned into given names.) If someone in your family has done genealogical research, your family tree can be an excellent place to brainstorm for name ideas. Even if you didn't know the relative in question personally, it can give your child a sense of history to be named after an ancestor.

Naming after friends and strangers

What more convincing way of expressing your admiration and friendship for someone than naming your child after him or her? Think about all the times you've seen an episode like that on a TV show or in a movie. It's used again and again because the act has such a strong emotional impact. Centuries ago, asking a friend to be godparent to your child, including being a namesake, was a serious lifelong commitment. Today the gesture is more symbolic, but still significant. If you're thinking of doing this, it's an extremely good idea to ask your friend's permission first. People feel proprietary about their names; if you ask, they can feel like they're giving a gift, but if you don't ask, it may feel a little like theft (or at least trespass).

The modern psychological equivalent of naming children after popular saints and royalty has to be the fashion of naming children after celebrities. Few parents are likely to think that doing so will automatically make their child talented, brilliant, or beautiful — and they certainly aren't likely to expect the celebrity to take any notice of a namesake — but celebrity names come with more than a bit of magic and glamour dusted onto them. They come with romantic stories and larger-than-life personalities attached. And that gives the names just a slight edge over the competition.

Evoking culture and heritage

In addition to drawing connections with individuals, names can be used to create a connection with your family's culture or heritage. Many of the popular "classic" names have variants that evolved in a wide variety of cultures and you could choose one that fits your family history. Or if your family includes a non-European heritage, using a name characteristic of that culture can be a reminder of the advantages of having a foot in more than one world.

Part II
Finding Names from Religion and Literature

The 5th Wave · By Rich Tennant

"They said we might notice some changes a week before she went into labor. Sure enough, 5 days ago, gas went up .06 cents at the pump, my lawn mower stopped working, and the guy across the street had his house painted."

In this part . . .

Whether I take names from the books of the great religions, or from novels, plays, and poetry, these names come with detailed and fascinating stories attached. One of the definitions of literature is that it endures across time, and for this reason literary names have been a way to bridge the centuries, reviving classic names again and again.

Chapter 4

Searching Scripture: Names from Judaism, Christianity, and Islam

In This Chapter

▶ Choosing Biblical names from the Old and New Testaments

▶ Understanding names that are prominent in Islamic history

*N*ames chosen for spiritual purposes reflect a capsule history of religion. Some names still in use preserve the veneration of pre-Christian deities. Mark, before it became the name of an evangelist, honored the Roman god Mars. Llewelyn holds traces of two ancient Celtic gods, Lugos and Belinos. Thurstan commemorates the great popularity of Thor in the north of Europe.

With the rise of Christianity, the names of the apostles and prominent Old Testament figures started spreading throughout Europe (John, David, and Anna), as well as names taken from words with Christian associations (Anastasia and Benedict). With an increasing emphasis on the veneration of saints, names like Katherine, Margaret, Nicholas, and Stephan shot up in popularity. When Protestant movements wanted to de-emphasize the veneration of saints (which they associated with Catholicism), an explosion of interest erupted in previously obscure Old Testament names (Benjamin and Jemima) as well as the use of "virtue" names such as Charity and Patience.

As American society has come to embrace its multicultural richness, names that previously were associated strongly with the Jewish community (Israel and Miriam) or Islam (Aisha and Jamal) have spread beyond their original communities. And New Age religious impulses have inspired the adoption of names celebrating the earth (River and Sierra) or spiritual awakening (Sage and Destiny).

Whether you are honoring a particular religious tradition or simply enjoying the name-wealth, the choices are many. This chapter explores names from the "peoples of the book": Judaism, Christianity, and Islam. If all the names that could fit in those categories were included, this chapter would take up half the book. So look for many religious-inspired names in other chapters as well.

Using Old Testament Names

The personal names found in the Old Testament come from a variety of languages: Hebrew, of course, but also its neighbors in the ancient Middle East, such as Egyptian, Persian, and so forth. Many of the oldest names, although commonly interpreted as if they were Hebrew, have origins that are now lost in the mists of time. Some of these names have been in continuous use in the Jewish community since Biblical times. A few were taken up in Christian use very early on, but the greatest fashion for Old Testament names came after the Reformation (see Chapter 9) when people turned away from names associated with Catholicism.

AARON: (m) Egyptian?; meaning uncertain. Many of the names in the early parts of Old Testament are not of Hebrew origin, and in the story of Moses, many of the main characters have Egyptian names. In that story, Aaron was the older brother of Moses and became one of the leaders of the Israelites as they set out for the Promised Land. Aaron has been consistently popular as a Jewish name, but was used only rarely by others before the Reformation. It has been moderately popular in the U.S. throughout the last century, peaking in the '70s. Well-known bearers of the name include Revolutionary War hero and vice president Aaron Burr, composer Aaron Copland, and TV producer Aaron Spelling. Variants: **Aron** and **Arron.**

ABDIEL: (m) Hebrew; servant. This was the name of a man mentioned in passing in the book of Chronicles. It has been revived at various times, but never with any major popularity. There has been some interest in it in recent years for unclear reasons. One bearer is in-line skater Abdiel Colberg.

ABEL: (m) Hebrew?; possibly "God is father," possibly "son," but it's uncertain that the name should be interpreted as Hebrew in the first place. Abel was the second son of Adam and Eve, killed by his brother Cain out of jealousy. The sympathies of those who have come after are clear in that Cain has been extremely rare while Abel has enjoyed occasional popularity. It has been increasing steadily in use over the last century. Famous bearers of the name have included Abel Tasman, after whom Tasmania was named, and French film writer and director Abel Gance.

ABIGAIL: (f) Hebrew; father's joy. The Biblical Abigail was a wise and generous woman who became the wife of King David. The name was popularized after the Reformation and became extremely common in the 17th century. It was then given some bad press by becoming a slang term for a lady's maid and largely fell out of use. Only the diminutive Abbie shows up on the popularity charts in the early 20th century, but the full name started coming back in midcentury and made it all the way up to number 6 in recent years. GAIL is another diminutive (see Chapter 19). Famous bearers include First Lady Abigail Adams and advice columnist Abigail Van Buren (actually a pen name used by a series of writers). Variants: **Abagail, Abbigail, Abigale,** and **Abigayle.** Diminutives: **Abbey, Abbie,** and **Abby.**

ASA: (m) Hebrew; created. This was the name of an early king of Judah. It was revived in recent centuries along with other Biblical names and was relatively popular in the 19th century. It fell completely out of fashion in the mid–20th century but has been making something of a comeback in the last couple decades. (There is also an unrelated Swedish feminine name Asa.)

ASHER: (m) Canaanite; the name of a god, used as a given name. Asher was a son of Jacob, and so a brother of Joseph of the many-colored coat. Historically it has never been particularly popular outside the Jewish community, although there has been a sudden more general interest in the last decade. The name may also sometimes be from the unrelated English surname meaning "dweller by an ash tree."

BATHSHEBA: (f) Hebrew; daughter of the oath. The story of how King David fell in love with Bathsheba has always had romantic appeal, although David's plot to get rid of her inconvenient husband tends to get swept under the rug. She then became the mother of Solomon. The name was used occasionally after the Renaissance but never seems to have caught on. One literary bearer is the central character of Thomas Hardy's novel *Far From the Madding Crowd.*

BENJAMIN: (m) Hebrew; son of the right hand; possibly originally a tribal name. This is the name of the youngest son of Jacob who played a key role in the story of Joseph (see under that name). It was a rare name before the Reformation, but after that it became quite popular. Around 1700 it was regularly in the top-ten most popular names, and though it's had ups and downs since then, it has always been a favorite. The name has lent itself to a number of diminutives, including BEN (Chapter 16), Benjy, and Benny. With such continued popularity, well-known bearers are easy to find: Revolutionary statesman Benjamin Franklin, Dr. Benjamin Spock (advisor to several generations of parents), U.S. president Benjamin Harrison, and composer Benjamin Britten. Diminutives: **Benjie, Benjy,** and **Benny.**

BETHIA: (f) Hebrew; daughter of God. This name appears for the daughter of an Egyptian pharaoh. When revived after the Reformation, it was probably helped by its resemblance to BETH (Chapter 10), but it has never been particularly popular.

CAIN: (m) Hebrew; spear. Cain was the son of Adam and Eve who killed his brother Abel out of jealousy. Given its background, it's not surprising that the name has never been seriously revived, although there has been a small amount of interest in the mid '90s. It may sometimes be confused with the unrelated surname KANE (Chapter 10).

DANIELLE (f), **DANIEL** (m): Hebrew; God is judge. This was the name of a prophet and a book of the Bible named after him. The Biblical Daniel may be best remembered for surviving unharmed in the lions' den. Dan can be a diminutive, although it also appears as the name of an Israelite tribe. Daniel is one of the minority of Old Testament names that became popular in the Medieval period, but unlike some of them, it also benefited from many of the

Biblical revivals. And unlike many Biblical names that declined after the 19th century, Daniel has been rising steadily over the last century and has been in the top-ten names for the last couple of decades. Feminine forms have been found in parallel with the masculine name. The French Danielle became popular quite rapidly in the second half of the 20th century, and unusual variants like Danica and Danette can also be found. Well-known bearers are plentiful. On the male side you can find pioneer folk-hero Daniel Boone, singer Danny Kaye, actors Daniel Day-Lewis and Daniel Radcliffe, senator and orator Daniel Webster, and for an unusual spelling variant, basketball player Donyell Marshall. On the female side, you can find have romance novelist Danielle Steel and actress Danica McKellar, among others. Variants: (f) **Danelle, Danette, Danica, Daniela, Daniella, Danika, Danita,** and **Danyelle;** (m) **Danial** and **Donyell.** Diminutives: **Dan.** (See also DANNY in Chapter 10.)

DAVID: (m) Hebrew?; possibly "darling, beloved," although the Hebrew origin is not entirely certain. The Biblical David had the sort of adventurous folk-hero's life that endeared his story to future generations. This would have been enough on its own to ensure the name's popularity, but it was, in addition, used by a 7th-century bishop who became the patron saint of Wales. In addition to becoming a wildly popular name in Wales, there were two early kings of Scotland named after the saint, which increased its popularity there. This saintly association caused the name David to suffer somewhat after the Reformation, and early use in America tends to be associated specifically with Welsh immigrants. Welsh use also contributed the nickname Davy as well as the surname Davis, which has also come to be used as a given name. David was quite popular coming into the 20th century and rose as high as number 2 in the '60s, with Davy and Dave tagging along for the ride. There have been many well-known bearers of this name, including U.S. president Dwight David Eisenhower, rock singer David Bowie, and soccer star David Beckham. The diminutives are found for jazz artist Dave Brubeck and semi-legendary frontiersman Davy Crockett. Variant: **Davis.** Diminutives: **Dave, Davey, Davie,** and **Davy.**

DEBORAH: (f) Hebrew?; a honeybee. As with many of the very early names, the Hebrew origin is not entirely certain. The Biblical Deborah was a judge and prophet — one of the few women with that type of prominence in the Old Testament. The name didn't catch on generally during the Medieval period, and had only a mild popularity after the Reformation, perhaps because the same people reviving Biblical names were a bit uncomfortable with Deborah's encroachment into "male" territory. It was fading out in the 19th century, but then saw an explosion of interest starting around the '30s, making it into the top ten in the '50s, both in the full form and the slightly shortened Debra. Well-known bearers include actress Deborah Kerr and linguist Deborah Tannen. See DEBBY (Chapter 10) for the diminutive. Variants: **Debbra, Debora, Debra,** and **Debrah.**

DELILAH: (f) Hebrew; delight. The treachery of the Biblical Delilah towards her lover Samson was not calculated to make her name popular during Biblical name revivals, but it has been used very occasionally since the 17th century. It tends to be more familiar from popular culture, such as Saint-Saëns' 19th-century opera *Samson and Delilah* and the 1917 pop song "Delilah," rather than from famous bearers.

DINAH: (f) Hebrew; judged, vindicated. If the latter meaning is more accurate, this may have been a nickname given to the Biblical character after her brothers avenged her seduction. The name was revived occasionally after the Reformation, but only became significantly popular in the 19th century. More recently it has a slight popularity in the mid–20th century. Variants on Dina are also found around that time, but this may be from an entirely separate origin. George Eliot named a character Dinah Morris in her 1859 novel *Adam Bede.* Today the best known bearer is probably singer and variety show host (and golf tournament sponsor) Dinah Shore. Variants: **Dina, Deena,** and **Dena.**

EDEN: (f) Hebrew; delight, paradise. This is the name of the idyllic paradise of the book of Genesis in which Adam and Eve first lived. It has been used occasionally as a given name since the Reformation, but has only become significantly popular in the last couple of decades. One bearer is actress Eden Riegel.

ELI: (m) Hebrew; lifted up, or possibly some unknown compound based on *el* "God." Some of the name's popularity may come from other names beginning with "Eli-" such as Elias or Elijah. Eli was revived after the Reformation and has enjoyed a mild and variable popularity over the last century. The name is familiar from bearers such as inventor Eli Whitney, actor Eli Wallach, and chemist Eli Lilly who founded the pharmaceutical company that bears his name.

ELIAS: (m) Hebrew; Jehovah is God. This is a Greek form of the same name as ELIJAH. It was quite popular during the Middle Ages when it gave rise to diminutives such as ELLIOT (Chapter 8). It is found for 17th century antiquarian Elias Ashmole, the founder of Britain's Ashmolean Museum. More recently it has been mildly popular, as for film director Elia Kazan. Variant: **Elia.**

ELIEZER: (m) Hebrew; help of God. There were a number of minor Biblical characters with this name. It has been rare outside the Jewish community, where it was borne by Eliezer Ben-Yehuda who led the modern revival of Hebrew as a living language.

ELIHU: (m) Hebrew; meaning uncertain, but most likely involving the element *el* "God." This is a rather rare name, but borne, for example, by politician Elihu Root.

ELIJAH: (m) Hebrew; Jehovah is God. This is the form of the name used in the King James Version of the Bible and it tended to replace ELIAS in the 17th century and later, although in the last century the names have had quite similar popularities. Familiar bearers include Black Muslim leader Elijah Muhammad and actor Elijah Wood. Variant: **Alijah.**

ELISHA: (m) Hebrew; God is salvation. Elisha was the name of an early prophet credited with a number of miracles. The name has been used only rarely since the Reformation. One familiar bearer is Elisha G. Otis, the inventor of the elevator.

ENOCH: (m) Hebrew; dedicated. This was the name of a grandson of Adam and Eve and the father of Methuselah. It has been used occasionally during Biblical revivals, both in this form and in the Greek version Enos, but has always been rare. Bearers include baseball hall-of-famer Enos Slaughter and big band leader Enoch Light. Variant: **Enos.**

ESTHER: (f) Persian?; myrtle. In the Biblical story of Esther, her name is identified as the Persian equivalent of Hebrew Hadassah, meaning the tree myrtle, but it is also similar to the Persian word for "star." (Hadassah is popular as a Jewish name.) Despite Esther's interesting and dramatic story, the name was never more than mildly popular during Biblical revivals. Nathaniel Hawthorne's use of Hester for the adulterous heroine of *The Scarlet Letter* may not have added to the name's popularity. Other literary bearers include Hester Bush in James Fenimore Cooper's *The Prairie,* and the central character of Charles Dickens's *Bleak House.* More recent bearers have included Olympic swimmer Esther Williams and fantasy novelist Esther Friesner. The variant Hester may sometimes have given rise to the diminutive Hettie, although this can also come from Henrietta. Somewhat confusingly, Esther was sometimes written as Easter. This group of names was quite popular in the early 20th century but has fallen off significantly since then. Variants: **Easter, Ester,** and **Hester.** Diminutive: **Hettie.**

EZEKIEL: (m) Hebrew; strength of God. Ezekiel was an early prophet famed for his visions and oracles. The name was revived occasionally since the Reformation, but has been enjoying something of a resurgence since the '70s, possibly for the sake of its diminutive Zeke. An early literary use is for the character Ezekiel Edgeworth in Ben Jonson's 1614 *Bartholomew Fair.* Variant: **Ezequiel.** Diminutive: **Zeke.**

EZRA: (m) Hebrew; help. The Biblical Ezra was a priest and scribe, prominent in the period after the Babylonian exile. It enjoyed a brief revival in the 18th century but has never been particularly popular since then. One recent bearer is poet Ezra Pound.

GENESIS: (f) Greek; birth, origin, creation. This is the name of the first book of the Old Testament, because it was concerned with the creation of the world. This name was not part of previous Biblical revivals but has suddenly become quite popular in the last two decades. Interest in the name has been too recent to produce well-known bearers, but one possible additional source of inspiration might be the rock band Genesis.

GIDEON: (m) Hebrew; one who hews or cuts down. As the Biblical Gideon was a general as well as a judge, this may originally have been a nickname. The name has been adopted occasionally since the Reformation but has always been fairly rare. Walter Scott used it for a minor character in his novel *The Heart of Midlothian,* but the name is primarily familiar today from the Gideon Society, which supplies free Bibles to many institutions.

HANNAH: (f) Hebrew; grace, favor. This was the name of the mother of the prophet Samuel. It is the same name as the ANNA of the New Testament (see Chapter 8). While Anna became extremely popular during the Medieval period, Hannah was not revived until the Reformation, when it became quite popular. This popularity fell off during the 19th century to almost disappear by the mid–20th, but in recent decades it has been shooting up again and has made it into the top ten. The name occurs for historian and political theorist Hannah Arendt, as well as the title character of the Woody Allen movie *Hannah and Her Sisters.* Variants: **Chana, Hana,** and **Hanna.**

HULDA: (f) Hebrew; weasel. Despite the name's meaning, the Biblical Huldah was a respected prophet. The name had some mild popularity around the turn of the 20th century. Variant: **Huldah.**

IRA: (f, m) Hebrew; watchful. The Biblical name is masculine, but it has been used for women as well, due to confusion of the "-a" ending (a gender rule that doesn't hold in Hebrew). It has been variably popular over the last couple of centuries, more so for men than women. Familiar bearers include author Ira Levin and lyricist Ira Gerschwin.

ISAAC: (m) Hebrew?; laughter. As with many early Biblical names, this may be a mistaken interpretation of a non-Hebrew name. The Biblical episode of how Abraham nearly sacrificed Isaac at God's command was a popular image in Medieval art, and the name is one of the few Old Testament names used in that period. It continued in popularity after the Reformation to the present day. The diminutive Ike was popular in the early part of the 20th century. Well-known bearers range from mathematician Isaac Newton to science and science fiction writer Isaac Asimov to pop singer Isaac Hayes. Variants: **Isaak** and **Issac.** Diminutive: **Ike.**

ISAIAH: (m) Hebrew; God's salvation. This was the name of one or more early prophets whose names may have become conflated at a later date. It has been used occasionally during the Biblical revivals but has enjoyed a sharp rise in popularity in the last few decades. Bearers include the philosopher Isaiah Berlin and conductor Isaiah Jackson. The Greek form Isaias is also sometimes found. Variants: **Isiah, Izaiah, Isai,** and **Isaias.**

ISRAEL: (m) Hebrew; ruling with God. Jacob took this on as a second name and it was also used for the twelve Jewish tribes as a whole — a use revived for the modern nation of Israel. It has never been more than mildly popular as a given name, with bearers such as Revolutionary general Israel Putnam and the title character of Herman Melville's novel *Israel Potter.*

JAEL: (f) Hebrew; generally understood as "wild mountain goat," but an alternate interpretation would derive it from two elements meaning "God," as the same ones Elijah uses in the opposite order. The name has been extremely rare during the Biblical revivals, perhaps because of the questionable behavior of its namesake. One current bearer is single-name science fiction book illustrator Jael.

JOEL: (m) Hebrew; God is God, or Jehovah is God. This was a popular name in the Old Testament with several bearers, most notably an early prophet. The name may have been especially popular during Biblical revivals for its shortness and the absence of the tongue-twister quality that many Old Testament names have. It has been moderately popular throughout the last century and bearers include children's writer Joel Chandler Harris and actor Joel Grey.

JONAH: (m) Hebrew; dove. A Greek version of this name, Jonas, is also found. The Biblical Jonah is famous for having been swallowed by a big fish (although pop culture has turned it into a whale), by which God rescued him from drowning. Both Jonah and Jonas have been in occasional use since the Reformation, although Jonas has been the more popular. Jonah has been making something of a comeback in recent decades. One famous bearer of this name is Dr. Jonas Salk, who developed the polio vaccine. Variant: **Jonas.**

JONATHAN: (m) Hebrew; God gave. This basic meaning is found in a variety of names, including the Hebrew Nathaniel and Nathan, and the Greek Theodore, Dorothea, and so on. The Biblical Jonathan, son of King Saul, was legendary for the strength of his friendship with his father's eventual successor, David. The Greek form Jonathas was used very rarely in the Medieval period, but the primary interest in this name came with the Reformation. It was probably helped by the name's resemblance to the extremely popular John. During the 17th and 18th centuries, Jonathan was consistently in the top-ten names. It became much less popular in the 19th century and has only significantly regained ground in the last half-century. Some of the spelling variants show influence from John, but the diminutive Jon is generally understood to stand for Jonathan. Bearers have included 18th-century author Jonathan Swift (of *Gulliver's Travels*) and actor Jon Voight. Variants: **Johathan, Johnathan, Johnathon, Jonatan,** and **Jonathon.** Diminutive: **Jon.**

JUDAH: (m) Hebrew; meaning uncertain, possibly "God will lead" or "he is praised." There were several Old Testament figures by this name, most notably a son of Jacob. The Greek version, Judas, is used in the New Testament, but never saw any general popularity due to its association with Judas Iscariot, although another association is with the Roman-era Jewish patriot Judas Maccabeus. Another variant, Jude, is most often associated with Saint Jude, the patron saint of hopeless causes, as well as with the Beatles's song "Hey, Jude." None of these names have been more than rare in recent centuries. Variants: **Judas** and **Jude.**

JUDITH: (f) Hebrew; woman of Judea, Jewish woman. There is a Judith in Genesis, but the popularity of the name derives primarily from the Judith who appears in the Apocrypha: a beautiful widow who, to save her people from the invading Assyrians, seduced and beheaded the Assyrian general, Holofernes. (This scene has been a popular one among painters.) The name was used occasionally in the Middle Ages, but was not seriously popularized until the Reformation. Its mild popularity in the 19th century picked up drastically in the '30s for no obvious reason, and the name made it into the top ten in the next decade. Some of the most famous bearers have used the diminutive JUDY (Chapter 18), but the full form is found for novelist Judith Kranz and astronaut Judith Resnik.

LEAH: (f) Hebrew?; sometimes interpreted as "weary," other times as "cow" or "antelope," although a Hebrew origin for the name is not certain in either case. The Biblical Leah was the first wife of Jacob. This has been used occasionally during the usual Biblical revivals and has risen to a moderate popularity in the last half century. It may sometimes fall together with LEE or LEIGH (Chapter 14) and may have contributed to those names becoming increasingly considered girls' names.

LEVI: (m) Hebrew; attached, joined. This was the son of Jacob and Leah whose descendents became the priestly class known as Levites. The name has been mildly popular in modern times, although strongly associated with the Jewish community. The best known bearer may be clothing manufacturer Levi Strauss (not to be confused with French anthropologist Claude Levi-Strauss).

MALACHI: (m) Hebrew; my messenger. While this may not have been intended as a personal name in the Bible, it has been interpreted as one by later ages and taken up for occasional use since the Reformation. It was particularly popular in Ireland where it was used to substitute for some similar-sounding Gaelic names. Novelist Walter Scott sometimes used the pseudonym Malachi Malagrowther, taken from one of his fictional characters. The name has seen a sudden interest in the last decade after being largely out of use for over a century. Variant: **Malaka.**

MEHITABEL: (f) Hebrew; God does good. The more standard Biblical form is Mehetabel, which is found for both male and female characters. When revived after the Reformation, it seems to have been considered exclusively feminine. It was quite popular for some time in the 18th century but fell largely out of use by the 20th. For most people today, it is familiar largely as Mehitabel the cat, companion to Don Marquis's poetic alter ego, the cockroach Archy. Variant: **Mehetabel.**

MICAH: (f, m) Hebrew; who is like God. This was the name of several men in the Bible, most notably an early prophet. A literary use is for the title character of Arthur Conan Doyle's novel *Micah Clarke*. Today Micah seems to have become somewhat confused with MICHAEL (Chapter 8) and came back into use after a long drought just at the time that Michael was taking the number-1 spot among boys' names. Interestingly, Micah is being used for both boys and girls currently.

MIRIAM: (f) Hebrew?; meaning uncertain, and possibly Egyptian in origin rather than Hebrew, given the name's connection to other characters with probably-Egyptian names, such as Moses and Aaron. This name also gave rise to MARY (Chapter 8), and the variants are often used to distinguish Old and New Testament bearers of the name. The name has been revived occasionally since the 18th century and has been mildly, but consistently, popular since then. Bearers include historical mystery novelist Miriam Grace Monfredo and actress Miriam Margolyes. Variants: **Maryam, Mariam,** and **Myriam.**

MORDECAI: (m) Hebrew?; possibly a Hebrew rendering of the Babylonian divinity name Marduk. Mordecai is a major figure in the story of Esther. The name seems to have been largely skipped over during the major Biblical revivals. Recent bearers include Canadian novelist Mordecai Richler and baseball hall-of-famer Mordecai Brown. Variant: **Mordechai.**

MOSES: (m) Egyptian?; possibly "son," as in the latter part of the name Rameses. Those who prefer to give the name a Hebrew origin connect it with a word meaning "to draw out," but if the Biblical story of Moses has any historic basis, then you would expect his name to be Egyptian, given by his adoptive mother. Moses is one of a small handful of names that have come to be popular among all three religious cultures influenced by the Old Testament: used as Moshe in Hebrew, as Moses among Christians, and as Musa by Muslims. It was revived to some extent after the Reformation and became particularly popular among African Americans for whom the story of Moses leading his people out of slavery had particular resonance. The name Moses itself has declined somewhat in popularity in the latter half of the 20th century, but the difference has been made up by the variants Moises and Moshe. One familiar bearer is actor Moses Gunn. Variants: **Moises, Moshe,** and **Musa.** Diminutive: **Mose.**

NAOMI: (f) Hebrew; pleasant, pleasure. In the Biblical story of Ruth and Naomi, the name is contrasted in a play on words with Marah "bitterness." It was revived after the Reformation and achieved a certain popularity around the turn of the 20th century. Familiar bearers include actress Naomi Watts and model Naomi Campbell. Variants: **Naoma** and **Noemi.**

NOAH: (m) Hebrew?; rest. The Hebrew origin is uncertain, however, and some consider Noah to be a shortening of a Hebrew translation of the Sumerian flood-survivor Zi-ud-sudda, "life of days long." The story of Noah building a ship to preserve two of every living creature from the Flood has been a favorite among artists since the Medieval period. There was some rare use of the name in the early Medieval period, including for a Breton saint, but the primary interest came after the Reformation. After a steady decline in popularity until the mid–20th century, it has seen a resurgence in recent decades and become extremely popular. One famous bearer is Noah Webster, who created the first specifically American dictionary in 1828 (and had a major influence on the distinctions in American and British spelling). Variant: **Noe.**

RACHEL: (f) Hebrew?; ewe, lamb. The origin of the name is not entirely certain. Rachel was the woman that Jacob worked seven years to marry — only to have her sister Leah substituted in her place, forcing him to work another seven years. The name was revived after the Reformation but was not among the more popular Biblical names until the 20th century. It had a particular boost around the '70s and has remained high on the charts since then. The spelling Rachael has also been popular, due to confusion with other Biblical names ending in "-ael," as well as the Spanish form Raquel. Well-known bearers include conservationist Rachel Carson, author of *Silent Spring,* and actress Raquel Welch. Variants: **Rachael, Racheal, Rachelle, Racquel,** and **Raquel.**

REBECCA: (f) uncertain; meaning uncertain, although some have tried to connect it with a Hebrew root meaning "heifer, cow." In the Bible, Rebecca was something of a mail-order bride fetched by Abraham for his son Isaac. Although there isn't as much drama in her story as in some others, the name became quite popular after the Reformation and has continued so to the present. Rebecca has been an extremely common literary name, being given to prominent figures in Walter Scott's *Ivanhoe,* William Makepeace Thackeray's *Vanity Fair,* and to the title characters of Daphne du Maurier's *Rebecca* and Kate D. Wiggin's *Rebecca of Sunnybrook Farm.* The usual diminutive is Becky, but Reba or Reva is also found. Prominent bearers have included pro basketball player Rebecca Lobo and country singer Reba McEntire. Variants: **Rebeca** and **Rebekah.** Diminutives: **Becky, Reba,** and **Reva.**

REUBEN: (m) Hebrew; meaning uncertain, but probably ending in *ben* meaning "son." One common interpretation is, "Behold, a son!" The name was revived mostly in the 18th and 19th centuries, but suffered somewhat from becoming a nickname for a country hick (especially in the diminutive Rube). It has been only moderately popular in the last century. The Woody Guthrie song "Reuben James" commemorated the ship of that name, the first to be lost by the U.S. Navy in World War II. The ship in turn was named after a boatswain's mate famous for his heroism during the Barbary Wars in the early 19th century. Another musical connection for the name is boxer Reuben "Hurricane" Carter, whose legal struggles were immortalized in a song by Bob Dylan. Variants: **Ruben, Rubin, Rueben.**

RUTH: (f) uncertain; meaning uncertain — if her story is historical, then her name is presumably Moabite, after the culture of her birth, and attempts to understand it as Hebrew, meaning "beloved," are misguided. The attractiveness of the Biblical story of Ruth, involving romance, faithfulness, friendship, and conversion, no doubt made this a particularly popular name and it was taken up fairly early after the Reformation. It may also have received a boost from the fashion for virtue names as "ruth," taken as an English word, means "compassion, mercy." After some ups and downs, Ruth was solidly in the top-ten names by the late 19th century and only began to decline with the shifts in name fashion in the mid–20th century. Some well-known bearers of the name have included British novelist Ruth Rendell, children's author Ruth Plumly Thomson, who continued the Oz books after Frank L. Baum, and psychologist Dr. Ruth Westheimer. Variant: **Ruthe.** Diminutive: **Ruthie.**

SAMSON: (m) Hebrew; sun. There are some clues in the Biblical story of Samson that he was originally a sun god, later diluted down into a folk hero. The story is very dramatic, what with slaying lions and super-strength magically bound up with un-cut hair, love and betrayal, and the final pulling down of the temple by the blinded Samson. This sort of imagery evidently appealed to Medieval folk, who made the name popular (including use by a saint or two), but was perhaps less attractive during the post-Reformation revivals. More recent use may come indirectly from the surname, but today the name is quite rare.

SAMUEL: (m) Hebrew; name of God, or perhaps "heard by God." The Biblical Samuel was involved in the establishment of Saul in the kingship, as well as in the choice of David to succeed him. Samuel was used occasionally in the Medieval period and became immensely popular after the Reformation, making it into the top ten by the late 18th century. It has fallen off only gradually, and the diminutives Sam and Sammy have held high places on the charts over the last century alongside the full name. In the early part of the 20th century, Sammie is also found occasionally for girls, at a time when it isn't likely to be a diminutive of Samantha or some other specifically feminine name. Given Samuel's popularity, it isn't hard to find well-known bearers: Revolutionary patriot Samuel Adams, Texas icon Sam Houston, Morse code inventor Samuel Morse, author Samuel Clemens (also known as Mark Twain), and baseball superstar Sammy Sosa. Diminutives: **Sam, Sammie,** and **Sammy.**

SARAH: (f) Hebrew; princess. The wife of the patriarch Abraham was originally named Sarai, interpreted as if it was Hebrew meaning "contrition," and the story of her name change may simply represent the reinterpretation of an originally non-Hebrew name as a more familiar word. This is one of the few feminine Old Testament names that was taken up into general use as early as the Medieval period, but its popularity increased significantly after the Reformation and it made it into the top five names in the 17th century. This very popularity eventually made it seem common and old-fashioned, causing it to fall off somewhat in the late 19th century, but in the later part of the 20th century it has picked up again and made it back into the top five. It has also given rise to popular diminutives: SADIE and SALLY (Chapter 9). Well-known actresses with this name have included Sarah Bernhardt, Sarah Jessica Parker, and Sarah Michelle Gellar. Variants: **Sara, Sarai, Sarina,** and **Sarahi.**

Preferring or avoiding religious names

Religious names are so much a part of our culture we often don't examine our attitudes towards them unless we bump into someone with a radically different background. On one side, you may be boggled to run into someone named *Jesus* or *Christ* (but not someone named *Joshua* or *Christine*), or on the other side you might observe the bogglement of a traditional Muslim encountering an American named one of the attributes of God, such as *Raheem* (the merciful), rather than using a devotional form such *as Abd-al-Raheem* (servant of the Merciful).

Neither the use nor the avoidance of particular religious names is obvious or logical. Today, the use of saints' names like Patrick, Bridget, and Colm is strongly associated with Irish naming. But until around the 16th century, the Irish considered these names too holy to be used directly, and instead used compounds meaning "devotee of so-and-so" such as *Gilbride, Malcolm,* and *Gospatrick.* It was only after significant exposure to English naming patterns that the use of "bare" saints' names became fashionable in Ireland.

When the Reformation swept through northern Europe, many of the popular names of the day (taken from saints' names) were considered too closely associated with the Catholic Church for comfort, so parents looked to more obscure Biblical inspirations (conveniently available in the native-language Bible translations that had helped spark the Reformation in the first place).

Sometimes the extreme popularity of a holy name led people to substitute an associated nickname that then turned into an independent name. So in Spanish, "Mary of the sorrows" produced *Delores* (sorrows) and "Mary of the mercies" produced *Mercedes* (mercies), while the surname of St. Frances Xavier took off on its own as *Xavier* or *Javier* (thus giving us one of the very few Basque-origin names in American circulation).

SOLOMON: (m) Hebrew; peace. Some historians believe that King Solomon's name may originally have been a nickname, due to the peace and prosperity of his reign. One reason for the name's popularity was the association of Solomon with wise judgments. Solomon was used in the earlier Medieval periods, then fell out of favor until revived again with the Reformation. It is no more than moderately common today. Diminutive: **Sol.**

URIEL: (m) Hebrew; God is light. The two Biblical figures with this name are obscure and unimportant — not that that has ever kept a Biblical name from being used. The very recent interest in the name may come more from the tradition that it belongs to one of the archangels (along with Michael, Gabriel, and others).

YADIEL: (m) Hebrew; may God cause rejoicing. This appears to be a Spanish variant of a name that appears in the King James Version of the Bible as Jahdiel. Neither version has ever been particularly common, but Yadiel has hit the charts just in the last few years. One bearer is in-line skating champ Yadiel Cruz.

Resurrecting New Testament Names

The most popular New Testament names will be covered in Chapter 8, as their greatest use began in the Medieval period. Here you see some of the less prominent (although still popular) names from the time of Christ, as well as some names (such as Alpha and Veronica) associated with events in the New Testament, even though they do not appear there as names.

ALPHA: (f, m) Greek; the first letter of the alphabet, used as a symbol for "the beginning." The use of Alpha as a name most likely comes from the passage where Jesus says, "I am the alpha and the omega," meaning the beginning and the end (omega being the last letter in Greek). The name may sometimes have been given to a first child and was popular for a while around the turn of the 20th century.

BARTHOLOMEW: (m) Hebrew; son of Talmai (where Talmai is a personal name meaning "abounding in furrows"). This was the nickname of the apostle Nathanael and was sometimes taken for a given name. An early saint named after him popularized the name in the Medieval period and a market fair originally held in honor of the saint is the setting for Ben Johnson's play *Bartholomew Fair* (the name also being borne by his main character, Bartholomew Cokes). A more recent fictional character, Bart Simpson, uses the name's most popular diminutive. The full name has not been used much over the last century. Diminutive: **Bart.**

BAUTISTA: (m) Spanish; baptist, one who baptizes. By far the most popular New Testament figure for whom names were given was John the Baptist. In addition to using JOHN (Chapter 8) in all its many variants, the compound "John-Baptist" was popular in several cultures, including Italian (Gianbattista), French (Jean-Baptiste), and Spanish (Juan Bautista). In time, these compounds were treated as if they were two separate given names and some variants of Baptist became independent names. Despite the "-a" ending, showing that the word is grammatically feminine, the connection with John the Baptist has been strong enough to keep the name masculine.

BERENICE: (f) Greek; bringer of victory. The name is only mentioned in passing in the New Testament, and despite an early martyr who bore it, it wasn't taken up in general use until after the Reformation. It became moderately popular by the late 19th century but then came to be seen as somewhat old-fashioned. The name was used by the title character of Jean Baptiste Racine's 1670 play *Berenice,* and more recently was borne by photographer Berenice Abbott. Variants: **Berneice, Bernice, Berniece,** and **Burnice.**

DAMARIS: (f) Greek?; meaning uncertain. The name is mentioned in passing as an Athenian woman converted by Paul. It was popular for a while after the Reformation but fell largely out of use in the 19th century. It has been enjoying a slight revival in the last half century. Well-known bearers have included 17th-century philosopher Damaris Masham and actress Damaris Hayman.

DORCAS: (f) Greek; a gazelle. The name is given as an alternate or translation for the Hebrew TABITHA (Chapter 16), the name of a woman known for her good works and alms. It was fairly popular after the Reformation, and particularly in early new England, but came to be viewed as outdated and disappeared from the popularity charts in the early 20th century. Early film actress Dorcas Matthews is one bearer. Despite the beautiful meaning of this name and its honorable history, it would be hard today to recommend naming a daughter something that shortens to "dork."

EMANUEL: (m) Hebrew; God is with us. This was originally an epithet of Christ, and has only rarely been used as part of Biblical revivals in English. It came into use much earlier, however, in Greek and Spanish, among others, and American use typically comes from those venues. Well-known bearers have included philosopher Immanuel Kant and actor Emmanuel Lewis, and using the name's diminutive, baseball player Manny Ramirez. Variants: **Emmanuel, Immanuel,** and **Manuel.**

EUNICE: (f) Greek; good victory. The Biblical Eunice is the mother of Timothy, the namesake of one of the books of the New Testament. The name has been moderately popular since the Reformation but has declined greatly over the last century. Bearers have included actress Eunice Gayson and track star Eunice Barber.

GABRIELA (f), **GABRIEL** (m): Hebrew; mighty God, or God is mighty. The Archangel Gabriel is God's messenger in the Nativity story and the name became popular in both male and female forms during the Middle Ages. Its use was not significantly changed by the Reformation and in recent decades it has been seeing renewed popularity. The French and Italian feminine forms Gabrielle and Gabriella became somewhat popular in the 19th century, but in general, the feminine forms have only been hitting the charts in the latter half of the 20th century, working their way up fairly quickly. Familiar male bearers include Colombian novelist Gabriel Garcia Marquez, actor Gabriel Kaplan, and TV character Gabe Kotter on the show *Welcome Back Kotter.* Female bearers have included tennis star Gabriela Sabatini and Canadian novelist Gabrielle Roy. Variants: (f) **Gabriella** and **Gabrielle.** Diminutive: (m) **Gabe.**

JESUS: (m) Hebrew; God is generous, or God helps. This is technically the same name as JOSHUA (Chapter 10), but the difference is used to distinguish Christ from others of the same name. In many cultures, the name Jesus has been considered too sacred for ordinary use, and its American popularity today is primarily through the Hispanic community. One bearer is television director Jesús Salvador Treviño.

JOACHIM: (m) Hebrew; may God raise up or exalt. The Apocrypha give this name to the father of Mary, and this led to its popularity in the Medieval period. It fell largely out of use in English by the Reformation and, not being a strictly Biblical name, was not part of the usual revivals. Current American use is generally taken from German or a similar source. One bearer is Flemish Renaissance painter Joachim de Patinir. The Spanish version, JOAQUIN (Chapter 18) is more common.

JOSEPH: (f, m) Hebrew?; increase. The name may, however be of unknown origin. As a name closely associated with the life of Jesus, this was in regular use in the Medieval era, but the Old Testament Joseph (he of the many-colored coat) guaranteed that the name would remain popular after the Reformation and it has regularly held a place in the top-ten male names at various times since then. Throughout the last century, it has never dropped out of the top twenty names, and cultural variants such as Italian Giuseppe and Spanish Jose have also been on the charts. Women have used the forms Joseph and the diminutive Joe occasionally as well, although specifically feminine forms such as JOSEPHINE (Chapter 9) and JO (Chapter 10) have been more common. Joey became popular for boys in the latter half of the 20th century and was used rarely by girls in that period as well. The commonness of Joseph can be seen in its use in World War II for the generic American soldier, G.I. Joe. Real-life bearers include folklorist Joseph Campbell, Connecticut senator Joseph Lieberman, and composer Giuseppe Verdi. All fields of sport have their Josephs, including Joe DiMaggio (baseball), Joe Frazier (boxing), Joe Namath and Joe Montana (football), Jose Canseco (baseball), and Jose Santos (horseracing). Variants: (m) **Giuseppe, Guiseppe, Jose, Josef, Yosef,** and **Yusuf.** Diminutives: (both) **Joe** and **Joey.**

JUDE: (m) Hebrew; a variant of JUDAH. This version of the name is often used for the apostle Judas Thaddaeus to distinguish him from less savory Judases. It has been used occasionally since the Reformation, including for the title character of Thomas Hardy's novel *Jude the Obscure.* Current bearers include actor Jude Law. Variant: **Judd.**

LAZARUS: (m) Hebrew; a Latin form of the name ELIEZER. This form is associated with the story of the man Lazarus who was raised from the dead, as well as the diseased beggar of the parable of Dives and Lazarus, from which the name came to be synonymous with "a leper." This probably goes a long way towards explaining why the name has been used very rarely during Biblical revivals. The only version that has hit the popularity charts in the last century has been the Spanish Lazaro. Variant: **Lazaro.**

LUKE: (m) Greek; a man from Lucania, a region of southern Italy. This name is not to be confused with the name Lucius, from a Latin word for "light." As the name of one of the four evangelists, this came into use in the Medieval period, although nowhere near as commonly as JOHN (Chapter 8). It has had a steady, if mild, popularity ever since, and has been increasing significantly in the last several decades. The Latin form, Lucas, is also found — a connection that film director George Lucas used to name the hero of his *Star Wars* movies Luke. Other bearers have included Renaissance artist Lucas Cranach, actor Luke Perry, and soap opera character Luke Spencer, of *General Hospital*'s perennial "Luke and Laura" romance. Variants: **Luc, Luca, Lucas,** and **Lukas.**

MARK: (m) Latin; belonging to Mars, the god of war. Despite being the name of one of the evangelists, Mark was uncommon both during the Medieval period and after the Reformation. And revivals have as often been classical (after Mark Anthony) as Biblical. This changed coming into the 20th century when the name hit a run of popularity that took it up to the top ten in the '50s and '60s. The Latin form, Marcus, has been only slightly less popular, and Spanish or Italian versions such as Marco and Marcos are also currently in the competition. Bearers have included Mark Twain (the pen name of Samuel Clemens), baseball star Mark McGwire, actor Mark Hamill, Olympic swimming champion Mark Spitz, beloved television character Marcus Welby, and artist Marc Chagall. Variants: **Marc, Marco, Marcos, Marcus,** and **Markus.**

MARTHA: (f) Aramaic; woman, lady. The Biblical Martha is mostly seen doing household chores and cooking, while grumbling that her sister Mary is hanging out with the apostles rather than helping her. This sort of background can be seen as either a plus or minus depending on your point of view. The name was rarely used in the Medieval period but became popular after the reformation, and in America especially in the 19th century in honor of First Lady Martha Washington. It continued in high popularity through the first half of the 20th century but has fallen out of favor since then. Another connection with domesticity comes through decorating and entertaining guru Martha Stewart. Variant: **Marta.**

PAUL: (m) Latin; small. This was the name taken on by Saul of Tarsus after his conversion. As one of the major shapers of early Christianity, you may expect the name Paul to have been extremely popular, but it was only in occasional use in the Middle Ages and was not significantly taken into use in English until the 18th century. Since then, however, it has held a consistently high position, spending the first half of the 20th century in the top twenty names. The Spanish form Pablo has also been mildly popular and the Russian form Pavel is occasionally found. Given the name's recent popularity, it isn't hard to find well-known bearers, including singers Paul Robeson, Paul Anka, Paul Simon, and Paul McCarney, actor Paul Newman, artist Paul Gauguin, and Olympic gymnast Paul Hamm. Variants: **Pablo** and **Pavel.**

PRISCILLA: (f) Latin; a diminutive of Prisca, the feminine form of the Roman name Priscus, meaning "old, primitive, strict." Both Prisca and Priscilla appear briefly in the New Testament, possibly for the same person. Only Priscilla enjoyed a significant revival after the Reformation and has enjoyed a mild popularity. Bearers have included actresses Priscilla Lane and Priscilla Presley as well as folksinger Priscilla Herdman. Variants: **Prisca** and **Priscila.**

SALOME: (f) Hebrew; peace. The name comes from the same roots as Solomon. Based purely on her story, you would hardly expect the Biblical Salome to have inspired emulation. Although she is mentioned by name only in non-Biblical sources, Salome was the daughter of Herod who demanded the head of John the Baptist in payment for her dancing. (There was another Biblical Salome, the mother of the apostles James and John.) This episode was a popular one among Medieval artists, but the name was not taken up into use until after the Reformation — although whether this was in spite of Salome's notoriety, because of it, or ignoring it in favor of the apostles' mother is impossible to tell. Salome hit the popularity charts briefly around the turn of the 20th century and has been borne by 19th century artist Salome Hensel and by actress Salome Jens.

SAUL: (m) Hebrew; asked for; desired. This was the name of the first king of Israel and the original name of Saint Paul, before his conversion. The saint's preconversion name might be expected to be less popular than his postconversion name, and Paul itself was surprisingly rarely used. In an Old Testament context, the tension between King Saul and his much more popular successor, David, may also have discouraged the use of Saul. In any event, it was revived fairly late and with only minor success and has never been more than very mildly popular. One well-known bearer is novelist Saul Bellow.

THADDEUS: (m) uncertain, possibly Aramaic; meaning uncertain, but if the Aramaic origin is correct, then perhaps "praise." This was the surname of the apostle Lebbaeus, but is generally used as the primary name to refer to him. In the Medieval period, the name was taken up mostly in the Eastern Orthodox church, rather than in the west, although it can be found occasionally in Ireland as a substitution for the Gaelic name Tadhg. It had a more general revival after the Reformation and especially around the 19th century, but has declined substantially over the last century. Jane Porter used it for the title character of her 1803 historical novel *Thaddeus of Warsaw.* Interesting bearers of the name have included Thaddeus Sobieski Lowe, who pioneered the use of balloons in military intelligence during the Civil War, and Mississippi senator Thad Cochran. Diminutives: **Tad** and **Thad.**

TIMOTHY: (m) Greek; honored by God; or perhaps honoring God. This was the name of Saint Paul's companion in the Book of Acts. It came back into use after the Reformation, and after some ups and downs has become quite popular in the latter part of the 20th century. Well-known bearers include actor Timothy Dalton and filmmaker Tim Burton. Variant: **Timmothy.** Diminutives: **Tim, Timmie,** and **Timmy.**

VERONICA: (f) Latin; true image. This was originally the name of a relic, a cloth with the image of Christ's face. The legend later elaborated this into the cloth used to wipe his face during the crucifixion, and the name was transferred to the woman who used it (who is unnamed in the Bible). Thus Saint Veronica was created. The name was used occasionally in Europe before the Reformation, but seems to have been revived more by 19th-century romantics than as part of a Biblical revival. Famous bearers include actress Veronica Lake and British historian Veronica Wedgwood.

Identifying Islamic Names

Islam arose among Arabic speaking people, and so the most prominent names in Islamic faith and history are in that language. Some of the current use of names with Islamic associations in America comes through immigrant communities, but there has also been a significant interest in these names in the African American community for cultural, not only religious, reasons, due to the historic significance of Islam in many parts of Africa.

ABDUL: (m) Arabic; either a diminutive of ABDULLAH or a shortening of various names beginning with "Abd-al-' meaning "servant of the." This group of names is formed from epithets of God or of Muhammad, such as Abd-al-Rahman, "servant of the Merciful." But when the names have been borrowed by those unfamiliar with Arabic or with this style of name, they have often been reinterpreted as two independent given names, for example, "Abdul" and "Rahman," and used separately. Abdul hits the popularity charts very briefly in the '70s.

ABDULLAH: (m) Arabic; servant of God. This is a very common name in Islamic cultures that has been showing up on the popularity charts in the last couple of decades. One famous bearer is South African jazz musician Abdullah Ibrahim.

AHMED: (m) Arabic; commendable, praiseworthy. The Medieval jurist and theologian Ahmad ibn Hanbal founded one of the four major Sunni schools of law. The name has enjoyed a mild popularity since the '70s. Variant: **Ahmad.**

AISHA: (f) Arabic; life, lively. This was the name of one of Muhammad's wives, famous for her scholarship and teaching. It has been in occasional use since the '70s, as for actress Aisha Tyler. Variants: **Aishah, Iesha,** and **Ieshia.**

ALIYAH: (f) Arabic; exalted, outstanding. (See Chapter 17.)

FATIMA: (f) Arabic; weaning. This is the name of a daughter of Muhammad and therefore greatly popular in Islamic cultures. The name also has the distinction of having picked up Christian associations due to an apparition of the Virgin at the village of Fatima in Portugal in the early 20th century. It hits the popularity charts in the '70s and has become moderately popular.

HAKIM: (m) Arabic; ruler, sovereign. Hakim ibn Hazm was a nephew of Muhammad and one of his early followers. The name has had a low-level popularity in the last couple of decades. One current bearer is basketball player Hakeem Olajuwon. Variants: **Akeem** and **Hakeem.**

HASIM: (m) Arabic; decisive. This has been a rare name recently, but is familiar from boxer Hasim Rahman.

HASSAN: (m) Arabic; handsome, good. This is a rare name that has been in use since the '70s. The name may be familiar from the late King Hassan of Morocco.

IMANI: (f) Arabic; faith, belief. The usual Arabic word is *iman,* but the form *imani* is used to name the seventh day of the modern Kwanzaa festival, and this may be a more immediate source of the name. This has been showing up as a feminine name for the last couple of decades, as for rapper Imani Coppola.

JABARI: (m) Arabic; brave, courageous. The name has hit the charts, although it is still relatively rare, within the last several decades. One bearer is poet and literary critic Jabari Asim.

JAHIM: (m) Arabic; fire, blaze. This is something of an unusual name to be taken up, as *al-Jahim* is a name for one part of Hell. It's also possible that this is simply a coined name (see Chapter 11) that is coincidentally similar to an Arabic word. Variants: **Jaheem, Jaheim,** and **Jahiem.**

JALIL: (m) Arabic; exalted, pure. This shows up on the charts briefly in the '90s, possibly inspired by child actor Jaleel White on the TV show *Family Matters.* A rather more startling appearance of a similar name is in the colonial Brenton family of Rhode Island, where several generations of Jahleel Brentons served as officers of the British navy in the 18th and 19th centuries. But here you have an Old Testament name generally interpreted as meaning "waiting for God." It's likely that the two names have become conflated today. Variants: **Jahleel** and **Jaleel.**

JAMAL: (m) Arabic; beauty, grace. This is one of the more popular Arabic names in American use, and consistently so since its first appearance on the charts in the '70s. One current bearer is basketball player Jamal Mashburn. Variant: **Jamaal.**

JAMILA (f), **JAMIL** (m): Arabic; elegant, graceful. This name has been mildly popular in both the masculine and feminine versions ever since the '70s. Jamila is also popular in India, and there may be an unrelated Hindi name that sounds the same. Variant: (m) **Jamel.**

KARIM: (m) Arabic; generous, noble. Taken from an epithet of God, this is a short form of the name Abd-al-Karim "servant of the Generous One," as seen for the Medieval philosopher and theologian Abd-al-Karim al-Jili. The short version of the name is familiar from basketball great Kareem Abdul-Jabbar and has been mildly popular since the '70s. Variant: **Kareem.**

KHADIJAH: (f) Arabic; born prematurely. Khadijah was a rich widow who first employed and then married the prophet Muhammad before his revelation, and later became his first follower. Her story represents some of the interesting puzzles in the place of women in Islamic history. The name hit the American popularity charts briefly in the '90s and is borne by actress Khadijah Karriem.

KHALID: (m) Arabic; glorious, eternal. One of the early followers of Islam, Khalid ibn al-Walid led the conquest of Syria in the 7th century. The name has been showing up occasionally on the popularity charts in the last couple of decades.

MUHAMMAD: (m) Arabic; praiseworthy, commendable. The name of the Prophet Muhammad is one of the most popular boys' names in Islamic cultures, although interestingly it is not the most popular Arabic name in American use. It may as often be used in honor of more recent bearers, such as boxing great Muhammad Ali. Variants: **Mohamad, Mohammad, Mohammed,** and **Muhammad.**

NASIR: (m) Arabic; helper. This name is related to the title of one of the sections of the Qur'an, "al-Nasr," that is, "help, assistance." It has appeared very suddenly on the charts in the last decade for no identifiable reason, as there seem to be no prominent American bearers. Elsewhere in the world, it can be found for Indian film writer and director Nasir Hussain.

RAHIM: (m) Arabic; compassionate. This is a short form of the name Abd-al-Rahim, "servant of the Compassionate," based on an epithet of God. One current bearer is football player Raheem Brock, but the name has not become more than occasionally used in the last couple of decades. Variant: **Raheem.**

RASHAD: (m) Arabic; integrity, maturity. The name has enjoyed mild popularity since the '70s. Variant: **Rashaad.**

RASHID: (m) Arabic; rightly guided. This was a nickname of the caliphs, who led the Islamic community after the death of Muhammad. It begins showing up on the popularity charts in the '70s but has never been more than rare. One bearer is basketball player Rasheed Wallace. Variant: **Rasheed.**

SAMIR: (m) Arabic; entertaining companion. This name has shown up rarely in the last few decades.

SHAKIRA: (f) Arabic; thankful, grateful. This is a recently popular name, although still fairly rare. One bearer is Latin pop singer Shakira Mebarak.

ZAIDA: (f) Arabic; increasing, growing. This is the feminine form of the name borne by Zayd al-Khayr, an early convert to Islam. It is possible, however, that another unrelated name is involved, as the appearance of Zaida on the popularity charts in the '40s and '50s is significantly before the major interest in Islamic names. One bearer is Cuban painter Zaida del Rio.

Chapter 5

Living the Legends: Names from Myth and Saga

In This Chapter

▶ Tracing names that come from Greek and Roman legend

▶ Looking at names from Norse mythology and history

▶ Enjoying names from Celtic sources

Mythical and legendary names come down to us through several routes. Some never went out of style in the first place. Others have been revived by way of literary retellings of the old legends. And some have been taken up directly from the ancient myths during periods of historic revival.

Carrying Names Down from Mount Olympus

There have been fads for names from myth and literature at many times across the ages. Some names simply never went out of style in the first place. Greek and Latin names were common among early Christians, and so among early saints, which meant they were perpetuated in the community. In this group, you can include names like Denis, Martin, and Helen.

The first classical revival came from the Medieval interest in stories like the Iliad and the exploits of Alexander the Great, retold in Medieval clothing alongside the romances of Arthur and Charlemagne. This fad brought names like Cassandra, Hector, and all the many forms of Alexander and Alexandra into use.

Of course, an explosion of interest in classical authors and images pretty much defines the Renaissance. (After all, the thing that was "reborn" — re+naissance — was the culture of the ancient Greek and Roman civilizations.) At this period, you find parents naming their children Diane, Penelope, Hercules, and even Julius-Caesar.

Another infusion of classical names into turn-of-the-century America comes from the combination of immigration with nationalist interest in traditional names. So you have Greek immigrants popularizing names like Achille, Aristotle, and Ariadne.

ACHILLES: (m) Greek; meaning unknown (although sometimes given as "lipless"). Achilles was a nearly immortal warrior who played a significant part in the siege of Troy in the Iliad. This is an uncommon name, perhaps more often seen in the French version Achille, as for former Belgian Prime Minister Achille van Acker. Variant: **Achille.**

ADONIS: (m) Greek; taken originally from a Phoenician word meaning "lord." The name has become a byword for a man built "like a Greek god," so it may set up rather high expectations. Adonis was handsome enough to catch the eye of the goddess of love. The name has achieved an occasional popularity in the last couple of decades.

AMBROSIA: (f) Greek; the name of the food of the gods, now meaning any sort of delicious food. Related to AMBROSE (Chapter 8).

ARCADIO: (m) Greek; Arcadia is a region in Greece that came to represent something of a paradise on earth; the given name means "Arcadian, man from Arcadia." There was an early saint Arcadius, of which Arcadio is an Italian form. The Russian version Arkady is also sometimes found, as in one of the science fiction writing brothers Arkady and Boris Strugatsky. Variants: **Arcadius** and **Arkady.**

ARIADNE, ARIANA: (f) Greek; very pure, very chaste. Ariadne had the brilliant idea of saving Theseus from the Minotaur's labyrinth by using a ball of string to keep track of the way out. One of Agatha Christie's fictional detectives is Ariadne Oliver. Another bearer is journalist and politician Arianna Huffington. Variants: **Arianna, Ariane, Aryana,** and **Aryanna.**

ATHENA: (f) Greek; the Greek goddess of wisdom and patron of the city of Athens. The name has had a steady low popularity in the U.S. since the '60s, but for interesting namesakes you can look abroad to Greek heiress Athina Onassis and Philippine cyclist Athena Beltran. Variant: **Athina.**

AURORA, AURORE: (f) Latin; dawn, the goddess of the dawn. Several literary Auroras, including Byron's Aurora Raby and Elizabeth Barrett Browning's Aurora Leigh spurred interest in the name in the 19th century, although it declines somewhat in popularity after that. The French version Aurore was born by writer Aurore Dupin, better known by her pen name George Sand.

CASSANDRA: (f) Greek; possibly "one who ensnares men." The Cassandra of the Iliad was doomed to make true prophecies that no one would believe. (Even today someone may be called "a Cassandra" for predicting dire events that people find more comfortable to ignore.) The name was revived in the Medieval period and has always been somewhat in fashion. It shot up to rather high popularity in the second half of the 20th century, and variants spelled with "K-" have become quite popular even more recently. Novelist Jane Austen had a mother, sister, and two cousins named Cassandra. More recently, you have jazz singer Cassandra Wilson. In addition to the diminutives listed here, the SANDRA group (Chapter 10) can be used for this name as well as Alexandra. Variants: **Casandra, Cassondra, Kassandra,** and **Kasandra.** Diminutives: **Cassie** and **Kassie.**

CYNTHIA: (f) Greek; a nickname for Artemis, goddess of the hunt, after her birth on Mount Kynthos on the isle of Delos. This is another of the classical names revived during the Renaissance, but today it's known for having hit the top-ten girls' names in the '60s. It was a popular name in Elizabethan verse, probably due to poetic comparisons of Elizabeth with the virgin goddess. Well-known bearers today include actress Cynthia Nixon, model Cindy Crawford, singer Cyndi Lauper, and designer Cynthia Rowley. Variant: **Cinthia.** Diminutives: **Cindy, Cindi, Cyndi,** and **Cinda.**

DAMON, DAMIAN: (m) Greek; one who tames or subdues. Damon and Damian are independent names historically, but once you toss in the range of variants used today, it's hard to insist that they have stayed distinct. In legend, Damon and Pythias were legendary for the strength of their friendship. There was an early saint named Damian. This group of names saw a significant increase in popularity throughout the 20th century, peaking in the '70s. Damian currently tops the lot, despite some bad publicity as the demon-child of the movie *The Omen.* More auspicious bearers include author Damon Runyon and actor Damon Wayans. Variants: **Damien, Damion,** and **Dameon.**

DAPHNE: (f) Greek; a laurel tree. According to myth, Daphne was a nymph who, to escape sexual harassment at the hands of Apollo, turned into a tree. Not one to give up, he made a wreath of her branches and took it for his symbol. It has been in rare use, although it has somewhat increased in popularity in the mid–20th century. Bearers include author Daphne du Maurier, actress Daphne Zuniga, and a continuing character on the TV show *Frasier.* Variant: **Dafne.**

DEIANEIRA: (f) Greek; meaning uncertain but perhaps having to do with battle. In Greek legend, she was the wife of Hercules, although their marriage came to a tragic end through jealousy. The name appears briefly on the popularity charts in 1993 suggesting that this use is connected with Dayanara Torres of Puerto Rico winning the Miss Universe pageant in that year, rather than with any of the various film and television productions of the Hercules legend. Variants: **Dayanara, Deianira,** and **Deyanira.**

DEMETRIA (f), **DEMETRIUS** (m): Greek; belonging to Demeter, goddess of the harvest. The male name has been more popular than the female, thanks to an early martyr who bore it, but both have had their greatest popularity in the later 20th century. A Russian form Dmitrii is seen in the name of chemist Dmitrii Mendeleyev. Women bearing this name include poet Demetria Martinez. Variants: (m) **Demetris, Demetri, Dimitri, Dmitrii,** and **Dmitriy.**

DENISE (f), **DENIS** (m): Greek; belonging to Dionysios, god of wine. The connection with Greek mythology had little to do with the popularity of this name, rather you can look to Saint Denis, long considered the patron saint of France. The name broadened into feminine use in the Middle Ages. In the 20th century, both names reached their peak around the '50s. Bearers include actor Dennis Hopper and basketball personality Dennis Rodman on the men's side, and actress Denise Richards on the women's side. Variants: (f) **Denice** and **Denisse;** (m) **Dionisio, Dionisius,** and **Dennis.** Diminutives: (m) **Dennie** and **Denny.**

DIANA, DIANE: (f) Latin; the goddess of the hunt, also associated with the moon. The name has been popular in both the Latin form Diana and the French form Diane, and both in some variants have been spelled to associate the name with ANNE or ANNA (Chapter 8). An early popularizer in the Renaissance was Diane de Poitiers, mistress of King Henry II of France. Shakespeare used the name for a minor character in *All's Well That Ends Well,* and there were Dianas in several popular 19th century novels including Walter Scott's *Rob Roy,* Charlotte Brontë's *Jane Eyre,* and George Meredith's *Diana of the Crossways.* But it wasn't until the 20th century that the name really took off, with both main spellings hitting a peak in midcentury. Diana saw a slight revival in the '80s, almost certainly inspired by the popularity of Diana, Princess of Wales. Famous Dianes today include California senator Diane Feinstein and actress Diane Keaton. Dionne or Dion is generally considered a short form of Dionysia, but its behavior in the popularity charts in America suggests that people are using it as a variant for Diane. Well-known bearers include singer Dionne Warwick and mystic Dion Fortune. Rather unusual spellings are borne by singer and actress Diahann Carroll and actress Dyan Cannon. Variants: **Dayana, Diahann, Dian, Diann, Dianna, Dianne, Deana, Deann, Deanna, Deanne** (and perhaps sometimes **Dean**), **Dion, Dionne,** and **Dyan.**

DORIS: (f) Greek; a sea nymph, mother of the nereids. The name burst on the scene with little warning in the late 19th century and by the '20s had shot up to number 8 in the ratings before declining back into obscurity. Some of its popularity may have been from its resemblance to Dorothy. Actress and singer Doris Day made the name synonymous with wholesomeness. More recently the field has expanded to include writer Doris Lessing and philanthropist Doris Duke. Variant: **Dorris.**

ERIS: (f) Greek; the goddess of chaos who set events in motion to cause the Trojan War. This is a somewhat unusual name to find making the charts briefly in the '20s — most likely it was actually being used as a variant of some other name (for example, IRIS [see later in this chapter]).

HECTOR: (m) Greek; possibly "holding fast," but this is uncertain. Hector became popular in the Middle Ages through retellings of the siege of Troy, and as Ector it moved into the Arthurian romances as well. Later the name became associated with Scotland where it was used to translate an unrelated Gaelic name. Well-known bearers include composer Hector Berlioz and author Hector Hugh Munro (except that nobody knows that, even if they know that H.H. Munro is the real name behind the stories with the byline Saki). The name has risen steadily in popularity throughout the 20th century. Variant: **Ector.**

HELEN: (f) Greek; bright one (although it's equally likely that the name is non-Greek and means something unknown). Helen is one of those wildly popular names that has spawned a number of distinct variants. So I cover the Helen group here, the ELAINE group with Arthurian literature (Chapter 6), the ELLENs under Medieval names (Chapter 8), and EILEEN with 20th-century names (Chapter 10). Helen of Troy was "the face that launched a thousand ships" in the Iliad, but the woman who really popularized the name was Saint Helena, the mother of the Emperor Constantine. (St. Helena was popularly credited with having rediscovered the True Cross.) Characters named Helen appear in two of Shakespeare's plays. At the turn of the 20th century, Helen occupied the number-2 spot for a couple of decades and declined in popularity only slowly. So it's not surprising that you have famous recent Helens in abundance: blind and deaf celebrity Helen Keller, actresses Helen Hunt and Helen Hayes, Australian singer Helen Reddy, anti-death-penalty activist Sister Helen Prejean, and perhaps I should add geologic celebrity Mount St. Helens. Variants: **Helena, Helene,** and **Hellen.**

HERCULES: (m) Greek; glory of Hera (the queen of the gods). The Hercules of legend was the superhero of the day, performing impossible feats of strength and daring. The name hasn't been particularly used in English, but the French form Hercule is familiar from Agatha Christie's Belgian detective Hercule Poirot. The legendary Hercules has been a perennial favorite in movies, television, and even an animated movie or two, but it's possible that the name is too closely associated with the mythic character for parents to feel comfortable using it. (Or perhaps they feel it would be too hard a name to live up to!) Variant: **Hercule.**

HOMER: (m) Greek; possibly "hostage." The modern name can also come from a French surname meaning "maker of helmets." It seems quite a descent from the blind poet Homer, declaiming "I sing of arms, and the man" to cartoon character Homer Simpson declaiming, "Doh!" The name was moderately popular in the late 19th century, but fell gradually out of use and has been quite rare since the '70s. Between the above scale from the sublime to the ridiculous, you find the name for painter Winslow Homer and country singer Homer Haynes.

IRIS: (f) Greek; goddess of the rainbow. See Chapter 12.

JASON: (m) Greek; meaning uncertain. Early uses of the name are more likely from the Biblical Eason, probably a Greek variant of JOSHUA (Chapter 10). In Greek legend, Jason led a shipload of heroes, known collectively as the Argonauts, on the quest for the legendary Golden Fleece. A movie version of the story in 1963 may have given the name a nudge at a time when it was already becoming popular. The name was given some early use in William Faulkner's novels and another pop culture influence was the TV series *Here Come the Brides,* set in frontier-era Seattle, featuring the brothers Jason, Joshua, and Jeremy. Jason shot up to popularity in the '60s and '70s and, paired with JENNIFER (Chapter 10) for girls, became symbolic of the new tendency towards name fads. Prominent Jasons include actors Jason Robards and Jason Lee. Variants: **Eason, Jasen,** and perhaps sometimes **Jayson** when it isn't from a surname meaning "Jay's son." Diminutive: **Jase.**

JUNE: (f) Latin; Juno, the queen of the gods. Current users may be thinking more of the month (see Chapter 13), but as the month is named for the goddess, it all comes to the same thing. It might sometimes be given for the birth month. See MAY and APRIL for similar names (Chapter 13). The name had its highest recent popularity in the '20s then declined rapidly. June Cleaver of *Leave it to Beaver* was the archetypal traditional TV mom. Another bearer was country singer June Carter Cash. In the early 20th century, there are examples of June as a male name, but this use has disappeared for the most part.

LEDA: (f) Greek; possibly from a Lycian word meaning "a woman." In legend, Leda was the mother of Helen of Troy. You may see her in various mythological paintings being seduced by Zeus in the form of a swan. The name has been rare but shows up as a character in Dashiell Hammett's novel *The Thin Man.*

LUNA: (f) Latin; the moon. In Roman mythology, the moon was personified as the goddess Luna, although DIANA (see earlier in this chapter) was also associated with the moon. This name has only hit the popularity charts in last year or two.

MARTINA (f), **MARTIN** (m): Latin; belonging to Mars, the god of war. See Chapters 8 (m) and 19 (f).

MINERVA: (f) Latin; the root may be Latin *men-* meaning "mind." Minerva was the goddess of wisdom, although she was rather active dabbling in war on the side. The name is found occasionally in the 19th century and figures in Charles Dickens's *Pickwick Papers.* There have been occasional media personalities with the name: actress Minerva Urecal and comedian Minerva Pious. Recently, people are more likely to think of the character of Professor Minerva McGonagall in the *Harry Potter* books by J.K. Rowling.

NARCISSUS, NARCISO: (m) Greek; the name of a man turned into a flower (see Chapter 12).

NEREIDA: (f) Greek; a nymph, especially one of the sea-nymphs. There was a mild interest in the name in the mid–20th century. One bearer is Puerto Rican television reporter Luz Nereida Velez, and if the name has been popular in Puerto Rico, this may account for its brief appearance in U.S. statistics. A related name is Nerissa, used in Shakespeare's *The Merchant of Venice.* This is similar in sound to Nerys, a popular girl's name in Wales, but that name comes from a short form of the Welsh name Generys and is unrelated. Variant: **Nerissa.** Similar names: **Nerys** and **Generys.**

NESTOR: (m) Greek; one who returns home. Nestor was one of the Greeks at the siege of Troy. He was an old man at the time but, true to the meaning of his name, one of the few who got home safely. For unclear reasons, the name became mildly popular in the late 20th century, particularly in the Hispanic community.

OLYMPIA: (f) Greek; from Olympus, home of the Greek gods. This is a rare name in the U.S., but familiar from actress Olympia Dukakis and also borne by Maine senator Olympia J. Snowe.

ORION: (m) Greek; light. Orion was a legendary hunter turned into a constellation when he died. The use of the name is likely to be directly from the constellation, which is one of the most easily recognized in the northern hemisphere. In other cases, the name may be taken from the Irish surname O'Ryan. The name has only appeared recently, but has risen sharply in popularity in the last decade.

PARIS: (f, m) multiple origins; meaning uncertain. The male name is usually the Greek Paris (the man who eloped with Helen of Troy and thus started the Trojan War), but the female name is more likely from the city of Paris, and so from the Gaulish tribal name *Parisi.* As a boy's name it has been used occasionally in the last few decades, but there has been a sharp interest in it as a girl's name starting more recently and this is likely to displace the male use, especially given the current media saturation of Paris Hilton.

PENELOPE: (f) Greek; the name may be connected with a word meaning "a bobbin." This ties in with the legendary Penelope's ruse of vowing not to consider any suitors to replace her husband Ulysses until she'd finished a piece of weaving. (She unraveled the work every night to ensure it was never finished.) The name was first revived for use in the Renaissance and has never been particularly common. In the U.S., the short form Penny has been more popular than the primary name, as for actress and director Penny Marshall. Diminutives: **Penni, Pennie,** and **Penny.**

PERSEPHONE: (f) Greek; bringer of death. Fortunately, few people are fluent in ancient Greek these days, so one can ignore the rather morbid literal meaning of the name and contemplate the legend of the maiden representing Spring who was abducted by the god of the underworld. There are also pomegranates involved. It's complicated. The name has been used only rarely and deserves better. Perhaps interest may be spurred by the character of Persephone in the *Matrix* movie series. Variant: **Proserpine.**

PHOEBE: (f) Greek; shining, or shining one. Phoebus was a nickname of the god Apollo. There is a Phebe mentioned in the New Testament, which is the source of more recent American use. One famous bearer is Phoebe A. Hearst, mother of newspaper magnate William Randolph Hearst, and a major philanthropist in her own right. The name has remained in very limited use until a spike of interest in the last couple decades. The character of Phoebe in the TV series *Charmed* may encourage this popularity. Variant: **Phebe.**

RHEA: (f) Greek; flowing. Rhea was the mother of the major pantheon of Greek gods. Another famous maternal Rhea was Rhea Silva whose sons, Romulus and Remus, were the legendary founders of Rome. The name had a mild popularity around the turn of the 20th century then trailed off, although more recent bearers include actress Rhea Perlman and astronaut Margaret Rhea Seddon.

SYBYL, SIBYL: (f) Greek; meaning unknown. The sibyls gave prophecies thought to be inspired by Apollo. Interestingly, St. Augustine and some other early Christians ranked the sibyls as equivalent to the Old Testament prophets in being truly divinely inspired. The name became quite popular in the Middle Ages but fell out of use somewhat after the Reformation. It appears sporadically in the early 20th century but nearly disappears after the '60s. It has been used for literary characters by Benjamin Disraeli, Oscar Wilde, and more recently as the multiple-personality title character of a book by Flora Rheta Schreiber. See also astrologer and occult writer Sybil Leek. A variant is found for actress Cybill Shepherd. Variants: **Sybil, Sybille, Syble, Sibylla, Sibilla,** and **Cybill.** Diminutives: **Sibley** and **Sib.**

ULYSSES: (m) Latin; meaning uncertain. This is a Roman version of Odysseus, the hero of the *Odyssey*. The Latin name may be unrelated to the Greek one and come instead from an older Etruscan name. The Greek Odysseus has never made it into significant common use, but the more familiar Latin form shows up on occasion. Civil War General and U.S. president Ulysses S. Grant may be responsible for the mild popularity the name enjoys towards the end of the 19th century. James Joyce's novel by this name also keeps it in mind, although anyone who struggled through the book may be disinclined to be reminded of the experience by using it for a son's name! Variant: **Odysseus** and **Ulises.**

VENUS: (f) Latin; the goddess of love. (See Chapter 19.)

VESTA: (f) Latin; the goddess of fire and the hearth, patroness of the Vestal Virgins. This was occasionally used around 1900, perhaps inspired by a character in Theodore Dreiser's novel *Jennie Gerhardt*. (The best known bearers seem to have adopted it as a stage name rather than being born with the name.)

Naming Northern Heroes

Many names from Norse myth and saga have been in continuous use in Scandinavia since Medieval times while others have been revived there during the last few centuries. These names have been brought to America by Scandinavian immigrants, especially in the early 20th century. Also included here are a few nonmythic names from early Scandinavian history.

Normally it is a failing of name books to label entries vaguely as "Norse," "Germanic," "Slavic," and the like. When discussing the origins of names at a time before the divergence of the modern Scandinavian languages, however, making a finer distinction than "Norse" would be misleading.

ASTRID: (f) Norse; beloved of gods. In the saga of Olaf Trygvason, Astrid is the title character's mother. She had to skip town in a hurry when her husband was murdered and had all manner of adventures keeping little Olaf safe to eventually become king of Norway. The story sits at the cusp between legend and history as well as on the border between the pagan and Christian eras in that region. Astrid Lindgren is well known as the author of the Pippi Longstocking books. As an immigrant import, the name quickly fell out of use in the early 20th century, but recently there has been a revival of interest.

BRUNILDA, BRUNHILDA: (f) Norse; battle-armor. These Viking gals were tough. The most famous Brunhilda is the Valkyrie made famous in Wagner's opera *Siegfried*. As Brunilda it shows up occasionally in the mid–20th century and, curiously, seems to have come in through the Hispanic community. It is truly a multicultural name!

DAGMAR: (f) Norse; day-maiden (maybe). Dagmar was the name of a Medieval queen of Denmark who became the subject of numerous folk ballads. The name is occasionally found in the early 20th century, and in midcentury was used as the sole name of actress Dagmar.

DAGNY: (f) Norse; new day. (See Chapter 19.)

EINAR: (m) Norse; lone warrior (one of several possible meanings). Einar was a relatively common name in Viking times and there are characters by this name in *Eric the Red's Saga* and *Egil's Saga* among others. The name enjoyed a small popularity in the early part of the 20th century.

ERIC: (m) Norse; possibly "ever rich" or "rich one." Eric the Red could have given lessons to modern real-estate salesmen: he named a glacier-covered chunk of rock "Greenland" and convinced his friends and relations to sail there with him. (Actually, it was a much pleasanter place at the time.) His son, LEIF (see below), led the Viking expeditions to North America. Eric is one of the few Scandinavian men's names to survive beyond the first generation of immigrants. It rises steadily in popularity through the 20th century to reach number 14 in the '70s. The reason is mysterious, although it's possible that the connection of Eric and his son to what would become America made the name more attractive. With that kind of popularity, it isn't surprising to find famous Erics coming out your ears including rock musician Eric Clapton and Olympic speed-skater Eric Heiden. More recently, a feminine form ERICA has developed (see Chapter 16). Variants: **Aric, Erik, Erick,** and **Erich.**

GUDRUN: (f) Norse; secret of the gods. In the Norse version of the Nibelungen legend, Gudrun (the sister of GUNNAR; see later in this chapter) was the scorned lover of SIGURD (who instead loved BRUNHILDA; see earlier in this chapter). Who says that soap operas are a new invention? The name continued in use in Scandinavia up through the current day and immigrants probably account for the name's appearance in the U.S. around the turn of the 20th century.

GUNNAR: (m) Norse; possibly battle leader. Like GUDRUN (see earlier in this chapter), Gunnar appears in the Norse version of the legend of the ring of the Nibelungen. In Wagner's opera on the topic, the German form Gunther is used. The name occurs rarely around the turn of the 20th century but has been seeing new interest in the last decade. More recent bearers have included actor Gunnar Hansen. Variants: **Gunner** and **Gunther.**

HERTHA: (f) Norse; the name of the goddess of fertility. This seems an odd name to find popular in the early 20th century, even if it appears only rarely. The best explanation may be Victorian poet Algernon Charles Swinburne's poem *Hertha.* Variant: **Herta.**

LEIF: (m) Norse; heir, one who inherits. Given the historic connection between Leif and ERIC (see above), it may not be surprising that this name shows up occasionally at the same time that Eric saw its highest popularity. Leif Ericsson led the Viking expeditions that found Vinland, in other words, North America. Another Leif Erickson was a prolific actor, appearing in *On the Waterfront* among many others.

OLAF: (m) Norse; heir of the ancestors. This name was famous in early Norwegian history as the name of two early kings, including one who became the patron saint of Norway. It enjoyed the usual mild popularity in the early 20th century only to fall out of favor, although the variant Ole remained the name of the archetypal Norwegian immigrant used by comedians. Variant: **Ole.**

SIGMUND: (m) Norse; victory-protection. Sigmund is the main character of the Volsunga Saga, chronicling the legendary origins of various Germanic tribes. The story is rife with feuds and the slaying of in-laws, making it a popular subject for literary and theatrical treatments over the centuries. Sigmund's son SIGURD (see later in this chapter) moves on to become the hero of the Nibelungen Saga. The name Sigmund was mildly popular in the early 20th century, the same period when psychologist Sigmund Freud was making his reputation. Variant: **Zigmund.**

SIGURD, SIEGFRIED: (m) Norse; victory-protection. Under the German form Siegfried, the legendary dragon-slayer was immortalized in Wagner's opera of that name. Siegfried has never been particularly popular in the U.S. The most famous current bearer is entertainer Siegfried Fischbacher of "Siegfried and Roy." The Scandinavian form Sigurd, however, shows up occasionally at the beginning of the 20th century.

THORA: (f) Norse; a short form of any of several names beginning with *Thor-* referring to the god of thunder. There are rare examples of the name early in the 20th century. Today, British actress Thora Hird and American actress Thora Birch share the name.

THURGOOD: (m) Norse; possibly "Thor's Gottlander" (that is, a person from Gottland), but the second element may have other meanings. This is one of many Norse names attesting to the popularity of devotion to the god Thor. While the name is of Norse origin, this particular form became an English sur-name, and that is the source for the name of Supreme Court justice Thurgood Marshall.

THURMAN: (m) Norse; multiple origins including "Thor's protection" and "Thor's wrath." This is best known as the surname of actress Uma Thurman, but it enjoyed a mild popularity as a given name in the first half of the 20th century.

THURSTON: (m) Norse; Thor's stone. The name is found rarely in the early 20th century. In a certain generation it may be best known as the name of the oblivious millionaire of *Gilligan's Island,* Thurstan Howell III.

Choosing Celtic Names

In contrast to Greek and Norse names, the interest in names from Celtic myth and legend is somewhat more of an American phenomenon rather than being driven by immigrants. It has also been a fairly recent phenomenon. While people tend to associate the word "Celtic" primarily with the Gaelic names of Ireland and Scotland — and these represent the majority of this section — a small handful of names from Welsh legend have also become popular, often through fairly circuitous routes.

ANGUS: (m) Gaelic; one choice (or perhaps "chosen one"). There are Anguses aplenty in Irish legend, the best known being one of those unfortunate men who saw a fairy woman in a dream and made everyone around him miserable until he won her for his bride. Now popularly associated more with Scotland than Ireland, the name was mildly popular in the early 20th century. It features in William Butler Yeats's poem *Song of the Wandering Angus* and appears for a character in Shakespeare's *Macbeth*.

BRENDAN: (m) Gaelic; a borrowing of a Welsh word meaning "king." The early Irish saint Brendan is one of various semi-legendary individuals competing for the title of "European discoverer of the New World." The name became suddenly popular in the mid–20th century and seems to have started the fad for names in the Brendan-Brandon-Braydon group. Variants: True variants of this name include **Brennan, Brennen,** and possibly **Brannon;** similar-sounding names with different origins include **Brandan, Brendon, Brenden,** and **Brennon.** The whole group tends to be treated as a continuum today without regard for origin.

BRIDGET: (f) Gaelic; high one. Many of the legends and attributes of the Irish saint Bridget point to an earlier goddess of the same name, probably associated with fire, whose attributes the saint took on. At the time of major Irish immigration to America, this was an extremely popular name in Ireland and it became the archetypal Irish immigrant woman's name. This may have influenced its fall from popularity in the first part of the 20th century, but having shaken off any lingering shreds of anti-Irish prejudice, it saw a resurgence around the '70s. In the Medieval period, the name was more used outside of Ireland than inside (the Irish feeling it was too sacred to use on its own and substituting names meaning "devotee of Bridget) and one Swedish Birgitta added another saint to the roster, thus spreading the name further. A diminutive appears for the title "character" in the book *The Search for Bridie Murphy*. In all its many varieties, you see the name for actresses Bridget Fonda, Brigitte Bardot, and Brigette Nielsen. Variants: **Birgitta, Bridgette, Bridgett, Brigitte, Brigette,** and **Brighid.** Diminutive: **Bridie.**

BRONWEN, BRANWEN: (f) Welsh; either "fair raven" (Branwen) or "white breast" (Bronwen). Since the earliest sources for the name alternate between the two forms, it isn't clear which is the original (and true meaning) and which the variant (and mistaken meaning). Branwen is one of those tragic heroines who, through no fault of her own, ends up having vast numbers of people die in a battle over her (although she can't quite compete with Helen of Troy for sheer numbers). For some reason, in American (and Australian) use, people prefer to change the "-wen" to "-wyn," which would turn this into a boy's name in the original Welsh. Nonetheless, you now see variants such as Branwyn, Branwynne, and so forth. Some of the modern popularity may derive from the character Bronwen Morgan in Richard Llewellyn's novel *How Green Was My Valley* and the 1941 film version of the story. Variants: **Branwyn,** and **Branwynne.**

Discovering obscure names with intriguing stories

Only a handful of legendary names have become significantly popular, but the less common mythical characters are a rich source of unusual names. Here are a few others that have interesting stories attached. (But it's best to look up the story before you give your child the name!)

Atalanta (f; Greek)

Balder (m; Norse)

Cadmus (m; Greek)

Calypso (f; Greek)

Ceridwen (f; Welsh)

Danu (f; Irish)

Dermot (m; Irish)

Electra (f; Greek)

Frey (m; Norse)

Freya (f; Norse)

Gwydion (m; Welsh)

Hyperion (m; Greek)

Iduna (f; Norse)

Lir (m; Irish)

Lugh (m; Irish)

Maeve (f; Irish)

Melusine (f; French)

Minos (m; Greek)

Morrigan (f; Irish)

Orpheus (m; Greek)

Ossian (m; Irish)

Tyr (m; Norse)

CONNOR: (m) Gaelic; hound-lover. In the Irish legends of Cuchulainn, Connor MacNessa is the king of Ulster. The name continued in popularity from Medieval times onward, rather than being a recent revival, although it has shot up considerably in popularity in the last couple of decades. It may also be taken from a surname of the same origin. Well-known bearers include Irish author and diplomat Conor Cruise O'Brien and the film character Connor MacLeod of the *Highlander* movies. Variants: **Conor, Conner, and Konnor.**

DEIRDRE: (f) Gaelic; meaning uncertain, possibly "murmurer." When you learn that the Irish legendary character's nickname was "Deirdre of the Sorrows" you just know this is another one of those "everybody dies" stories. Sure enough, she falls in love with the wrong man, elopes, and massive bloodshed ensues to get her back. Her story was retold in William Butler Yeats's *Deirdre* and William Sharp's work of the same name. There was a brief fad for the name around the '60s but it has fallen out of fashion. Variants: **Deidre, Deidra,** and **Dedra.**

DYLAN: (f, m) Welsh; a wave. There are only traces of the Medieval legend about Dylan: As soon as he was born, he gave his mother Aranrhod the slip and headed for the ocean, then later he was accidentally killed by an uncle. But between Welsh poet Dylan Thomas and songwriter Bob Dylan, the name caught enough people's imagination to shoot up to number 19 among boys' names in the '70s. It has been spotted more recently as a girl's name. Variants: **Dylon** and **Dyllan.** There is an unrelated, but sound-alike, Irish name that may appear as **Dillon, Dillan,** or **Dillion.**

ERIN: (f, m) Gaelic; belonging to Ireland. This is taken from the possessive form of the Irish name for Ireland (Eire), and has often been used in English as a poetic name for the country. As a boy's name it enjoyed a mild popularity just after the mid–20th century but was pushed out by feminine use peaking in the '80s. Female bearers include activist (and movie subject) Erin Brockovich and actress Erin Moran. Variant: **Eryn.**

FINN: (m) Gaelic; white, fair. There are other possible origins for this name. There is an entire cycle of Medieval Irish legends centering around the character of Finn MacCool who was also known in Scotland under the name Fingal. The name has popped up only in the last few years, so famous bearers will need to wait a while. It's equally possible that this modern use is from some other inspiration, for example, the surname of literary character Huckleberry Finn, created by Mark Twain.

MAEVE: (f) Gaelic; intoxicating, the name is related to the word "mead." Queen Maeve (or Meadhbh, to use the Gaelic form of the name) was a powerful figure in early Irish legend, famous for wealth, her lovers, and for starting a war over a bull. The name Maeve has been continuously popular in Ireland since medieval times, although it has only started appearing on the American charts in the last year or so. One current bearer is novelist Maeve Binchy.

NEIL: (m) Gaelic; meaning uncertain: possibly "warrior," possibly "cloud," possibly something else. The name may often be from one of the surnames using it, as O'Neil or MacNeil, but its appearance in the 19th century suggests it may have been part of the romantic Celtic Revival. The name rose to a moderate popularity in the mid–20th century, then declined again. Bearers include playwright Neil Simon, astronaut Neil Armstrong, and singers Neil Sedaka and Neil Diamond. **Niles** and **Nelson** are surnames taken from this root that have also evolved into given names, as for politician Nelson Rockefeller and South African president Nelson Mandela. In addition, the surname **Oneal** is sometimes found as a given name. Neil has been Latinized as NIGEL (see Chapter 6). Variant: **Neal.**

RHIANNON: (f) Welsh; queen. (See Chapter 17.)

SABRINA: (f) Brittonic; a river name, the Severn. (See Chapter 16.)

TARA: (f) Gaelic; possibly: eminence. The name of the seat of the ancient kings of Ireland. (See Chapter 18.)

Chapter 6

Writing Your Child's Story: Literary Names from Shakespeare and Others

* *

In This Chapter

▶ Seeking inspiration from Medieval literary heroes

▶ Playing with Shakespeare's names

▶ Identifying with the characters of popular novels

* *

*L*iterature has long been a path for names to travel between cultures and to cross the barriers between imagination and everyday life. These names may invoke heroic virtues and qualities for a child, or simply provide an air of romance or adventure. Not all eras have considered literature an appropriate source for children's names, but the books and plays have still been there waiting at the next surge of interest.

Arthur and Roland: Names from Great Medieval Literature

The practice of using names from literature probably started with the mythical history of Troy and the Medieval revival of Achilles and Hector and the like. The widest literary influence comes from the tales of King Arthur. They were the pop fiction of most of Europe in the 12th and 13th centuries, and you soon started seeing Arthurs, Percivals, and even a scattered Merlin or two.

ALEXANDER: (m) Greek; defender of men. This was a nickname of Paris in the Iliad, but its popularity is due to Alexander the Great — not so much because of the historic person, but because his exploits were expanded and mythologized in a cycle of Medieval romances. Apart from that, there was a startling number of early saints named Alexander. It was the name of several Scottish kings and so became rather popular there, where it became Alastair. A variety of feminine forms evolved, such as ALEXANDRA (Chapter 9). ALEC (Chapter 18) and ALEX (Chapter 10) are diminutives, while ALEXIS (Chapter 16) is sometimes considered one as well and used for both boys and girls. SANDY (Chapter 10) is another unisex diminutive, while for boys you also find XANDER (Chapter 16) and for girls you have SANDRA (Chapter 10). The most popular form of the boy's name is Alexander, which has been increasing in popularity throughout the 20th century. A Spanish form Alejandro is only slightly less popular. Famous bearers (in addition to Alexander the Great) include Scottish novelist Alastair MacLean and artist Alexander Calder. Variants: **Alastair, Alejandro, Aleksandr, Alessandro, Alexandre, Alexandro, Alexzander,** and **Alistair.**

ARTHUR: (m) multiple possibilities; possibly of Brythonic origin, meaning "bear," but a Latin origin (of uncertain meaning) is also possible. This confusion and uncertainty is par for the course for the name of King Arthur — whose own historic existence is the subject of much debate. The one certain thing about King Arthur is that he was the focus of an enormous amount of Medieval literature and imagery, and continues to be to this day. The name occurs rarely in the Middle Ages, generally in honor of the legendary king, and has seen a boost in popularity every time a new version of the Matter of Britain becomes popular. The Victorian revival of interest in King Arthur also corresponded with the fame of Arthur Wellesley, duke of Wellington, which assured the name lasting popularity in England. In the U.S., the name has been falling somewhat in popularity through the 20th century, although it still remains quite popular, however the Spanish and Italian form Arturo has been rising on the lists and surpassed it. Well-known recent bearers of this name and its diminutives include tennis great Arthur Ashe, conductor Arturo Toscanini, singer Art Garfunkel, early TV host Art Linkletter, and band leader Artie Shaw. Variants: **Arther** and **Arturo.** Diminutives: **Art** and **Artie.**

ELAINE: (f) Greek; see ELLEN (Chapter 8). This is a Medieval French form of Helen that was used by Malory in his *Morte D'Arthur* and has come to be associated with the woman who fell hopelessly in love with Lancelot and bore his son, Galahad. It was given another boost in Tennyson's *Idylls of the King* and continued rising in popularity until the mid–20th century, after which it has declined somewhat. Variants: **Elaina** and **Elaynne.**

ENID: (f) coined; from the Breton place name Vannes (in an older form *Wened*) and most likely not, as some would have it, from a Welsh word meaning "woodlark." The tale of *Erec and Enid* (or, in some versions, Gereint and Enid) is a Medieval addition to the earlier Arthurian material. Enid is one of those long-suffering heroines who only wins true love by putting up with a lot of nonsense. The name doesn't seem to have moved into common use until the publication of Tennyson's version of the story in the mid–19th century. It appears occasionally through the first half of the 20th century then falls out of use. Children's author Enid Blyton was born at the height of the fashion for this name.

FAUST: (m) Latin; fortunate, lucky. The name is best known today from the legend of the sorcerer Faust (based on a 16th-century German Johann Faust) who made a bargain with the devil. The story was popularized in many forms, beginning with a play by Christopher Marlowe in 1592. If it had depended entirely on him, the name is unlikely to have become popular, but it was also the name of an early Roman martyr and had already been widespread enough to produce the sorcerer's surname. Variant: **Faustino.**

GAVIN: (m) multiple origins; several names have merged here: a Welsh name *Gwalchwyn* (white hawk) that became the Arthurian name Gawain, a French name *Gauin,* perhaps meaning "a piece of land," and an Irish surname meaning "smith." The Gawain of legend was a nephew of King Arthur and features in the story *Gawain and the Green Knight.* Today the name is closely associated with Scotland. One American bearer is actor Gavin MacLeod. Variants: **Gaven** and **Gavyn.**

GUINEVERE: (f) Welsh; white spirit. The name of King Arthur's queen didn't catch on as quickly as some other names from the stories — perhaps because the most common versions of the stories gave her something of a loose character. But it was picked up enough to produce variants like Italian Ginevra, Welsh Gaynor, English Wander, and Cornish Jennifer. Of these, only JENNIFER has achieved any significant popularity (see Chapter 10). Variants: **Gaynor, Ginevra,** and **Wander.**

GWENDOLEN: (f) Welsh; originally a misreading of *Gwendoleu* "white meadow." In ancient Welsh legend, Gwendoleu was the patron and lord of the magician Myrddin (Merlin), but later Medieval stories turned the character into his wife, and it's as a woman's name that it has come into general use. The spelling Gwendolyn has enjoyed moderate popularity from the 19th century to the present. The Arthurian character was not the direct cause of this name's use, rather you see a run of 19th-century romantic heroines, including Guendolen in Robert Browning's *A Blot in the 'Scutcheon,* Gwendolen Harleth in George Eliot's *Daniel Deronda,* and Gwendolyn Fairfax in Oscar Wilde's *The Importance of Being Earnest.* Variants: **Guendolen** and **Gwendolyn.** Diminutive: **Gwen.**

KAY: (m) Latin; rejoice (the form was Caius). The female name Kay is more often a diminutive of Katherine (Chapter 8.) Sir Kay figures as one of King Arthur's most constant companions. The use of Kay as a girl's name has largely crowded out masculine use, although it saw a brief fashion in the mid–20th century. Variant: **Kai.**

LINETTE: (f) French; moon (an older form of the name is *Lunette*). The name comes from the heroine of the Arthurian tale of *Owein*. The name is often mistakenly believed to be Welsh, and a later Welsh adoption Eluned has also become popular. The name was somewhat popularized by Tennyson in the 19th century, but is only rarely found more recently. It is sometimes considered to be a diminutive of LYNN, but the two are unrelated in origin. Variants: **Eluned, Lynette,** and **Lynnette.**

LORELEI: (f) German; uncertain meaning. The Lorelei of legend was a siren who sang sailors to their deaths along the banks of the Rhine. The name was popularized in a 19th-century German song, based on a poem by Heinrich Heine. The name Lorelai features prominently among characters in the TV series *Gilmore Girls*. Variant: **Lorelai.**

MERLIN: (m) coined; an adaptation of the Welsh name for King Arthur's magician, *Myrddin,* which in turn is taken from a place name meaning "fortress by the sea." This was one of the Arthurian names used occasionally in the Medieval period and revived in the Victorian era. It even enjoyed an increasing popularity in the early part of the 20th century. Football player turned actor Merlin Olsen bears this name. Variant: **Merlyn.**

MORGAN: (f, m) Welsh; the male and female names have different origins. The supernatural Morgan la Fey of Arthurian legend had a name that meant "sea-born," while the masculine name Morgan also involves the word "sea," but the second part may mean "edge, boundary." As a male name, Morgan came to the U.S. with Welsh immigrants, primarily as a surname turned back into a given name. Actor Morgan Freeman is a modern example. As a female name, Morgan has been popularized only very recently. The traditional versions of the Arthurian stories made Morgan somewhat of a villainess and not someone you'd name your daughter after. Some of the modern popularity is due to feminist retellings of the legends, such as Marion Zimmer Bradley's *The Mists of Avalon,* which turned her into the hero of the story. Actress Morgan Fairchild predates this phenomenon and may be an example of the male name being transferred.

OLIVER: (m) uncertain; generally identified with Latin *olivarius* "olive (wreath) bearer," but the name is more likely to be from an unknown Germanic root. In legend, Oliver was one of Charlemagne's warriors and the companion of ROLAND. In the Medieval period, the name became quite popular, but during the early colonization of America it had fallen drastically out of favor due to its association with Oliver Cromwell. A more recent association that has increased it somewhat in popularity is Charles Dickens's *Oliver Twist* and the musical *Oliver!* based on that story. Diminutive: **Ollie.**

OWEN: (m) Welsh; generally considered to derive from Latin *Eugenius* "well-born." The Owein of the oldest Arthurian legend is associated with a troop of magical raven-warriors, but later Medieval stories turn him into a relatively ordinary knight-errant. The Irish name Eoghan may also appear as Owen but has a different origin. Owen was relatively popular into the early part of the 20th century and has recently been seeing a revival. Actor Owen Wilson is one current bearer.

PERCIVAL: (m) coined; the name appears to have been invented by Medieval writer Chretien de Troyes for a character known earlier as Peredur (a Welsh name of uncertain meaning). There are rare examples of Percival in Medieval use, but the main popularization seems to have come in the 19th century. The name Percy is sometimes used as a diminutive for this, but is also an independent family name derived from a place in France. A famous bearer of the latter name is the poet Percy Bysshe Shelley. Diminutive: **Percy.**

REYNARD: (m) French; hard advice. The name Reynard was given in the Middle Ages to the fox and the satirical tale of Reynard the Fox and his animal friends was quite popular at the time. Variant: **Raynard.**

ROLAND: (m) French; fame-land (from a Germanic root). The greatest literary competition for King Arthur in the Middle Ages came from the hero Roland, hero of legendary tales associated with Charlemagne. The name has had a steady popularity since then in several countries. The Italian form Orlando became prominent in its own right for the hero of Ariosto's *Orlando Furioso.* Both characters have continued to have their stories retold through the years. Over the course of the 20th century, you see Roland and Orlando switching places in the popularity charts, with Roland starting out on top and being supplanted. The current popularity of actor Orlando Bloom is likely to continue the trend. There is a rare feminine form Rolanda. Variants: **Rolando, Rolland, Rollie, Rollin, Rowland, Orland,** and **Orlando.**

ROWENA: (f) uncertain; meaning uncertain. The name first appears in the 12th century in Geoffrey of Monmouth's *History of the Kings of Britain,* an early expansion of the Arthurian legends. The name is variously attributed to a Welsh or Anglo-Saxon origin. Sir Walter Scott considered it a quintessentially Saxon name in his *Ivanhoe,* and it was that character who popularized it for general use. It has been fading steadily through the 20th century, however. One modern bearer is fantasy artist Rowena Morrill.

SHERWOOD: (m) English; wood belonging to the shire. This name is probably most used from the surname, rather than being taken directly from the legends of Robin Hood. One prominent bearer is author Sherwood Anderson.

TRISTAN: (f, m) Brythonic; meaning uncertain, possibly "tumult." The earliest form of the name appears as Drustan, but Medieval French writers taking up the story of Tristan and Iseult connected the name with the French word *triste* "sad" and altered its spelling to match. (The connection may have been enhanced by the tragic nature of the story.) In English, the name generally became Tristram, as for American folklorist Tristram Coffin. While that variant has largely dropped out of use, many other versions have sparked significant interest in the last couple of decades. The feminine name Trista may derive from this name or directly from the French word, while feminine use of Tristen is quite recent and more likely to be a borrowing of the male name. Variants: (both) **Tristen;** (f) **Trista;** (m) **Tristian, Tristin, Triston, Tristram,** and **Trystan.**

URIEN: (m) Welsh; city-born. Urien is a prominent figure in early Welsh versions of the Arthurian tales, but later French versions turn him into King Arthur's enemy. It is a rare name.

VIVIAN: (f, m) Latin; lively, living. This name was popular in the Medieval period as a man's name, rather less so as a woman's name in the form Viviana. But the name Vivian came to be used for the Arthurian character of the Lady of the Lake, most likely as a substitute for an older, less familiar name, either Niniane or Nimue (of uncertain meaning). This connection swung the name over firmly to the feminine side in people's minds and today male use is nearly nonexistent. This is aided by famous bearers such as actress Vivien Leigh. Variants: (f) **Viviana, Vivien,** and **Vivienne.**

Shakespeare and the Romantic Writers

Shakespeare not only gave us English forms of the names he found in his story sources (Jessica and Cordelia), but coined new names with staying power (Miranda). The nymphs of 16th- and 17th-century pastoral poetry gave us Phyllis and Chloe, although the names of their shepherd lovers were less commonly adopted. The rising genre of romantic novels in the 18th and 19th centuries was fond of unusual and poetic names for its characters and these names began making an impact on ordinary use. (The writers of the Romantic movement are to be distinguished from modern romance novelists, although they may be considered literary ancestors of a sort.)

AMANDA: (f) Latin; worthy of being loved. This began as a name invented by 17th-century poets to address anonymous ladies. Its diminutive is MANDY (see Chapter 17).

ANABEL: (f) Scottish; meaning uncertain, possibly a variant of Amabilis. In Edgar Allen Poe's poem *Annabel Lee,* this name encapsulates the Victorian gothic sensibility. The name's popularity trailed off in the early 20th century, but very recently Annabelle has made an astounding leap up the popularity charts. Variants: **Annabel, Annabell,** and **Annabelle.**

ARDEN: (m) English; several possible origins including "dwelling place" and "eagle valley." The forest of Arden features in Shakespeare's *As You Like It* and is one of those places where all manner of marvelous things may happen. There is also a surname taken from one or more of the place names and this produced the given name sometime in the 19th century. The name fell out of popularity in the mid–20th century.

BELINDA: (f) German, via French; uncertain meaning, but the second part of the name means serpent or snake. Some of the Charlemagne romances give this as the name of Roland's wife and later it was used by Alexander Pope for the heroine of *The Rape of the Lock*. It was taken up by several Victorian novelists, but doesn't seem to have been very popular in ordinary use until the mid–20th century when it became quite fashionable for several decades. Current bearers include pop singer Belinda Carlisle.

BYRON: (m) English; cow shed (a variant of Byrom). This is most famous as the title of early 19th-century poet Lord Byron, who helped define the romantic style of the day. The name has held relatively steady in popularity, possibly helped by its resemblance to the popular BRIAN (see Chapter 10). It was borne by director Byron Haskin.

CHARMIAN: (f) Greek; joy. The name appears to have been invented for (or at least first popularized by) a minor character in Shakespeare's *Antony and Cleopatra*. A variant appears in John Dryden's 17th-century play *All for Love*. Some of the name's popularity may come from its resemblance to the English word "charming." In the 20th century, the most popular variant has been Charmaine, possibly involving a blend with GERMAINE (see Chapter 13). One interesting bearer is political and social analyst Charmaine Yoest. Variants: **Charmaine** and **Charmion.**

CHLOE: (f) Greek; a growing shoot or branch. The name appears once in the New Testament, making it a candidate for the Biblical name revivals of the Reformation. But during the same period it became a favorite of pastoral poets, used as a favorite name for nymphs and shepherdesses in verse. The name faded in popularity in the early 20th century but recently has shot back up the charts, making it to number 24 in 2003. The name may be familiar from actress Chlöe Sevigny.

CORDELIA: (f) uncertain; this is the name of the heroine and daughter of Shakespeare's *King Lear*, suggesting a possible connection with the Welsh name Creiddylad, which appears for a similar character, however another possible origin is a German name Cordula. Alternately, the name may be pure invention on Shakespeare's part, perhaps blending the Latin root *cord-* "heart" with a name such as Delia. Although popular in Victorian times, the name declined in use in the early 20th century. Recently it has been used for the character of Cordelia Chase in the TV show *Angel*. Variants: **Cordia** and **Cordie.**

DULCINEA: (f) Spanish; sweet. The name seems to have been invented by Miguel de Cervantes for his novel *Don Quixote de la Mancha.* The name Dulce could be used as a diminutive of this name but is also an independent name from the same root. The latter has been used occasionally in the last few decades. Variant: **Dulce.**

EVANGELINE: (f) coined; invented by the poet Henry Wadsworth Longfellow for his poem of that name, most likely as a blend of "evangel(ist)" and the feminine ending "-ine." This root word fit well for Salvation Army leader and songwriter Evangeline Booth. The name has been mildly popular through the early parts of the 20th century. Variant: **Evangelina.**

GLORIANA: (f) coined; from the root "glory" with the Latin feminine ending "-iana" added. This was used as a poetic name for Queen Elizabeth I, especially by Edmund Spenser.

HAMLET: (m) Norse; meaning uncertain. Shakespeare took the name of his tragic hero from Amleth in the original version of the story by Saxo Grammaticus. Shakespeare's own son was named Hamnet (after his godfather), but this is an entirely different name. The name Hamlet has never been particularly popular.

IMOGEN: (f) coined; the Imogen of Shakespeare's *Cymbeline* is based on the Innogen of Geoffrey of Monmouth, centuries earlier, which appears to have been borrowed from a Breton source. The name is most familiar from early TV actress Imogene Coca. Variants: **Emogene** and **Imogene.**

JESSICA: (f) coined; this name is another of Shakespeare's coinages, apparently based on the Biblical name Iscah. It is given to one of the clever heroines of *The Merchant of Venice.* The name Jessica was queen in the 1980s, supplanting the previous favorite Jennifer, and supplanted in turn the next decade by Ashley. The name has been borne by actresses Jessica Lange, Jessica Tandy, and TV sleuth Jessica Fletcher (of *Murder, She Wrote*). Variants: **Jesica, Jessika, Yesica,** and **Yessica.**

JIMENA: (f) Spanish; possibly a borrowing of SIMON. In the great Medieval Spanish epic of *El Cid,* the title character's wife is named Chimene, an early form of this name. Both Jimena and the variant Ximena have been hitting the popularity charts recently, primarily from use in the Hispanic community. Variants: **Ximena** and **Chimene.**

JULIET: (f) English; an adaptation of the Italian Giulietta, in turn a diminutive of JULIA (Chapter 17). The name has become synonymous with young love, although the heroine of Shakespeare's *Romeo and Juliet* can't really be considered an advertisement for healthy relationships. It is something of a rule that all books on naming must quote Juliet's line, "What's in a name?" Famous bearers of this name include Juliette Gordon Low, founder of the American Girl Scouts. Variant: **Juliette.**

LEANDER: (m) Greek; lion-man. Appearing originally in the Greek myth of Hero and Leander, this name became a favorite of romantic novelists, often for characters who achieved their ends with a bit of trickery. It had a mild popularity around the turn of the 20th century.

LENORE: (f) English; a variant of ELEANOR (Chapter 8). This name was a favorite of 19th-century romantic writers, the most familiar example appearing in Edgar Allen Poe's poem *The Raven* where the narrator is pining for his "lost Lenore." The name has remained popular in several variants through the mid–20th century. Poet and novelist Lenore Marshall is the namesake of a prize given by the Academy of American Poets. Variants: **Lenora, Leonor, Leonora,** and **Leonore.**

LESLIE: (f, m) Brythonic; meaning uncertain, possibly "court of the holly tree." Use as a given name may have come from the surname or directly from the Scottish place name. But the surname has an alternate origin in a given name based, in a roundabout way, on Latin LETICIA (Chapter 8). It seems to have been revived as a given name first by Scottish poet Robert Burns in his poem *Bonnie Lesley,* where it is used as a woman's name. Following the general pattern for names taken from surnames, it also came to be used as a man's name. The common wisdom in name books has been that the spelling Leslie is a male name and Lesley its female counterpart, however this distinction seems to be artificial. In American usage, coming into the 20th century, only the spelling Lesley had significant popularity for either sex, and the name as a whole was more commonly used for men. But while male use held steady until midcentury, female use rose sharply, and around the time that the numbers were roughly equal, Leslie started showing up for both, also in equal numbers. In the second half of the 20th century, male use for both spellings declined, and the name has come to be considered nearly exclusively a girl's name, with male examples like actor Leslie Howard coming to seem rather old-fashioned. Female examples are plentiful, including actresses Leslie Caron and Lesley Ann Warren. Variants: (both) **Lesley;** (f) **Lesli** and **Lesly.**

MALVINA: (f) coined; in the 18th century, James Macpherson invented a collection of "ancient Gaelic poetry" known as the Ossian poems. These became wildly popular across Europe in the way that invented traditions often do and inspired the use of a number of personal names. The name may have been modeled after some unknown Gaelic name. This name is unrelated to that of the Malvinas Islands (known in English as the Falklands). The best known bearer is probably folk-song writer Malvina Reynolds of *Little Boxes* fame. Variants: **Melvina** and **Melva.** Diminutive: possibly **Vina.**

MAVIS: (f) English; a song-thrush (a type of bird). This seems to have been popularized in use by poets such as Robert Burns and Sir Walter Scott. It had a moderate popularity through the first half of the 20th century but has fallen out of use. Mavis Staples is the lead singer for the Staples Singers.

MIRANDA: (f) Latin; admired one. This is a slightly shortened version of Admiranda. The English word Admire can also be found occasionally as a name. Shakespeare's Miranda is a main character in *The Tempest* and has been the major impetus for use of this name. A more recent bearer is actress Miranda Richardson. The name has been increasing steadily in popularity through the second half of the 20th century. Variants: **Admiranda, Admire, Maranda, Meranda,** and **Myranda.**

OPHELIA: (f) coined; possibly inspired by the Greek word *ophelia* "help." It appeared in Sannazaro's *Arcadia* in 1504, which may be where Shakespeare found the name for the character in *Hamlet.* It is the latter use that has popularized the name more generally. The name enjoyed a mild popularity through the first half of the 20th century but has fallen somewhat out of fashion since then. One interesting current bearer is Native American poet and linguist Ofelia Zepeda. Variant: **Ofelia.**

OSCAR: (m) English; divine spear. This is another of the names used by 19th-century poet James Macpherson in his pseudo-historical Ossianic Cycle where it is used for the son of the title character Ossian. It was this use that spread the name into general use and it became surprisingly popular in Scandinavia. One famous bearer is Victorian poet and author Oscar Wilde.

PHYLLIS: (f) Greek; leafy. This was a popular name in Greek and Latin pastoral poetry, and so was revived by Renaissance poets working with the same images. It fell out of favor for a while but was revived again in the late 19th century and was quite popular through the first half of the 20th century. Mystery novelist P.D. James's initials stand for Phyllis Dorothy. Comedian Phyllis Diller is another well-known bearer. Variants: **Phillis** and **Phylis.**

PORTIA: (f) Latin; a Roman family name, possibly from *porcus* "pig." Shakespeare's Portia in *The Merchant of Venice,* like many of his heroines, cleverly saves the day from the somewhat bumbling men in the play. The name is found today for Australian actress Portia De Rossi. Variant: **Porsha.**

REGAN: (f, m) various origins; the feminine name is generally from Shakespeare's character in *King Lear,* which is adapted from an older name Regau of uncertain origin. The masculine name is from an Irish surname based on a root meaning "king." Variants: (both) **Reagan;** (f) **Raegan.**

ROMEO: (m) Italian; one who has been to Rome. The name was already popular when Shakespeare used it for the hero of *Romeo and Juliet,* and this may account for the relative popularity of the name. In general, male literary names are less likely to catch on in general use, but this one has seen scattered bouts of popularity throughout the 20th century.

Shakespeare's villains

If literary heroes don't appeal to you, you could always consider the names of the villains. Not all of Shakespeare's plays have true villains — and in some cases one is tempted to put the protagonists in that role.

Sometimes the villains have perfectly ordinary names: Frederick *(As You Like It),* John *(Much Ado About Nothing),* Aaron *(Titus Andronicus),* Sebastian *(The Tempest),* Edmund *(King Lear),* and Claudius *(Hamlet).*

The plays with classical settings often use unusual names for the less central characters, including villains: Aufidius *(Coriolanus),* Iachimo *(Cymbeline),* Thaliart *(Pericles),* and Chiron *(Titus Andronicus).*

Rarely, the villain's name gives him away: Malvolio "bad will" *(Twelfth Night),* Hotspur *(Henry IV* part 1), and Shylock *(Merchant of Venice).*

In other cases, the name may simply be unusual and so become closely associated with the Shakespearean character: Iago *(Othello),* Brutus *(Julius Caesar),* and Leontes *(The Winter's Tale).*

ROSALIND: (f) French; from Germanic roots meaning "horse-serpent." Shakespeare seems to have been very fond of the name, using it in *As You Like It* and in the form Rosaline in *Love's Labors Lost* and for an offstage character in *Romeo and Juliet.* Some of the popularity may come from combining the imagery of roses with the favorite name element *lynn.* One famous modern bearer is actress Rosalind Russell. Variants: **Rosalinda, Rosalina, Rosaline, Rosalyn, Roselyn,** and **Roslyn.**

SELMA: (f) coined; another of James Macpherson's invented Ossianic names. In the text it is assigned the meaning "beautiful appearance," but there is no clear source for this. Some of its popularity may come from a fashion for the sound pattern also found in Velma, Thelma, and so on. Variants: **Salma** and **Zelma.**

UNA: (f) multiple origins; the Una in Spenser's *The Faerie Queene* is simply the Latin word for "one," however this name is long predated by an Irish Gaelic name Úna, of uncertain meaning. As the name has chiefly been popularized from Irish sources, you can assume that the latter name is the main influence. The best known example may be Oona Chaplin, wife of actor Charlie Chaplin. The name was mildly popular in the early 20th century. Variant: **Oona.**

Popular Names from Popular Novels

The rise of the modern novel in the 18th century saw generations of girls named after literary heroines (Pamela and Edna) and the occasional boy named after the heroes (Cedric). The fashion isn't limited to realistic fiction.

Fantasy writer J. R. R. Tolkien's *Lord of the Rings* has inspired the occasional Galadriel and Strider, although these have not become common enough for general notice. But throughout the 20th century, the influence of written literature on names has largely been replaced by that of television and movies (Chapters 16 and 18).

AMYAS: (m) Latin; loved. Compare the meaning of this name with the feminine names AMANDA (see earlier in this chapter) and AMY (see Chapter 16). It was used for the character of Captain Sir Amyas Leigh in Charles Kingsley's novel *Westward Ho!* And this seems to have inspired at least occasional imitators.

ANGHARAD: (f) Welsh; well-loved. Several Welsh names were popularized more broadly via Richard Llewellyn's novel *How Green was my Valley* and the film made from it.

BAMBI: (f) coined; although the character of Bambi in Felix Salten's novel of that name is male, the name seems to have struck the general imagination as more feminine in sound. It enjoyed a mild popularity for a few decades after the animated Disney movie based on the book came out.

BRENDA: (f) coined; possibly intended as a feminine variant of Brand derived from a Norse root meaning "sword." The name appears to have been invented by Sir Walter Scott for the heroine of his novel *The Pirate*. It soared to extreme popularity in the mid–20th century and has continued to be very common. Well-known bearers include pop singer Brenda Lee and the character of Brenda Walsh on the TV show *Beverly Hills 90210.* The popularity of Brenda ushered in a great fad for names beginning with "Br-."

CEDRIC: (m) coined; invented by Sir Walter Scott for his novel *Ivanhoe.* It is most likely an adaptation of Cerdic, the name of an Anglo-Saxon king, although that name itself is probably of Brythonic origin. Another literary bearer was the title character of Frances Hodgson Burnett's *Little Lord Fauntleroy,* which might have been expected to put coffin nails into the name's popularity. Instead you see it becoming popular in several variants in the latter half of the 20th century. Current bearers include basketball player Cedric Maxwell. Variants: **Cedrick** and **Sedrick.**

CLORINDA: (f) coined; perhaps a blend of Clara and Florinda or similar names. An early use of the name is in Torquato Tasso's 1580 novel *Jerusalem Delivered.*

DARCY: (f, m) multiple origins; either a French surname "from Arcy" or from the Irish surname Ó Dorchaidhe "descendant of the dark man". Although the best-known literary Darcy is the hero of Jane Austen's novel *Pride and Prejudice,* the name only seriously makes the popularity chart as a girl's name, appearing in the second half of the 20th century. Given that it shows up at the same time and in the same spelling variants as Marcy (see MARCIA in Chapter 10), it's possible that the feminine name is a coined blend involving Marcy instead of a borrowing of the masculine name. Variants: **Darci** and **Darcie.**

DORIAN: (m) Greek; a person from the Doric region of Greece. Rather surprisingly, the name seems to have been popularized by the somewhat sinister title character of Oscar Wilde's *The Picture of Dorian Gray*. It has been rising in popularity for the last several decades.

DORINDA: (f) coined; a blend of Dora with any of various names ending in "-linda." It has been a favorite of novelists, used in George Farquhar's 1707 *The Beaux Stratagem* and Ellen Glasgow's 1925 *Barren Ground*. It had a mild popularity in the mid–20th century, including author Dorinda Kamm.

EBENEZER: (m) Hebrew; stone of help. This is a Biblical place name that was adopted as a given name during the Reformation and was relatively popular in colonial New England. It seems to have been undermined, rather than popularized, by its use in Charles Dickens's *A Christmas Carol* for the miser Ebenezer Scrooge.

FANNY: (f) English; a diminutive of FRANCIS (Chapter 8). It was quite popular in England starting in the 18th century, when it was used for the title character in John Cleland's *Fanny Hill* as well as a character in Henry Fielding's *Joseph Andrews*. But in the 20th century, British use virtually disappeared when the name developed into a term of vulgar slang for a portion of female anatomy. American popularity continued well into midcentury. Variant: **Fannie.**

FINNEGAN: (m) Gaelic; a diminutive of FINN "white, fair." This is the title character of James Joyce's novel *Finnegan's Wake*. It may also be used directly from the Irish surname but is relatively rare.

FIONA: (f) coined; intended as a feminine form of Irish Fionn or FINN (Chapter 5). This name was used as a pen name by Scottish author William Sharp in the 19th century. The name has become quite popular in the last decade or so.

HEIDI: (f) multiple sources; in Johanna Sypri's novel of the name, it is said to be a diminutive of Adalheid, but there is also a name Haidee used in Lord Byron's *Don Juan* and several other works, often for girls of foreign origin where it may be intended to carry a sense of "heathen." The forms Heidi and Haydee have both been mildly popular in the later 20th century. Variants: **Haidee** and **Haydee.**

HOLDEN: (m) English; hollow valley. This is a transferred use of the surname. The name is familiar from the character of Holden Caulfield in J. D. Salinger's *Catcher in the Rye,* but the recent spate of popularity seems likely to be simply from a fashion for this sound pattern.

ISHMAEL: (m) Hebrew; God hears. Like many names in Genesis, this may alternately be a non-Hebrew name of unknown meaning. The name features in Herman Melville's *Moby Dick* and is found for author Ishmael Reed. The spelling Ismael has been much more popular throughout the 20th century. Variant: **Ismael.**

KIM: (m) English; a diminutive of various names beginning with "Kim-." In Rudyard Kipling's novel of the name, it is short for Kimball. (In female use, Kim is almost always short for KIMBERLY, see Chapter 14.) The name enjoyed a brief intense popularity in the mid–20th century.

LAURA: (f) Italian; either a feminine form of LAURENCE (Chapter 8) or taken directly from *laurus,* the name of the laurel tree. Laura was the addressee of most of Italian Renaissance writer Petrarch's poetry. The name has been wildly popular throughout the 20th century and gave rise to many variants. Bearers include singer Laura Nyro, actress Laura Dern, and the character of Laura Vining (of the "Luke and Laura" romance) in the soap opera *General Hospital.* Another variant is found for basketball player Lorri Bauman. Variants: **Lara, Lora; Larissa; Lauri, Laurie, Lori, Lorie, Lorri,** and **Lorrie.**

LEMUEL: (m) Hebrew; God is bright. The name occurs in passing in the Old Testament and was revived after the Reformation. Jonathan Swift's Lemuel Gulliver features in the novel *Gulliver's Travels.* The name was mildly popular in the late 19th century and on into the first half of the 20th century.

LILLIOM: (f) coined; most likely adapted from LILLIAN (Chapter 9). This name appears for the title character in Ferenc Molnar's novel *Liliom.* The rare use of Lilliam in the mid–20th century is likely to be an independent coinage, though. Variant: **Lilliam.**

LORNA: (f) coined; possibly taken from the place name Lorne in Scotland. This name appears as the title character for R. D. Blackmore's novel *Lorna Doone* and is moderately popular throughout much of the 20th century. It is found for actress and singer Lorna Luft, the daughter of Judy Garland.

MANFRED: (m) German; peace-strength. Literature rarely popularizes male names, and the use of Manfred may be entirely independent from its use in Horace Walpole's *The Castle of Otranto* and Lord Byron's poem *Manfred.* In any event, the name has been rare and, when used, is often an immigrant name, as for mystery writer Manfred B. Lee.

MARMION: (m) French; a monkey, a brat. It seems unlikely that Sir Walter Scott had the original meaning of the name in mind when he gave it to the title character of *Lord Marmion.*

MEDORA: (f) coined; the origins of the name are unclear. There are several U.S. towns named Medora where the name may be of Native American origin, but Edith Wharton may have invented it independently for the character of Medora Mingott in *The Age of Innocence.* It never seems to have caught on in popularity, despite its similarity to the very popular Dora.

MELVILLE: (m) French; bad town. As a surname, this is familiar from novelist Herman Melville, famous for his sea-faring stories especially *Moby Dick.* Like many surnames, it was taken up as a given name in the 19th century and continued to enjoy a small popularity in the early part of the 20th century. Melville Dewey was the inventor of the Dewey Decimal System for organizing library books. (He was also interested in spelling reform and later wrote his name "Melvil Dui.")

NIGEL: (m) Latin; black. This name is sometimes found as a Latin form of NEIL but is unrelated. It may be one of the few men's names popularized through use in 19th-century literature. Nigel Loring is the main character of Arthur Conan Doyle's *The White Company* and Nigel Olifaunt of Scott's *The Fortunes of Nigel.* The name has a connection to another of Arthur Conan Doyle's characters in actor Nigel Bruce, who played Dr. Watson to Basil Rathbone's Sherlock Holmes.

NYDIA: (f) uncertain; possibly a coined name, blending the initial "N" with Lydia. There is a minor character named Nydia in Edward Bulwer-Lytton's novel *The Last Days of Pompeii.* The name enjoys some small popularity in the mid–20th century, but it isn't clear whether this comes from the novel or is an independent coinage.

OSWALD: (m) English; divine power. This name was in occasional use since the Medieval period, but it became a favorite of 19th-century novelists due to its impression of antiquity. Variants: **Osbaldo, Osvaldo,** and **Oswaldo.**

PAMELA: (f) coined; invented from Greek roots meaning "everything sweet." Sir Philip Sidney came up with this name for a character in his *Arcadia* after which it languished until used by Samuel Richardson for the title character of his 1740 novel *Pamela.* It didn't become popular in the U.S. until the mid–20th century when it shot up from obscurity to number 13 in the course of four decades. It is known from actresses Pamela Anderson and Pamela Sue Martin. Variants: **Pamala** and **Pamella.** Diminutive: **Pam.**

PEREGRINE: (m) Latin; pilgrim, foreigner. The name had been used occasionally but was first popularized by Tobias Smollett's 1751 novel *Peregrine Pickle.* One diminutive is Perry, as for fictional investigative lawyer Perry Mason. Diminutive: **Perry.**

PERSIS: (f) Greek; persian woman. This is a Biblical name used occasionally after the Reformation. The name was popularized by the character of Persis Lapham in William Dean Howells's *The Rise of Silas Lapham.* One modern bearer is actress Persis Khambatta.

PRECIOUS: (f) English; something valuable. This might be thought of as similar to the virtue names popular after the Reformation, but it appears to be relatively recent in use. The protagonist of Alexander McCall Smith's mystery series *The No. 1 Ladies' Detective Agency* is named Precious Ramotswe.

RAMONA: (f) Spanish; a feminine version of RAYMOND (Chapter 8). Helen Hunt Jackson's 1884 novel *Ramona* was written in part to draw attention to the situation of Native Americans in California at the time but also became a romantic classic. The name was fairly popular through the mid–20th century but has fallen off somewhat since then. Variants: **Ramonita** and **Romona.**

ROHAN: (m) Breton; from a place name. Recent popularity may be influenced instead by the place name in J. R. R. Tolkien's *The Lord of the Rings.*

SILAS: (m) Latin; a variant of Silvanus (see SYLVESTER in Chapter 12). This was originally the name of a Roman tree-god, but found in the New Testament as an ordinary name where Silas is Paul's companion on his travels. Despite this, the name was not much used until the Reformation. It became a favorite of 19th-century novelists, appearing for title characters in William Dean Howells's *The Rise of Silas Lapham,* George Eliot's *Silas Marner,* and Joseph Sheridan Le Fanu's *Uncle Silas.* The name has been in use throughout the 20th century, although of variable popularity.

THOMASINA: (f) English; a feminine form of THOMAS (Chapter 8). In Thomas Hardy's 1878 novel *The Return of the Native,* the character of Thomasin Yeobright is known familiarly as Tamsin. Variants: **Tamsin** and **Thomasin.**

UNDINE: (f) coined; from the Latin for "wave." This is the name of a water-nymph sort of character in Fridrich de La Motte-Fouqué's 1811 novel *Undine.* It was taken up into at least occasional use and appears for a rather more solidly human character in Edith Wharton's *The Custom of the Country.*

URIAH: (m) Hebrew; God is light. The Biblical Uriah is a rather admirable figure, but the name has been spoiled for many by its association with the slimy Uriah Heep in Charles Dickens's *David Copperfield.* In spite of it all, it is found occasionally in the mid–20th century.

VANESSA: (f) coined; the name was created in the 18th century by Jonathan Swift for his friend Esther Vanhomrigh as a cut-and-paste of her names. It was used occasionally after that but got its greatest boost from the novels of Hugh Walpole, including the self-titled *Vanessa* in 1933. Not long after that, the name shot up to extreme popularity and has held its position ever since. One famous bearer is actress Vanessa Redgrave. Variants: **Vanesa** and **Venessa.**

WENDY: (f) coined; the name appears to have been invented by J. M. Barrie for the character in his 1904 novel *Peter Pan*. One theory is that it comes from a baby-talk phrase "friendy-wendy." It rises quickly in popularity in the '40s and has only dropped off somewhat from its peak. Current bearers include art historian Sister Wendy Beckett. Variant: **Wendi.**

WILFRED: (m) English; one who desires peace. This is another of the names popularized by Sir Walter Scott's novel *Ivanhoe,* here the given name of the title character. Its popularity was aided by a general Victorian interest in antique-sounding names. Since that time it has only slowly declined in popularity, and some of that has been made up by a rise in the Spanish variant Wilfredo. Other bearers include poet Wilfred Owens and former Canadian Prime Minister Wilfrid Laurier. Variants: **Wilfredo** and **Wilfrid.**

ZANE: (m) uncertain; the most likely origin of this name is as a form of JOHN (Chapter 8), but it comes most immediately from a surname of uncertain origin. The name is most familiar from prolific Western author Zane Grey. It has been increasing slowly in popularity through the 20th century and recently has been picking up spelling variants. Variants: **Zain** and **Zayne.**

ZULEIKA: (f) Persian; brilliant beauty. The name is commonly found in Persian poetry but was popularized in English by Lord Byron's poem *The Bride of Abydos.* Another literary use is in Max Beerbohm's novel *Zuleika Dobson.* Variant: **Zuleyka.**

Part III
Naming through the Ages

The 5th Wave — By Rich Tennant

"That's a telecast of parade balloons used in Macy's Thanksgiving Day Parade. Your ultrasound images are over here."

In this part . . .

1f you hear the name Jennifer, Emily, or Heather, you'll immediately have an idea of when that person was born. And although you may be wrong in individual cases, the fact remains that naming fashions have changed over time, and that particular names are characteristic of particular eras. This section takes a brief tour through the centuries, examining names that were popular in various eras.

Chapter 7

Building Empires: Classical Names

In This Chapter

▶ Finding Greek names

▶ Searching through Latin names

▶ Checking out names from the Barbarians

M any cultures have contributed names to the current repertoire, but the names of classical Greece and Rome hold a special place due to the history of the early Christian church. While many people featured in the New Testament bear Aramaic names (the version of Hebrew that was spoken at the time), the church expanded and evolved in the middle of the Roman Empire, and many early followers (and so also many early leaders, saints, and martyrs) had names of Latin or Greek origin. So when later parents named their children after prominent figures in Christianity, a great many of the names were Latin or Greek.

Picking a Name That's Not All Greek to You

Why were Greek names so popular? Greek was the language of philosophy and learning, even among the Romans. Just as Latin became the language of scholars in the Middle Ages, Greek was the language that showed fellow citizens of the empire how cultured and cosmopolitan you were.

ANASTACIUS: (m) Greek; resurrection. (For the feminine version, see ANASTASIA in Chapter 9.) There were several early popes named Anastasius, but the name never caught on much in English. A Spanish form shows up occasionally around the turn of the 20th century and was used by 19th-century Mexican president Anastacio Bustamante. Variant: **Anastacio.**

CHARISSA: (f) Greek; grace. It began to be used after the Reformation as a "virtue name." An early literary use appears in Spenser's *The Faerie Queen.* In the 20th century, it appeared on the charts suddenly in the '70s and several forms have been quite popular since then. One bearer is actress Charissa Chamorro. Variant: **Carisa, Carissa, Charisse,** and **Karissa.**

CLEO: (f, m) Greek; glory. As a feminine name, it is often short for Cleopatra ("father's glory"), the name of the most famous early Egyptian queen. It is less obvious what the origin of the name is for men, although one possibility is Cleon (which hits the charts briefly in the '20s). Curiously, the male and female uses have had very similar popularities, appearing sometime in the 19th century and dropping out of fashion by the mid 20th. One woman with this name is British jazz singer Cleo Laine. Variant: (f) **Cleopatra;** (m) **Cleon.**

EUDORA: (f) Greek; good gift. The name has been used occasionally since the 19th century, but in general is quite rare. One bearer is novelist Eudora Welty.

EULALIA: (f) Greek; good speech, sweet speech. The word was an epithet of the god Apollo and the name of an early Christian martyr. It has been more common in France and Spain than in English-speaking areas but is found around the turn of the 20th century.

EUSEBIUS: (m) Greek; pious. The name was borne by an early church historian who wrote a biography of the emperor Constantine; later use is often in honor of him. A modern bearer is Portuguese soccer star Eusebio da Silva Ferreira. Variant: **Eusebio.**

GALEN: (m) Greek; calm. The 2nd-century Greek physician Galen's work on anatomy was not improved on for one and a half millennia. The name seems to have become popular only in recent times, particularly in the mid–20th century. One bearer is early TV host Galen Drake. Variant: **Gaylon.**

HIPPOLYTA (f), **HIPPOLYTUS** (m): Greek; one who sets horses loose. In Greek mythology, Hippolyta was the queen of the Amazons, who bore a son named Hippolytus to the hero Theseus. (Shakespeare's *A Midsummer Night's Dream* features both Hippolyta and Theseus.) An early pope bore the name Hippolytus which inspired later use. One more modern bearer was early photographic artist Hippolyte Bayard. Variants: (f) **Hipolita;** (m) **Hipolitus, Hipolito,** and **Hippolyte.**

LYSANDER: (m) Greek; one who frees men. In ancient Greek history, Lysander commanded the Spartan fleet against Athens. The name occurs occasionally in literary contexts, as for a character in Shakespeare's *A Midsummer Night's Dream,* but has also been in more ordinary use, as for 19th-century anarchist Lysander Spooner. Variant: **Lisandro.**

MELANIE: (f) Greek; black. Two early saints of this name gave it a basis for later use, but it had never been common before it was used for a character in Margaret Mitchell's *Gone With the Wind* and leapt onto the popularity charts in the '40s. Since then it has been quite common, as for actresses Melanie Lynskey and Melanie Griffith. Variants: **Melany** and **Melonie.**

MELISSA: (f) Greek; a bee. The name was used in classical Greek but was revived in the Renaissance through literary use when it appeared in Ludovico Ariosto's *Orlando Furioso* and Spenser's *The Faerie Queen.* It became extremely popular in the late 20th century, reaching as high as number 3 in the '70s. Well known bearers include actress Melissa Gilbert and singers in a variety of genres including Melissa Manchester, Melissa Etheridge, and Missy Elliott. Variants: **Melisa, Mellisa,** and **Mellissa.** Diminutives: **Mellie** and **Missy.**

PHILOMENA: (f) Greek; one who remains loving. The name has been used occasionally in poetry. Chretien de Troyes wrote a poem of this name based on a character in Ovid's *Metamorphoses,* and Henry Wadsworth Longfellow wrote one about Saint Philomena which he dedicated to Florence Nightingale. The name was moderately popular in the 19th and early 20th centuries but has fallen out of fashion. One bearer was British sculptor Philomena Davidson Davis. Variant: **Filomena.**

SOPHIA: (f) Greek; wisdom. This is an abstract concept mistakenly turned into a saint in the Medieval period. Its use as a name spread gradually from Greece throughout Europe and came into English use in the 17th century. Over the last century, it has been quite popular in a variety of forms, although the spelling Sophia has become particularly popular in recent decades. The Russian diminutive Sonia has also enjoyed a fair amount of popularity, especially in the middle of the 20th century. The name is familiar from actress Sophia Loren, singer-songwriter Sophie B. Hawkins, and Norwegian ice skater Sonja Henie. Variants: **Sofia** and **Sophie.** Diminutives: **Sonia, Sonja,** and **Sonya.**

THALIA: (f) Greek; good cheer. Thalia is the muse of comedy and of idyllic poetry. The names of the eight muses have not, in general, been taken up for use as given names, but in the last couple of decades, Thalia has been making a small splash. One bearer is rocker Thalia Zedek.

THEODORA (f), **THEODORE** (m): Greek; God's gift. The same elements in a different order are found in DOROTHEA (Chapter 8). The male name may sometimes be confused with THEODORIC (see later in the present chapter). These names first became popular under the Byzantines and in the Eastern Orthodox church. There were several early popes named Theodore, and several Byzantine empresses named Theodora. The names came into English use beginning in the 17th century but were not particularly popular at first. Theodore enjoyed a growing fashion beginning in the mid-19th century and has never seriously fallen out of fashion. At the same time, Theodora has never made it past fairly modest numbers. For diminutives, people may use Theo or Thea, but Theodore has also borrowed the diminutive Ted from EDWARD (Chapter 8). Bearers have included U.S. president Theodore Roosevelt and anthropologist Theodora Kroeber. A character named Thea Kronborg features in Willa Cather's novel *The Song of the Lark*. Variants: (m) **Teodoro** and **Theadore**. Diminutives: (both) **Theo**; (f) **Thea**.

THERON: (m) Greek; a wild beast. This was the name of a ruler of ancient Sicily, but there seems to be no clear reason why it was revived in the late 19th century. It has enjoyed a rather mild popularity through much of the 20th century and one example is basketball player Theron Smith.

ZOE: (f) Greek; life. This was originally used as a Greek translation of the name EVE (Chapter 8) and caught on due to an early Christian martyr who bore it. It has appeared rarely since the 19th century but has been shooting up the charts in the last couple of decades. Bearers have included historic novelist Zoe Oldenbourg and actress Zoe Wanamaker. Variants: **Zoey** and **Zoie**.

Loving Latin Names

The Latin language was a constant presence in Europe, particularly among the educated or upper classes, and when people wanted to create new names, they often used some descriptive name or phrase in that language. Latin forms of Christian names were kept alive through church liturgy and were always available for new use.

ADRIANNA (f), **ADRIAN** (m): Latin; someone from the Adriatic region. The name was popular in classical times, as for the Roman emperor Hadrian. It shows up rarely in England in the Middle Ages, perhaps in honor of the only pope of English birth, who took the name Adrian IV. The feminine form, Adriana, occurs in Shakespeare's *A Comedy of Errors,* but modern use dates mostly from the 19th century. The name increased in popularity for both women and men through most of the 20th century, but feminine use has been dropping in recent decades. Bearers include actors Adrian Paul and Adrien Brody, and poet Adrienne Rich. Variants: (f) **Adrian, Adriana, Adriane, Adrianne,** and **Adrienne;** (m) **Adrien** and **Hadrian**.

ALMA: (f, m) Latin; soul. Although the Latin word is familiar, especially from the collegiate phrase *alma mater* (mother of the soul), the use of Alma as a name began mostly in commemoration of the 1854 battle of Alma in the Crimean War. This accounts for it being used as both a male and female name, given that the word itself would be expected to be feminine. Even so, it has always been much more popular for women, and the male name fell out of fashion in the early 20th century. Bearers include opera singer Alma Gluck.

ANTONIA (f), **ANTHONY** (m): Latin; meaning uncertain, from an old Roman family name. In classical times, the name is closely associated with Marcus Antonius, the contemporary of Julius Caesar and lover of Cleopatra, and the combination Mark Anthony is often used in reference to him. Another early popularizer was Saint Anthony of Padua. For the diminutives TONY and TONIA, see Chapters 18 and 10, respectively. Other feminine variants are discussed under ANTOINETTE (Chapter 9). As a boy's name, this has been relatively popular in several variants over the last century, especially Anthony, Anton, and Antonio. More recently, the French form Antoine, and phonetic spellings of it such as Antwan, have become popular, too. The feminine form Antonia has also been moderately popular, although declining somewhat in recent decades. Male bearers have included composer Antonio Vivaldi, actors Anthony Hopkins, Antonio Banderas, and Anthony Quinn, and the title character of the movie *Antwone Fisher*. Female bearers have included historian and biographer Antonia Fraser and novelist Antonia (A. S.) Byatt. Variants : (m) **Antoine, Anton, Antone, Antonio, Antony, Antwan, Antwon,** and **Antwone.**

AURELIA (f), **AURELIUS** (m): Latin; golden. This may not have been the original meaning of the Roman family name, but is now solidly associated with it. The name was mildly popular in the earlier parts of the 20th century. One historic bearer was Italian renaissance painter Aurelio Luini. Variants: (f) **Aurea;** (m) **Aurelio.**

CAESAR: (m) Latin; possibly "hairy," although it is not entirely certain that the name is of Latin origin at all. This was originally an old Roman family name, but became synonymous with "emperor" when the Caesar branch of the Julius family brought an end to the Roman Republic. It's sometimes used in the compound name Julius Caesar, which can be found occasionally from the Renaissance onward. The name has naturally been popular in Italy, and is most common in the U.S. in the Italian or Spanish form Cesar, as for actor Cesar Romero. Variant: **Cesar.**

CECIL: (m, rarely f) Latin; blind. This is an old Roman family name that may have originated in a personal nickname of the family's founder. While the feminine form CECILIA (Chapter 17) was popularized by an early saint, modern use of the masculine Cecil comes mainly from the surname which, just to confuse the issue, comes more immediately from the Welsh name Seisyllt, which may be from Latin Caecilius or possibly from Latin Sextillius. Cecil was moderately popular around the turn of the 20th century but has fallen slowly out of fashion since then. Prominent bearers have included Cecil Rhodes, the founder of Rhodesia (now Zimbabwe), and film producer Cecil B. DeMille. Variant: **Cecilio.**

CICERO: (m) Latin; chickpea, garbanzo bean. This name was the personal nickname of famous Roman orator Marcus Tullius Cicero (possibly named for a mole or wart shaped like a chickpea). The name has been popular during several revivals of interest in classical literature but has always been fairly rare.

CLAUDIA: (f) Latin; lame. This is an old Roman family name, probably taken from a personal nickname. For the masculine name, see Chapter 10. Claudia occurs once in the New Testament, and interest in this name has been driven by a combination of classical and Biblical revivals. The Welsh name GLADYS (Chapter 10) is sometimes thought to be derived from this name. Claudia has been quite popular ever since the late 19th century, with some additional contributions from the French forms CLAUDETTE (Chapter 18) and CLAUDINE (Chapter 9). Bearers include film director Claudia Weill and model Claudia Schiffer. Variant: **Claudie.**

CORNELIA (f), **CORNELIUS** (m): Latin; meaning uncertain, but based on the word *corn* meaning "horn." This old Roman family name also appears in the New Testament. There are several saints named Cornelius, including one particularly popular in the Netherlands which has caused the name to be common there, as for Dutch-American financier Cornelius Vanderbilt. Another source of popularity comes from the Irish use of the name to substitute for the Gaelic name Conchobhar. Cornelius has been quite popular over the last century, only dropping off somewhat in the last decade or two. The fashion for Cornelia was more confined to the late 19th and early 20th centuries.

DONATUS: (m) Latin; given; gift. The name was made popular by several early martyrs but also by the author of an early Latin grammar book. His work so set the standard for this type of work that in some places in the Middle Ages "Donatus" came to be the ordinary word for "grammar textbook." The name is found rarely around the turn of the 20th century. Variant: **Donato.**

DRUSILLA: (f) Latin; meaning unknown. The Latin name was adapted from the Gaulish Drausos and was used in both the masculine form Drusus and the feminine diminutive Drusilla. These were originally used in the Livian family, from which the second wife of the emperor Augustus came, and that connection brought them into more prominence. (They may be quite familiar from the television mini-series *I, Claudius,* or the series of novels by Robert Graves on which it was based.) One Drusilla is mentioned in the New Testament, which is the primary source for modern use. A character of the name features in Thomas Hardy's novel *Jude the Obscure,* and more recent bearers include British writer Drusilla Beyfus and historian Drusilla Dunjee Houston. It is a very rare name, found mostly around the turn of the 20th century. Variant: **Drucilla.**

FABIOLA: (f) Latin; bean. The name is a diminutive of Fabia, from the same root as FABIAN (Chapter 17). There was an early saint of this name, but it has always been rather rare. It shows up on the popularity charts only recently, and a recent bearer is Brazilian in-line skating champion Fabiola da Silva.

GALILEA: (f) Latin; a person from Galilee. Galilea is the Latin name for the place, but the personal name may also have arisen as a feminine form of the name of Renaissance astronomer Galileo Galilei. One current bearer is Mexican actress Galilea Montijo, and the name has very recently been hitting the popularity charts.

HILARY: (f, m) Latin; cheerful. The same root is seen with a slight shift in meaning in the word "hilarious." Early use was primarily in honor of St. Hilarius of Poitiers and so faded somewhat after the Reformation. The name was revived a bit in the late 19th century primarily as a masculine name (and so, most likely from the surname), but for unclear reasons this use fell out of fashion well before the resurgence of interest in feminine use in the second half of the 20th century. Well-known female bearers include New York senator Hillary Rodham Clinton and actresses Hilary Swank and Hilary Duff. Variants: (f) **Hillary;** (m) **Hilario.**

HORTENSIA: (f) Latin; a garden, one who lives in a garden. This old Roman family name became popular in English primarily through romantic 19th-century novels such as Charlotte Brontë's *Shirley* and Charles Dickens's *Bleak House.* The name was mildly popular around the turn of the 20th century but fell rapidly out of fashion. One bearer is anthropologist Hortense Powdermaker. Variants: **Hortencia** and **Hortense.**

JULIUS: (m) Latin; meaning uncertain, possibly "downy, bearded." This is an old Roman family name said to derive from the name of Aeneas's son Iulus. The variant Julian has been equally popular. (For feminine names in this group, see JULIA in Chapter 17, JULIET in Chapter 6, and JULIANA in Chapter 8.) As the family name of the first Roman emperor, Gaius Julius Caesar, Julius was used directly in his honor during the various classical revivals, while Julian was popularized by a variety of early saints, especially Saint Julian the Hospitaller. Several variants of the name have been quite popular throughout the last century, including a Spanish form, Julio, and the French Jules, as borne by early science fiction writer Jules Verne. Variants: **Jules,** and **Julio; Julian** and **Julien.**

JUNIUS: (m) Latin; possibly from the same root as JUNE (Chapter 5), from the name of the goddess Juno. This old Roman family name has been revived especially in honor of Roman revolutionary hero Marcus Junius Brutus, better known to history simply as Brutus, the friend and assassin of Julius Caesar. It is often used in the combination "Junius Brutus," as by 19th-century painter Junius Brutus Stearns. The name enjoyed a mild popularity in the late 19th and early 20th centuries. Variant: **Junious.**

LAVINIA: (f) Latin; meaning uncertain. The name was borne by the wife of Aeneas in Virgil's *Aeneid* and so popularized during various classical revivals, starting in the Middle Ages. It became quite fashionable in the 18th century and only fell off the charts in the early 20th. Bearers include British writer Lavinia Greenlaw and nursing reformer Lavinia Lloyd Dock. Variant: **Lavina.**

LOUVENIA: (f) Latin; meaning uncertain, but most likely from a place name derived from the Latin personal name Lupinius, with a root meaning "wolf." The name was mildly popular in the 19th and early 20th centuries and may sometimes have been used as a variant of LAVINIA (see earlier in this chapter).

LUCIUS: (m) Latin; light. This Roman family name also gave rise to the feminine name LUCY (Chapter 16). It was borne by an early saint and two Medieval popes, but doesn't seem to have become popular in general use until the Renaissance. The name was mildly common in the early 20th century. Also found at that time is the form Lucious, which is presumably intended to be a spelling variant of this name, although it also evokes the ordinary word "lucious," as in, "delicious." Variant: **Lucious.**

SERGIUS: (m) Latin; an ancient Roman family name, possibly meaning "servant." Historically, this name has been more common in eastern Europe, however, a Spanish or Italian form, Sergio, has become increasingly popular in the late 20th century. Examples include Latin musician Sergio Mendez and director Sergio Leone. Variants: **Sergey** and **Sergio.**

TATIANA: (f) Latin; meaning uncertain; from the Roman family name Tatius. There were several early saints and martyrs bearing both the feminine and masculine versions of this name, but only the feminine form became generally popular, mostly in the Eastern Orthodox Church, especially in Russia. Modern use is primarily taken from the Russian name, either in the full form or using the diminutive Tania. It's the latter that has been most popular in the U.S., especially in the second half of the 20th century. Bearers include opera singer Tatiana Troyanos and country singer Tanya Tucker. Variants: **Tatianna** and **Tatyanna.** Diminutives: **Tania, Tanya, Tawny, Tawnya,** and **Taniya.**

TERRANCE: (m) Latin; meaning unknown; from the old Roman family name Terentius. The name was kept in mind by 2nd-century playwright Publius Terentius Afer, but it came into use largely in 19th-century Ireland as a substitute for various similar-sounding Gaelic names. In the U.S. it has been most popular in the second half of the 20th century, while the diminutive Terry has been significantly more popular than the original name. (Terry also appears as a woman's name, primarily as a diminutive of THERESA — see Chapter 10.) Bearers include film writer and director Terrence Malick, actor Terry Gilliam, and football player Terry Bradshaw. Variants: **Torrance, Terence,** and **Terrence.** Diminutive: **Terry.**

TITUS: (m) Latin; meaning uncertain; an old Roman given name. The name appears in the New Testament, but has been associated in the popular imagination more with the Roman emperor Titus. This accounts for it becoming popular in the 19th century as part of the romantic revival, rather than during periods when Biblical names were revived. It has been used rarely in the later part of the 20th century. The name is found for the main character of Mervyn Peake's Gormenghast novels (Titus Groan). The Spanish variant is borne by musician Tito Puente. Variant: **Tito.**

VALENCIA: (f) Latin; strong, healthy. This name comes from the same root as VALENTINE (Chapter 18). The name Valencia is perhaps more familiar as that of a region in Spain. It enjoyed a mild popularity just after the mid–20th century.

VERGIL: (m) Latin; meaning uncertain, although later (and probably falsely) associated with *virgo* "virgin, maiden." It is an old Roman family name made famous by the poet Publius Vergilius Maro, author of the *Aeneid*. As such, it tended to be revived during times of classical interest and has been quite popular from the late 19th century through most of the 20th. The name was used for the main character, Virgil Tibbs, in the movie and later TV series *In the Heat of the Night*. Variants: **Virgil** and **Virgilio.**

VICTOR: (m) Latin; victor, conqueror. The name was rare in the Middle Ages, despite having been borne by early popes and martyrs, and modern use has probably been inspired more by the meaning than by historic tradition. It became popular in the early 19th century when it was used by Mary Shelly for the title character of her novel *Frankenstein*. Bearers have included several kings of Italy, French novelist Victor Hugo, pianist and comedian Victor Borge, and actor Vic Morrow. Victor has enjoyed a consistently high popularity throughout the last century. Diminutive: **Vic.**

VITUS: (m) Latin; life. The name was popularized by an early saint. It has been used in the U.S. primarily in the Italian or Spanish form Vito, familiar from one of the main characters of Mario Puzo's novel *The Godfather*. A familiar bearer of the original form of the name is tennis star Vitus Gerulaitus. Variant: **Vito.**

Storming the Gates with Barbarian Names

The Roman Empire wasn't the only force in the world in classical days. The barbarians — which at that time meant anyone who wasn't Greek or Roman — have sent a few names down the ages to join the name pool. Often they were the names of kings or queens, or of people who became prominent in the early church.

ALARIC: (m) Gothic; ruler of all. This was the name of several Gothic kings, and most notably the one who sacked Rome in the early 5th century, generally counted as marking the end of the western Roman Empire. The name was revived in the 19th century but has never been particularly popular. One bearer is bicycle racer Alaric Gayfer.

AMELIA: (f) German; industrious, working. Originally a short form of various names like Amalburga (an early saint) or Amalswintha (a queen of the Ostrogoths), today it has come to be treated more as a variant of EMILY (Chapter 9). This name came into English use in the 18th century via German connections of the Hanoverian kings and was a favorite of romantic novelists, as in Henry Fielding's 1751 *Amelia*. It was surpassed in popularity by Emily in the 19th century, but has continued to enjoy a relatively high popularity through the last century. Well-known bearers include early feminist Amelia Bloomer, aviator Amelia Earhart, and tennis pro Amelie Mauresmo. Variants: **Amelie** and **Emelia.**

BARBARA: (f) Greek; foreigner. The ancient Greeks called all foreigners "barbarians" meaning "those who babble; those who can't speak Greek." The name was first popularized by the 3rd-century Saint Barbara and only fell out of favor with the Reformation. *Barbara* began rising in popularity again in the early 20th century — perhaps inspired by several minor characters of the name in 19th-century novels — and made it as high as the third most popular girls' name in the '30s and '40s before declining somewhat. There's a strong streak of romanticism associated with the name, from prolific romance author Barbara Cartland to the tragic and disdainful heroine of the folksong *Barbara Allen.* Superstar singer and actress Barbra Streisand sports a variant spelling, and diminutives include *Barb* and *Babs.* Another diminutive, *Barbie,* has become irretrievably associated with the popular fashion doll. Variant: **Barbra.** Diminutives: **Babs, Barb,** and **Barbie.**

CAMILLA: (f) uncertain; meaning uncertain. Camilla appears in Vergil's *Aeneid* as the name of a foreign warrior-queen and may have been an invention by the author. (If so, then it should probably be classed as a Latin name.) Like many romantic literary names, it became popular in the 19th century especially via novels such as Fanny Burney's *Camilla.* It has been mildly popular through much of the 20th century, but more recently only the French variant Camille has been making the charts. Well-known bearers include feminist Camille Paglia and British socialite Camilla Parker-Bowles. Variants: **Camila** and **Camille.**

CANDACE: (f) uncertain; meaning uncertain. In classical times, this was a popular name (or perhaps actually a title) of the queens of Ethiopia, one of whom is mentioned in the New Testament. The name is also sometimes attributed to the famed Queen of Sheba of Solomon's day. Chaucer has a passing reference to one of these queens under the name Canace in his *Canturbury Tales,* but the name was not taken up into ordinary use until the early 20th century. William Faulker used it for a central character in his novel *The Sound and the Fury.* Candace has been popular largely in the second half of the 20th century, especially in the '80s, perhaps influenced somewhat by popular actress Candice Bergen. The diminutive Candy has been similarly popular. Variants: **Candice, Candis, Kandace,** and **Kandice.** Diminutives: **Candi, Candy, Kandi,** and **Kandy.**

CLOTILDE: (f) Frankish; loud battle. The 5th-century Saint Clotilde is credited with influencing the Christian conversion of her husband, King Clovis I of France. The name was revived during the neo-Medieval fashion of the 19th century but became rare in the early 20th.

CLOVIS, LOUIS: (m) Frankish, French; one who hears battle. When the barbarian Franks took control of Gaul in the decline of the Roman empire, the name Clovis or Chlodovicus was popular among their kings. As they settled in to become French rather than Franks, the name evolved into Louis, a name that continued to be popular among French kings up until the Revolution. In England it became Lewis, while Germany preferred the more conservative form Ludwig and Italy worked through a Latin variant to get Ludovico. In American use, the Spanish form Luis is also popular. Several of these variants have been moderately common at various times in the last century. Clovis itself has never seriously been revived, although it is used for the central character of Saki's short-story collection *The Chronicles of Clovis*. Well-known bearers of various forms of the name include German composer Ludwig von Beethoven, scientist Louis Pasteur, and jazz trumpeter Louis Armstrong. Variants: **Lewis, Ludwig,** and **Luis.** Diminutives: **Lew, Lou,** and **Louie.**

CYRUS: (m) Persian; throne; royal. The Cyrus mentioned in the Bible was the great founder of the Persian Empire, however he was even more familiar through the historical works of classical writers like Herodotus and Xenophon. The name was a late-comer in the fashions for Biblical names, only showing up around the late 18th century, but it has held a steady, if mild, popularity since then. Bearers include former Secretary of State Cyrus Vance. The diminutive Cy is familiar from baseball legend Cy Young. Diminutive: **Cy.**

DARIUS: (m) Persian; meaning uncertain. The name of a famous early Persian king who, like Cyrus, was mentioned in the Bible but is better known through classical historians such as Herodotus. It has been revived to some extent since the 19th century but has only become significantly popular in the last several decades, perhaps as part of a sound fashion for names like Darren and Daryl. One famous bearer was French composer Darius Milhaud. Variants: **Dario** and **Darrius.**

DIDO: (f) uncertain; meaning uncertain. The name of the founding queen of Carthage in Vergil's *Aeneid* whom Aeneas loved and left. It is perhaps more familiar from various musical productions of the story, such as Henry Purcell's opera *Dido and Aeneas*. It is a rarely used name.

HANNIBAL: (m) Phoenician; grace of God. This is the name of the Carthaginian general famous for attacking Rome by coming over the Alps with an army that included war-elephants. The Italians held no grudge against the name and took it up in the form Anibal, as for painter Annibale Caracci. Hannibal has been used occasionally in English during various classical revivals, starting in the 16th century, but especially since the 19th century. Recent fictional bearers include the character of Hannibal Hayes in TVs *Alias Smith and Jones,* and — less appealingly — murderer Hanibal Lecter in the book and movie *The Silence of the Lambs*. Variants: **Anibal, Annibale,** and **Hanibal.**

Uncovering the influence of Latin on the idea of names

Both by sheer weight of numbers and because of the use of Latin as a scholarly language, Latin has had a disproportionate influence on the ideas about names. Greek never managed the same impact — indeed only French comes close to competing with Latin, and the Normans had a lot to do with that. Here are some ways Latin has influenced the idea of names:

✔ While Latin is not the only language in which women's names normally end in "-a," it has been the strongest cause of this apparent "rule." Because of Latin, names ending in "-a" tend to be made feminine even when they weren't feminine to start with, as in Andrea or Sasha. And when new names get invented, one of the easiest ways to indicate that a name is intended to be a girl's name is to end it in "-a" (see Chapter 11).

✔ Many Latin names came in two versions: a basic form like August(us) or Julia, and a form ending in "-i(a)n", such as Augustine or Juliana. Originally these endings meant something like "belonging to, associated with." Not only have they been added to other, non-Latin names (for example, Geraldine), but the commonness of women's names ending in "-ian(a)" combined with the popularity of the name Ann(a) encouraged the idea of compound names (see Chapter 11).

✔ When names are in popular use, they tend to change and adapt over the years until they look nothing like their original roots. A parent fond of the name Edith is unlikely to consider naming her daughter the original Eadgyth. But because the original Latin forms of names have always been available, familiar, and perhaps more elegant and sophisticated, the parent contemplating Mark may choose Marcus instead. So the original forms of Latin names keep getting reinjected into use.

MONICA: (f) uncertain; meaning uncertain. The name was originally popularized by the mother of Saint Augustine, herself a saint, which suggests that the name may come from some unknown North African language. Its principal revival has been in the 20th century, and it became most popular in the '60s and '70s. Well-known bearers include athletes Monica Seles (tennis) and Monique Hennagan (track), as well as the TV character Monica Geller from the series *Friends*. Variants: **Monika** and **Monique.**

OTTO: (m) German; rich. When control of the Roman Empire passed from the hands of Romans to that of barbarians, Otho or Otto was one of them. The name was in occasional use in English during the Middle Ages but fell out of fashion until reintroduced from German use in the 19th century. It fell out of fashion by the mid–20th century, perhaps influenced by a distaste for names with obviously German associations. Interestingly, the older forms Otha and Otho have been just as popular as the more modern Otto. One famous bearer is symphony director Otto Preminger. Variants: **Otha** and **Otho.**

ROXANNE: (f) Persian; dawn. Originally famous as one of the wives of Alexander the Great, the name was kept in mind by the popularity of romances about Alexander and revived in literary use for the title character of Daniel Defoe's 1724 novel *Roxana* and for the romantic object of *Cyrano de Bergerac* by Edmond Rostand. Coming into the 20th century, only the diminutive Roxie was on the popularity charts, but there was a brief fashion for the full name centered around the '50s and '60s, with variants that show that people have falsely associated the latter part of the name with Anne. Variants: **Roxana, Roxane, Roxann,** and **Roxanna.** Diminutive: **Roxie.**

THEODORIC: (m) Gothic; ruler of the people. Not to be confused with THEODORUS, of Greek origin. The Ostrogothic king Theodoric was immortalized by the early historian Jordanes and the name continued to be popular in various Germanic languages. The most popular forms today come from diminutives such as Derick (Chapter 9) or Dirk (Chapter 16). The full name Theodoric is quite rare.

ZENOBIA: (f) uncertain, but possibly of Semitic origin; meaning uncertain. This was the name of a famous 3rd-century queen of Palmyra. It was also the name of an early martyr but seems to have been taken up for ordinary use through classical associations. Nathaniel Hawthorne used it for a character in his 1852 novel *The Blithedale Romance,* but it has never achieved any significant popularity.

Chapter 8

Getting Medieval: The Rise of the "Old Standards"

In This Chapter

▶ Surviving fashion's ups and downs

▶ Discovering forgotten Medieval gems

*A*round the time that you usually think of as the start of the Middle Ages, a curious thing happened. Before that time, there tended to be a lot of different names in use and while names were reused, there didn't tend to be a lot of people with any one name at the same time. Then things changed — and they changed throughout Europe in a surprisingly short period of time. Increasingly, children were being named *after* someone. A relatively small number of names became extremely popular, and many names fell out of use altogether.

In the current chapter, you see this transition: The names that would reign supreme for centuries were in the process of establishing themselves and the others were jockeying for a place (however small) in posterity. The next major change would signal the end of the Medieval period in naming, as the Reformation (in those countries where it took hold) led people to move away from the names of saints and to look to some interesting new sources of names as you discover in Chapter 9.

Enduring Through the Ages with Popular Medieval Names

When you look at the popular names of the Medieval period, you realize how many of the current favorites — both given names and surnames — were established at that time. Among the most popular boys names today, perhaps

70 percent were given names in use in the Middle Ages, for girls it's only slightly less at 60 percent. The names at the top of the charts during the 12th to 15th centuries gave rise to a large variety of nicknames still in use, as well as many that remain only as family names. In this section, I explore some of these "chart toppers," and the wealth of variants they produced.

ADAM: (m) Hebrew; red. (It's also possible that the name is not Hebrew and of unknown meaning.) Old Testament names that were popular in the Middle Ages tend to fall into two groups: names used by saints who became popular namesakes and names of characters whose stories particularly caught the Medieval imagination. Adam falls in the second group and, along with Eve, was quite popular. There was a pair of popular Irish saints who bore the variant Adamnán, but they had little influence on naming outside Ireland. One might have expected Adam to have been popular during the post-Reformation fashion for Old Testament names as well, but it seems to have taken a bit of a hit in popularity, perhaps due to the emphasis on Adam's role in Original Sin, rather than his status as the first man. Still, the name has been moderately popular up through modern times and has become quite fashionable again in the last few decades, although not reaching as high as the top ten. Well-known bearers include actors Adam West and Adam Sandler and economist Adam Smith. Adam gave rise to a number of popular diminutives in the Medieval period but none have survived in current popularity. you see a trace of the diminutive Addy in the surname Addison which has recently become popular for both boys and girls — more so for girls, most likely by association with MADISON (Chapter 10). Variant: (both) **Addison.**

AGATHA: (f) Greek; good. Popularized by an early saint, this name became extremely common by the early Middle Ages. Like the names of many non-Biblical saints, it fell out of favor during the Reformation but continued to hold a small place up until the early 20th century. Today it is considered rather old-fashioned. A familiar bearer is mystery writer Agatha Christie.

AGNES: (f) Greek; pure, chaste. This was an extremely popular name during the Middle Ages, taken from that of an early saint. At that time the pronunciation was the one seen in the variant Annis, but when the name was revived in more recent times — after being nearly exterminated by the Reformation — it was with the classical pronunciation still used today. This name has been used by French writer Anaïs Nin, minimalist painter Agnes Martin, actress Agnes Moorehead, and prolific creator of successful soap operas Agnes Nixon. Variants: **Anais** and **Annis.**

ALANNA (f), **ALAN** (m): Breton; meaning uncertain. This name was first popular in Brittany but was given wider scope by Breton participants in William's conquest of England. It gained a particular foothold in Scotland. Some modern use may be via the surname, typically in the spelling Allen. A feminine form, Alanna, can be found extremely rarely in the Medieval period and has been reinvented in the last century. Alan was most popular around the '50s while Alanna is still increasing in popularity today. There is no shortage of well-known bearers of this name. On the male side you have poets Edgar Allan Poe and Allen Ginsberg, mathematician and cryptographer Alan Turing, and actors Alan Alda, Alan Arkin, and Alan Rickman. On the female side you have mystery writer Alanna Knight and rock musician Alannah Myles. Variants: (f) **Alaina, Alana, Alannah,** and **Alayna;** (m) **Allan, Allen,** and **Allyn.**

ALICE: (f) English; from German roots meaning "noble type." This name has the same origin as ADELAIDE (Chapter 9). It was extremely popular during the Middle Ages despite the lack of prominent saintly namesakes. Perhaps for this reason it survived the Reformation, although it was declining in popularity at that time and didn't begin to recover until the 19th century. The general interest in older and Medieval names started the revival, but one can't discount the influence of Lewis Carroll's *Alice in Wonderland* and its sequel. Around the turn of the 20th century it was among the top-ten most popular girls' names, but it has declined again to a fairly mild level. Alice produced a diminutive, Alison, which was also extremely popular in Medieval times, especially in Scotland. (This is the same method of forming diminutives as seen in Mary and Marion.) Alison fell out of use except as a surname and when the surname was turned back into a given name in the 19th century, it was given primarily to boys — an unusual case of a girl's name turning into a boy's name. Male use of Allison drops off the charts after the '30s, and in the '40s you see the name being revived as a girl's name again. Today it has become quite popular again. Well-known bearers of these names include novelist Alice Walker, chef Alice Waters of Chez Panisse, and actress Alyson Hannigan. Variants: (both) **Allison;** (f) **Alize, Alyce, Alyse,** and **Elease;** (f) **Alison, Allyson,** and **Alyson.**

ANDREA (f, m), **ANDREW** (m): Greek; manly. The immense popularity of the name in the Middle Ages comes from the apostle and saint who bore it. Saint Andrew became the patron saint of both Russia and Scotland, but was venerated and used as a namesake throughout Europe. The name dropped off a bit in popularity after the Reformation but began rising again in the 19th century and has made it up into the top ten within the last decade. Variants from several languages have been on the charts in America, including the French Andre and Italian Andrea — a form that has been reinterpreted as a girl's name due to the "-a" ending and which became quite popular in that use in the last half century. The surname Anderson has also been used as a given name with some regularity. Famous bearers have included U.S. president Andrew Jackson, philanthropist Andrew Carnegie, and artist Andrew Wyeth, while more recently you have seen composer Andrew Lloyd Weber, artist Andy Warhol, actor Andy Griffith, and tennis star Andre Agassi. Variants: (both) **Andrea;** (f) **Andria;** (m) **Anderson, Andra, Andre, Andreas,** and **Andres.** Diminutives: **Andy** and **Andrey.**

ANNE: (f) Hebrew; the same name as HANNAH (Chapter 4) meaning "grace, favor." As the name given in apocrypha for the mother of the Virgin Mary, this name became one of the Medieval top ten throughout Europe and developed many variants and diminutives. Versions covered in other chapters, in addition to Hannah, include ANNETTE (Chapter 18), ANNIKA (Chapter 19), ANNIE (Chapter 17), and NANCY (Chapter 10). By the 16th century, Anne was consistently among the top five most popular women's names, which insulated it from the general rejection of saints' names. In American use it has typically been among the top-ten names up through the early 20th century. It slipped a little in midcentury but has recently been coming back again. Well-known bearers have included diarist Anne Frank, novelists Anne Rice and Anne Perry, poet Anne Sexton, advice columnist Ann Landers, singer Anne Murray, and actresses Anna Paquin and Anne Bancroft. Variants: **Ana, Ann,** and **Anna.**

AUGUST: (m) Latin; venerable. Augustus was a name used by several Roman emperors, although one is particularly associated with this name. This led to it being revived as a nickname by several of the German Holy Roman Emperors in the Middle Ages, and from that it came to be used as a given name in Germany. English use of August or Augustus is fairly recent, but the variant AUGUSTINE (Chapter 9) early became popular in honor of two saints, one of them being the first archbishop of Canturbury and so particularly of interest in England. The diminutive Gus can be used for any of the names in this group. None of these names has been more than mildly popular over the last century, but notable bearers include novelist and publisher August Derleth, aviator Charles Augustus Lindbergh, movie director Gus Van Sant, and astronaut Virgil "Gus" Grissom. Variant: **Augustus.** Diminutive: **Gus.**

BEATRICE: (f) Latin; one who blesses. The 4th-century Saint Beatrice inspired the popularity of this name in the Middle Ages, but after the Reformation it suffered the common fate of saintly names. Dante's Beatrice kept the name popular in literary circles, though, and it benefited from the romantic revivals of the 19th century, leading to a fairly high popularity around the turn of the 20th century. The name has been popular in the Dutch royal family and other well-known bearers include children's writer Beatrix Potter and actress Beatrice (Bea) Arthur. Variants: **Beatrix** and **Beatriz.** Diminutive: **Bea.**

BENEDICT: (m) Latin; blessed. Medieval popularity of this name was largely in honor of the 6th-century Saint Benedict, founder of the Benedictine order of monks, although there were also several popes who took the name. In English it developed into Bennett, and after the Reformation this form survived as a surname to appear again during the 19th-century revival of surnames as given names. One of the better-known bearers in U.S. history, Benedict Arthur, may not be the sort of person to name your children after, but humorous poet Bennett Cerf may be. Another famous bearer is the Dutch philosopher Benedict de Spinoza. This group of names has only been mildly popular over the last century. Variants: **Benito** and **Bennett.**

CARL: (m) German; a man. This name has the same origin as CHARLES (Chapter 9) and is thought of today as the German form of the name (especially in the variant Karl) although it has always been used more widely than that. The Latin form Carolus gave rise to CAROL (Chapter 17), although the feminine use of this name took a longer route to get there. Carl itself has been used very rarely for women, but feminine use has much more often been in the forms CHARLOTTE (Chapter 9), CAROLINE (Chapter 14), and its variant CAROLYN (Chapter 10), or using the feminized variant CARLA (Chapter 10) and its diminutive CARLY (Chapter 17). The Medieval emperor Charlemagne (that is, Carl le Magne "Carl the great") first popularized this name. Recent American use has tended to come via German immigrants, and it had a long run of high popularity from the late 19th through mid–20th centuries. The Spanish form Carlos has recently been increasing in popularity. Well-known bearers have included poet Carl Sandburg, psychologist Carl Jung, actor Karl Malden, and musician Carlos Santana. Variants: **Carlo, Carlos,** and **Karl.**

CHRISTIAN: (f, m) Latin; a Christian. This developed as a given name in the Medieval period from the ordinary word and became popular across most of Europe in various forms. The male name has been less popular in English than the female variants, although the two have been becoming more equal in the last half century. A vast variety of girls' names have spun off of this root, including CHRISTINE (Chapter 9), the Scandinavian KIRSTEN (Chapter 18), and the diminutives TINA (Chapter 10), CHRISTY (Chapter 19), and CHRISSY (Chapter 16). There is no similar variety in boys' names, although they share with the girls the diminutive CHRIS (Chapter 19), as well as sharing it with CHRISTOPHER. With the exception of Christine and its variants, the girls' names in this group have largely been popular in the mid- and late 20th century, while the boy's name Christian has had a more consistent presence. One famous bearer is heart transplant pioneer Christiaan Barnard. Variants: (both) **Kristian;** (f) **Christa, Christen, Christiana, Krista, Kristan, Kristen,** and **Krysta;** (m) **Christion** and **Cristian.** Diminutives: (both) **Chris** and **Kris.**

CHRISTOPHER: (m) Greek; Christ-bearer. The name originally simply indicated a Christian, but a literal reading inspired the image of the (fictitious) St. Christopher carrying the Christ child across a river. The name was widely popular throughout Europe in the Middle Ages, and was common enough in England at the time of the Reformation that it suffered very little from the turning away from saints' names. In the mid–20th century it shifted gears from merely common to extremely popular, making it up to the number 2 spot in the '70s through '90s. The diminutive Chris has been similarly popular while other variants have tagged along in recent decades. Famous bearers have included 17th-century architect Christopher Wren, multiple kings of Denmark, frontiersman Kit Carson, and actors Kris Kristofferson and Christopher Reeve. Variants: **Christoper, Cristobal, Cristopher, Kristofer, Kristoffer,** and **Kristopher.** Diminutives: **Chris, Cris, Kit,** and **Kris.**

CLARA: (f) Latin; bright, clear. The name is very often used in honor of St. Clare of Assisi, a contemporary of St. Francis. After falling out of favor during the Reformation, it was revived in the 19th century and has retained a mild popularity since then, although fashions shift between the several variants. The version Clarine developed in parallel with other names ending in "-ine," but never caught on. Well-known bearers have included nursing pioneer Clara Barton and actress Claire Danes. Variants: **Claire, Clare,** and **Clarine.**

CLEMENT: (m) Latin; merciful, mild. The name was popular in the Middle Ages as the name of several saints and popes. It was revived in the 19th century but fell out of fashion during the first half of the 20th. Clement C. Moore is the author of the famous poem *A Visit from St. Nicholas.* Variant: **Clemens.** Diminutive: **Clem.**

DOROTHY: (f) Greek; gift of God. The same elements produced the name THEODORA (Chapter 7). There was an early martyr named Dorothy, but the name seems to have become popular on its own merits and rather late in the Medieval period. It was revived late in the 19th century and spent several decades among the top-ten names before slipping down the charts again. The diminutive Doll or Dolly was transferred to the toy (previously called a puppet or poppet), which took it out of use as a given name. Dottie is another diminutive, as is Dora, which rapidly became an independent name and quite popular in its own right. Famous Dorothys include the fictional Dorothy Gale of the *Wizard of Oz* books, U.S. first lady Dolley Madison, literary critic Dorothy Parker, mystery writer Dorothy L. Sayers, actress Dorothy Dandridge, and ice skater Dorothy Hamil. Variants: **Dorathy, Doretha, Dorotha, Dorothea, Dortha,** and **Dorthy.** Diminutives: **Dora, Dori,** and **Dottie.**

EDITH: (f) English; from the Anglo-Saxon Eadgyth, "rich-war." The name was popularized by a 10th-century saint, which helped it survive the Norman Conquest at a time when most Anglo-Saxon names fell out of fashion. Like many saints' names, it fell out of use with the Reformation and was revived in the late 19th century. Well-known bearers include author Edith Wharton, French singer Edith Piaf, and TV character Edith Bunker of *All in the Family.* Variants: **Edyth** and **Edythe.**

EDWARD: (m) English; fortunate guardian. An Anglo-Saxon name, popularized by king and saint Edward the Confessor. It was one of only a few Anglo-Saxon names to survive the Norman Conquest in any numbers, and the later use of the name by a string of English kings cemented its popularity and spread it more widely in the world such that you have the Spanish Eduardo and the Norwegian Edvard. The great popularity of this name also shows in the number and variety of diminutives it gave rise to. It spent several decades around the turn of the 20th century in the top-ten names. Namesakes include vaccination pioneer Edward Jenner, poet Edward Lear, artist Edvard Munch, longtime Massachusetts senator Edward Kennedy, TV producer Ted Turner, actors Ed Asner, Eddie Murphy, and Edward G. Robinson, and baseball star Ted Williams. Ted and Teddy can also be diminutives of THEODORE (Chapter 7), and when Eddie is used as a girl's name, it may be a diminutive of Edith. Variants: **Edgardo, Eduardo, Edvard, Edwardo,** and **Edison.** Diminutives: **Ed, Edd, Eddie, Eddy, Ned, Ted,** and **Teddy.**

ELEANOR: (f) French; meaning uncertain, but possibly a blend of Ellen and Honora, or simply a variant of Ellen. The name was greatly popularized by Eleanor of Aquitaine who was in turn queen of France and England. It was also a great favorite in the 19th-century romantic revival and a wide selection of variants are on the charts in the first half of the 20th century. The most famous modern bearer may be Eleanor Roosevelt who completely transformed the role of First Lady. Variants: **Eleanora, Eleanore, Elenor, Elenora, Elinor, Elinore,** and **Elnora.**

ELIZABETH: (f) Hebrew; God has sworn. As the name of the mother of John the Baptist, Elizabeth had a popularity across Medieval Europe rivaled only by Anne and Margaret. At a time when the Reformation was frowning on other saintly names in England, it was borne by the enormously popular Queen Elizabeth I and has rarely been out of the top-ten girls' names from then until today. This is reflected in the range of variants and diminutives that have become popular: Bess, BETH and BETSY (Chapter 10), BETTY (Chapter 18), Lizbeth, ELIZA (Chapter 18), ELSA (Chapter 9), ISABEL (below), LIBBY (Chapter 10), LILY (Chapter 12), LILLIAN (Chapter 9), LILLIOM (Chapter 6), LISA (Chapter 10), and LIZ (Chapter 18). Choosing representative namesakes is a matter of paring down a long list: poet Elizabeth Barrett Browning, mystery novelist Elizabeth George, North Carolina senator Elizabeth Dole, 19th-century women's rights activist Elizabeth Cady Stanton, children's book illustrator Lisbeth Zwerger, blues singer Bessie Smith, U.S. first lady Bess Truman, and actress Elizabeth Taylor. Variants: **Elisabeth, Lisbeth, Lizabeth,** and **Lizbeth.** Diminutives: **Bess** and **Bessie.** (See also the other headings listed previously.)

ELLEN: (f) English; a variant of HELEN (Chapter 5). This arose as an independent name during the Middle Ages and was revived in the 19th century and has been moderately popular ever since. Well-known bearers include actress Ellen Burstyn, columnist Ellen Goodman, and comedian and talk-show host Ellen Degeneres. Variants: **Elena, Ellen,** and **Eleni.**

ELLIOT: (m) English; a diminutive of ELIJAH (Chapter 4). The popular Medieval diminutive gave rise to a surname which is the immediate source for the modern use of Elliot. Bearers include composer Elliott Carter and actor Elliott Gould. Variants: **Eliot** and **Elliott.**

EMMA: (f) English; possibly from a Germanic root meaning "whole, universal." This was a popular name among the Normans in England, but it fell out of fashion in the 16th century. It was revived as a romantic name in the late 19th century but has seen yet another revival in the last couple of decades, shooting up to the number 2 position. A number of popular actresses bear this name, including Emma Thompson and Emma Watson, in addition to Statue of Liberty poet Emma Lazarus.

EVE: (f) Hebrew?; possibly "life-giving" but the identification of the name as Hebrew is not at all certain. Like ADAM, this was a popular name in the Middle Ages without benefit of saints or royalty bearing it. It became much less popular after the Reformation but has enjoyed a slight comeback in the last century or so. Some well-known bearers illustrating the popular variants are the actresses Ava Gardner, Eve Arden, and Eva Marie Saint. Variants: **Ava** and **Eva.**

EVELYN: (f, m) English; from Germanic roots of uncertain meaning. The Medieval name seems to have been used only by women, but it gave rise to a surname that was turned into a masculine given name as early as the 17th century. Bearers have included (male) novelist Evelyn Waugh and (female) dancer Evelyn Cisneros. Variants: (f) **Evalyn, Evelin, Eveline,** and **Evelyne.** Diminutive: **Evie.**

FRANCIS & FRANCES: (f, m) Latin; a Frank, a French person. Greatly popularized by Saint Francis of Assisi, although that is not the only source of interest in the name. The spelling Francis was used by both men and women, although other variants such as French Francois(e) had different forms to distinguish the genders. Only within the last century has the custom arisen of differentiating a masculine Francis and a feminine Frances. Frank has become the most popular male form in modern times, but variants from a number of languages have made the charts in the 20th century. On the female side, you have author Frances Hodgson Burnett and Frances Perkins, the first female cabinet officer (serving as Secretary of Labor under FDR). On the male side, you have Saint Francis Xavier, U.S. national anthem writer Francis Scott Key, biologist Francis Crick, film director Francis Ford Coppola, actor Franco Nero, singer Frank Sinatra, architect Frank Lloyd Wright, and novelist Franz Kafka. Variants: (both) **Frank;** (f) **Francesca, Franchesca, Francheska,** and **Francisca;** (m) **Francesco, Francisco, Franco,** and **Franz.** Diminutives: (both) **Frankie;** (f) **Fran.**

GEOFFREY: (m) English; multiple origins, from Germanic roots meaning "district," "traveler," or "pledge" plus a second element meaning "peace." The name was popularized by the Normans in England, where it developed variants starting with "Jeff-." Geoffrey, while continuously in use, has never been extremely popular, and the diminutive Jeff may sometimes be more immediately from the surname Jefferson, turned into a given name. Well-known bearers have included Medieval author Geoffrey Chaucer, Confederate president Jefferson Davis, and actor Jeff Bridges. Variants: **Jefferey, Jefferson, Jeffery, Jeffrey,** and **Jeffry.** Diminutive: **Jeff.**

GERALD: (m) English; from Germanic roots meaning "spear rule." The name was made popular by the Normans but fell out of fashion after only a few centuries. It was revived in the 19th century, but more recently the diminutives JERRY (Chapter 19) and GARY (Chapter 18) have become more popular than the original name. Well-known bearers have included U.S. president Gerald Ford, travel and nature writer Gerald Durrell, TV host Geraldo Rivera, and baseball player Jerald Clark. Variants: **Garold, Gerald, Geraldo, Gerold, Jerald, Jerold, Jerrell, Jerrold, Jarrell, Jarret, Jarrett,** and **Jerel.**

GERARD: (m) English; from Germanic roots meaning "spear-hard." This is another name popularized by the Normans, but much rarer at all times than the similar-sounding Gerald. Familiar bearers include French actor Gérard Depardieu and German chancellor Gerhard Schröder. Variants: **Gerardo** and **Gerhard.**

GILBERT: (m) English; from Germanic roots meaning "bright pledge." The Medieval diminutives Gib and Gibbon fell entirely out of use and today the usual diminutive is Gil. Bearers include chemist Gilbert Newton Lewis and silent movie director and actor Gilbert M. "Broncho Billy" Anderson, known as the father of the cowboy movie. Variant: **Gilberto.** Diminutive: **Gil.**

GREGORY: (m) Greek; watchful. The name was popularized by a large number of Medieval popes and became common in England in time to produce a wide variety of surnames. It has been increasing in popularity throughout the 20th century but has never made the very top ranks. Bearers have included early geneticist Gregor Mendel, rock guitarist Greg Lake (of Emerson, Lake, and Palmer), and actor Gregory Peck. Variants: **Greggory, Gregor,** and **Gregorio.** Diminutives: **Greg** and **Gregg.**

HAROLD: (m) English; army-power. The name dates to Anglo-Saxon times and was the name of two key players (on losing sides) in the Norman Conquest. It was used rarely in the Medieval period (which may account for the lack of variants and diminutives) but was revived enthusiastically in the 19th century. It made the top-20 names for several decades early in the 20th century but has been fading since then. Well-known bearers include playwright Harold Pinter, Nobel Prize–winning chemist Harold C. Urey, literary critic Harold Bloom, and U.K. prime minister Harold Wilson.

HARVEY: (m) English; from a Breton name meaning "battle-worthy." The name was introduced to England by Bretons accompanying William the Conqueror (similarly to Brian and Alan). It was revived, along with other Medieval names, in the 19th century and was moderately popular for a while but has fallen down the charts since then. Well-known bearers include the actors Harvey Keitel and Harvey Korman.

HENRY: (m) English; from Germanic roots meaning "home-rule." In English, the everyday name became Harry, with the diminutives Hal and Hank, but in other languages the Latin form Henricus gave rise to versions like German

Heinrich and Italian Enrico. The name's use by a series of English kings assured its popularity, but it became less fashionable after the 16th century despite not suffering the burden of association with Catholicism. Both Harry and Henry were revived at a high level of popularity in the late 19th century and have remained at least moderately popular since then. Several surnames based on Henry, such as Harris and Harrison, have also found their way back as given names. Well-known bearers have included poet Henry Wadsworth, U.S. president Harry S. Truman, writer and philosopher Henry David Thoreau, automobile magnate Henry Ford, children's book character Harry Potter, musicians Harry Belafonte and Henri Mancini, actors Henry Fonda and Harrison Ford, country singer Hank Williams, science fiction author Hal Clement, pop singer Enrique Iglesias, and Nobel Prize–winning physicist Enrico Fermi. Variants: **Enrico, Enrique, Harris, Harrison, Harry,** and **Henri.** Diminutives: **Hal** and **Hank.**

ISABEL: (f) French; a variant of ELIZABETH that became an independent name in the Medieval period. These forms of the name tended to be used in Romance-speaking countries, as for Queen Isabella of Spain (patron of Columbus), Chilean author Isabel Allende, and actress Isabella Rossellini. Variants: **Isabela, Isabell, Isabelle, Isobel, Izabella,** and **Izabella.**

JACOB: (m) Hebrew; commonly interpreted as "he supplanted" or "he seized the heel," but both translations are doubtful. In the early Middle Ages this Biblical name evolved into JAMES (Chapter 9), but both versions continued to be used independently even though the connection between them was still well-known (as when supporters of James Stuart were referred to as Jacobites). One great popularizer of this name was Santiago (that is, Saint James) of Compostela whose shrine was a major pilgrimage destination. Shakespeare's villain Iago in *Othello* bears a variant of the name. Other bearers include painter Jacob Lawrence and folklorist Jakob Grimm. The surname Jacobi, taken from this name, has been revived in recent decades as a given name as is the more probable origin for the name KOBE (Chapter 15). The French Jacques is also derived from this name. Although the name has never been less than popular, in the last few decades it has shot up quickly to inhabit the number 1 position ever since 1999. Variants: **Jacoby, Jakob,** and **Jakobe; Jacques, Jacquez,** and **Jaquez.** Diminutive: **Jake.**

JOAN (f), **JOHN** (m): Hebrew; God has favored. Given the enormous popularity that the name John — in both male and female versions — came to have, it's surprising to note that it was a very rare name for the first millennium of Christianity. But after that there came a number of changes in naming fashions in Europe, one of which was to focus interest on a relatively small number of saints' names. With the various names associated with Jesus being considered too sacred for everyday use in much of Christianity, the greatest interest in male names came to focus on John the Baptist, who was considered the man most closely connected with Christ. In the space of only a few centuries, John went from being an obscure name occasionally adopted by men with religious vocations, to the number-1 male name, often accounting for a fifth to a quarter of all boys being named. With the rise in popularity of the male name, interest in a female version began to appear, and while it was never as dominant as John itself, it settled into a comfortable residence in the top-ten popular girls' names — often with more than one variant being among that top ten. John held its place at or very near the top spot from the Middle Ages up through the early 20th century and has only gradually faded to the lower end of the top 20 since then. (This considers the specific variant "John" only — with all the different variants of the name combined, it has been even more tenacious.) The feminine name hasn't been quite as dominant, and has been diluted over a larger number of established variants. Most of the current variety in male forms of John comes from other languages. The forms popular over the last century have included EVAN (Welsh, Chapter 10), Ivan (Russian), HANS (German, Chapter 18), Johan (German), IAN and SEAN (Gaelic, Chapter 10), Jean (French), Giovanni (Italian), and Juan (Spanish). Common female variants include some non-English borrowings, including Ivana (Russian), Jeanne and Jeannette (French), Johanna (various languages including Latin and German), Juana and Juanita (Spanish), SINEAD (Chapter 17) and SIOBHAN (Chapter 10), both Gaelic, and GIOVANNA (Italian, Chapter 18). But while the English versions of the male name are mostly limited to John, Jack, and their diminutives, the female name has produced JAN and JANE (Chapter 10), Janet, Jenny, Joan, Joanne, and a whole host of diminutives from them. A very brief tour of famous bearers might include, on the men's side, U.S. president John F. Kennedy, French film director Jean Cocteau, behaviorist Ivan Pavlov, Medieval Italian writer Giovanni Boccaccio, beat poet Jack Kerouac, and baseball hall-of-famer Juan Marichal; and on the women's side, author Johanna Sypri, marathoner Joan Benoit, actress Joanne Woodward, former attorney general Janet Reno, singer Jenny Lind, astrologer Jeane Dixon, author Jean Auel, singer and actress Jeanette MacDonald, and socialite Ivana Trump. Variants: (f) **Ivana; Jacque; Jean, Jeane, Jeanne, Jeana, Jeanna,** and **Jena; Janel, Janell, Janelle,** and **Jenelle; Janet, Janette, Jannette, Jeanette,** and **Jeannette; Janie, Jannie, Jeanie, Jeannie, Jenny, Joann, Joanne, Joana, Joanna, Jonna, Johana, Johanna, John,** and **Johnna; Juana** and **Juanita;** (m) **Ivan; Gian, Gianni, Giovani, Giovanni, Giovanny,** and **Gino; Jack; Jan** and **Jean; Johan** and **Johann;** and **Juan.**

JULIANA: (f) Latin; a variant of JULIA (Chapter 17). The name became JILLIAN and JILL (Chapter 10) in everyday use. It was particularly popular in the Netherlands — a connection that still holds today — and came to England from there. One Medieval bearer was the mystic Juliana of Norwich. A more modern example is actress Julianne Moore. Variants: **Juliann, Julianna, Julianne,** and **Yuliana.** Diminutives: **Liana** and **Lyanne.**

KATHERINE: (f) Greek; meaning unknown. This name was later assumed to be from Greek *katharos* "clean, pure," but as the Greek form of the name is Aikaterine, this is unlikely to be accurate. The cult of Saint Katherine of Alexandria was popularized by returning crusaders beginning around the 12th century, and it shortly became one of the most consistently popular names in England. Katherine was among those saintly names that were so common at the time of the Reformation that they received little or no back-lash. (The popularity of Katherine in the 16th century is attested by the fact that three of King Henry VIII's six wives bore this name.) With a few ups and downs, the name has remained extremely popular to this day, although its true place on the popularity charts has been disguised by the profusion of variants and spellings in common use. A few of the popular versions come from non-English forms of the name, such as Spanish Catalina, Russian Katrina, Danish KAREN (Chapter 10), and Gaelic CAITLIN (Chapter 10), but English has produced plenty of variants and diminutives on its own, including Cathleen, CARRIE (Chapter 10), KATHY (Chapter 10), KATE (Chapter 10), KITTY (Chapter 12), and Kay. Some well-known bearers have included actresses Katherine Hepburn, Catherine Deneuve, and Catlin Adams, Kansas governor Kathleen Sebelius, Olympic ice skater Katarina Witt, and Texas senator Kay Bailey Hutchison. Variants: **Katlin, Katlyn,** and **Katlynn; Catalina; Cathleen, Catlin, Cathaleen, Kathleen,** and **Kathlyn; Caterina, Catharine, Catherine, Cathrine, Cathryn, Katharina, Katharine, Katherine, Katheryn, Kathrine, Kathryn,** and **Kathryne; Catina, Katina, Catrina, Katarina, Katerina,** and **Katrina.** Diminutives: **Katia; Kay, Kaye;** and **Trina.** (See also the variants listed separately as previously mentioned.)

LAURENCE: (m) Latin; from the town of Laurentium (whose name means "place of laurel trees"). The name was popularized in the Middle Ages by the martyr Saint Laurence and has been revived to some extent in the last century. Prominent bearers have included actor Laurence Olivier and poet Lawrence Ferlinghetti. Variants: **Lars, Lawerence, Lawrence, Lawson, Lorenz,** and **Lorenzo.**

LUCIA: (f) Latin; light. This name is the origin of the name LUCY (Chapter 16) and was popularized by the saint and martyr. The name was used for the title character of Donizetti's opera *Lucia di Lammermoor* based on a novel by Walter Scott.

MAGDALENA: (f) Hebrew; woman from Magdala. Although the Bible identifies Mary Magdalene as having been healed of seven devils, Medieval tradition also associated her with the story of the forgiven prostitute — a story that caught the Medieval imagination but was much less popular after the Reformation. Modern interest has primarily been in French variants such as Madeline. Bearers have included former secretary of state Madeleine Albright, actress Madeline Kahn, and sculptor Magdalena Abakanowicz. Variants: **Madaline, Madalyn, Madalynn, Madeleine, Madeline, Madelyn, Madelynn, Madilyn, Magdalen, Magdalene,** and **Migdalia.** Diminutive: **Madie.**

MARGARET: (f) Greek; pearl. The French Marguerite also means "a daisy." Along with Saint Katherine, Saint Margaret of Antioch became enormously popular starting around the 12th century — a popularity reflected in the range of variants and diminutives that developed. Today these are supplemented with variants from other languages such as the German Gretchen. Margaret itself spent the early part of the 20th century in the top-ten girls' names but has fallen off since then. Familiar bearers include authors Margaret Mitchell, Marguerite Henry, and Marge Piercy, anthropologist Margaret Mead, actresses Greta Garbo and Meg Ryan, and champion ice skater Peggy Fleming. Variants: **Margarete, Margarett, Margaretta, Margarette, Margarita, Margit, Margret, Margrethe,** and **Marguerite; Marge, Margery, Margie, Margy, Marjorie,** and **Marjory.** Diminutives: **Greta, Gretchen, Meg, Peggie,** and **Peggy.**

MARTIN: (m) Latin; associated with the Roman war-god Mars. Due to the popularity of an early saint of this name, it has seen continuous popularity since classical times. Famous bearers include Protestant reformer Martin Luther, and his more recent namesake Martin Luther King, Jr. Diminutive: **Marty.**

MARY: (f) English; from the Hebrew name MIRIAM (Chapter 4). Latin speakers interpreted the original Mariam as a grammatical form of Maria and used that as the root name. Somewhat surprisingly, Mary didn't come into general use until the general fashion for using saints' names around the 12th century. One very popular variant of it was MARION (see later in this chapter), as in Robin Hood's Maid Marion. Mary was consistently in the top-ten names during the Medieval period and in recent centuries has spent most of its time in the number-1 slot, only dropping out of it in the last half century. With that kind of popularity, no list of bearers can be more than random examples: author Mary Shelly, actresses Mary Pickford , Maura Tierney, and Mary Tyler Moore, singers Mary Chapin Carpenter and Marie Osmond, physicist Marie Curie, and astronomer Maria Mitchell. Variants: **Mari, Marie, Maira, Mara, Maria, Maura, Mayra,** and **Moira.**

MATHILDA: (f) English; from Germanic roots meaning "strength-battle." The more everyday form of the name was Maude, and Medieval bearers of the name were often recorded alternately with both versions. Both names were revived around the 19th century but fell out of fashion in the early 20th. Names in this group are borne by the title character of Roald Dahl's children's book *Mathilda,* human rights activist Matilda Joslyn Gage, children's novelist Lucy Maud Montgomery, the title character of the TV show *Maude* played by Bea Arthur, actress Tilda Swinton, and author and labor activist Tillie Olsen. Variants: **Mafalda, Mathilde, Matilda,** and **Matilde; Maud, Maude,** and **Maudie.** Diminutives: **Tilda** and **Tillie.**

MATTHEW: (m) Hebrew; gift of God. Not all of the apostles' names were equally popular in the Medieval period. Matthew was adopted earlier, more often, and more widely than most other male New Testament names, but failed to achieve the superstardom of, for example, John and Thomas. One popular Medieval variant was Macy — a name familiar today primarily as a surname, although somewhat inexplicably it has seen some interest in the last decade as a girl's name. Matthew has been rising in popularity over the last century and has been in the top-ten boys' names since the '70s. Some familiar bearers include arctic explorer Matthew A. Henson, theologian Matthew Fox, and actor Matthew Broderick. Variants: **Mateo, Mathew, Mathias,** and **Matteo.**

MICHAEL: (f, m) Hebrew; who is like God. Like Gabriel, Michael appears in the Bible as an archangel, not as a human being, but Medieval people turned him into a saint and considered him to be the patron of soldiers, which no doubt accounts for his popularity. The name was not among the very common ones, however, and fell even more out of favor after the Reformation. By the 19th century in America it was associated primarily with Irish immigrants (to the point where "Mick" was a derogatory nickname for an Irishman). Eventually Irishness lost its stigma, and Michael rose sharply in the charts to hold the number 1 position for the entire second half of the 20th century. Some recent bearers have been actors Michael Landon, Mike Myers, and Michael J. Fox, and basketball star Michael Jordan. Female use of Michael is rare, but thanks to actress Michael Learned, people are unlikely to think it strange. Variants: **Michale, Micheal, Michel, Miguel, Mikal, Mikel, Mikhail, Mitchel, Mitchell, Mychal,** and **Mykel.** Diminutives: **Mike** and **Mitch.**

NICHOLE (f), **NICHOLAS** (m): Greek; victory of the people. Although the name is found earlier, the cult of Saint Nicholas became popular in the 12th century and the main use of the name dates from that time. The name was often shortened to Colin, although it is fashionable today to connect that name with an entirely different and Gaelic origin. Nicholas was popular enough that the Reformation had only a little impact on its use, but current American use also draws on a number of non-English variants. Feminine variants came into use very early in the name's career. Bearers have included, on the male side, astronomer Nicolaus Copernicus, actors Nicolas Cage, Nick Nolte, and Colin Firth, and inventor Nikola Tesla, and on the female side, actress Nicole Kidman. Variants: (both) **Nicola;** (f) **Nichol, Nicole, Nicolle, and Nikole;** (m) **Nels, Nicholaus, Nichlaus, Nickolas, Nicolas, Nikhil, Nikola, Nikolas,** and **Nils.** Diminutives: (f) **Nicki, Niki,** and **Nikki;** (m) **Colin, Collin, Nick, Nicky, Nico, Nikko,** and **Niko.**

PETER: (m) Latin; a rock, a stone. The apostle Simon was renamed Peter in a play on words indicating that he would be a stable foundation. The close association of the name with Saint Peter's in Rome helped its popularity during the Middle Ages but hurt after the Reformation. It has revived to some extent, but not into the top ranks of popularity. In Medieval England, the forms Pierce and Pernell were more popular than the original name, and in America today the English forms are joined by variants such as French Pierre, Spanish Pedro, and Italian Pietro. Some examples include actors Pernell Roberts and Pierce Brosnan, film director Peter Jackson, former Canadian prime minister Pierre Elliott Trudeau, and tennis pro Pete Sampras. Variants: **Pedro, Pernell, Pierce, Pierre, Piers,** and **Pietro.** Diminutive: **Pete.**

PHILLIP: (m) Greek; lover of horses. The popularity of Phillip in the Middle Ages went far beyond what might be expected to be inspired by a relatively minor apostle, and much of the use may be credited instead to royal use in places like France and Spain. The lack of strong saintly associations kept it in use after the Reformation and, although it has never been in the top ranks, it has remained consistently popular. Notable bearers include renaissance poet Philip Sidney, composers John Philip Sousa and Philip Glass, and folk singer Phil Ochs. Variants: **Felipe** and **Philip.** Diminutive: **Phil.**

RALPH: (m) English; from Germanic roots meaning "wolf-counsel." While one major theme in popular Medieval names was the use of saints' names, another was the use of a group of names with no saintly associations and primarily of Germanic origin that became a sort of "international fashion." This group includes names like Ralph, Richard, Robert, and William. After its Medieval popularity, Ralph fell largely out of use for several centuries and then was revived in the 19th century. It has declined again in recent decades, but familiar bearers include poet Ralph Waldo Emerson, actor Ralph Fiennes, and in a Spanish version, actor Raul Julia. Variants: **Raoul** and **Raul.**

RICHARD: (m) English; from Germanic roots meaning "hard rule." The use of Richard in the English royal family, for example, for King Richard the Lionhearted, accounts for much of its popularity there, although it was also common in several other countries. It spent several centuries in the top-ten names and then fell slightly out of fashion for a while, returning to the top ten only in the mid–20th century. Familiar bearers include actors Richard Burton and Ricardo Montalban, physicist Richard Feynman, ice skater Dick Button, and U.S. vice president Dick Cheney. Another diminutive is RICK (Chapter 10). Variant: **Ricardo.** Diminutives: **Dick** and **Dickie.**

ROBERT: (m) English; from Germanic roots meaning "bright fame." Robert is a fascinating example of a name that, despite the lack of early prominent namesakes, has regularly been among the top-ten names and has spread significantly beyond its cultural origins. Modern diminutives are based on ROB and BOB (Chapter 10), but historically there have also been forms based on Hob and Dob. The popularity of the name has ensured that there have been prominent Roberts throughout history, including the Medieval Scottish king Robert the Bruce, legendary folk hero Robin Hood, poets Robert Burns and Robert Frost, and Confederate general Robert E. Lee. Variant: **Roberto.**

ROGER: (m) English; from Germanic roots meaning "spear-fame." After its Medieval popularity, the name fell largely out of fashion for several centuries and has had only a modest revival in recent times. Well-known bearers include football players Roger Craig and Roger Staubach and actor Roger Moore. Variants: **Rodger** and **Rogers.**

SIMON: (m) Hebrew?; meaning uncertain; even the identification of the name as Hebrew is uncertain. Simeon was the name of one of the tribes of Israel in the book of Genesis and later appears as a given name, including the original name of the apostle Peter. Some of the name's New World popularity has been in honor of 19th-century South American liberator Simon Bolivar. The name has remained steadily in use, although never in the top ranks of popularity. Variant: **Simeon.** Diminutive: **Sim.**

Comparing Gothic names, old and new

People have used the word "gothic" repeatedly across the centuries to give a sense of the barbaric, sinister, or anticivilized. The original Goths were a Germanic tribe, one of various groups who spread across Europe in the waning days of the Roman Empire. In the Middle Ages, the Goths were remembered as barbaric and uncouth, so those who didn't care for the new cutting-edge style of architecture dismissed it as "Gothic" and ugly. To 19th-century people, "Gothic" had become synonymous with "Medieval," evoking the romantically sinister (or sinisterly romantic) moldering Medieval ruins in which sensational romance novels were set — lending the name "Gothic" to the literary genre. Blended with the Victorian fixation on the monuments and rituals of mourning, the sense of "Gothic" as dark, gloomy, and morbid led to a particular subset of the punk rock scene being christened "Goths" and, as in every previous case, people embraced the label and made it their own.

In each age, personal names have formed part of Gothic fashion, but the specific names have been very different. In the names of Visigoths and Ostrogoths, you can glimpse some of the same Germanic roots as more familiar names:

✔ **Male:** Amalafrid, Gesimund, Hermanaric, Oduulf, Theodoric, Thiudimer, Valaravans, and Vinitharius.

✔ **Female:** Amalaberga, Brunhild, Erelieva, Ermenberga, Gunthswinth, Mathesuentha, Thiudigoto, and Vadamerca.

The characters in Victorian Gothic novels are likely to have long, multisyllabic Italian names, although there is also a scattering of Old English names:

✔ **Male:** Abellino, Biandetto, Ferdinand, Hyppolitus, Lionardo, Ludovico, Pharamond, Theodore, and Udolpho.

✔ **Female:** Almalhide, Cassandra, Cinthelia, Clarinda, Dianora, Emmeline, Ethelwina, Pamela, Rosalba, and Valambrosa.

It can be hard to distinguish between often tongue-in-cheek "Goth nicknames" and any real naming fashions coming out of the current Goth community, but an Internet discussion among Goths about what they named their children gives some ideas: seasonal and nature-based names like Wynter (or Winter), Autumn, Solstice, and Rain; names with religious associations like Nirvana, Mercy, and the names of obscure angels; names connected with pop culture popular among Goths, such as Vincent (Price), (Jane) Eyre, and Wednesday (Addams); names with "dark" associations in myth or history, such as Morrigan, Dracos, and Salem; or words with similar associations, such as Talon, Tragedia, and Tristessa. But most Goth children seem to enjoy the same names as their neighbors: Alexander, Brianna, Emily, and Lucas.

STEPHAN: (m) Greek; a crown. The saint and martyr of this name inspired the name's popularity and, although it has never been in the top ranks, it has remained steadily in use since around the 12th century. The form Steven has been the most popular recently in the U.S. Bearers include horror writer Stephen King, physicist Stephen Hawking, film director Steven Spielberg, actor Steve McQueen, and musicians Stevie Ray Vaughan and Stevie Wonder. Variants: **Esteban, Estevan, Stefan, Stephen, Stephon, Stevan,** and **Steven.** Diminutives: **Steve** and **Stevie.**

THOMAS: (m) Aramaic; a twin. This is the name of one of the apostles. Interestingly, there is some evidence that when Medieval people were naming twin boys, the name Thomas was used more commonly than it was in single births, suggesting that ordinary people were aware of the name's meaning. In England, the martyrdom and canonization of Thomas Becket made this name especially popular, and it was commonly among the top-ten names. It continued in common use after the Reformation and was borne by several famous Revolutionary figures, including Thomas Jefferson and Tom Paine. More recently, it spent the middle part of the 20th century in the top ten again, and has been borne by inventor Thomas Alva Edison, singer Tom Jones, and actor Tommy Lee Jones. A feminine form, Tomasa, has also been used, although the more common feminine version is THOMASINA (Chapter 6). Variants: (f) **Tomasa;** (m) **Tomas.** Diminutives: (both) **Tommie;** (m) **Tom** and **Tommy.**

WALTER: (m) English; from Germanic roots meaning "ruler of the people." This is another name popularized by the Normans, although it has rarely been in competition for the highest ranks. It briefly broke into the top ten around 1900 but has dropped to a more moderate popularity today. Currently, the usual diminutive is Walt, although the Medieval choice, Wat, still shows up via the surname-turned-given-name Watson. Some familiar bearers include poet Walt Whitman, news anchor Walter Cronkite, and actor Walter Matthau. Variant: **Watson.** Diminutives: **Wally** and **Walt.**

WILLIAM: (f, m) English; from Germanic roots meaning "will helmet." This name was perfectly positioned for success in England as the name of William the Conquerer who became the first Norman king of that land. It enjoyed a position high in the top-ten names but, like many of the Germanic names, lost ground after the Reformation, not from the active avoidance given to saints' names, but simply by being displaced by the fashion for Biblical names. In the 19th century, with that fashion fading, William moved back into the top ten and since then has spent all but the last few decades in that group. Diminutives have been based on both Will and BILL (Chapter 10). Women have sometimes used the male name as is, but the most common specifically feminine variant has been WILMA (Chapter 19), with WILHELMINA (Chapter 10) having specifically German associations. Familiar male bearers have included playwright William Shakespeare, publishing magnate William Randolph Hearst, actors Will Smith and Willem Dafoe, baseball players Willie Mays and Willie McCovey, and R&B musician Wilson Pickett. On the female side you have author Willa Cather. Variants: (f) **Willa** and **Willia;** (m) **Guillermo, Wilhelm, Willard, Willem, Williams, Willian,** and **Wilson.** Diminutives: (both) **Willie;** (m) **Will, Willis,** and **Willy.**

Remembering Forgotten Fashions in Medieval Names

Many of the common names of the Middle Ages never made the top of the charts, but have hung on (or been revived) through the ages. The names in this section never had the popularity of a Michael or Margaret but each is rich with history and worth another look.

ADA: (f) English; a diminutive of Adela, Adelaide, or Adeline. Medieval English use of this name died out and it was reintroduced from Germany in the late 18th century. Ada Lovelace, daughter of the poet Byron, is considered by many to be the first computer programmer, for her work with Charles Babbage on his analytical engine. Variant: **Adah.**

ALBAN: (m) Latin; from Alba, in other words, Britain. Popularized by an early British martyr. A variant is borne by sculptor Albin Polasek. Variant: **Albin.**

ALFONSO: (m) Spanish; from Germanic roots meaning "noble-ready." A whole succession of Medieval Spanish kings of this name did much to popularize it, but the name has been less popular outside that region. Other bearers have included artist Alphonse Mucha and Nobel Prize–winner Alfonso Garcia Robles. Variants: **Alfonzo, Alphonse,** and **Alphonso.**

AMBROSE: (m) Latin; ambrosial, divine. The name was most commonly used in honor of the 4th-century saint, but has never been seriously popular. It is familiar from writer and satirist Ambrose Bierce.

ANSELM: (m) German; God-helmet. The name was brought to England in the 11th century by a man appointed to be Archbishop of Canterbury. Photographer Ansel Adams bears a variant of the name. Variants: **Ansel** and **Anselmo.**

AVICE: (f) English; from Germanic roots of uncertain meaning. A lovely name that was popular in the Middle Ages but failed to have staying power, most likely due to a lack of saintly or noble namesakes. One modern bearer is British comedian Avice Landon. Variant: **Avis.**

BALTHAZAR: (m) Hebrew; God protect the king. Medieval legend assigned this Biblical name to one of the wise men of the Nativity, and it was on that basis that it came into use. It has always been quite rare, but one recent bearer is actor Balthazar Getty.

BERNARD: (m) German; bear-hard. The popularity of Saint Bernard of Clairvaux helped to popularize this name in the Medieval period. Familiar bearers include dramatist George Bernard Shaw and movie director Bernardo Bertolucci. The diminutive Bernie may come from other names as well. Variants: **Bernardo** and **Bernhard.** Diminutive: **Bernie.**

BERTRAM: (m) English; from Germanic roots meaning "bright raven." Modern use of the name is likely to be from the romantic revival of the 19th century rather than from continuous use. A variant of the name is borne by philosopher Bertrand Russell. Variant: **Bertrand.**

BLAISE: (m) Latin?; possibly from the Roman family name Blaesus, but this is uncertain. Medieval use comes through Saint Blaise who, among other things, was the patron of wool workers, and so was popular in England. Despite bearers like mathematician Blaise Pascal, the name has been out of fashion for quite some time, but has been showing up on the charts in the last decade. Variant: **Blaze.**

BLANCHE: (f) French; white, fair. This was a popular name for the heroines of Medieval romances and was also borne by Queen Blanche of Castille. More recently it has been associated with the hapless Blanche Dubois of Tennessee Williams's *A Streetcar Named Desire.* The Spanish form Bianca has been slightly more popular, as for celebrity human rights activist (and former rock star wife) Bianca Jagger. Variants: **Bianca, Blanca,** and **Blanch.**

DREW: (f, m) English; from a Germanic root meaning "to draw or carry." The Medieval variant Drogo has not kept its popularity. Recently, this male name has been given to girls as well, thanks to the prominent example of actress Drew Barrymore.

EDWIN: (m) English; rich friend. This is an Anglo-Saxon name that, like Edward, survived the Norman Conquest, although not as successfully. It benefited from the 19th-century romantic revival and has been moderately popular over the last century. Bearers include poet Edwin Arlington Robinson and astronomer Edwin Hubble.

ELDRED: (m) English; old counsel. The Anglo-Saxon name survived long enough to produce some surnames, from which current use is taken. Eldred was the birth name of actor Gregory Peck, and another variant is borne by Black power activist Eldridge Cleaver. Variant: **Eldridge.**

ELFRIEDA: (f) English; elf strength. This is another Anglo-Saxon name that did not survive beyond the Norman Conquest until it was revived in the 19th century. One bearer is magazine editor Elfrieda Abbe.

ELVIN: (m) English; multiple origins: noble friend, or elf friend. Like most of the names beginning in "El-," this name dates to Anglo-Saxon times. It survived in various forms as a surname and was transferred to use as a given name in the 19th century. One bearer is basketball player Elvin Hayes. Variants: **Elwin** and **Elwyn.**

EMERY: (m) English; from Germanic roots, one of which means "ruler." This name has never been more than rare. The surname Emerson is also sometimes used for both boys and girls. Bluegrass musician Emory Lester is one bearer. Variants: (both) **Emerson;** (m) **Emory.**

EMMET: (m) English; a diminutive of EMMA that became a male name by way of surname use. Football player Emmitt Smith bears a variant of this name. Variants: **Emmett, Emmit,** and **Emmitt.**

ERASMUS: (m) Greek; beloved. This was the name of an early Medieval martyr, although much of the name's popularity may come by way of theologian Desiderius Erasmus. One bearer is naturalist Erasmus Darwin, the grandfather of Charles Darwin. Variant: **Erasmo.**

ESME: (f) French?; meaning uncertain. The name was masculine in the Middle Ages but today is used almost exclusively for women, as for the title character of J. D. Sallinger's *For Esme, with Love and Squalor.* One exception is actor Esme Percy.

FERDINAND: (m) Spanish; from Germanic roots meaning "risky journey." The name has only occasionally been taken up in English, but was a favorite of Spanish kings. Another bearer is early explorer Ferdinand Magellan. Variants starting with "H-" also occur in Spanish. Variants: **Fernand, Fernando,** and **Hernan.**

GARRET: (m) English; a variant of GERARD (see earlier in this chapter), taken from use as a surname. This name was borne by inventor Garrett A. Morgan. Variants: **Garett** and **Garrett.**

GENEVIEVE: (f) French; from the Gaulish name Genoveva, of uncertain meaning. Interestingly, this ancient form of the name has been revived for use in recent times. The name has mostly been taken directly from French use and so has not been particularly common. One familiar bearer is actress Genevieve Bujold. Variant: **Genoveva.**

GILES: (m) French; by a roundabout route through Latin from a Greek root meaning "a kid, a young goat." The name was popularized in the Middle Ages by an early saint but is extremely rare today.

GISELLE: (f) French; from a Germanic root meaning "a pledge." The modern use is generally taken directly from French. The name only shows up on the American charts in the last few decades, and may be inspired by the ballet of that name. Variant: **Gisselle.**

GRISELDA: (f) Italian; from Germanic roots possibly meaning "gray battle." The Medieval tale of "Patient Griselda" would hardly recommend the name to today's parents, but this name is probably the source of Zelda, famous as the name of writer F. Scott Fitzgerald's wife. Diminutive: **Zelda.**

GUY: (m) English; from a Germanic root of uncertain meaning. Although the name was common in the Middle Ages, the Guy Fawkes plot in the early 17th century made it abruptly unpopular in England. It was revived to some extent by the romantic movement but has been hampered somewhat by becoming a slang word for a person (especially a man) in general. The reasons for that use are unclear. Bearers have included French writer Guy de Maupassant and actor Guy Pearce. Variant: **Guido.**

HELOISE: (f) French; from Germanic roots meaning "healthy and wide." While the name was brought to England by the Normans, it was mainly popularized by the romantic story of Heloise and Abelard. The name has largely fallen out of use in the latter part of the 20th century, but is familiar from the literary persona behind the advice column "Hints from Heloise" (written by a series of authors). Variants: **Elois, Eloisa, Eloise,** and **Elouise.**

HILDA: (f) English; from a Germanic root meaning "battle." After falling into long disuse, it was part of the romantic revival and enjoyed some popularity in the early 20th century. Poet Hilda Doolittle is one bearer.

HILDEGARD: (f) German; war knowledge. This name was not particularly used in England in the Middle Ages, but modern interest in the sainted abbess Hildegard of Bingen has caused some revival of the name. Variant: **Hildegarde.**

HUBERT: (m) English; from Germanic roots meaning "bright heart." As the patron saint of hunting, Saint Hubert was naturally very popular among Medieval nobility. After long disuse, it was revived slightly in the late 19th century but has slipped down the charts again. The name is familiar from U.S. vice president Hubert Humphrey. Variants: **Hobart** and **Hobert.**

HUGH: (m) English; from a Germanic root meaning "heart, mind." Like many names popularized by saints, it fell out of fashion after the Reformation. Recent revivals have covered both the English form Hugh and the French form Hugo. Bearers include actor Hugh Jackman and musician Huey Lewis. Variant: **Hugo.** Diminutive: **Huey.**

ISIDORA (f), **ISIDORE** (m): Greek; the meaning is debated, but the second part is clearly "gift." Medieval use centered on the male name, due to the popularity of encyclopedist Saint Isidore of Seville. Today the female version is also popular, as for dancer Isidora Duncan. Variants: (m) **Isadore** and **Isidro.**

JOCELYN: (f, m) English; a diminutive from a Germanic root meaning "Goth." In the Middle Ages it was a man's name, but modern revivals have turned it primarily into a woman's name, by analogy with other names using Lynn. Variants: (f) **Jocelyne, Joselyn, Joslyn, Joycelyn,** and **Yselin.**

LETICIA: (f) Latin; gladness, joy. In everyday use, this became Lettice, but that form was not part of the 19th-century revival of the name. Instead, people returned to the Latin form and to the diminutive Lettie. Leta may be another variant, as borne by psychologist and early feminist Leta Stetter Hollingworth, and Leticia may also be the origin of the coined name LATISHA (Chapter 11). Variant: **Letitia.** Diminutive: **Leta** and **Lettie.**

LINUS: (m) Greek; linen, a net of linen fiber. The name had only a mild popularity in Medieval times, after an early pope and saint, but it has continued in occasional use. Some familiar bearers include chemist Linus Pauling and Linus Torvalds, the inventor of the computer operating system Linux.

LUCRETIA: (f) Latin; meaning uncertain, possibly either from "light" or "profit." Medieval popularity of this name seems to be simply a continuation of the Roman name and the best known bearer — Lucretia Borgia — is counted as notorious rather than famous. The name was revived in the 19th century when you find it for abolitionist and women's rights activist Lucretia Mott.

MARION: (f, m) English; a diminutive of Mary. This version rivaled the original in popularity in Medieval times and gave rise to a surname that later made this name available to boys as well (as in the birth name of actor John Wayne: Marion Michael Morrison). The variant Marian was reinterpreted as a compound of Mary and Ann (see Chapter 11). Familiar bearers include track star Marion Jones and science fiction author Marion Zimmer Bradley. Another popular diminutive of Mary was Marisa, as for actress Marisa Berenson. Variants: (f) **Marian, Mariana, Marisa,** and **Marissa.**

MILLICENT: (f) English; from Germanic roots meaning "strong work." The name was mildly popular in the Middle Ages and was revived early enough in the 19th century to be already considered old-fashioned by the mid 20th, contradicting the title of the musical *Thoroughly Modern Millie.* Variant: **Milisendia.** Diminutive: **Millie.**

NICOLETTE: (f) French; a feminine diminutive of NICHOLAS (see earlier in this chapter). In addition to using Nichola, the form Nicolette developed, as in the Medieval romance of *Aucassin and Nicolette.* Just as the original name shortened to Colin, this form shortens to Colette, as for the French short-story writer who wrote under that single name. Diminutives: **Colette** and **Collette.**

PETRA: (f) Latin; a rock. While Petra is the simplest feminine form of PETER, the most common feminine form used in Medieval times was Petronilla, corresponding to the male name Pernell. Variant: **Petronilla.**

PHILLIPPA: (f) Greek; horse lover. A feminine form of PHILLIP. This has been in only spotty use in modern times, but one example is historic novelist Philippa Gregory. Variant: **Felipa.**

RANDAL: (m) English; from Germanic roots meaning "shield wolf." This name survived after the Middle Ages primarily as a surname while a different form, RANDOLPH (Chapter 10) was revived in the 19th century. One bearer is poet Randall Jarrell. Variants: **Randall, Randel, Randell,** and **Randle.** Diminutive: **Rand.**

RAYMOND: (m) English; from Germanic roots meaning "counsel-protection." It fell out of fashion before the end of the Middle Ages but was revived at a relatively high popularity in the 20th century. Familiar bearers include actor Raymond Burr and science fiction writer Ray Bradbury. Variants: **Ramon, Raymon,** and **Raymundo.** Diminutive: **Ray.**

REYNOLD: (m) English; from Germanic roots both meaning "force, power." This name worked its way through a variety of forms, including REGINALD (Chapter 19). Modern use is primarily from revivals or from various surnames. Variants: **Reinaldo, Reinhold, Reynaldo,** and **Reino.**

RICHILDA: (f) French; from Germanic roots meaning "battle ruler." This name was popular among the Medieval French nobility, but it was not particularly used in England. Modern use seems to be taken directly from the French. Variant: **Richelle.**

ROSAMOND: (f) English; from Germanic roots meaning "horse-protection" although the name was also reinterpreted as Latin "rose of the world" and associated with the Virgin. The most famous Medieval bearer was "Fair Rosamund," the mistress of King Henry II rumored to have been poisoned by his queen, Eleanor. The name was quite popular during the Victorian romantic revival.

SEBASTIAN: (m) Latin; from the city of Sebastia. Although the cult of Saint Sebastian was fairly popular, the name never seriously caught on. It has been quietly present, however, borne by people like actor Sebastian Cabot. Variant: **Sabastian.**

SIMONE: (f) French; a feminine variant of SIMON. Feminine use was rare in the Middle Ages, and the recent popularity of this name is most likely taken directly from French. One well-known bearer is novelist and sociologist Simone de Beauvoir. Variant: **Symone.**

TIFFANY: (f) English; from the Greek Theophania "manifestation of God," a synonym for the Epiphany. The name was mildly popular in the Middle Ages and gave rise to the surname that is now solidly associated with fine jewelry. It is that association that has likely driven the revival of the name in the late 20th century. One bearer is actress Tiffani-Amber Thiessen. Variants: **Tiffani** and **Tiffanie.**

URSULA: (f) Latin; little bear. In Medieval times, this name was associated with Saint Ursula and the (apocryphal) story of the 11,000 virgins. Modern bearers include actress Ursula Andress and science fiction author Ursula K. LeGuin.

YOLANDA: (f) French?; possibly a variant of Violante, from VIOLA (Chapter 12). It was a rare name in Medieval times but has been revived with some popularity in the 20th century. One bearer is basketball player Yolanda Griffith. Variant: **Yolonda.**

Chapter 9

Naming Revolutions: From the Reformation to the Victorians

Among the changes at the end of the Medieval period were shifts in naming practices, both in the specific names in circulation and in how those names were used. This chapter examines some of the new types of names being used in this era, but the period also traces the rise of middle names and the use of surnames as given names from their faint beginnings to their established practice. Even more than these specific changes, you can see an increase in the rate of change. Tradition was still important, but people were increasingly attracted to new name fashions simply for their novelty.

Reforming Name Ideas: Protestant Naming Fashions

Several shifts in thinking affected names around the 16th to 17th centuries. Religion had always been a strong influence on name choice, so it's not surprising that the Reformation and the rise of Protestant religions affected naming. While some names with religious associations were too popular to be affected (like Anne, Margaret, and John), many Protestants wanted to shift away from the saints' names that were strongly associated with Catholicism, while still using ones with religious associations.

One solution was to choose other Biblical names, especially more obscure Old Testament names such as Jeremiah, Lydia, and Nathaniel. Care was taken to find characters with uplifting and moral lives, but there was also the technique of opening the Bible at random and pointing at a verse with closed eyes, which led to some rather odd choices indeed. Another approach was to use a word or phrase with spiritual meaning. The fanatic extremes of the Puritans (like "Sorry-for-sin") didn't survive, but many of the "virtue names," such as Charity or Prudence have enriched the name pool.

In this section, I discuss the names resulting from the revival discussed above as well as virtue names.

ABNER: (m) Hebrew; father is light, or perhaps more literally, father is Ner, since the Biblical Abner's father was named Ner. In the Bible, Abner is the commander of King Saul's armies. This is one of the revived Biblical names that sounds a bit old fashioned now, although it was moderately popular around the turn of the 20th century. The use of it for Melville Davisson Post's backwoods detective as well as for the comic strip character L'il Abner may have helped to make the name less fashionable. Real life bearers include Abner Doubleday, who is mistakenly credited with the invention of baseball and football player Abner Naynes.

ADLAI: (m) Hebrew; interpretations differ with some giving the meaning as "lax, weary" and others as "my adornment." The name has never been particularly popular but is familiar today from several generations of use in a certain Stevenson family, including U.S. vice-president Adlai Stevenson.

AMOS: (m) Hebrew; burden-bearer. This name became quite popular in early New England and continued in common use through most of the 20th century. Amos is associated with the radio, and later TV, show *Amos 'n' Andy* and appears as the surname of musician Tori Amos.

CALEB: (m) Hebrew; dog. This was the name of one of the scouts sent by Moses to explore the Promised Land. Less popular than many Biblical names in the 19th century, it has recently seen a sudden revival, making it as high as number 34 on the popularity charts in 2003. This name appears for the title character of William Godwin's 1794 novel *Caleb Williams*. Current bearers include novelist Caleb Carr. Variant: **Kaleb.**

CHARITY: (f) English; originally "love," but now more in the sense "generosity." The name was originally inspired by the phrase in I Corinthians, "And now abideth faith, hope, charity," all of which became popular names in the Reformation. The name has been undergoing another revival in recent decades. you see it for actress Charity Rahmer and the title character in the musical *Sweet Charity*. For a variant, early TV actress Charita Bauer played the longest running single character in a television drama. Variant: **Charita.**

CHASTITY: (f) English; chasteness, chastity; originally with a sense of faithfulness rather than celibacy. After enjoying some popularity after the Reformation, this name was revived again around the '70s. Celebrity daughter Chastity Bono dates from this general era. Variant: **Chasity.**

ESPERANZA: (f) Spanish; hope. In addition to virtues used in their English forms, a number of names have become popular that are either borrowed from similar name fashions in other languages, or simply borrow the words and turn them into names. Esperanza was fairly common in the early part of the 20th century.

FAITH: (f) English; faith, belief, confidence. Although not particularly common in early America, this name has transcended its faddish origins and become an extremely popular name in the later 20th century. Bearers include novelist Faith Baldwin and singer Faith Hill.

GAMALIEL: (m) Hebrew; my reward is God. Although never a particularly popular name, Gamaliel is interesting for being the "G" in the name of U.S. president Warren G. Harding.

GRACE: (f) English; in its original sense, the word means "the favor or mercy of God," but today the ordinary sense is "a graceful person, a pleasant and smooth movement." While greatly popularized after the Reformation, this name has actually been in use since the Middle Ages. It was wildly popular in the late 19th century and has become so again in the last couple of decades. The name particularly brings to mind the fairy-tale story of actress Grace Kelly who became Princess of Monaco. Comedian Gracie Allen was half of a famous comedy team with George Burns. On recent television, you have the character of Grace Adler on the show *Will and Grace.* Variants: **Gracie, Graciela,** and **Grayce.**

HIRAM: (m) Phoenecian?; meaning uncertain. The Biblical Hiram was a king of Tyre contemporary with David and Solomon. The name was popular in the 19th century and well into the 20th, although it has fallen out of fashion in recent decades. In literary use, it is strongly associated with specifically American use, as for the character of Hiram B. Otis in Oscar Wilde's story *The Canterville Ghost.*

HONOR: (f) English; honor, the quality of being honorable. The name has been used since the Medieval period, when it had variants such as Annora and Latin Honoria. As it had been the name of a saint, it fell somewhat out of fashion in the Reformation, but revived piggybacking on the virtue names. Current bearers include actress Honor Blackman and artist Annora Spence. Variants: **Annora, Honora,** and **Honoria.**

HOPE: (f) English; hope. As well as the simple name, phrases such as Hope-still and Hope-for had an isolated fashion after the Reformation. Although somewhat rare in the 19th century, it has been climbing steadily up the charts during the 20th. Bearers have included actresses Hope Lange and Hope Davis.

HOSEA: (m) Hebrew; God is help. This minor prophet got his own book in the Bible, ensuring that the name would be picked up during the Reformation. It was never particularly common, but was used by James Russell Lowell for his stereotypical 19th-century New Englander Hosea Bigelow.

JEDEDIAH: (m) Hebrew; friend of God. This was a nickname of King Solomon in the Bible. The name became popular in early New England but then fell out of fashion. It retains associations with the period of western expansion, as for 19th-century explorer Jedediah Smith. There was a brief revival of it in the '80s. Variant: **Jedidiah.** Diminutive: **Jed.**

JEREMIAH: (m) Hebrew; God is exalted, or perhaps "made exalted by God." This was the name of a major prophet in the Bible, with a book named after him. The somewhat ranting nature of the prophecies associated with him gave rise to the word "jeremiad" for this type of composition. The name became quite popular in early New England. An English variant JEREMY (Chapter 10) eventually outstripped it in popularity in the mid–20th century. It can have many of the same diminutives as GERALD (Chapter 8). Bearers include composer Jeremiah Clarke and the title character of the movie *Jeremiah Johnson,* set in the Old West.

JUSTICE: (f, m) English; justice, a judge. The name originally shows up as Latin Justus and was used in the Medieval period. It fell out of fashion during the Reformation, as it had been a saint's name, but was revived occasionally on the tails of the virtue names, both in the Latin form, and in the English form Justice. In recent decades it has been seeing another revival, perhaps as part of a returning fashion for "J" names. Variant: (m) **Justus.**

LUTHER: (m) German; lute player, or lute maker. This is hardly an activity that one would associate with Protestant reformer Martin Luther, who is responsible for this being adopted as a given name. It was quite popular in the later 19th century and continuing for some time into the 20th. Famous bearers have included botanist Luther Burbank and musician Luther Vandross.

LYDIA: (f) Greek; a woman from Lydia. One Lydia is mentioned briefly in the New Testament, and as women's personal names are rare in that book, nearly all of them have been seized on for use at some point. The name has maintained a fairly steady popularity for the last couple centuries and has been popular as a literary name, used by novelists such as Tobias Smollett and Jane Austen. Bearers have included singer Lydia Mendoza and poet Lydia Lunch. Variants: **Lidia** and **Lyda.**

MERCEDES, MERCY: (f) Spanish, English; mercy. In English use, this is a straightforward virtue name, but the Spanish version comes indirectly from an epithet of the Virgin *Maria de Mercedes* "Mary of the mercies". The form Mercy was common in early New England but has fallen almost completely out of fashion. In contrast, Mercedes has held a steady popularity throughout the last century. One bearer is actress Mercedes Ruehl.

NATHAN: (m) Hebrew; He gave, that is, God gave. While it is used as an independent name, it is sometimes thought of as a short form of NATHANIEL (see later in this chapter). The name was quite popular during the colonial era, as for American patriot Nathan Hale. It has remained quite popular through the 20th century, even increasing somewhat in recent decades. Variant: **Nathen.**

NATHANIEL: (m) Hebrew; God gave, gift of God. The name makes a brief appearance in the New Testament, but it seems to have been treated more as an Old Testament name in terms of when it became popular. The name was very popular in the 18th and 19th centuries, for figures such as General Nathaniel Greene and author Nathaniel Hawthorne. It has been increasing steadily in popularity through the 20th century. Nat can be a diminutive for either this or Nathan, or for feminine names such as NATALIE (Chapter 13), and Nat was an independent name around the turn of the 20th century. Variants; **Nathanael** and **Nathanial.** Diminutive: **Nat.**

NEHEMIAH: (m) Hebrew; God has consoled. There were several Old Testament figures by this name. It has been used occasionally since the Reformation but has never been particularly popular. One literary example is the character of Nehemiah Holdenough in Sir Walter Scott's *Woodstock.*

OREN: (m) Hebrew; pine tree. There is only a brief mention of this name in the Old Testament, but it's enjoyed enough popularity to pick up a range of variants. All of them fall out of fashion in the early part of the 20th century. Some bearers include long-time Utah senator Orin Hatch and Native American leader Oren Lyons. Variants: **Oran, Orin,** and **Orrin.**

PATIENCE: (f) English; patience, the quality of being patient. This virtue name is strongly associated in the popular imagination with the Pilgrims and the colonial era. The name has recently seen a slight revival.

PROVIDENCE: (f) English; something (especially God) that will provide, often used in the sense of "fate, destiny." This name has never been particularly common. Variant: **Providenci.**

PRUDENCE: (f) English; wisdom, forethought. Like Patience, this name is strongly associated in the popular mind with the early colonies of the Pilgrims, although it had been in use for some centuries before that, thanks to a St. Prudentius. It fell out of fashion around the mid–20th century, but current bearers include TV producer Prudence Fraser.

SETH: (m) Hebrew?; compensation, substitute. Many of the names from the Book of Genesis can only tentatively be identified as Hebrew, but in this case the apparent meaning would make sense for the character, who was born to Eve and Adam after the tragedy of Cain and Abel. The name enjoyed a fairly mild popularity in the 18th and 19th centuries, but has been rising steadily in the charts in the later part of the 20th century. Current bearers include actor Seth Green.

TOBIAS: (m) Hebrew; God is good. Tobias is a Greek form of the original Tobiah. This was not a particularly popular name as it appears in the Apocrypha rather than in more canonical scripture. It has been enjoying a certain revival of interest lately, and is even more popular in the diminutive Toby, as for actor Tobey Maguire. Diminutives: **Tobey** and **Toby.**

Going for Baroque: New Patterns in the 17th and 18th Centuries

People are always looking for ways to make old names new — to combine the benefits of tradition with the joys of fashion. Through the 17th and 18th centuries, new, fancier forms of girls names were created by adding "-ina" or "-ette" to old names, such as Georgina or Henriette, or by reviving older Latin forms of the names, such as Alicia. Intermarriage among the noble families of Europe brought in new names or variants of names already in use, such as James, Charles, George, Caroline, and Gertrude.

In addition to these two groups, this section includes other names that first became fashionable around the Baroque era.

ADELINE: (f) French; from a Germanic root meaning "noble." The name was popular in Medieval times and was revived at a time when names ending in "-ine" were becoming fashionable. It's featured in the song *Sweet Adeline,* beloved of barbershop quartets. Variants: **Adaline, Adelina,** and **Adilene.**

ALETHA: (f) Greek; truth. Perhaps originally popularized in English via Princess Maria Aletea of Spain, who was offered in marriage to King Charles I. Aleta fell out of fashion in the early 20th century, but the variant Aleta enjoyed a brief fashion in the mid century, perhaps at least partly due to the character of Queen Aleta in the comic strip *Prince Valiant.* Variant: **Aleta** and **Alethea.**

ALICIA: (f) Latin; a "fancy" Latin form of ALICE (Chapter 8). Around the 18th century, people started looking for ways to make familiar names a little more exclusive and exotic. One method was to revive Latin forms like Alicia. In this spelling, it has been increasing steadily in popularity through the 20th century, and lately variants based on phonetic spellings have been hitting the charts as well. Current bearers include musician Alicia Keys and actress Alicia Silverstone. Variants: **Alecia, Alesha, Alesia, Alisha, Alycia, Alysha, Alysia,** and **Alyssia.**

ALOYSIUS: (m) Latin?; possibly a Latinized form of LOUIS (Chapter 7). It first became popular in honor of 16th-century Jesuit St. Aloysius Gonzaga, but by the 18th century had become more generally used. Diminutive: **Alois.**

ANASTASIA: (f) Greek; resurrection. This is another name that had been in use for some time in familiar forms such as Anstey, but was revived in its original form in the 18th century. The name had been more popular in eastern Europe and is often associated today with Russia. Several film versions have been made of the story of Anastasia, the daughter of the last Russian Tsar, who was sometimes rumored to have survived her family's slaughter during the Russian Revolution. Lately it has been creeping up the charts again. Diminutive: **Tasia;** see also STACY (Chapter 10).

ANTOINETTE: (f) French; a variant of ANTHONY (Chapter 7). French connections among the English aristocracy brought in an infusion of French forms of names that had become less fashionable in their original versions. Historically, the name is most familiar from the tragic fate of French queen Marie Antoinette during the French Revolution. Bearers include ballerina Antoinette Sibley and Antoinette Brown Blackwell, active in the women's suffrage movement. Antoinette has held a mild but steady popularity through the 20th century, but the other variants are confined mostly to the early decades. Variants: **Antionette, Antonetta, Antonette, Antonietta,** and **Antonina.**

APHRA: (f) Hebrew; dust. This arose from a misunderstanding in Biblical translation, turning the ordinary word into a name. It was never a common name, however one very intriguing bearer was 17th-century dramatist and spy Aphra Behn.

AUGUSTINA (f), **AUGUSTINE** (m): Latin; variants of AUGUST (Chapter 8). The masculine name became popular early in the Medieval era in honor of Saint Augustine, the founder of a successful monastic order. The name eroded down into Austin but has regularly been revived in its full form. The feminine form Augusta became popularized through the German mother of England's King George III and variants such as Augustina were not far behind. The diminutive Gussie was borne by tennis player Gussie Moran. The women's names in this group have largely fallen out of popularity in the early part of the 20th century. Of the men's names, only Austin has been increasing in popularity recently. Variants: (both) **Augustine** and **Austin;** (f) **Augusta;** (m) **Agustin, Austen, Auston,** and **Austyn.** Diminutive: (f) **Gussie.**

CAROLINE: (f) English; a feminine form of CHARLES. This began as Carolina, an Italian feminine form of Charles, which spread first to Germany and then came to England as Caroline with George II's queen. It quickly became fashionable, aided by the fame (or notoriety) of Lady Caroline Lamb, mistress of the poet Byron. This name has held steady at a moderate popularity through the 20th century, although the development of CAROLYN (Chapter 10) surpassed it by a large margin. Familiar examples include Caroline Kennedy and the title character of the TV show *Caroline in the City.*

CELESTE: (f) French; heaven, heavenly. This was originally a Latin name, inspired by Saint Celestina. There are corresponding male forms of the name but only the Italian Celestino has been popular enough to hit the charts. Celeste itself has been mildly popular through much of the 20th century. Bearers include actress Celeste Holm. Variant: (f) **Celestine;** (m) **Celestino.**

CHARLES: (m) French; a variant of CARL (Chapter 8), from a Germanic root meaning "man." Although forms of this name had been used in English occasionally in the Middle Ages, it wasn't until the reign of two kings by that name in the 17th century that it became somewhat popular, and not until the 19th did it reach the high ranking it enjoys today. It has a longer history in France where the original Frankish name borne by Charlemagne (Carl-le-magne, that is, Charles the Great) was Latinized as Carolus and then evolved into Charles. After the run of kings (and would-be kings) with this name, it became firmly established in England and so spread to America where it seems to have created its own momentum without the benefit of prominent early bearers. Yet it made its way up into the top-ten male names in the later 19th century and remained there until the mid–20th century, dropping only slightly after that. The usual diminutive is Charlie, which was popularized as early as the 18th century in the time of "Bonnie Prince Charlie" and has continued in popularity through the present. More recently, a specifically American diminutive, Chuck, has developed but is apparently too informal to have made the charts yet as an independent given name. The variant Chas began life as a written abbreviation, and examples of it around the turn of the 20th century almost certainly stand for the full name. But in recent decades it has reappeared as Chaz, evidently as a name in its own right. It took some time for feminine forms to develop. For these, see CAROLINE and CHARLOTTE in this chapter, as well as CAROLYN (Chapter 10), CAROL, and CARLA (both Chapter 17). Current examples of the male name include actors Charles Bronson, Charlie Chaplin, and Charlie Sheen, and musician Charlie Parker. Some other prominent historic bearers include French prime minister Charles de Gaulle and Charles Babbage, inventor of the computer. Diminutives: **Charley, Charlie, Chas,** and **Chaz.**

CHARLOTTE: (f) French; a feminine version of CHARLES. Despite the French origin, the name became popular in the English-speaking world largely through the influence of the German wife of King George II, Charlotte Sophia.

The name quickly appealed to authors of popular fiction, spreading its influence even further. The name has had very similar popularity to Caroline in the 20th century but their fortunes have reversed, with Charlotte declining as Caroline rose. The usual diminutive is LOTTIE (Chapter 10). Well-known bearers of the name have included novelist Charlotte Brontë and one of the pioneers in books on personal names, Charlotte Yonge. Variants: **Carlotta** and **Charolette.**

CHRISTINE: (f) English; a variant of CHRISTIANA (Chapter 8). The fashion for names ending in "-ine" made this variant a natural, and it has become popular in a wide variety of variants, many drawn from other languages. The epicenter of this collection of names appears to be the '70s and '80s. It is often shortened to CHRIS (Chapter 19) or CHRISSY (Chapter 16). Current bearers include actresses Christina Ricci and Kristin Kreuk. Variants: **Christeen, Christene, Christin, Christina, Cristin, Cristina, Kristin, Kristina, Kristine, Kristyn, Krystina, Krysten,** and **Krystin.**

CLAUDINE: (f) French; a variant of CLAUDIA (Chapter 7). Although this name fits in with the fashion of names ending in "-ine," it came into use from French somewhat later than most, in the later 19th century. The novels of French writer Colette feature a character of this name. It enjoyed a mild popularity through the first half of the 20th century.

CLEMENTINE: (f) English; a variant of CLEMENT (Chapter 8). Rather than being borrowed from French, as Claudine was, this name seems to have been coined directly, similarly to GERALDINE. Like many of this group of names, it was picked up and popularized in literature. A Clementina features in George Eliot's *Daniel Deronda* and another is a major character in Samuel Richardson's *Sir Charles Grandison.* In the form Clementine, the name is familiar from the 19th-century song addressing "My darling, Clementine." It seems to have fallen out of fashion in the early 20th century. Variant: **Clementina.** Diminutive: **Clemmie.**

CORA: (f) Greek; maiden, daughter. Despite its classical origins, the name seems to have been a new coinage, probably specifically an American one. There may also have been some influence from Corinna, which has an older history. Cora Munro was the unfortunate heroine of James Fenimore Cooper's *The Last of the Mohicans* and there are some theories that this was the first use of the name. It remains in use throughout the 20th century, although declining somewhat. As noted above, Corinna shows up earlier, at least as early as Robert Herrick's 1648 poem *Corinna's Going A-Maying.* It had neither the significant popularity of Cora nor its fall from fashion, instead holding steady in the middle ground. A French variant was popularized by Madame de Staël's 1807 novel *Corinne.* The name was also immortalized in Ray Peterson's song *Corinna Corinna.* In the '70s and '80s there was a brief fashion for several variants of Cory, possibly as a diminutive of this name but more likely as cross-over from the popularity of the male name (see Chapter 10). To complete the musical references, the traditional song *Darling Corey* was popularized by the Weavers. Variants: **Corene, Corina, Corine, Corinna, Corinne, Corrine,** and **Coraima.** Diminutives: **Corey, Cori, Corrie, Cory,** and **Kori.**

EMMELINE: (f) English; from a Germanic root (by circuitous paths) meaning "work, labor." The name was popular in the Middle Ages but fell out of use only to be revived in the 18th century. Although similar in appearance, it isn't directly connected with EMMA (Chapter 8). A character with this name appears in Harriet Beecher Stowe's novel *Uncle Tom's Cabin,* and another well-known bearer was English suffragist Emmeline Pankhurst.

ERNEST: (m) German; earnest, serious, steadfast. It was introduced into English use in the late 18th century via the German connections of the English royal family. A feminine form, ERNESTINE (see later in this chapter), developed somewhat later. The origins of the name support the pun found in the title of Oscar Wilde's play *The Importance of Being Earnest.* Other well-known bearers include Antarctic explorer Ernest Shakelton, physicist Ernest Rutherford, and novelist Ernest Hemingway. The name has been fairly popular throughout the 20th century in several variants. Variants: **Earnest, Ernesto,** and **Ernst.** Diminutive: **Ernie.**

EUGENIE: (f) French; a feminine form of EUGENE (Chapter 18). This name was popularized by the Empress Eugenie, wife of Napoleon III. The variant Eugenia has been more popular in the U.S. Variant: **Eugenia.**

FLORINE: (f) English; a variant of Flora, which is itself a variant of FLORENCE (Chapter 12). The name is not, as one might think, related to fluorine gas, a component of fluorescent lighting. This is another "fancy" name coined by adding "-ine" to an existing name. It was mildly popular in the early 20th century. Variant: **Florene.**

FREDERICK: (m) German; peace ruler. Although there are scattered earlier examples, this name seriously entered English use in the 18th century under the influence of the Hanoverian kings. It came into American use shortly afterward, despite the lack of a similar connection, and rose rapidly in popularity to a peak around 1900. It has declined slightly but steadily through the 20th century. The common diminutives are FRED and FREDDY (Chapter 18). Frederick may be the only name with its own international organization, the Fred Society. Membership only requires being named with some form of Fred or Frederick. (Those interested in this rather tongue-in-cheek organization can check out their Web site at www.fredsociety.com.) Well-known bearers include abolitionist Frederick Douglass, physiologist Frederick C. Robbins, and film director Federico Fellini. Feminine versions such as Frederica have not really caught on in the U.S. Variants: **Federico, Frederic, Fredric, Fredrick,** and **Friedrich.**

GEORGE: (f, m) Greek; farmer. This was the name of a possibly apocryphal early saint who was adopted by English crusaders and so ended up becoming the patron saint of England. Despite this connection, the name was slow to take root in ordinary use, and it wasn't until the beginning of the run of Kings George in the 18th century that it started heading for the top of the charts. For American use, the dislike of the third English king of that name might have killed the name if not for the coincidence of a certain General Washington. By the beginning of the 20th century, it was enjoying a top-ten slot and only began falling from that position in midcentury. Famous Georges, in addition to Washington, have included composer George Gershwin, director George Lucas, boxer George Foreman, rock musician George Harrison, and actor George Clooney. The occasional examples of Geo in the early 20th century are most likely abbreviations rather than a diminutive. However the Spanish form, Jorge, has been rising steadily through the ranks over the last century, as for Argentine writer Jorge Luis Borges. Several feminine forms of the name arose (in addition to the occasional use of George for women), especially Georgiana in the 18th century and Georgette in the early 20th. The variant Georgina has shown the most longevity in the mid–20th century. Well-known female bearers have included romance novelist Georgette Heyer and pre-Raphaelite poet Christina Georgina Rossetti, author of *Goblin's Market*. Variants: (f) **Georgene, Georgette, Georgiana, Georgianna, Georgie, Georgina,** and **Georgine;** (m) **Geo** and **Jorge.**

GERALDINE: (f) English; a feminine form of GERALD (Chapter 8). This first appears as a poetic nickname in the 16th century for Lady Elizabeth Fitzgerald, where it simply meant "member of the Gerald family." It doesn't seem to have become an actual given name until just after 1800 when you find it used in Coleridge's poem *Christabel* as well as for the writer Geraldine Jewsbury. It was fairly popular through the early mid–20th century but has fallen out of fashion since then. It has the same diminutives as the masculine Gerald, mostly variants of Gerry. Well-known bearers have included actress Gerladine Chaplin, politician Geraldine Ferraro, and model Jerry Hall. Variant: **Jeraldine.** Diminutives: **Geri** and **Gerri.**

GERTRUDE: (f) German; spear strength. This name was occasionally used in England in the Middle Ages but increased significantly in popularity leading into the 17th century. It enjoyed another revival in the later 19th century but fell out of fashion half a century later. Shakespeare gives the name to Hamlet's mother and more recently it has been borne by writer Gertrude Stein and actress Gertrude Astor. The most popular diminutives are Gertie and Trudy, with the latter taking over from Gertrude towards the end of its popularity. Diminutives: **Gertie, Trudie,** and **Trudy.**

HENRIETTA: (f) French; a feminine version of HENRY (Chapter 8). The importation of this name can be traced to Henrietta Maria, the queen of Charles I. The name quickly became naturalized, substituting the usual English root

Harry to get Harriette and then simply Harriet. While all of these variants have been moderately popular coming into the 20th century, even more so is the diminutive Hattie. The entire group, however, fell out of fashion by the '60s. The name is familiar from bearers like activist and novelist Harriet Beecher Stowe, early TV icon Harriet Nelson, and painter Henriette Wyeth (sister of the more famous artistic Wyeth). Variants: **Harriet, Harriett, Harriette,** and **Henriette; Enriqueta.** Diminutives: **Hattie** and **Hettie.**

JAMES: (f, m) French; a development of the Hebrew name JACOB (Chapter 8). The history of this name is complex. In the Latin form Jacobus, this name was wildly popular in the Middle Ages, thanks in part to the popularity of the pilgrimage to the shrine of Saint Jacob/James at Compostela. By shifts in pronunciation, Jacobus became Jacomus and then James. But both names continued to be used in parallel, and in the King James translation of the Bible, Jacob was used for a number of Old Testament figures of the name, while James was used to translate the same name in the New Testament. James itself doesn't begin showing up significantly in English use until the 16th century, and didn't take off until popularized by the kings of that name in the 17th century. Coming into the 20th century, the name is steady in third place and rises to number 1 in the '40s. It declines after that but never out of the top-20 boys' names. The diminutive Jamie shows up in a variety of spellings and had some popularity in the later part of the 20th century. The other major group of diminutives, based on JIM are covered in Chapter 10. The Spanish version, Jaime, has been increasing in popularity over the last century. The surname Jameson has also been taken up as a given name, especially in recent decades, and very recently the Gaelic version Seamus has been making the charts, too. Well-known bearers of this name include painter James Whistler, musicians James Taylor and James Brown, actors James Cagney and James Earl Jones, and fictional character James Bond. James has also been mildly popular as a feminine name, and the diminutives in the Jamie group even more so. Feminine examples in use include TV character Jaime Sommers *(The Bionic Woman)* and Canadian ice skater Jamie Sale. Variants: (f) **Jaime, Jaimee, Jaimie, Jami, Jamie, Jammie,** and **Jayme;** (m) **Jaime, Jame, Jameson, Jamey, Jamie, Jamison, Jammie,** and **Jayme; Seamus.**

JEANINE: (f) French; a variant of Jean (see under JOAN in Chapter 8). Another of the popular name variants ending in "-ine." This one has recently been popular mostly in the mid–20th century. Interesting bearers include science writer Janine Benyus and Jeanine Salla, a fictional character created as a marketing gimmick for the movie *Artificial Intelligence.* Variants: **Janeen, Janine,** and **Jeannine.**

JOSEPHINE: (f) French; a feminine form of JOSEPH (Chapter 4). The name Josephine was popularized by the Empress Josephine, wife of Napoleon Bonaparte. The time was ripe for the name to catch on in English use, despite the distaste for things French at the time. It was moderately popular around the turn of the 20th century but has declined somewhat in the later part of the century. Diminutives used independent names include Josette, Josie, and JO (Chapter 10). Familiar bearers include actress Josephine Baker, mystery novelist Josephine Tey, and comic book character Josie of *Josie and the Pussycats* (also appearing in TV cartoon and live-action movie versions). Variants: **Josefa** and **Josefina.** Diminutives: **Josette, Josie,** and **Joetta.**

LOUISE: (f) French; a feminine form of LOUIS (Chapter 7). The name came into English use during the same period as many other French names were being imported in the 17th century. In addition to the basic name's popularity (which held out until well into the mid–20th century), it gave rise to many diminutives and blended variants such as Louella. The name is familiar from actress Louise Lasser, golfer Louise Suggs, and gossip columnist Louella Parsons. Variants: **Louis, Louisa, Loyce,** and **Luisa.** Diminutives: **Lou, Louella, Louie, Lu, Luela, Luetta, Lula,** and **Lulu.**

LUCINDA: (f) coined; apparently a blend of LUCY (Chapter 16) with a name like BELINDA (Chapter 6). It showed up in literary use in the 17th century and later, as for Lucinda Roanoke in Anthony Trollope's 1873 *The Eustace Diamonds*. In came into general use around the 19th century and held a fairly steady moderate popularity through most of the 20th. Country singer Lucinda Williams is one bearer.

MARCELLA: (f) Latin; a feminine form of MARCEL (Chapter 18). It comes into the 20th century with a moderate popularity and several variants. One bearer was opera star Marcella Sembrich. Variants: **Marcela, Marcelina, Marceline,** and **Marcelle.**

MAXIMILLIAN: (m) German; taken from the Latin Maximus "great." It became popular in Germany beginning in the 16th century and slowly filtered out to other countries, entering English use around the 19th century. It has been relatively rare and has only regularly hit the popularity charts in the last few decades. There is a whole family of names derived from this Latin root, or diminutives of those names, such as Max. Some of the most familiar examples still come from German-speaking countries, such as actors Maximilian Schell and Max Von Sydow. Russian novelist Maxim Gorky bears another variant. Variants: **Maximilian, Maxim, Maximino, Maximo,** and **Maximus.** Diminutives: **Max** and **Maxie.**

MAXINE: (f) English; a feminine form of Max (see MAXIMILLIAN). This name was coined on the "-ine" pattern, but later than the main group of such names. It was relatively popular in the early part of the 20th century but rapidly fell out of favor. Famous bearers include Maxene Andrews of the singing group the Andrews Sisters and writer Maxine Hong Kingston. Variant: **Maxene.** Diminutive: **Maxie.**

PAULETTE, PAULINE: (f) French; variants of PAULA (Chapter 10). As with many of the extremely popular male names, Paul was put through its paces with all the fashionable feminine endings. Paulina is found as early as Shakespeare in *A Winter's Tale*. Pauline immediately brings to mind the popular film serial *The Perils of Pauline*. Variants: **Pauletta** and **Paulina.**

SALLY: (f) English; a diminutive of SARAH (Chapter 4) that has become an independent name. The *r*-to-*l* shift is seen in a number of diminutives, such as Mary to Molly. As the main fashion for Biblical names declined, this informal diminutive struck out as an independent name and by the mid–20th century briefly overtook its parent. But Sally then fell out of fashion while Sarah found a renewed interest. Well-known bearers include actresses Sally Field and Sally Struthers and astronaut Sally Ride. Variant: **Sallie.**

STEWART: (m) English; a steward, a caretaker. A very important version of this job fell to the hereditary stewards of Scotland, who took the occupation as their family name and eventually sat on the throne of that land. And because James VI of Scotland was the closest relative of Elizabeth I, he also became King James I of England. This brought the name, in the form Stuart, into major prominence. With the declining fortunes of the Stuart dynasty the name passed from having the cachet of success to having the mystique of failure, as well as being thoroughly entangled in a sense of romantic Scottishness. And it was in the early 19th century, when Stuart politics were safely far behind, that it was taken up as a given name. Bearers include movie director Stuart Rosenberg. Variant: **Stuart.**

Romanticizing Victorian Ideas

The era named after Queen Victoria (roughly equivalent to the 19th century) is famous for its indulgence in romanticism, sentimentality, and a renewal of interest in things Medieval. These interests revived many older names for both men and women, such as Wilfred, Edgar, and Edith. Girls were often given "fancy" names inspired by the heroines of popular novels, such as Winifred. Boys were increasingly likely to be given surnames as first names, especially surnames associated with prominent families in English history. you also see a new generation of diminutive forms of names achieve independence, such as Sadie for Sarah or Willie for William.

ABRAHAM: (m) Hebrew; father of a multitude. This name was taken up in use with many other Biblical names but saw an increase in popularity in the early 19th century, including a certain Abraham Lincoln. The name was becoming old-fashioned in midcentury but was redeemed from obscurity by the popularity of President Lincoln and has remained moderately popular ever since. The diminutive Abe fell out of fashion as an independent name in the early part of the 20th century, and the diminutive Bram, as for horror author Bram Stoker, was never particularly common. An Arabic form of the name, Ibrahim, is also in use. Variants: **Abram** and **Ibrahim.** Diminutives: **Abe** and **Bram.**

ADELAIDE: (f) French; from Germanic roots meaning "of a noble kind." This name was quite popular in the Medieval period, but it was abandoned in favor of its descendent ALICE, only to rise again in the early 19th century, partially due to the popularity of the queen of William IV, who bore the name. It had the sort of gothic Medieval feel that was popular at the time. In America, it had become moderately popular by the turn of the 20th century, although it fell out of fashion midcentury. Variant: **Adelaida.**

ADELBERT: (m) English; noble and bright. This is the same name as German ALBERT (see later in this chapter). It was revived in the 19th century from a combination of the popularity of its German variant Albert and a renewed interest in medieval-sounding names. The variant Delbert has been moderately popular over the last century, although Adelbert fell out of use in the early 20th century. Variants: **Adalberto** and **Delbert.**

ADELE: (f) English; from a Germanic root meaning "noble." Although the name has been used since the Middle Ages, it was never particularly common, but received a boost in the 19th century, due in part to being featured in the operetta *Die Fledermaus.* It remained popular in a variety of forms through the early 20th century. Some examples are nutritionist Adele Davis the character of Adela Quested in E.M. Forester's novel *A Passage to India.* Variants: **Adela, Adelia, Adell, Adella,** and **Adelle.**

ADOLPHUS: (m) German; noble wolf. This was brought into English use in the 19th century from both German and Swedish use (the combination Gustavus Adolphus features prominently in Swedish history). In the mid–20th century, the association with Adolf Hitler pretty much killed that form of the name, although the Spanish variant Adolfo has remained popular. Other bearers include Arctic explorer Adolphus W. Greely and lyricist Adolph Green. Variants: **Adolf, Adolfo,** and **Adolph.**

ALBERT: (m) German; noble and bright. Although an Old English version of the name, ADELBERT (see earlier in this chapter), had been in use in the Middle Ages, modern use of Albert was reintroduced via Prince Albert, the husband of Queen Victoria. His name became extremely popular; by the end of the 19th century it was in the top-20 men's names in the U.S. and has retained a fairly high ranking. Famous people of this name include humanitarian Albert Schweitzer and physicist Albert Einstein. Two diminutives have had roughly equal popularity: Al, as for racer Al Unser and singer Al Jolson; and Bert or Bertie, as for actor Bert Lahr. Variants: **Alberto** and **Elbert.** Diminutives: **Al, Bert, Berton,** and **Bertie.**

ALBERTA: (f) English; a feminine form of ALBERT. This was coined as a feminine form of the name of Queen Victoria's consort, Prince Albert, and popularized by her daughter, Louise Caroline Alberta, after whom the Canadian province Alberta was named. Another bearer was blues singer Alberta Hunter. The name was quite popular in the early 20th century but declined soon after. Variants: **Albertha, Albertine,** and **Alverta.** Diminutive: **Bertie.**

ALEXANDRA: (f) Greek; a feminine form of ALEXANDER (Chapter 6). Although the name Alexandra in various forms has been in use since Medieval times, modern popularity is closely linked to the name of Princess Alexandra, wife of the future Edward VII. In fact, through tangled family connections, it was a popular name in many of the 19th century royal families of Europe and so carried an air of nobility. Both the male and female versions of this name have given rise to a wide variety of diminutives, some of which can be found under ALEX and SANDRA (Chapter 10), ALEXIS and LEXIE (Chapter 16). Variants: **Alejandra, Alejandrin, Alessandra, Alexandrea,** and **Alexandria.** Diminutives: **Alexa** and **Alexia.**

ALFRED: (m) English; elf-counseled. Relatively few Anglo-Saxon names survived in serious popularity past the Middle Ages. Despite the fame of King Alfred the Great, this name became very rare after the Norman Conquest and was only revived in popular use with the Victorian obsession with all things Medieval. It was extremely popular for several decades around the turn of the 20th century. Most of its diminutives are shared with other names: Al with Albert, Fred with Frederick, although you sometimes find Alf or Alfie used (as for the title character of the movie *Alfie*). Famous bearers include inventor and philanthropist Alfred Nobel and film director Alfred Hitchcock. A feminine version, Alfreda was coined in the late 19th century and enjoyed at least a mild popularity into the early 20th. Variant: **Alfredo.** Diminutives: **Alf** and **Allie.**

ALMEDA: (f) uncertain; a name of unclear origin, although from the form it looks like it may have come from an Italian or Spanish source, and so may have been popularized through literary use. It enjoyed some small popularity in the late 19th century and into the early 20th. Variant: **Almeta.**

ALMIRA: (f) coined?; possibly from Arabic *amir* "prince," especially given the variant Amira. In rare use in the later 19th century, as for actress Almira Sessions. Variant: **Amira** and **Elmira.**

ALONZO: (m) Spanish; a variant of ALFONSO (Chapter 8). The name Alonso shows up in Shakespeare's *The Tempest* for one of the foreign characters, but common use seems to come from the 19th century penchant for Medieval names. Various forms of this name have been moderately popular continuing throughout the 20th century, and the diminutive Lonnie has outstripped the original name. The various forms of the diminutive are familiar from bearers such as actor Lon Chaney and blues musician Lonnie Johnson. Variants: **Alonso** and **Alonza.** Diminutives: **Allie, Lon, Lonnie, Lonny** and **Lonzo.**

ALVA: (f, m) multiple origins; in some cases, possibly from the Biblical name Alvah, but also possibly from the old English name Alvin, which in turn has multiple origins (Ealdwine "old friend," Æthelwine "noble friend," or Ælfwine "elf-friend"). Alvin fell out of use in the Medieval period and when it appears again in the late 19th century it isn't clear whether it's a revival or simply a coincidental coinage. The use of Alva for both men and women suggests that the original source was masculine but that the final "a" has led people to consider it a feminine name. Examples of this group of names include track star Alvin Harrison and inventor Thomas Alva Edison. With the exception of the continuing popularity of Alvin, most of these names fell out of fashion in the mid–20th century. Variants: (f) **Alvera, Alvena,** and **Alvina;** (m) **Alvah, Alvie,** and **Alvin.**

ARABELLA: (f) uncertain; early examples suggest that this may either be a variant of the English name ANABEL (Chapter 6) or an adaptation of the Latin name Orabilis "entreatable." One might expect it to pick up all the usual variants of a name ending in "-bella," but none of them have become popular enough to make the charts. The name has been in use since Medieval times (one prominent bearer was Arabella Stuart, the niece of Mary, Queen of Scots), but it was one of the names revived in the Medievalist fad of the 19th century.

ARCHIBALD: (m) French; from Germanic roots meaning "genuine and bold." The name became especially popular in Scotland where, for curious reasons, it was regularly used to translate the Gaelic name Gillespie. These Scottish associations continued during its more recent revival, as for poet Archibald MacLeish. The full name fell out of fashion early in the 20th century, but its diminutive Archie continued in much greater popularity until fairly recently. The name brings to mind TV character Archie Bunker of *All in the Family.* Diminutives: **Arch** and **Archie.**

ARNOLD: (m) German; eagle-power. This is yet another name originally brought to England by the Normans that fell out of fashion in the later Middle Ages and then was revived in the late 19th century. It may have fallen in the "German imports" or "Medieval revivals" categories, or possibly both. It has been moderately popular throughout the 20th century, borne by such familiar figures as golfer Arnold Palmer and actor-turned-governor Arnold Schwartzenegger. Variants: **Arnaldo** and **Arnoldo.** Diminutives: **Arne** and **Arno.**

ARVID: (m) Swedish; eagle tree. Unlike many immigrant names, this one remained at least mildly popular through the '30s. One literary reference comes in science-fiction author Poul Anderson's novel *The Queen of Air and Darkness.*

BERTHA: (f) French; from Germanic roots meaning "bright." The name fell out of favor in the Medieval period but was revived in the later 19th century and was quite popular leading into the early 20th. Despite some negative associations from the nickname "Big Bertha" given to a German heavy gun in World War I, it continued in mild popularity well past midcentury. Variant: **Berta.**

BEULAH: (f) Hebrew; she who is married. This was originally a nickname for Israel, referring to a metaphoric marriage with God. The name was quite popular around the turn of the 20th century, but may have suffered somewhat by a too-close association with the title character of the early TV show *Beulah.* Variants: **Beaulah** and **Bulah.**

CARLETON: (m) English; town of the free peasants. Interestingly, this name has the same origins as CHARLTON (see Chapter 18). It arose from a surname but was picked up possibly not because of a specific family heritage but for its aristocratic associations with London's Carlton Club. It has remained moderately popular through much of the 20th century, as for actor Carleton Carpenter. Variant: **Carlton.**

CARLYLE: (m) Brythonic; the fortress of Luguvalos (a personal name). This name is taken from the surname. The name enjoyed mild popularity through the first few decades of the 20th century. Bearers include two generations of actors named Carlyle Blackwell.

CASIMIR: (m) Polish; proclamation of peace. The name may have come into English use via German connections. It was mildly popular through the early 20th century. An early American connection for the name comes from Casimir Pulaski, a Polish exile who embraced the American cause during the Revolution. Variant: **Casimer.**

CLARENCE: (m) English; originally a noble title, derived from the place name Clare. When the title Duke of Clarence was revived for the eldest son of Edward VII, it slipped over into use as a given name, although this doesn't clearly explain why it shot up in popularity in America at the same time. It was extremely popular around the turn of the 20th century and has declined only slowly since then. Mark Twain used it for a character in *A Connecticut Yankee in King Arthur's Court,* showing how well it had been established at that time. Currently, it is familiar from Supreme Court Justice Clarence Thomas. Variant: **Clarance.**

CLARISSA: (f) Latin; a diminutive of CLARA (Chapter 8). The name seems to have been coined for (or at least popularized by) Samuel Richardson's 1748 novel of the same name and was used again by Virginia Woolf for Clarissa Dalloway, the title character of *Mrs. Dalloway* in 1925. By the early 20th century, the more English-looking Clarice was the most popular form, but over the course of the century the original Clarissa has overtaken it again. Variants: **Clarice** and **Clarisa.**

CONRAD: (m) German; bold counsel. This was the name of several Holy Roman Emperors in the Middle Ages, this name has always had strong German associations. The fashions for both Medieval and German names in the 19th century brought it into use, and it features in various romantic novels and poems of that era. It came into the 20th century with a fairly steady moderate popularity. Well-known bearers include hotelier Conrad Hilton and animal behaviorist Konrad Lorenz. Variant: **Konrad.** Diminutive: **Connie.**

CORDELL: (m) English; from a surname meaning "a little cord," possibly occupational in origin. The name has become fashionable in recent decades for unclear reasons. Cordell Hull was awarded the Nobel Peace Prize in 1945 for his work on the economic basis of world peace. Variant: **Kordell.**

DARWIN: (m) English; dear friend. This Anglo-Saxon given name survived as a surname and is most familiar as the surname of 19th-century naturalist Charles Darwin, whose observations of variation between species led to an understanding of the process of evolution. The name has been mildly popular over the last century, perhaps due in part to his influence.

DERICK: (m) Dutch; a diminutive of the Greek name THEODORIC by way of German Diederich (Chapter 7). The reasons for the names sudden fashion-ability in the late 19th century are unclear, but the name has been common enough to develop a multitude of variants. American popularity has some-what lagged that of England, with the latter peaking early in the 20th century and the former peaking around the '80s. Familiar bearers include actors Derek Jacobi and Dirk Bogarde. Variants: **Dedric, Dedrick, Darrick, Dereck, Derek, Deric, Derik, Derrick,** and **Dirk.**

EDGAR: (m) English; rich spear. This was a very popular name in the Anglo-Saxon period but in declining use through the Middle Ages. It was revived among Romanticists, occurring in 19th century novels like Charles Brockden Brown's *Edgar Huntly.* Edgar was quite popular coming into the 20th century and unlike many names of this type has retained that level of use fairly con-sistently to the present. Familiar examples include the authors Edgar Allan Poe and Edgar Rice Burroughs. One diminutive could be Ed, although this is more commonly associated with Edward.

EDMUND: (m) English; rich protection. This was the name of kings and saints of the Anglo-Saxon era, but like many such names it fell out of fashion in the later Medieval period, although never completely out of use. And, like many such names, it was revived for its Medieval associations in the 19th century. Well-known bearers include mountain climber Edmund Hillary and writer Edmund White. Variant: **Edmond.**

EDNA: (f) uncertain; a name of unknown origin and meaning appearing in the Biblical Apocrypha. Although it resembles many Anglo-Saxon names, this is coincidental. It was popularized through literary use in the 19th century, as in C.M. Yonge's novel *Hopes and Fears* and the pen name of novelist Edna Lyall. The name was wildly popular around the turn of the 20th century and has declined only slowly since then. Famous bearers include poet Edna St. Vincent Millay and novelist Edna Ferber.

ELECTA: (f) uncertain; possibly a variant of the Greek Electra, or possibly a learned name from the word "elect." This name had a very brief fashion in the late 19th century.

ELMER: (m) multiple origins; either from the Medieval French name Aylmer or from an Anglo-Saxon name Ethelmer. Another possibility is that it is a modification of Elmo, popularized in the late 19th century by Augusta Jane Evans' novel *St. Elmo.* American use may be influenced by an Elmer family prominent in the Revolutionary War. But all in all the 19th century popularity seems to come simply from a borrowing of surnames in general. Sinclair Lewis used it for the title character of his novel *Elmer Gantry.* A certain generation may associate it more closely with the cartoon character Elmer Fudd. The name was relatively popular in the early 20th century but has declined somewhat since then. Variant: **Elmore.**

ELSA: (f) German; a diminutive of ELIZABETH (Chapter 8). The use of this name in English derives most likely from its use for the bride of Lohengrin in Richard Wagner's opera on the topic. It has had a mild but declining popularity over the last century. One of the more familiar examples is the name of the lioness featured in Joy Adamson's book *Born Free.* Elsa is distinct in origin from another diminutive Elsie, which developed in Scotland and has been somewhat more popular. This name was used for the title character of Henry Wadsworth Longfellow's poem *Elsie Venner.* Variants: **Else, Elsie,** and **Elza.**

ELVIRA: (f) Spanish; from a Germanic root of unclear meaning. It may sometimes be an independent coinage, following names such as Elmira or Elvina. An Elvire appears in Moliere's 1665 play *Don Juan.* More recently, it has been associated with the stage character of TV movie hostess *Elvira, Mistress of the Dark,* which does not seem to have helped its popularity much. Variant: **Elvera.** Diminutives: **Elva, Elvia,** and **Elvie.**

EMIL: (m) German; from the Latin family name Aemilius, and so equivalent to EMILY (see later in this chapter). The name has been mildly popular in several variants. The German form is found in Erich Kästner's children's novel *Emil and the Detectives,* the French version is familiar from novelist Emile Zola, and the Spanish form is used by actor Emilio Estevez. Variants: **Emile, Emiliano,** and **Emilio.**

EMILY: (f) English; from the Latin family name Aemilius. The name became popular at first from literary use, as in Boccaccio and Chaucer, but it was not seriously taken up until the 19th century, in part substituting for AMELIA (Chapter 7). Also contributing to its popularity is the similarity to the unrelated names EMMA and EMMELINE. Towards the end of the 19th century it was enjoying some moderate popularity, only to decline towards the middle of the 20th century like most names of the same type. The surprise comes around the '70s when the name began climbing the charts again, bringing it currently to first place. Historic bearers include novelist Emily Brontë and poet Emily Dickinson. No doubt the current crop of Emilys will produce a few notable examples in their day. Variants: **Emely, Emilee, Emilia, Emilie,** and **Emmalee.** Diminutives: **Emmie,** and **Emmy.**

ERNESTINE: (f) English; a feminization of the German ERNEST (see earlier in this chapter). This is a development after the male name became popular. Ernestine was moderately popular around the turn of the 20th century and only declined in midcentury. One example is jazz singer Ernestine Anderson; however, the name may also bring to mind Lily Tomlin's comic character of Ernestine the phone operator. Variants: **Earnestine** and **Ernestina.**

ETHELENE: (f) English; possibly a development from Ethelind "noble serpent," influenced by the fashion for names ending in "-ine." The name has an unfortunate resemblance to the chemical name for ethylene gas. It had a mild popularity around the turn of the 20th century. Variant: **Ethelyn.**

EVERARD, EVERETT: (m) English; from Germanic roots meaning "hard as a boar." During the Middle Ages, Everard evolved into Everett and survived as a surname. Everett was revived as a given name in the late 19th century and remained moderately popular for much of the 20th century. Everardo has recently been flirting with the low end of the popularity charts. C. Everett Koop was Surgeon General of the U.S. during the Reagan administration. Another bearer was pre-Raphaelite painter John Everett Millais. Variants: **Everardo, Everette,** and **Evert.**

FRANCINE: (f) English; a variant of FRANCES (Chapter 8). This was a late development in the fashion for names ending in "-ine." It sees its greatest popularity in the mid–20th century.

GODFREY: (m) English; from Germanic roots meaning "peace of God." It enjoyed a brief revival around the turn of the 20th century, either from the surname or as a revival of the medieval given name. The name appears for the title character of the 1936 movie *My Man Godfrey.*

GUSTAVE: (m) German; meaning uncertain, although the second part is equivalent to "staff, stick." This name was popularized in part by the Protestant hero King Gustaf Adolf of Sweden, often known by the Latin form of his name, Gustavus Adolphus. It came into English popularity with the fashion for German names and survived the early 20th century primarily in the diminutive Gus, and the Spanish or Italian form Gustavo. Another familiar bearer is composer Gustav Mahler. Variants: **Gustav** and **Gustavo.** Diminutives: **Gus** and **Gust.**

HERBERT: (m) English; the name comes via French from Germanic roots meaning "famous army." It survived the Medieval period primarily as the surname of a noble family and from this context became popular again in the mid–19th century. It remained quite popular through the early 20th century and declined only slowly. U.S. president Herbert Hoover was born at the height of the fashion for this name. Variant: **Heriberto.** Diminutive: **Herb.**

HERMAN: (m) English; from Germanic roots meaning "army-man." This is another name popularized by the intersection of fashions for Medieval and German names. Well-known bearers include novelists Herman Melville and Herman Wouk. Variants: **Hermann, Herminio,** and **Hermon.**

HORACE: (m) Latin; from an old Roman family name, possibly based on a root meaning "hour, time." The name has had several waves of popularity. The popularity of the Roman poet known to later ages as Horace brought it to mind every time there was a fashion for classical names. Shakespeare used Horatio for a character in *Hamlet.* And for various of these associations it was picked up again in the 19th century, supported further by the popularity of Admiral Horatio Nelson. Further examples include educator Horace Mann, novelist Horatio Alger who gave his name to the genre of "poor boy makes good through hard work," and editor Horace Greeley (to whom is misattributed the exhortation, "Go west, young man!"). The name continued in moderate popularity through the first half of the 20th century but declined after that. Variant: **Horatio.**

HOWARD: (m) English; possibly the same origin as HAYWARD (Chapter 13). This was the name of a prominent family, and seems to have been turned into a given name for no reason beyond that. It was quite popular around the turn of the 20th century. The diminutive Howie has never quite caught on as an independent name. Well-known bearers include eccentric millionaire Howard Hughes.

HOWELL: (m) Welsh; uncertain in meaning, but the first part of the name means "good, well." This was a popular Medieval name in Wales, with the best known bearer being the 10th-century king Hywel Dda (the Good). In due time it became a surname, and the modern English use is from this.

IRVING: (m) English; a surname taken from a place name in Scotland. The name has come to be confused with Irwin or Erwin, which can be of either English or German origin and means "boar friend." The whole group of names show similar patterns of popularity, beginning in the later 19th century and remaining relatively popular throughout the 20th. Bearers include composer Irving Berlin and physicist Erwin Schrödinger. Variants: **Ervin, Erwin, Irvin,** and **Irwin.**

JEROME: (m) Greek; holy name, one who bears a holy name. The original Greek name was Hieronymos, and variants of this are also found. As it had been the name of an early saint, the name fell somewhat out of favor during the Reformation, but came back with the Victorian interest in Medieval-sounding names. It shows up for songwriter Jerome Kern and ballet dancer and choreographer Jerome Robbins. The original Greek form of the name is most familiar from Dutch Renaissance artist Hieronymous Bosch. Variant: **Hieronymus.**

JOANIE (f), **JOHNNY** (m): English; diminutives of JOHN (Chapter 8). While many variants of John and Joan have been popular over the centuries, the establishment of Johnny as an independent name belongs primarily to the 19th century. Like many diminutives of this type, it appears first as Johnnie and is overtaken by the spelling Johnny in the mid–20th century. For women, the corresponding diminutives are based on Joan. Familiar male examples include country music legend Johnny Cash, actor Johnny Depp, and football star Johnny Unitas. Female examples include folk singer Joni Mitchell. Variants: (both) **Jonnie, Johnie,** and **Johnnie;** (f) **Joni.**

JUDSON: (m) English; a surname based sometimes on the Biblical name JUDE (Chapter 4) or on a diminutive of JORDAN (Chapter 14). The name has been only mildly popular and came in with the general fashion for turning surnames in to given names.

LAFAYETTE: (m) French; a surname taken from a place name. The surname of the French Marquis de Lafayette who assisted the American side in the Revolution. Naturally, this did not lead to the name being as popular in England as in the U.S. It enjoyed a mild popularity well into the early 20th century.

LEOPOLD: (m) German; bold people. The name was popularized through several kings of Belgium, one of whom was the uncle of Queen Victoria. The name was also borne by the central character of James Joyce's *Ulysses*. Another familiar bearer was conductor Leopold Stowkowski. It fell somewhat out of fashion in the mid–20th century. Variant: **Leopoldo.**

LILLIAN: (f) English; a diminutive of ELIZABETH (Chapter 8). It shows up occasionally as early as the 16th century but became particularly popular in the 19th century, perhaps as a romantic name. Well-known bearers include actresses Lillian Russel and Lillian Gish, author Lillian Hellman, and presidential mother Lillian Carter. Variants: **Lilian, Liliana, Lilliana,** and **Lilyan.**

MAIDA: (f) Italian; a place name in southern Italy. One curious fashion of the 19th century was to name children after the sites of famous battles. The battle of Maida in 1806 was significant in the Napoleonic wars and led to the name being used for girls (the final "a" no doubt fixing it as a female rather than unisex name). The name still occurs occasionally in the early 20th century.

MARVIN: (m) Welsh; from an ancient name Merfyn, of uncertain meaning, that survived as a surname. It was taken up for use as part of the fashion for converted surnames and became quite popular in the later 19th century. The form Marvin has remained quite popular to the present. Well-known bearers have included fantasy novelist Mervyn Peake, actor Mervyn LeRoy, and singer Marvin Gaye. The usual diminutive is seen in the name of TV host Merv Griffin. Variants: **Mervin** and **Mervyn.** Diminutive: **Merv.**

MAURICE: (m) Latin; a person from Mauritania, a Moor. As the name of a saint, this was quite popular in the Middle Ages, shifting into the more English form Morris. It went out of fashion in the Reformation but was revived in the 19th century for its historic associations. Both variants of the name have remained quite popular throughout the 20th century, although fashions for the various diminutives have shifted. Well-known bearers include actor Maurice Chevalier, rock singer Maurice Gibb, and track star Maurice Green. Variants: **Mauricio** and **Morris.** Diminutives: **Maury** and **Moe.**

MOLLY: (f) English; a diminutive of MARY (Chapter 8). The same *r*-to-*l* shift is seen in Sally as a diminutive of Sarah. In 18th- and 19th-century literature, the name is generally associated with servants and other lower class characters and in particular had Irish associations. But in American use these considerations seem to have had no effect on its popularity. It has remained consistently popular over the last century, even increasing somewhat lately. A related diminutive is Polly, following the same substitution as you see in Peg for Meg. The name is found for actress Molly Ringwald, columnist Molly Ivins, and actress Polly Bergen. Variants: **Mallie** and **Mollie; Polly.**

MORTIMER: (m) French; a surname taken from a French place name. As the surname of a prominent family, this fell under the fashion for Medieval-sounding names. It was falling out of fashion in the early 20th century.

NAPOLEON: (m) French; a person from Naples. The name of French emperor Napoleon Bonaparte naturally did not endear itself to the English, but it found somewhat more sympathetic ground in America and continued in mild popularity through the early part of the 20th century. One familiar example is TV character Napoleon Solo of *The Man from U.N.C.L.E.*

NELL: (f) English; a diminutive of either ELLEN or ELEANOR (Chapter 8). The earliest prominent bearer of the name was Nell Gwyn, the mistress of Charles II in the 17th century. Like several other diminutives, it saw a fresh popularity in the 19th century as an independent name. Nell has its own diminutive, Nellie, which gained even more popularity than the original. Bearers include actress Nell Carter and Nelly Bly, the pseudonym of journalist Elizabeth Cochrane Seaman. Variants: **Nella, Nelle, Nellie,** and **Nelly.**

NORBERT: (m) French; from Germanic roots meaning "north-bright". The medieval Saint Norbert founded the Premonstratensian order. The name was mildly popular around the turn of the 20th century, most likely due to the general revival of medieval-sounding names.

NORINE: (f) Gaelic; a diminutive of NORA (Chapter 17). The same ending is seen in other Irish diminutives such as Maureen. The name was mildly popular in the early 20th century but has declined since then. Variants: **Noreen** and **Norene.**

NORRIS: (m) French; a northerner. This became a prominent English surname, from which the given name use is taken. It remained popular through much of the 20th century.

ORA: (f, m) uncertain; possibly from a Latin word meaning "pray," especially from the phrase *ora pro nobis* "pray for us," found regularly in liturgy. If this origin is correct, it would explain the curious use of this feminine-looking name for both men and women, although it has been more common for the latter. Oralia may be a related name. Variants: (f) **Oralia.**

ORVILLE: (m) French; a surname taken from a place name. The surname occurs in Fanny Burney's 1778 novel *Evelina* and may in fact have been invented by her for that use. Aviation pioneer Orville Wright may also have helped popularize the name, and it stays on the charts well past the mid–20th century. Variants: **Orval** and **Orvil.**

RHETA: (f) Greek; possibly from a root meaning "orator, speaker." The name appears in the 19th century and was mildly popular through the first half of the 20th century. Bearers include journalist Rheta Dorr. Variants: **Reta, Retha,** and **Retta.**

RODERICK: (m) multiple origins; the name is primarily from a Germanic name meaning "famous-rule," but it is also sometimes found as a rendering of the Welsh name Rhydderch. Roderick became associated strongly with Scotland, at least partly due to Walter Scott's *Lady of the Lake.* A Spanish form of the name, Rodrigo, also has literary associations, being the name of Medieval hero Rodrigo Diaz de Vivar, known as El Cid. Broderick is also derived from this name, coming from the Welsh "ap Roderick" (son of Roderick). An example of that name is actor Broderick Crawford. Variants: **Broderick, Rodrick,** and **Rodrigo.**

ROSALIA: (f) coined; from the root ROSE (Chapter 12). This is one of a number of variants of the name Rose which are only related by their connection to that name. Rosalia has evolved an association with the element "lee," developing variants such as Rosalee and Rosaleigh. Variants: **Rosella, Rosetta, Rozella, Rosalee, Rosaleigh,** and **Rosalie.**

RUDOLPH: (m) German; famous wolf. This is one of the names popularized in the 19th century by the fashion for German things. Various forms of the name have been mildly popular throughout the last century. Familiar from legendary silent-movie actor Rudolph Valentino. Variants: **Rodolfo** and **Rudolf.** Diminutive: **Rudy.**

Why did people start using surnames for first names?

In Medieval times, there was a clear distinction between the set of names used as given names and the sort of thing that could be used as a surname. (In some cultures today, there is still a fairly strict distinction.) So how did it get to current practice, where surnames can be turned into given names at the drop of a hat?

Inheritance was one reason. Historically, there has been a strong connection in people's minds between a family inheritance (especially of land) and the family name. So sometimes when a child would be inheriting land associated with a different surname, he would be given that surname for a first name to show the connection. An early example is Warham St. Leger, whose mother was heiress of the Warham family.

Another reason was simply to introduce new names into use. The practice of naming children after godparents, combined with an emphasis on a small number of extremely popular names, meant that there were a lot of people running around named Elizabeth, Anne, or Margaret, and John, Thomas, or William. (There were several centuries in England when one in every five men was named John.) So, one way to name a child after a godparent and yet use a new name was to use the godparent's surname.

More recently, surnames have crept into use as given names by way of being middle names. Once the idea of middle names became established and people were using them both as a second first name and to include a second surname, it was only natural for names to cross the boundary that way.

SADIE: (f) English; a diminutive of SARAH (Chapter 4). This was moderately popular beginning in the late 19th century. One of the interesting associations is with "Sadie Hawkins Day," an occasion invented by Al Capp in the context of the *L'il Abner* comic strip, on which women were supposed to take the initiative in courting (a somewhat dated event). Variant: **Sadye.**

SHERMAN: (m) English; shearer, one who shears sheep. In the context of turning surnames into given names, the particular impetus for this name owes a certain amount to the Civil War's General Sherman. The name remained popular through the early part of the 20th century but has declined since then.

SIDNEY: (f, m) English; a wide marshy ground. This is taken from the surname of the prominent Sidney family. In the case of feminine use, there may also be contributions from an unrelated Medieval name Sidony, from a word meaning "shroud," specifically in reference to the shroud of Christ. While the popular wisdom is that the spelling Sidney versus Sydney distinguishes between male and female use respectively, the statistics show this to be nonsense in historic terms, with both spellings being used by both genders when the name first comes into use. But prescription from baby name books may have turned the myth into reality, as the spelling Sydney dropped out of male use in the mid–20th century and becoming much the preferred form for girls around the same time. Well-known bearers include actor Sidney Poitier on the male side and actress Cyd Charisse on the female side. Variants: (f) **Cydney, Sydnee, Sydney, Sydni,** and **Sydnie;** (m) **Sydney.** Diminutives: (both) **Sid;** (f) **Cyd.**

SPENSER: (m) English; dispenser, steward. The name is taken from the surname of a prominent English family. One influence on its popularity was its use in the Churchill family, but it had been in common use before that. It has been increasing steadily, if slowly, in popularity over the last century. One bearer is actor Spencer Tracy. Variant: **Spencer.**

TESS: (f) English; a diminutive of THERESA (Chapter 10). Like many other diminutives, this became established as an independent name in the 19th century, especially through literary use as for the title character of Thomas Hardy's novel *Tess of the D'Urbervilles*. It had fallen out of fashion except in the form Tessie by the early 20th century but has recently been making a comeback. Variants: **Tessa** and **Tessie.**

VICTORIA: (f) Latin; victory. The name came into English use via Queen Victoria, who was named after her German mother. Despite the length and influence of her reign (or perhaps because of it) the name did not become as popular as one might expect in her lifetime. In American use, it began the 20th century at a modestly high level, but has only made it up around the top 20 in the last decade or so. For diminutives it has an assortment of spellings of Vicky, whose greatest popularity centered around the '50s. The aristocratic associations of the name have made it popular for theater, including soap opera character Victoria Lord and actress Victoria Principal, as well as the character of Victoria Winters on the long-running serial *Dark Shadows*. Diminutives: **Vickey, Vicki, Vickie, Vicky** and **Vikki.**

WENDELL: (m) English; from the Germanic tribal name Wend. The name Windell may instead by an unrelated surname meaning "wind hill." This name was moderately popular through much of the 20th century, peaking in the '40s. One notable bearer was jurist Oliver Wendell Holmes. Variant: **Windell.**

WILBUR: (m) English; multiple origins: an Anglo-Saxon name meaning "bright will" or a nickname meaning "wild boar." One source of popularity for this name was aviation pioneer Wilbur Wright, but it had been in relatively common use before that. Variants: **Wilber** and **Wilbert.**

WINIFRED: (f) Welsh; meaning uncertain although it includes an element meaning "white." The form Winifred has been influenced by Anglo-Saxon names, and the Welsh form of Saint Winifred's name appears as Gwenfrewi. Like many Medieval-sounding names, this was popularized by the 19th century Romantics. It appears for a major character in John Glasworthy's *The Forsyte Saga* and was borne by social activist Winifred Holt. The usual diminutive is Winnie, familiar from the name of South African political activist Winnie Mandela. Variant: **Winnifred.** Diminutive: **Winnie.**

ZELLA: (f) uncertain; possibly a variant of Zelda (see GRISELDA, Chapter 8). This is supported by examples like film writer Zelda Young who sometimes used Zella Young. This name was moderately popular around the turn of the 20th century.

Chapter 10

Coming Up to Date: Names of the 20th Century

In This Chapter

▶ Exploring the popular names of the different decades

▶ Tracing modern fashions in naming

▶ Watching the development of a current name landscape

*T*his chapter presents, not necessarily the most popular names of each era, but names that are in some way characteristic of their time. Some are diminutives that made their mark as independent names in this century. Some are names that, for reasons known or unknown, shot up the charts at this time, even if they didn't make the top ranks. Some are names that represent a more general fashion or trend. In general, unless otherwise noted, the names included here were most popular only in the period where they are listed.

Bringing in the New Century: The First Three Decades

When you look at the ways in which popular names of the 1900s to 1920s distinguish themselves from following decades, you find a number of names clearly German in origin: Adolph, Emil, Gustav, Herman, Meyer, Otto. The wars with Germany had not yet made it desirable to shift to more "American" sounding names. Names popular among Jewish immigrants from central Europe are also prominent: Abe, Hyman, Isadore, Murray, Sol. Many girls are given diminutives ending in "-ie": Addie, Effie, Essie, Flossie, Goldie, Lizzie, Lottie, Nannie, Nettie, Ollie. And for some reason, the initial "E" is popular among girls' names: Edna, Elizabeth, Estelle, Ethel, Eula.

ADDY: (f) English; a diminutive of Adeline, Adele or similar names. Variant: **Addie.**

ARLEY: (f, m) English; eagle wood. The name may also come from other sources, as for baseball player Arlie Latham (born Walter Arlington Latham). A female bearer is sociologist Arlie Hochschild. Variant: **Arlie.**

BOYD: (m) multiple origins; a surname, either from the Scottish place name Bute (meaning uncertain), or from Gaelic *buidhe* "yellow-haired."

CLARE: (m) English; from the surname of multiple origins: either from the feminine name CLARA (Chapter 8), an occupation "clayer, plasterer," or the place name Clare (meaning uncertain). While the feminine name has long been popular, use as a masculine name is more limited. Variants: **Clair** and **Claire.**

CLAUDE: (m) French; from the Latin name Claudius, "lame," equivalent to the feminine CLAUDIA (Chapter 7). The name has had a long run of popularity in recent times. One bearer is actor Claude Rains. Variants: **Claud, Claudie,** and **Claudio.**

CYRIL: (m) Greek; Lord, master. While long popular in the Eastern Orthodox church, this name has been less popular in the usual sources for American names, although an early literary example is Kyrle Daly in Gerald Griffin's 1828 *The Collegians.* Variant: **Kyrle.**

EILEEN: (f) English; a variant of ELLEN (Chapter 8), possibly by way of Gaelic Eibhlin, but it may also be influenced by the common feminine name ending "-ine." Eileen and Aileen have been popular throughout the century and some variants have only shown up very recently. One bearer is actress Eileen Brennan. Variants: **Aileen, Aleen, Alena, Alene, Alina, Aline, Aliene,** and **Alline.**

ESTELLE: (f) French; star. This may possibly be a holdover from the romantic movement of the late 19th century. The name is borne by actress Estelle Parsons. Rarely, a masculine variant Estel may be found. Variants: (f) **Estela, Estell, Estella,** and **Estrella.**

ETHEL: (f) English; a diminutive of various old English names such as Ethelburg or Ethelinda, popularized by the romantic revival. Prominent bearers have included actress Ethel Merman, TV character Ethel Mertz on *I Love Lucy,* and political wife Ethel Kennedy. Variant: **Ethyl.**

EULA: (f) English; a diminutive of EULALIA (Chapter 7). The name may also be influenced by (or a diminutive of) BEULAH (Chapter 9). Variant: **Eulah.**

EUPHEMIA: (f) Greek; good speech. The full name is less common than its diminutive EFFIE (Chapter 11) but is found for mathematician and educator Euphemia Haynes.

GLADYS: (f) Welsh; origin uncertain, but sometimes thought to be from Latin CLAUDIA (Chapter 7). The late 19th century in Britain and Ireland saw a revival of interest in older names from Celtic cultures, and through most of the 20th century these waves of interest have washed up on American shores. Gladys made it into the top-20 names and has only gradually fallen from favor. One notable bearer is singer Gladys Knight. Variant: **Gladyce.**

HERSHEL: (m) German; little stag. This name is commonly associated with Jewish immigrants from Germany. Examples come from TV director Hershel Daugherty and football player Herschel Walker. Variant: **Herschel.**

HYMAN: (m) Hebrew; life, a variant of CHAIM (Chapter 15). Admiral Hyman G. Rickover has been called the "father of the nuclear navy."

IVA: (f) multiple origins; there is a Biblical place name Ivah, and an obscure Cornish martyr Iva, but the Slavic context of many modern examples of this name suggest that it's most commonly being used as a diminutive of Ivana (see JOAN in Chapter 8). Variant: **Ivah.**

LIBBY: (f) English; a diminutive of ELIZABETH (Chapter 8). Although often used as a diminutive by those formally named Elizabeth, this name had a slight run as an independent name. One bearer is champion dogsled racer Libby Riddles. Variant: **Libbie.**

LOTTIE: (f) English or German; a diminutive of CHARLOTTE (Chapter 9). The most famous bearer may be German singer and actress Lotte Lenya.

MAE: (f) English; a diminutive of MARY (Chapter 8). It is often used in compounds (see Chapter 11), but also as an independent name, as for actress Mae West.

MURPHY: (m) Gaelic; sea warrior. This is generally taken from the surname O'Murphy, and the popularity of the name is a consequence of the wave of Irish immigration at the turn of the 20th century. Variants: **Murray** and **Murry.**

NETTIE: (f) English; a diminutive of various names such as ANNETTTE, JEAN-NETTE, and so on. One bearer is geneticist Nettie Stevens. Variant: **Neta.**

WILHELMINA: (f) German; a feminine variant of WILLIAM (Chapter 8). Like many clearly German-sounding names, this fell out of favor during the early decades of the century, despite the immense popularity during the same period of Queen Wilhelmina of the Netherlands. Variants: **Wilhelmine, Willene.** Diminutive: **Mina.**

Names with a Bullet

Some names seem to come out of nowhere and shoot to the top of the charts. The following names have shown a major increase in popularity between the 1990s and the present. Two of these may be the "Jennifer and Jason" of the current decade. Go with the crowd or avoid like the plague? The fashion in sound for boys' names is clear: anything that rhymes with "-ayden." There's more variety among the girls.

Boys: Aidan, Aiden, Caden, Kaden, Jaden, Jayden, Malachi, Brayden, Carson, and Owen

Girls: Trinity, Ava, Ella, Avery, Sophia, Aaliyah, and Lily

Inventing Nostalgia: Midcentury Names

The '30s through '50s show a culture on the cusp of major changes. While old naming fashions started to fall away, the new ones were largely variants on tradition rather than the major break that happened in the '60s and '70s. This period, in many ways, shaped ideas about "ordinary" names.

For boys, you see a rising interest in short, one-syllable names: Bill, Bob, Brad, Don, Gene, Greg, Kim, Kirk, Mark, Rick, and Todd. Diminutives of traditional names such as James, Richard, Robert, and William become more prominent, and there seems to be a sound-fashion for two-syllable names with "r" in the middle, such as Barry, Darryl, Garry, Jerry, and Larry. Short names also become fashionable for girls, such as Jane, Jo, Joan, June, Kim, and Sue, as do names beginning with either "sh" or "p," including Sharon, Sheila, Sherry, Shirley; Pamela, Patricia, Paula, and Peggy. And in this period, girls start enjoying a larger variety of available names than before.

ANITA: (f) Spanish; a diminutive of ANNE (Chapter 8). A number of Spanish names began showing up in mainstream use at this time. One bearer is R&B singer Anita Baker.

AUDIE: (f, m) English; multiple possible origins: a diminutive of various names beginning with "Aud-" such as Auden or Audley; or by some suggestions a variant of Eddie. This name was popularized by World War II hero Audie Murphy.

BETH, BETTY: (f) English; a diminutive of ELIZABETH (Chapter 8). While these forms have long been used as informal diminutives, for a brief period in mid century, Betty surpassed the full name in the charts. Variants: **Betsy, Bettie, Betty,** and **Bettye.**

BILLY: (m) English; a diminutive of WILLIAM (Chapter 8). While these names have long been in use as informal diminutives, their period of greatest popularity as independent names came in mid century. Some men who go by these diminutives include jockey Bill Shoemaker, singer-songwriter Billy Joel, and actor Billy Crystal. Billie may also be used by women, as for singer Billie Holiday. Variants: (both) **Billie;** (m) **Bill.**

BOBBY: (f, m) English; a diminutive of ROBERT (Chapter 8). As with BILLY (see above), these diminutives have their greatest independence at this period, and you commonly find men using them as formal names (whether given at birth or not), for example, actor Bob Newhart, musician Bob Marley, chess champion Bobby Fisher, hockey star Bobby Orr, actor Rob Reiner. The feminine name Roberta also comes seriously on the scene at this time, as for singer Roberta Flack, and Bobbie may be used for girls as an independent name. Variants: (both) **Bobbie, Bobby, Robbie;** (f) **Bobbi, Bobbye,** and **Roberta;** (m) **Bob, Rob, Robb,** and **Robby.**

BRIAN: (m) multiple origins; high, noble. While most commonly thought of as Irish, recalling the 10th-century king Brian Boru, the popularity of the name in English traces historically to a related Breton name brought over by followers of William the Conqueror. Some current use may be from the transfer of surnames like Bryan and Bryant. This name comes at the intersection of several fashions: The beginning interest in "Celtic" names, and as a precursor for the fad for names beginning in "Br-." Well-known bearers include Olympic ice skater Brian Boitano and actor Brian Keith. Variants: **Brayan, Brien, Bryan, Bryant,** and **Bryon.**

CAROLYN: (f) English; a variant of CAROLINE (Chapter 14). This name may have begun simply as a variant of Caroline, but it quickly developed its own pronunciation and forged its own path, making it into the top-20 names in the '40s. Another variant of Caroline that became popular at this time is the French-sounding Charlene. Familiar bearers include the actresses Carolyn Jones and Charlene Tilton. Variants: **Carleen, Carlene, Carolynn, Charleen, Charlene, Charline, Karlene, Karolyn,** and **Sharlene.**

CHAD: (m) English; from the Anglo Saxon personal name Ceadda, of uncertain meaning. The revival of this name is something of a mystery, but it fit with the fashion for one-syllable names. A popular folk music group of the period is the Chad Mitchell trio. Chad may sometimes be used as a diminutive of Chadwick, from a surname meaning "Chad's farm." Variants: **Chadd, Shad, Chadrick,** and **Chadwick.**

CHERYL: (f) English; a variant possibly of CHERIE (Chapter 17). This name explodes on the scene with a number of variants and then falls out of fashion almost as quickly. Bearers include actress Cheryl Ladd and basketball player Sheryl Swoopes. Variants: **Cheryle, Sherrill, Sherryl,** and **Sheryl.**

COLLEEN: (f) Gaelic; a young girl. Despite the Gaelic origins, this is a purely American name and in Ireland is considered the equivalent of naming your daughter "Girl." One bearer is actress Colleen Dewhurst. Variant: **Coleen.**

DANNY: (m) English; a diminutive of DANIEL (Chapter 4). Like BOBBY and BILLY (see above), this diminutive came into its own in mid century. Memorable bearers include actors Danny Thomas and Danny DeVito. Variant: **Dannie.**

DARLA, DARLENE: (f) English; possibly from the word "darling," although possibly influenced by names like Charlene. The name is borne by child actress and singer Darla Hood and the character of Darlene Conner on the TV show *Roseanne*. Variants: **Darleen** and **Darline.**

DARYL: (f, m) French; from Airelle, a place in France, taken from the surname. This name benefited from the fashion for names with an "r" in the middle. Baseball player Darryl Strawberry is one example, and more recently the name has been taken up by women, such as actress Daryl Hannah. Variants: (m) **Darell, Darrel, Darrell, Derrell, Darryl,** and **Daryle.**

DEBBY: (f) English; a diminutive of DEBORAH (Chapter 4). The fashion for using the diminutive as an independent name was relatively brief, making it closely linked with a specific era. Notable bearers include actress Debbie Reynolds and U.S. senator Debbie Stabenow. Variants: **Debbi, Debbie,** and **Debi.**

DONALD: (m) Gaelic; world-strong. This is one of a handful of names brought by Scottish immigrants that became wildly popular (Kenneth is another). While it may have had some boost in the late 19th century by romantic writers such as Walter Scott, the name soars up into the top ten in mid century purely on its own merits. Notable bearers include actor Donald Sutherland, songwriter Don McLean, and rich guy Donald Trump. Variants: **Donal, Donell,** and **Donnell.** Diminutives: **Don, Donn, Donnie,** and **Donny.**

HARLAN: (m) English; boundary woods. There is also a group of variants of this name without the initial "H," some of which may be from the same origin. In general, all these names are taken from surnames. Bearers include science fiction author Harlan Ellison and Pennsylvania senator Arlen Specter. Variants: **Harland, Harlen, Arlen,** and **Arlin.**

JIMMIE: (f, m) English; a diminutive of JAMES (Chapter 9). While this group of diminutives remained popular over a long period, they peaked in mid century. Most likely it is the common use of Jim and Jimmy by prominent people named James that encouraged parents to use the short forms independently. Some of those prominent bearers include U.S. president Jimmy Carter, musician Jimi Hendrix, and comedian Jim Carrey. Jimmie also hits the charts as a woman's name. Variants: (m) **Jim, Jimi,** and **Jimmy.**

JACKIE: (f, m) English; a diminutive of JACK (Chapter 8) or JACQUELINE. Familiar bearers include baseball great Jackie Robinson, comic actor Jackie Gleason, and on the women's side, track star Jackie Joyner-Kersey. Variant: (m) **Jacky.**

JACQUELINE: (f) French; a feminine diminutive of Jacques, that is, JAMES (Chapter 9). While English produced some homegrown feminine forms of this name, like Jamesina, only Jacqueline has developed any real popularity over an extended period of time. Some prominent bearers are Jacqueline Kennedy-Onassis and actresses Jaclyn Smith and Jacqueline Bisset. Variants: **Jacalyn, Jackeline, Jacklyn, Jaclyn, Jacquelin, Jacquelyn, Jacquline, Jaquelin,** and **Jaqueline.**

JAN, JANE: (f) English; a variant of JOAN (Chapter 8). Jane had been a popular variant since the Medieval period, but Jan is a new development at this point. Starting a few decades later, Jana and its variants join the scene. Famous bearers have included novelist Jane Austen, actresses Jane Wyman and Jane Fonda, and mystery writer Jan Burke. Variants: **Jann, Jayne, Jana, Janae, Janay,** and **Janna.**

JO: (f) English; a diminutive of JOSEPHINE (Chapter 9), or directly from masculine JOE, but perhaps sometimes from JOAN (Chapter 8). Whatever its origins in individual cases, Jo has an extended run as an independent name in mid century, producing bearers such as science fiction author Jo Clayton.

KAREN (f) Danish, **KATHY** (f): English; a diminutive of KATHERINE (Chapter 8). The full name had long been a staple of the top-ranked names, but in mid century a profusion of diminutives found a place on the charts, with Karen making it into the top ten for two decades. Some familiar bearers are Olympic gymnast Cathy Rigby, golfer Kathy Whitworth, actresses Kathy Bates and Karen Black, and Danish author Karen Blixen (better know as Isak Dinesen). Variants: **Cathey, Cathi, Cathie, Cathy, Kathi,** and **Kathie; Caren, Caron, Caryn, Karan, Karin, Karina, Karon, Karren,** and **Karyn.**

KENNETH: (m) uncertain; the name comes via Gaelic but may be Pictish in origin, of unknown meaning. Kenneth had become popular in the later 19th century due to Scottish immigrants, but it spread to more general use and reached its peak in the mid–20th century with four decades in the top 20. The range of forms can be seen for actor Kenneth Branagh, economist John Kenneth Galbraith, country singer Kenny Rogers, and novelist Ken Follett. Variant: **Kennith.** Diminutives: **Ken, Kenney,** and **Kenny.**

KIRK: (m) English; church, from a Scottish variant of the word. This name fits the fashion for sharp, one-syllable names for boys, but it seems to have been given a boost in the '40s and '50s by actor Kirk Douglas.

LINDA: (f) multiple origins; sometimes from Spanish *linda* "beautiful," but sometimes a diminutive of names such as ROSALIND (Chapter 6). This name had been mildly popular since the beginning of the century, but it shot up to spend two decades in the number 2 spot in mid century producing bearers such as singer Linda Ronstadt and actress Linda Hamilton. Variants: **Lindy** and **Lynda.**

MARCIA: (f) Latin; belonging to Mars, the god of war. This is a feminine equivalent of Marcius, related to Marcus. Marcia had been in use for some time, but it hit its peak in the '40s and produced several variants. The TV character Marcia Brady (of *The Brady Bunch*) reflects the name's popularity at this time (in fact, all the names from that show reflect the prevailing fashions closely). Another bearer is astronaut Marsha S. Ivins. Variants: **Marci, Marcie, Marcy,** and **Marsha.**

MAUREEN: (f) Gaelic; a diminutive of MARY (Chapter 8). This is one of a number of Irish names that gained a much wider popularity at various points. Bearers include actress Maureen O'Hara and tennis pro Maureen Connolly. Variants: **Marina** and **Maurine.**

NANCY: (f) English; a diminutive of ANNE (Chapter 8). Alternate theories make this a diminutive of AGNES (Chapter 8). It had been mildly popular for centuries, but climbed up to spend several decades in the top ten in mid century. Notable bearers include fictional teenage detective Nancy Drew, golfer Nancy Lopez, singer Nancy Griffith, and actress Nanette Fabray. Variants: **Nan, Nanci, Nancie, Nanette, Nannette,** and **Nannie.**

PATRICIA (f), **PATRICK** (m): Latin; a patrician, a noble person. Saint Patrick having been of somewhat restricted interest in the Middle Ages, this name didn't make it high in the ranks at that time. But the growing interest in Irish names moved Patrick up to a relatively high level in mid century and Patricia caught people's fancy enough to spend four decades in the top ten. Pat and Patty have been used as diminutives for both sexes, although Patty has come to be considered exclusively female. Well-known bearers have included, on the men's side, Revolutionary hero Patrick Henry, historical novelist Patrick O'Brian, and guitarist Pat Donohue, and on the women's side, mystery novelist Patricia Cornwell, actress Patty Duke, and singers Pat Benatar and Trisha Yearwood. Variants: (f) **Patrica** and **Patrice.** Diminutives: (both) **Pat;** (f) **Patti, Pattie, Patty, Tricia, Trisha,** and **Tisha.**

PAULA: (f) Latin; small; a feminine version of PAUL (Chapter 4). In the 19th century, the favorite feminine form of Paul was Pauline, but Paula took its place in the early 20th century. Current bearers include singer Paula Abdul and comedian Paula Poundstone. Variant: **Paola.**

RANDOLPH: (m) English; from multiple sources, either a Norse name meaning "shield-wolf" or a German name meaning "raven-wolf." In Medieval times, the form RANDAL (Chapter 8) was more popular, but the Victorian romantic revival preferred Randolph. Bearers include actor Randolph Scott.

RANDY: (f, m) English; a diminutive of RANDOLPH (see above). When the diminutive Randy began showing up on the charts in the mid–20th century, it rapidly surpassed the full name. Male bearers include songwriter Randy Newman and country singer Randy Travis. As a woman's name, it may be a borrowing of the male name or may be a diminutive of MIRANDA (Chapter 6) or some similar name. Variant: (f) **Randi.**

RICKI: (f, m) English; a diminutive of RICHARD (Chapter 8). Before the mid–20th century, the most common diminutives of Richard were based on Dick, but starting in mid century a variety of forms of Rick and Ricky become popular, as for early TV heartthrob Ricky Nelson. There may be other sources for these names; baseball player Richie Sexson's original name was Richmond. Ricki is sometimes used as a feminine name, usually taken directly from male use, although it may sometimes be a diminutive for Richenda or similar names. One example is actress Ricki Lake. Variants: (f) **Rikki;** (m) **Rich, Richie, Rick, Rickey, Ricki, Rickie, Ricky, Rico,** and **Ritchie.**

RONALD: (m) English; from Norse roots meaning "strong force." This comes from the same roots as REYNOLD (Chapter 8) and REGINALD (Chapter 19). Ronald is associated with Scotland and may have benefited from a general interest in Irish and Scottish names. Well-known bearers have included U.S. president Ronald Reagan and TV actor and director Ron (Ronny) Howard. Variant: **Ronaldo.** Diminutives: **Ron, Ronnie,** and **Ronny.**

SANDY: (f, m) English; a diminutive of ALEXANDER (Chapter 6) or ALEXANDRA (Chapter 9). Both names are relative newcomers to the popularity charts in the 20th century and see their greatest interest in mid century. Male use of Sandy has always been rare. Female examples of the name and the related diminutive Sandra include actresses Sandra Bernhard, Sandra Bullock, and Sondra Locke, and British pop singer Sandy Denny. Variants: (f) **Sandi, Sandra, Saundra,** and **Sondra.**

SHARON: (f) Hebrew?; a Biblical place name. The name seems to have been borrowed from the phrase "rose of Sharon" in the Song of Solomon, and there are rare examples of that entire phrase being used as a name. For mysterious reasons, the name caught people's interest enough that it rose form obscurity to the top ten in the space of two decades. Bearers include actress Sharon Stone and historic novelist Sharon Kay Penman. Variants: **Sharen, Sharron, Sharyn, Sheron,** and **Sherron.**

SHEILA: (f) Gaelic; a variant of CECILIA (Chapter 17). Just as Shawn represents the name John processed through Gaelic pronunciation, Sheila results from Cecilia undergoing the same transformation. It rapidly became popular in a short period after first making the charts. One bearer is drummer and singer Sheila Escovedo. Variants: **Shelia, Shiela, Shayla,** and **Sheyla.**

STANLEY: (m) English; stone meadow. This surname was taken up as a given name in the 19th century and increased steadily in popularity until the mid 20th. It seems to have become fashionable on its own merits rather than from any significant namesakes. Notable bearers have included film director Stanley Kubrick and musician Stan Getz. Diminutive: **Stan.**

THERESA: (f) Spanish; meaning uncertain, but possibly from a Greek word meaning "woman from Thera." Saint Teresa of Avila became popular after the Reformation — the wrong time to directly influence English naming. But she provided an indirect inspiration through the use of the name in Catholic countries. A growing interest in Spanish names also contributed to the name's rise to just short of the top 20 in mid century, and it gave rise to a wide variety of diminutives at that period. A famous recent bearer is humanitarian Mother Theresa. Variants: **Teresa, Terese, Teresita, Teressa, Therese,** and **Theresia.** Diminutives: **Tresa, Tressa, Tressie; Teri, Terra, Terri, Terrie,** and **Terry.**

TINA: (f) English; a diminutive of various names ending in "-tina," especially CHRISTINA (Chapter 8). Tina had been used as an independent name for some time but enjoyed its greatest popularity in mid century. Singer Tina Turner is one well-known bearer. Variants: **Teena** and **Tena.**

WANDA: (f) German; possibly "stem, stock" and related to the tribal name of the Vandals. It had been used rarely since the 19th century but became particularly fashionable starting around the '30s. One example is rockabilly musician Wanda Jackson.

Exploding Tradition: The '60s and Their Aftermath

We tend to think of the '60s as signaling the shift in naming from "traditional" to "innovative," although the change shows up most strongly in the '70s. The fashion for short, compact names for boys continues (Brett, Brian, Cory, Eric, Ian, Kyle, Ryan, Seth), and you see the rise of groups of unrelated names that share certain sound patterns, such as the Brian/Brandon group and the Darren group. Girls see an increasing popularity of flowery three-syllable names (Amanda, Angela, Jennifer, Kimberly, Melissa, Samantha, Stephanie, Vanessa) as well as a fashion for names beginning with "T-" (Tammy, Tanya, and Tracey).

ALEX: (f, m) English; a diminutive of ALEXANDER (Chapter 6) or ALEXANDRA (Chapter 9). Alex had long been relatively popular for boys, but it reached a peak during this period and this is also when you see it appear most commonly for girls. One well-known bearer is author Alex Haley of *Roots.*

ANGELA: (f) Latin; an angel, from a Greek word meaning "messenger." This name may have benefited from a growing interest in Spanish names. Angela rose quickly into the top ten during this period, but has fallen back to only mild interest. One familiar bearer is actress Angela Lansbury. Variant: **Angelia.**

BARRETT: (m) uncertain; either from a Middle English word meaning "trouble, strife," or possibly a French occupation "cap maker, beret-maker." Although never particularly common, it begins showing up at this period as part of the fashion for "Br" names.

BRANT: (m) Norse; sword; fire-brand. This was taken up from the surname as part of the fashion for "Br" names, in contrast to the majority of surname-derived names which date back to the 19th century. One bearer is actor Brant von Hoffman. Variants: **Brandt** and **Brent.**

BRANDON: (m) English; broom hill; or hill by the river Brant. The variants of this name overlap with those for BRENDAN (Chapter 5) and today the two can be considered to have blended into a single name group. This name did not appear on the charts before the '50s but rapidly rose to spend two decades in the top 20. More recently it got a boost in popularity from the TV character Brandon Walsh on *Beverly Hills 90210.* Variants: **Branden** and **Brandyn.**

CARRIE (f), **KERRY** (f, m): English; Carrie is a diminutive of CAROLINE (Chapter 14), but some variants may have other origins, such as Kerry from the Irish place name, or Carey from the English place name. Bearers have included actresses Carrie Fisher and Keri Russell, and Olympic gymnast Kerri Strug. Variants: (f) **Carey, Cari, Carie, Carri, Cary, Kari, Karie, Karri, Karrie, Keri, Kerri,** and **Kerrie.**

CARLA: (f) Spanish; a feminine form of CARL (Chapter 8), or in some variants, of Charlene or Charlotte. One bearer is actress Carla Gugino. Variants: **Charla, Karla,** and **Sharla.**

COREY: (m) Norse; possibly "curly" or "bent, curved." A moderately popular name that did not appear on the charts before the second half of the century. Actor Corey Feldman is one example. Variants: **Cory, Korey,** and **Kory.**

COURTNEY: (f, m) French; place belonging to a man named Curt. Sometimes a name seems to come out of nowhere and head for the top of the charts for no obvious reason. Courtney is one of those, showing up first as a boy's name, but soon taken over by the girls. The most familiar examples are all female, such as actress Courteney Cox and Olympic gymnast Courtney Kupets. Variants: (both) **Cortney;** (f) **Courteney, Kortney,** and **Kourtney.**

DARIAN: (f, m) Latin a derivative of DARIUS (Chapter 7). Variants of this name blend into DARREN (see below) to some extent. Variants: (f) **Daria** and **Dariana;** (m) **Darien, Darion, Darrian, Darrien,** and **Darrion.**

DARREN: (m) Gaelic; great, large, from the surname Ó Dearáin. Despite the specific origin, the great variety of spellings suggest that this name also belongs to the "three consonant" pattern of invented names discussed under JADEN (Chapter 11). Memorable bearers include singer-songwriter Darren Hayes and TV character Darrin Stephens from *Bewitched.* Variants: **Daren, Darin, Daron, Darrin, Darron,** and **Deron.**

DEVON: (f, m) multiple origins; Devon is from the Brythonic tribal name Dumnonii, which meant something like "the world," while Davin is from a Gaelic root meaning "a deer or ox." The two names are in the process of merging and, like DARREN, the range of spelling variants suggests that this name is being treated in the "three consonant" invented name pattern (see under JADEN in Chapter 11). Variants: (both) **Devan, Devin,** and **Devyn;** (m) **Davin, Davion,** and **Deven.**

IAN: (m) Gaelic; a variant of JOHN (Chapter 8). This became popularized as a Scottish form of John, as part of the general interest in Scottish and Irish names (see also SEAN below). Well-known bearers include author Ian Fleming, the creator of James Bond, actor Ian McKellen, and Olympic swimmer Ian Thorpe.

JARED: (m) Hebrew; descent, descended. In the Bible, this is the name of Methuselah's grandfather. Although the name shows up very occasionally as part of the Biblical revivals, it doesn't show up on the popularity charts until the '60s and then explodes into a large number of variants. This timing suggests there may have been some influence from the character of Jarrod Barkley on the popular TV western *The Big Valley* (a show that also seems to have popularized the name Heath). Variants: **Jaret, Jarett, Jarod, Jarred, Jarrod, Jerad, Jered, Jerod,** and **Jerrod.**

JENNIFER: (f) English; a variant of GUINEVERE (Chapter 6). For no clear reason, Jennifer leaps onto the scene in the '40s and makes it up to number 1 by the '70s, becoming the archetype of the "new names" of this period. Familiar bearers include actress Jennifer Aniston and singer Jennifer Lopez. Sometimes Jenny is used as a diminutive for Jennifer, although it originates as yet another name derived from JOAN (Chapter 8). Variant: **Jenifer.** Diminutives: **Jenna, Jennie,** and **Jenny.**

JEREMY: (m) Hebrew; may God exalt; a variant of JEREMIAH (Chapter 9). Jeremy starts showing up around the '40s, but hits both its peak and its greatest range of variants in the '70s. A certain amount of credit might be given to the character of this name played by teen heartthrob Bobby Sherman on the late '60s TV show *Here Come the Brides.* Another bearer is actor Jeremy Irons. Variants: **Jeramie, Jeramy, Jeremey, Jeremie, Jermey,** and **Jeromy.**

JODY: (m) English; a diminutive of uncertain origin, possibly from Joe, George, or Jude (or for the feminine name, covered in Chapter 18, perhaps from Judy). Variant: **Jodie.**

JOSHUA: (m) Hebrew; God is salvation. Joshua was part of the Biblical revivals after the Reformation, but came into the 20th century at a relatively low popularity. It wasn't until the '60s that it began the rise that eventually brought it up to its current place in the top ten. There have been many interesting Joshuas across the years, including Joshua Slocum, the first man to sail solo around the world, and San Francisco personality Joshua A. Norton who, in 1859, proclaimed himself to be Emperor of the United States. Variants: **Joshuah** and **Josue.** Diminutive: **Josh.**

KEVIN: (m) Gaelic; beautiful birth. This is another of the Irish names that gained a more general popularity at this period. A number of actors have borne this name, including Kevin Costner, Kevin Bacon, and Kevin Sorbo. Variants: **Keven** and **Kevon.**

KYLE: (m) uncertain; possibly Brythonic "Coel's land," but perhaps Gaelic "a strait, a narrow place." Bearers include NASCAR racer Kyle Petty and Olympic gymnast Kyle Shewfelt.

LISA: (f) English; a diminutive of ELIZABETH (Chapter 8). Lisa first appears on the charts in the '40s and has jumped to number 1 by the '60s, dislodging Mary from that position for the first time in ages. A few of the many familiar Lisas are actress Lisa Kudrow, novelist Lisa Scottoline, and Apple's first paradigm-breaking personal computer, the Lisa. (Leonardo da Vinci's famous painting *Mona Lisa* may or may not be of a woman named Lisa.) Another diminutive of Elizabeth that becomes popular at this time is the French Lisette. Variants: **Leesa, Leisa, Lise, Lisha, Lissa; Lisette, Lissette, Lizeth,** and **Lizette.**

MISTY: (f) English; possibly a diminutive of MELISSA (Chapter 7), but sometimes from the everyday word. This name may be further popularized by Olympic beach volleyball player Misty May. Variant: **Misti.**

RORY: (m) Gaelic; great king; or possibly, red king. This is another beneficiary of the fad for Irish names, and is borne by Irish blues guitarist Rory Gallagher and pro golfer Rory Sabbatini.

RYAN: (f, m) Gaelic; a king. Taken from the surname O'Ryan, this name may have been helped in popularity by the soap opera *Ryan's Hope,* but another boost may have come from actor Ryan O'Neal. The name is sometimes found for girls, and one feminine variant blends it with Ann. Variant: (f) **Ryann.**

SEAN: (f, m) Gaelic; a variant of JOHN (Chapter 8). The general fashion for names of Irish and Scottish origin helped popularize this name. Sean occurs as a female name as well, but specifically feminine versions ending in "-a" also developed. A slightly different variant, but also fed through Gaelic, produced Sheena. The 1953 western movie *Shane* may have contributed some popularity. Other bearers are actors Sean Connery and Sean Penn, actress Sean Young, and singer Sheena Easton. Variants: (f) **Shana, Shanna, Shauna, Shawn, Shawna, Sheena, Shonna,** and **Zhane;** (m) **Shane, Shaun, Shawn, Shayne,** and **Shon.**

SHANNON: (f, m) Gaelic; either from the name of the river, or a personal name meaning "old one." Bearers have included, on the male side, boxer Shannon Briggs, and on the female side, actress Shannen Doherty and Olympic gymnast Shannon Miller. Variant: (both) **Shanon;** (f) **Shannan** and **Shannen.**

SIOBHAN: (f) Gaelic; a variant of JOAN (Chapter 8). It's somewhat surprising that this name became popular in its Gaelic form, rather than as something more phonetic. One source for its use may have been the character of Siobhan Ryan on the soap opera *Ryan's Hope.*

STACY: (f, m) English; the masculine name is a diminutive of Eustace (a Greek name possibly meaning "fruitful"), the feminine is a diminutive of ANASTASIA (Chapter 9). Both only start showing up on the charts in mid century and have their greatest popularity at this time, but the feminine name is considerably more popular and seems to have crowded out the male name. Examples are actress Staci Keanan and actor Stacy Keach. Variants: (both) **Stacey;** (f) **Staci, Stacia, Stacie,** and **Stasia.**

STEPHANIE: (f) French; a feminine form of STEPHAN (Chapter 8). Although it had some popularity over the centuries, Stephanie only really hits its stride in the later 20th century, when it spends two decades in the top ten. Some bearers have included actress Stephanie Zimbalist and chemist Stephanie Kwolek whose work led to the development of Kevlar. Variants: **Stefani, Stefanie, Stephani, Stephania, Stephany, Stephenie; Estefani, Estefania,** and **Estefany.** Diminutive: **Stevie.**

TONIA: (f) English; a diminutive of ANTONIA (Chapter 7). Toni is the first of this group to appear, influenced by the masculine name, but Tonia takes over by the '60s. An early literary use is in O. Henry's short story *The Red Roses of Tonia.* Another bearer is novelist Toni Morrison. Variants: **Toni, Tonia, Tonja,** and **Tonya.**

VALERIE: (f) French; from an old Roman family name meaning "to grow strong." Valerie has had a mild popularity since the 19th century, but sees its peak in the '60s, perhaps as part of a fashion for long flowery names. Bearers include actresses Valeria Golino and Valerie Bertinelli, and basketball player Valorie Whiteside. Variants: **Valarie, Valeria,** and **Valorie.** Diminutive: **Vallie.**

ZACHARIAH: (m) Hebrew; God has remembered. Others interpret it as "God is renowned." The name has been used occasionally during the Biblical revivals, as for U.S. president Zachary Taylor, but its major popularity has come since the '70s. Variants: **Zachary, Zachery, Zackary, Zackery, Zakary,** and **Zechariah.** Diminutives: **Zach** and **Zack.**

Entering the New Millennium: Names of the '80s and After

The previous fashion for short, one-syllable boys' names gave over to a fashion for two-syllable names, especially ones ending in "-n," such as Aidan, Brenden, Dillon, Ethan, and so on. The fashion for names beginning in "Br-" continues, and boys' names started to enjoy more variety than previously, including at the top ranks of popularity. Girls used a lot of two- and three-syllable names ending in a "-y" sound, such as Courtney, Lindsay, Whitney, and so on. Some specific names that are very characteristic of this period are Ashley, Brittany, Caitlin, and Chelsea or Kelsey.

AIDAN: (m) Gaelic; fire; firey. Within the space of a decade, Aidan came out of obscurity and shot up to number 39 in 2003. Much of the name's popularity seems to come purely from its sound, given the number of rhyming names that have made similar leaps during the same period (for example, Caden, Brayden, and Jaden). Actor Aidan Quinn bore this name well before the current fashion started. Variants: **Aden, Aiden,** and **Ayden.**

ALISA: (f) multiple origins; a variant of ALICE (Chapter 8). Some spellings of the name may also be influenced by the plant name Alyssum, and the name's popularity may also be an echo of the earlier fashion for LISA (see earlier in this chapter). One bearer is actress Alyssa Milano. Variants: **Alissa, Aliza, Allyssa, Alysa,** and **Alyssa.**

AMARI: (f, m) uncertain; there are multiple possible sources for this name: an anagram of MARIA (Chapter 8), a Yoruba name meaning "strength"; and perhaps even a Japanese name of uncertain meaning. (There is also a Thai hotel chain of this name.) The name jumps suddenly onto the charts for both boys and girls within the last half decade, and there is probably a specific inspiration for this trend that has not yet been identified.

ANAYA: (f) uncertain; possibly from a Spanish surname, as for Chicano writer Rudolfo Anaya. The "-a" ending would lead parents to treat it as feminine, as for actress Anaya Farrell. The name appeared suddenly in recent years.

ARMAND, ARMANI: (m) French; from a Germanic root meaning "warrior." The name has been mildly popular over the last century but several variants have been showing a new interest recently. The variant Armani is probably inspired by clothing designer Giorgio Armani. Variants: **Armando, Arman, Armani,** and **Armond.**

AXEL: (m) Swedish; a variant of Absalom, a Hebrew name meaning "father is peace." The Biblical Absalom was the wayward son of King David, but the recent popularity of Axel is more likely to be attributable to *Guns 'N' Roses* member Axel Rose.

AYANNA: (f) uncertain; possibly a diminutive of JULIANA (Chapter 8) or some similar name. A profusion of similar names have become popular in the last decade. An earlier bearer is NASA robotics specialist Ayanna Howard. Variants: **Aiyana, Ayana, Iyana,** and **Iyanna.**

BRAXTON: (m) English; probably a variant of Broxton "town of a man named Brock." The sudden recent popularity of this name is curious and although it may simply be tied in with the fashion for boys' names beginning with "Br-," one wonders how many mothers first considered it after experiencing Braxton-Hicks contractions.

BRAYDON: (m) English; meaning uncertain, although an origin meaning "broad valley" would produce something similar. The sudden popularity and variety of names in this group is due to its position at the intersection of the fashions for names beginning with "Br-" and names rhyming with Aidan. One bearer is baseball player Braden Looper. Variants: **Braden, Bradyn, Braeden, Braedon, Braiden,** and **Brayden.**

BRIANA: (f) English; a feminine variant of BRIAN (see earlier in this chapter). As a literary name, this can be traced back to the 16th century in Edmund Spenser's *The Faerie Queene,* but as a name in actual use, it appears suddenly on the scene in the '70s. One familiar bearer is Olympic soccer goalie Brianna Scurry. Variants: **Brianda, Brionna, Breana, Breann, Breanna, Breanne, Brenna, Breonna, Brian, Brianna, Bryana,** and **Bryanna.** Diminutives: **Bria, Brea, Bree,** and **Brielle.**

BRYCE, BRYSON: (m) uncertain; Bryce is probably of Breton origin, but of uncertain meaning. Bryson is originally an English surname meaning "son of Bryce." There was also an ancient Greek mathematician (mentioned by Plato and Aristotle) named Bryson, but this is an entirely unrelated name. Variant: **Brice** and **Brycen.**

CADE, CADEN: (m) multiple origins; Cade can have multiple origins, including an Anglo-Saxon personal name meaning "round, lumpy." Caden is sometimes from the German place name Kaden, as in Frank Lloyd Wright's Kaden Tower. The current fashion for these names, however, is likely to be based on sound alone (see AIDAN above). Some related bearers are child actor Cayden Boyd and artist Cady Noland. Variants: **Cady, Caiden, Cayden, Kade, Kaden, Kadin, Kaiden,** and **Kayden.**

CAITLIN: (f) English; an adaptation of the Gaelic Caitlín (that is, Kathleen), but pronounced as if "Caitlin" were an English spelling (see KATELYNN in Chapter 11). This name shot up the charts abruptly in the '80s. One bearer is swimmer Kaitlin Sandeno. Variants: **Caitlyn, Caitlynn, Kaitlin, Kaitlyn, Kaitlynn, Katelin,** and **Katelyn.**

CAMDEN: (m) English; valley with camps. The name has rapidly become popular in the last decade for obscure reasons.

CARSON: (m) uncertain; a surname from a Scottish place name of uncertain origin. This name has been in use since the 19th century, but has recently been given a boost in popularity, perhaps by MTV host Carson Daly. Variant: **Karson.**

CASSIDY: (f, m) Gaelic; meaning uncertain, but possibly "curly (haired)." As a boy's name, this had a brief and rare appearance in the '80s, perhaps partly in response to teen idols David and Shaun Cassidy (the timing being wrong for a connection with western movie characters Hopalong Cassidy or Butch Cassidy). But this has primarily become popular as a girl's name, so you can chalk it up to an interest in the sound, perhaps inspired by Cassie or similar names. Variant: (f) **Kassidy.**

CODY: (f, m) Gaelic; from the surname Mac Óda "son of Odo" (see OTTO in Chapter 7). In this case it is female use that is rare and brief. The male name begins appearing around mid century and gets as high as number 26 in the '90s. Some interest may come from the name's Irish origin, but it may also simply resemble popular diminutives such as Bobby. The title character of the movie *Agent Cody Banks* cashes in on this name's popularity. Variants: (m) **Codey, Codi, Codie, Coty,** and **Kody.**

COLTON: (m) English; town belonging to Cola. The name doesn't appear on the charts before the '80s and seems to be connected with the fashion for names ending in "-n." Variants: **Colten** and **Kolton.** Diminutives: **Colt.**

COOPER: (m) English; a maker of barrels. Another curious recent name fashion has been for surnames taken originally from occupations (such as Taylor). Since the meaning is unlikely to be the point of interest, this seems to suggest a sound fashion for names ending in "-r." Some familiar examples of this as a surname are actor Gary Cooper and author James Fenimore Cooper.

DEJA: (f) uncertain; possibly sometimes from the French phrase *déjà vu* "already seen," but one can't entirely discount the name of Edgar Rice Burroughs' Martian princess Dejah Thoris, which is almost certainly invented. Variants: **Daija, Daja,** and **Dejah.**

DESTINY: (f) English; destiny, fate. The popularity of this name has been increasing steadily since the '70s, so only some of the more recent interest in it can be attributed to the R&B group *Destiny's Child.* There also appears to be a rare masculine variant Destin. Variants: (f) **Destany, Destinee, Destiney,** and **Destini.**

EVAN: (m) Welsh; a variant of JOHN (Chapter 8). Evan has been increasing steadily in popularity since the early part of the 20th century. One bearer is Indiana senator and governor Evan Bayh. Variant: **Evans.**

GAGE: (m) English; someone who gauges or measures things. This name suddenly appears in the last decade for no obvious reason. Variant: **Gaige.**

JILLIAN: (f) English; a variant of JULIANA (Chapter 8). Jill itself saw its greatest popularity in the '70s, but Jillian and Gillian only seriously hit the charts after that. Some familiar bearers include actresses Gillian Anderson and Jill St. John. Variant: **Gillian.** Diminutive: **Jill.**

JUSTINE (f), **JUSTIN** (m): Latin; just. These names have been in use since Medieval times, but both have seen a new popularity in the last few decades. In the case of boys, some of the interest may be due to pop idol Justin Timberlake. Variants: (f) **Justina** and **Justine;** (m) **Justen, Justine, Justo, Juston,** and **Justyn.**

KATE: (f) English; a diminutive of KATHERINE (Chapter 8). To some extent, these names are only now recovering the popularity they have had at various times in the past. Kate was a popular name back in the Middle Ages and is now enjoying a comeback. Well-known bearers include actresses Kate Winslet and Cate Blanchett. Variants: **Cate, Kati, Katie, Kattie,** and **Katy.**

KEEGAN: (m) Gaelic; from the surname Mac Aodhagáin "son of Aodhagán," from a root meaning "fire." This name doesn't appear on the charts until the '80s but has rapidly become popular. One bearer is actor Keegan MacIntosh. Variants: **Keagan** and **Kegan.**

KENNEDY: (f, m) Gaelic; rough head. The more immediate inspiration for this name is the prominent political Kennedy family. Use as a girl's name has now been validated by its appearance for a character on the TV show *Buffy the Vampire Slayer.* Variant: (f) **Kennedi.**

MACKENZIE: (f, m) Gaelic; son of Coinneach, from a root meaning "fair, bright." Another variant of the name is MacKenna, which has only hit the charts as a girl's name. One early appearance of Mackenzie as a male given name is for a character on the soap opera *Another World* in the '70s and at a similar point actress Mackenzie Phillips became familiar for her work on the TV show *One Day at a Time*. The name begins showing up on the charts for both boys and girls in the '80s, but the boys rapidly abandoned the field. Variants: (f) **Makenzie, Mckenzie; Kenzie, Kinsey; Makena, Makenna,** and **McKenna.**

MADISON: (f, m) English; Matthew's son. Madison has an unusual recent history. It was used as a male name, like many surnames, beginning in the 19th century but fell out of popularity in the mid–20th century. Then in the '80s it suddenly appears as a girl's name — as best as anyone can tell, entirely inspired by the name of Daryl Hannah's character in the movie *Splash* — and shot up to spend a few years at number 2. It made a brief comeback as a boy's name recently, but this hasn't lasted. Variants: (f) **Maddison, Madisen, Madisyn,** and **Madyson.**

MEGAN: (f) Welsh; a diminutive of Meg, from MARGARET (Chapter 8). Megan is often mistakenly thought of as an Irish name and its popularity can no doubt partly be as part of the fashion for Irish and Scottish names. Bearers include actress Megan Mullally and tennis player Meghann Shaughnessy. Variants: **Maegan, Magen, Meagan, Meaghan, Meghan,** and **Meghann.**

MICHAELA: (f) English; a feminine variant of MICHAEL (Chapter 8). Michaela shows up as popular beginning in the '70s, and in the next decade you can track its development through Micaela and Mikayla to McKayla (which otherwise might appear to be from a Scottish surname). There's also some influence from a separate name, Kayla, which shows up in the '60s. Variants: **Makaila, Makala, Makayla, Mckayla, Micaela, Micayla, Mikaela, Mikaila, Mikala, Mikayla; Kaela, Kaila, Kailey, Kayla, Kaylah, Keila, Keyla,** and **Kyla.**

PAIGE: (f) English; a page-boy, a servant. There's no obvious inspiration for the popularity of this name. It starts showing up in mid century and has been rising in popularity ever since.

RHIANNA: (f) Welsh; maiden. This may sometimes perhaps be used as a diminutive of RHIANNON (Chapter 17). One bearer is British singer-songwriter Rhianna Kenny, but the popularity of this name is too recent for much fame yet. Variants: **Reanna** and **Rianna.**

SKYLAR: (f, m) Dutch; scholar, student. This shows up on the charts as a boy's name in the '80s, and for girls in the next decade, although the girls have started to edge ahead in recent years. The name is still too recent for many famous bearers, but one example is actress Skyler Shaye. Variants: (both) **Skyler;** (f) **Skyla;** (m) **Kyler.**

Chapter 11

Designing the Future: Created and Constructed Names

*I*t hasn't always been the case that creativity in names was admired. In many times and places, tradition and heritage have been all-important. In other situations, new names may have been created, but only by certain rules on what you could combine and how. The Anglo-Saxons put together names with a "one from column A, one from column B" method, often repeating one of the parts for all their children as a sort of family tie. So you might have named your sons Edward, Edmund, and Edwin, and your daughters Edith and Ediva.

Another way of creating new names — especially nicknames — has been to take a short chunk of the original name and add any of a smorgasbord of endings to it. So from John you get the male names Johnny, Jenkin, and so on, and the female names Janet, Janelle, Janessa, Janis, Janine, and so forth.

This chapter looks at some other ways new names have been produced: compounds of existing names, names created from initials, and names constructed by cutting and pasting parts of existing names together. Note that, in general, name listings in this section do not include meanings as any meaning they might be assigned comes from their component parts — just look at the chapter referenced to check out the meaning of the component parts.

Turning Two Names into One

With the fashion for giving children two given names, some combinations have been so popular that they have become glued together to form new names. In English, this has happened more for girls' names, such as Annabeth or Emmylou. In Italian, it's common for boys' names to turn into compounds as well, especially when they start with the very common "Gian-" (John), while in French, the same compounds (using Jean) are written with hyphens that keep the two names more distinct (for example, Jean-Claude).

But not all names that look like compounds started out that way. Many Latin names come in two variants, one "plain" and one ending in "-ian" such as Julie and Juliana, and in the case of girls' names, this can be reinterpreted as a compound with ANN(A). Similarly, a number of older French names end in "-elyn" (such as Joscelyn or Catelyn), and when used for girls they are sometimes turned into compounds with LYNN. These two groups in turn have encouraged the creation of new compounds ending in "-ann(a)" or "-lynn."

ANNABELLE: (f) uncertain; ANNE (Chapter 8) + BELLE (Chapter 13); a variant of ANABEL (Chapter 6). While the name Anabel was not originally a compound name, it is now treated as one, with all the available variations on Belle/Bella used for the ending. One current bearer is actress Annabella Sciorra. This name first appears in the 19th century and fell out of fashion in the early 20th, but in recent years several variants have been making a comeback. Variants: **Annabel** and **Annabella.**

ANNABETH, ANNALISE: (f) multiple origins; ANNE (Chapter 8) + ELIZABETH (Chapter 8). For many centuries, the names Anne and Elizabeth were among the very most popular girls' names in Europe, so they were a natural for forming compounds. Each language has its own favorites: Annalise comes from German and has only recently become popular in the U.S.; Annabeth uses more familiar forms and is used by TV actress Annabeth Gish of *The X-Files.*

ANN-MARGARET: (f) English; ANNE (Chapter 8) + MARGARET (Chapter 8). The distinction between the use of two given names and the use of a compound name can be subtle in some cases. But some cultures will hyphenate the two when the combination is meant to be treated as a single name. Another pair of extremely common names appear in the name of actress Ann-Margaret, which she considers distinctive enough to use without a surname. Variant: **Anna-Margaret.**

ANNMARIE: (f) various origins; ANNE (Chapter 8) + MARY (Chapter 8). One of the earliest patterns in giving multiple given names was the use of Mary as a second name, in honor of the Virgin. In some cultures this could be so automatic that even men were given the second name Maria (as for composer Carl Maria von Weber). Compounds ending in Mary haven't often hit the popularity charts, especially if ROSEMARY (see later in this chapter) is discounted. It seems to be a peculiarly American fashion (and a southeastern one) to use the variant Mae for Mary as a second name. Annmarie has been the most popular of the compounds of Ann and Mary, appearing on the charts consistently for the last half century. Variants: **Annamae, Annamarie,** and **Annemarie.**

BILLIE JEAN: (f) English; WILLIAM (Chapter 8) + JOAN (Chapter 8). Sometimes it is usage that fixes a pair of names as a compound rather than two independent elements. There are a number of compounds starting with Billie, used as girls' names, that are normally written as separate words but used as a single name. Tennis star Billie Jean King is a good example of this phenomenon.

CAROLANN: (f) English; CAROL (Chapter 17) + ANNE (Chapter 8). Compounds based on Carol show up most commonly during the period when that name was at its peak of popularity, around the '40s. Carolann seems to be a spontaneous creation from Carol and Anne, but the various forms of CAROLYN (Chapter 10) combine a development of CAROLINE (Chapter 9) and a reinterpretation of the name as a compound of Carol and Lynn.

CARRIE-ANNE: (f) English; CARRIE (Chapter 10) + ANNE (Chapter 8). As with Ann-Margaret, the hyphen is the only clue that this name is to be taken as a compound. The recent popularity may be inspired by actress Carrie-Anne Moss.

CLARIBEL: (f) English; CLARA(Chapter 8) + BELLE(Chapter 13). This is most likely a blend of Clara and names like ISABEL (Chapter 8) or ANABEL (Chapter 6), and so not directly from the Spanish word *bella* "beautiful." Claribell showed up first in the 16th century as a literary name, as in Spenser's *The Faerie Queen.* Recently it has been popular primarily in the early 20th century. A current bearer is poet Claribel Alegria. Variants: **Clarabelle** and **Claribell.**

ELLAMAE: (f) English; ELLA (Chapter 17) + MARY (Chapter 8). Ordinarily one might suspect that this compound comes from ELLEN (Chapter 8) rather than Ella, but it appears during the period when Ella was most popular as an independent name.

EMMYLOU: (f) English; EMMY (Chapter 9) + LOUISE (Chapter 9). The popularity of this name may come from the inspiration of particular bearers, such as country singer Emmylou Harris, as the component names, while popular, are not enormously so.

GERALYN: (f) English; GERALD (Chapter 8) + LYNN (Chapter 14). This group of names appears in the mid–20th century, following closely on the heels of the greatest popularity of GERALDINE (Chapter 9) and its diminutive JERRY (Chapter 19), as well as the fashion for MARILYN (Chapter 18). Rather than being a new coinage from Jerry and Lynn, it is more likely a combination of a shortening of Geraldine and a blend of that and Marilyn. Variants: **Jerilyn** and **Jerline.**

IVELISSE: (f) uncertain; IVONNE (Chapter 19) + ELIZABETH (Chapter 8). Ivelisse had a brief popularity around the '70s at a time when IVONNE (Chapter 19) had reached its peak of popularity, but the compound is rather unusual and it's likely that some use in popular culture gave it a push. One bearer is artist Ivelisse Jimenez.

JOANNE: (f) English; JO (Chapter 10) + ANNE (Chapter 8). The name Joanna or Joanne is sometimes treated as a compound of Jo and Anne, but in origin it is simply a variant of JOAN (Chapter 8). Variants: **Joann** and **Joanna.**

JOELLEN: (f) English; JO(EL) (Chapter 10) + ELLEN (Chapter 8). As the name Joel has never been commonly used for women, this is more likely to be a blend of Jo, although Jolene may be influenced by the many feminine names ending in "-ine." These names were most popular around the '50s and of the two, Jolene is much more popular, perhaps assisted by Dolly Parton's 1974 song of that name. Variant: **Jolene.**

JOHNPAUL: (m) English; JOHN (Chapter 8) + PAUL (Chapter 4). The only masculine compound name in English that hits the charts is almost certainly being given in honor of the present pope, John Paul II.

JOSELUIS: (m) Spanish; JOSEPH (Chapter 4) + LOUIS (Chapter 7). The Spanish versions of Joseph and Louis are among the most popular boys' names in the Hispanic community, so the appearance of this compound on the popularity charts may be purely a result of statistics.

JUANCARLOS: (m) multiple origins; JOHN (Chapter 8) + CARL (Chapter 8). While compound names are just as common for boys and girls in places like Italy and France, American culture seems less likely to create or use them for boys. The only masculine compound names that hit the popularity charts are imported direct from other cultures. The Spanish compound of these two names, in particular, may be popularized by several kings of Spain named Juan Carlos. Variant: **Giancarlo.**

JULISA: (f) English?; JUDY (Chapter 18) or JULIA (Chapter 17) + ELIZABETH (Chapter 8). While older compounds from Elizabeth are likely to use Beth, the enormous popularity of LISA (Chapter 10) in the last century has brought it into compounds as well. While Judy and Julia are equally possible origins for the first part of this name, the way that Julia blends into Lisa makes it a better candidate. But for another possible origin, see JALISA in the next section.

KATELYNN: (f) English; KATE (Chapter 10) + LYNN (Chapter 14). Cateline shows up as a variant of KATHERINE (Chapter 8) as early as the Medieval period. Whether directly, or more likely by way of the Gaelic form Caitlín, people have re-interpreted the spelling of this name as if it were a compound of Kate and Lynn. The forms listed here make this re-interpretation clear, while more traditional spellings of this name appear in Chapter 10. Variant: **Katelyn.**

KAYLEIGH: (f) English?; KATHERINE (Chapter 8) + LEE (Chapter 14). The collection of names included here are likely to be from a variety of origins. Kayleigh, as in the popular song of the '80s, is clearly influenced, at least in spelling, by the names Kay (Chapter 8) and Leigh, but a name like Callie might be intended as a rather traditional diminutive of Callista (supported by the fact that it has been consistently popular over the last century), and some variants look like they may be variants of KELLY (Chapter 14). Another group of similar names are discussed under KYLIE (Chapter 17). And some name books will suggest a connection with Gaelic word *ceilidh,* a term for a musical party, which is pronounced similarly. The way that each group shades into each other points out the difficulty in classifying fashionable name variants as if they were more traditional names. With the exception of Callie, this group of names has only hit the charts in the last couple of decades. Variants: **Caleigh, Cali, Callie, Kailee, Kaleigh, Kaley, Kalie, Kallie, Kaylee, Kayley, Kayli,** and **Kaylie.**

KAYLYNN: (f) English; KATHERINE (Chapter 8) + LYNN (Chapter 14). Usually, compound names appear at a time when the component names are fairly popular. The various forms of Kaylynn have only begun showing up in the last decade or so, while Kay and Lynn have been out of fashion for some time, so there may be some other explanation for the explosion of interest in this name group. Variants: **Kaelyn, Kailyn, Kalyn, Kaylin,** and **Kaylyn.**

LEEANN: (f) English; LEE (Chapter 14) + ANNE (Chapter 8). For the most part, these names appear to be a compound of Leigh and Anne, but it's possible that there's some influence from the Greek name Leandra (see LEANDER in Chapter 6). One familiar bearer is musician LeAnn Rimes. These names have been popular during the second half of the 20th century. Variants: **Leandra, Leann, Leanna,** and **Leanne.**

LORIANN: (f) English; LAURA (Chapter 6) + ANNE (Chapter 8). This is a fairly straightforward compound of Lori and Ann, showing up in the '60s when Lori was at its peak of popularity.

LOUANNE: (f) English; LOUISE (Chapter 9) + ANNE (Chapter 8). These names were popular for a short time in the mid–20th century, towards the end of the greatest popularity of Lou and Louise. One version of the name is found for education writer Louanne Johnson. Variants: **Louann, Luana, Luann,** and **Luanne.**

MARIANNE: (f) multiple origins; MARY (Chapter 8) + ANNE (Chapter 8). While this name is treated today as a compound of Mary and Anne, it originates in two independent names, Latin Mariana and English Marion, both variants of Mary (see Chapter 8). But the re-interpretation as a compound has led to spellings that create a new name, and one especially popular during the mid–20th century. The connection can be seen for novelist Mary Ann Evans, who also used Marian Evans (but is better known under her pen name of George Elliot). Another bearer is musician Marianne Faithfull. Variants: **Mariann, Marianna, Maryann,** and **Maryanne.**

MARICRUZ: (f) Spanish; MARY (Chapter 8) + CRUZ (Chapter 15). This is a compound of two names quite popular in the Hispanic communities. It has only recently been popular enough to appear on the charts.

MARILEE: (f) English; MARY (Chapter 8) + LEE (Chapter 14). In addition to being a compound of two popular names, this group may be encouraged by an association with the word "merrily." One familiar bearer is actress Marlee Matlin. Variant: **Marlee.**

MARILOU: (f) English; MARY (Chapter 8) + LOUISE (Chapter 9). This name was popular more towards the early part of the 20th century, the time when Lou itself was most common for girls. One bearer is poet Marilou Awiakta. Variant: **Marylou.**

MARISOL: (f) Spanish; MARY (Chapter 8) + Sol "sun". This is a condensed form of a nickname for the Virgin, "Mary of the sun." One bearer is sculptor Marisol Escobar.

MARYBELLE: (f) English; MARY (Chapter 8) + BELLE (Chapter 13). This compound may also derive from a blend of Mary and ISABEL (Chapter 8), although the spelling Marybelle connects it with French *belle* "beautiful." It's also possible that the name may sometimes be a back-construction from MABLE (Chapter 17), treating it as Mae + Belle. The name has been popular primarily in the last half century. Variant: **Maribel.**

MARYBETH, MARLYS: (f) English; MARY (Chapter 8) + ELIZABETH (Chapter 8). Given the enormous popularity of both Mary and Elizabeth, it would be startling if there were no popular compounds produced from them. In fact, you see two groups, using the diminutives Beth and Lis(a), both popular around the mid–20th century. Variant: **Maribeth.**

MARYJANE: (f) English; MARY (Chapter 8) + JANE (Chapter 10). This was a somewhat popular compound in the earlier part of the 20th century. It may have gone out of fashion simply because Jane itself became less popular, but there may have been negative associations from the use of "Maryjane" as a nickname for marijuana.

MARYJO: (f) English; MARY (Chapter 8) + JO (Chapter 10). Many of the compounds starting with Mary had their greatest popularity in the mid–20th century, perhaps as a warm-up exercise for the even greater inventiveness in naming that was about to explode on the scene. Maryjo shows up when Jo is at its most popular as a girl's name.

ROSEANNE: (f) English; ROSE (Chapter 12) + ANNE (Chapter 8). In addition to deriving from the very popular names Rose and Anne, this may occasionally be a variant of ROXANNE (Chapter 7). An early literary use of this name is in Wilkie Collins' 18th century novel *The Moonstone,* but it follows the pattern for more recent compounds in hitting the charts primarily in the mid–20th century. Roseanne has been quite popular in show business, including for singer Rosanne Cash and actresses Rosanne Arquette and Roseanne Barr. Variants: **Rosann, Rosanna, Rosanne, Roseann,** and **Roseanna.**

ROSEMARY: (f) English; ROSE (Chapter 12) + MARY (Chapter 8). The earliest known example of this name, in the mid–18th century, connects it clearly with a compound of Rose and Mary, as it was borne then by a woman originally christened Mary but born at Rose Castle in England. The popularization of the name by the 1924 musical *Rose Marie* also makes this connection. But the connection with the plant name rosemary must certainly have been a major influence on the name's popularity, especially in the late 19th century when plant names were fashionable. Well-known bearers have included singer Rosemary Clooney and children's writer Rosemary Sutcliff, as well as the fictional title character of the book and movie *Rosemary's Baby.* Variant: **Rosemarie.**

SUELLEN: (f) English; SUSAN (Chapter 17) + ELLEN (Chapter 8) or ELEANOR (Chapter 8). Given that the mid–20th century saw a general fashion for compounds of popular names, you probably don't need to connect this name specifically with the character in Margaret Mitchell's *Gone with the Wind.*

Making a Point with Initialisms

It has been fashionable for quite some time to use initials rather than full names for the first or middle name or both. This has been particularly popular among men, but because the fashion can conceal the bearer's gender, it has been used by professional women or female authors in male-dominated fields to get a foot in the door.

If the initials have the right sound, they may be treated — at least in spoken form — as the equivalent of a given name. And some combinations of initials are pronounced identically to existing names, so that name may be substituted for them. (The classic example is of Olympic track star J.C. Owens, known to history as Jesse.) Some Caseys may no doubt originally be K.C.s, and the Kaycees almost certainly are. Going in the other direction, on the TV show *M*A*S*H,* Captain B.J. Hunnicutt explained that he was named for his parents: Bea and Jay and that the initials don't stand for anything. Some names, like the Indian name Vijay, may be mistaken for initialism names but aren't yet being used for that purpose.

ARTIE: (f, m) English; R.T. The masculine name is normally a diminutive of ARTHUR (Chapter 6), but this seems unlikely in the case of the feminine use. The two are popular at different eras as well, with the feminine name appearing in the early part of the 20th century, while the masculine name appears in the '30s and '40s, perhaps inspired by swing band leader Artie Shaw. Another bearer is comic actor Artie Johnson.

DEE, DEEDEE: (f, m) English; D., D.D. Dee is popular as a male name around the turn of the 20th century, then trails off in the '60s when it had become most popular for girls. One bearer is actor Billy Dee Williams. The duplicated form Deedee is found primarily for girls and is sometimes a diminutive of Deirdre.

EFFIE: (f) English; F.E. This is more often a diminutive of EUPHEMIA (Chapter 10) than taken from initials. One bearer is poet Effie Walker Smith. The name was quite popular around the turn of the 20th century and remained on the charts for another half century.

ELLE: (f) English; L. This is much more likely to be a diminutive of any of various names ending in "-elle," such as Gabrielle or Michelle. Inspiration may also come from the fashion magazine *Elle* (French for "her"). The main character of the movie *Legally Blonde* bore this name. The name has only become popular in the last few years.

ELLIE: (f) English; L.E. This is more commonly a diminutive of ELLEN (Chapter 8) than from the initials L.E. After being moderately popular around the turn of the 20th century, this name has suddenly been revived in the last decade or so.

ESSIE: (f) English; S.E. This may instead by a diminutive of a name such as ESTELLE (Chapter 10). (In one isolated case, it is short for the obscure name Eslanda.) Bearers include Australian musician and activist Essie Coffey and actress Essie Davis.

EXIE: (f) English; X.E. This is possibly a diminutive of ALEXANDRA (Chapter 9), perhaps via LEXIE (Chapter 16). It shows up occasionally in the late 19th and early 20th century. An origin in the initials is made unlikely by the rarity of popular names beginning with "x".

ICIE: (f) English; I.C. It's difficult to know where this name could come from, if not from the initials I.C. and it is quite rare, only occurring in the early 20th century. One bearer is nutritionist Icie Gertrude Macy.

JAYCEE (f), **JAYCE** (m) English; J.C. The distinction between the variants found for men and women suggest that you may be seeing distinct origins (although the spellings Jaycee and Jaycie would normally be interpreted as more feminine in any case). As a masculine name, this may sometimes be a diminutive of JASON (Chapter 5) and may be pronounced to rhyme with "face" rather than as the initials. Note that "Jaycee" is also an initialism for the Junior Chamber of Commerce organization (the Jaycees). The name has only become popular in recent decades for both boys and girls, although it appears earlier for boys. Variants: (f) **Jacey** and **Jaycie;** (m) **Jace** and **Jase.**

KAYCEE: (f) English; K.C. The specific form Kaycee suggests an initialism, but ordinarily this should be considered a variant of CASEY (Chapter 19).

OBIE: (m) English; O.B. This may sometimes be a diminutive of the Biblical name Obadiah, which may account for some of the early 20th century uses, but an origin in initials seems equally likely. One bearer is rapper Obie Trice.

OCIE: (f, m) English; O.C. Ocie occurs for both men and women in the early part of the 20th century and there seems to be no obvious source other than the initials.

ODIE: (f, m) English; O.D. There is an English surname Odie that derives originally from an Anglo-Saxon personal name Odd. But given that the name is found equally commonly for men and women around the early 20th century, an origin in initials seems more likely. One bearer is blues drummer Odie Payne.

OPIE: (m) English; O.P. The name of the character of Opie Taylor on *The Andy Griffith Show,* was most likely inspired by that of '40s bandleader Opie Cates, whom the show's producers admired. But this only shifts the question, and it's quite likely that Cates' given name derives originally from initials.

VIJAY: (m) Hindi; Victorious. Not an initialism name from V.J. at all, although those unfamiliar with Indian names may take it for one. The prominence of pro golfer Vijay Singh may make this name more familiar.

Putting the Pieces Together for Invented Names

Just as some historic cultures created new names by pasting together an established menu of beginnings and endings, people today are creating new menus of "name parts" to assemble in creative ways. Some of these new creations may be relatively isolated, while other parts may be added or substituted in to a wide variety of names.

One of the most fascinating and creative versions of this comes out of the African American community and is a good example of how even arbitrary invention can have rules and a history. The fashion has its roots in names like the French surnames Leroy, Laverne, and Dubois. From these, people took the prefix (Le-, La-, De-, and so on) and added it to an existing name, producing names like Deshawn and Lawanda. Then more prefixes were added to the palatte (Sharonda, Jamarkus, and Rashawn), and they got added to purely invented roots, not just existing names (Lakeisha and Shanika). Sometimes traditional names can be re-spelled to fit them into this fashion (Duwayne from Dwayne, ShaVonne from the Irish Siobhan).

The most common prefixes used in this type of created name are as follow:

- ✔ **Da-, De-:** Originally from Romance language surnames starting with *de, di, da,* and so forth, meaning "of". This prefix is used in both male and female names.

- ✔ **Ja-, Jay-:** This prefix appears to be inspired by the sound of Arabic names such as Jamal or Jalil and is much more commonly found in boys' names.

- ✔ **K-, Ke-, Key-:** This is a less common prefix and seems to appear only as a substitute for other prefixes in existing names.

- ✔ **La-, Le-:** French and Spanish nicknames beginning with *le* or *la,* meaning "the," inspired this prefix and it is found equally commonly in boys' and girls' names.

- ✔ **Sha-:** This is most commonly found in feminine names and was popular early in the fashion for this type of name. It may be inspired by the sound of some Arabic or African names.

- ✔ **Ta-, Ty-:** The prefix "Ta-" shows up fairly early in the fashion and appears to substitute for other prefixes in existing names. "Ty-" has most likely been borrowed from names like Tyrone and Tyrell and is now used mostly in creating boys' names.

In addition to created names, this section includes some of the traditional names that have provided the models and patterns for this fashion, as well as names that have been fit into it by creative spelling.

ARLENE: (f) English; this is most likely either a blend of any of various names starting with "Ar-" and the ending "-line" from Caroline or a similar name, although it may instead simply be a shortening of Charlene or a similar name. It was already quite popular in the late 19th century and hits its peak in the '30s. One well-known bearer is actress Arlene Francis. Variants: **Arleen** and **Arline.**

DAISHA: (f) coined; the ending "-isha" is extremely common in feminine coined names, perhaps originally borrowed from names like Tisha and Trisha (see LATRISHA below) or blended using AISHA (Chapter 4). Related names: **Tiesha** and **Tyesha.**

DAVON(TE): (m) multiple origins; Davon, may be connected with names such as DEVON (Chapter 10), but there is also a surname Devante of unclear origin. DeVaughn occurs as a surname as well, although possibly not connected with the Welsh name VAUGHAN (Chapter 13). But, the set of names including Deonte, Devonte, and Javonte strongly point to invention as another source. These were most popular in the early '90s and didn't hit the charts much before that. R&B musician DeVante Swing is featured on the soundtrack of the movie *Dangerous Minds.* Another variant is borne by actor DeVaughn Nixon. Kavon is often a derivative of this name. Variants: **Davante, Davonta, Devante, Devaughn, Devonta, Devontae,** and **Devonte.** Related name: **Kavon.**

DEANDRE: (m) French; this is taken from the surname DeAndre or D'Andre, meaning "descendent of Andrew." Deandre shows up as early as the '60s, but the others are more recent. Bearers include gospel singer DeAndre Patterson. Many of the most popular names prefixed with "De-" have parallels beginning with "Ke-" as in Keandre, which appears briefly in the '90s. Variants: **Dandre, Deondre,** and **Dondre.** Related name: **Keandre.**

DEANGELO: (m) Italian; this name comes from the surname De Angelo or D'Angelo meaning "descendent of Angelo." It shows up on the leading edge of the fashion in the '80s, as for football player DeAngelo Hall. Variant: **Dangelo.**

DEASIA: (f) coined; this is perhaps taken from the continent, but the sound "sha" is very common in coined names, so this may be coincidence. The continental connection is sometimes emphasized in the spelling as DeAsia. A similar name uses the prefix "Ny-" which is not otherwise a major player in the creation of coined names. Pop singer Nyasia Batista bears this name. Related name: **Nyasia.**

DEJUAN: (m) Spanish?; possibly this comes from a surname. It shows up on the charts in the '70s. One bearer is football player DeJuan Groce.

DELISA: (f) Italian; this comes from an Italian surname DiLisa or DeLisa, possibly meaning "descendent of a woman named Lisa." It hits the charts only briefly in the '60s, before the major fashion starts. One bearer is pro basketball player Delisha Milton. This name no doubt inspired the creation of Jalisa. Variants: **Delisha** and **DiLisa.** Related names: **Jaleesa** and **Jalisa.**

DELOIS: (f) French; the name is taken from a surname meaning "descendent of Louis." It is used now as a feminine name because of being connected with the name Lois.

DEMARCO, DEMARIO: (m) Italian, Spanish; these names come from the surnames DeMarco and DeMario. The form DeMarcus is likely to be a more recent coinage. All three are in the leading edge of the fashion, around the '80s. Bearers include singer and actor DeMario Thornton and boxer DeMarcus Corley. Variant: **Demarcus.**

DEMONTE: (m) Italian; from the mountain. While this name may have influenced the Devonte group of names, you don't see new coinages ending in "-monte" hitting the charts. One bearer is football player Demonte Bolden. A related origin and meaning produced the French name Lamont. It begins showing up on the charts in the '30s, perhaps not coincidentally the decade that saw the debut of the radio show *The Shadow,* where the title character's alter ego was named Lamont Cranston. Related name: **Lamont.**

DENISHA: (f) coined?; this may be a variant of DENISE (Chapter 5), adapted to the sound pattern of coined names, but it may also be an independent invention. This name may have inspired Kenisha. Several names have been created by substituting initial "K" for "D." Related names: **Kanisha** and **Kenisha.**

DEQUAN: (m) coined; there appears to be a Chinese name Dequan, but it's unlikely to be the source. Dequan has only become popular in the last decade or so, but already has a Hollywood namesake in child actor Dequan Henderson. One reason to doubt a Chinese origin is the pattern of names using this ending with all the popular prefixes. Jaquan, Laquan, Raquan, Shaquan, and Tyquan have all become popular as boys' names only in the '90s, although an early example named basketball player JaQuan Hart. This ending appears to be exclusively masculine, although a feminized Shaquana also appears. Variant: **Daquan.** Related names: **Jaquan, Laquan, Raquan, Shaquan,** and **Tyquan.**

DESHAWN: (m) coined; this name appears to be a compound of the prefix "De-" with the name SEAN (Chapter 10). Some forms of this name appear as early as the '70s, making it a leader in the fashion, given that it is not derived from a surname. With that lead time, you have a variety of notable bearers including basketball player DeShawn Stevenson, football player DeShaun Foster, and actor Deshaun Hill. Shawn appears with other prefixes, including "Ke-," as for football player Keyshawn Johnson, "Ra-," as for actor Rashaan Nall, and "Ty-," as for jazz percussionist Tyshawn Sorey. See also Lashawn. Variants: **Dashawn** and **Deshaun.** Related names: **Keshaun, Keshawn, Keyshawn; Rashaan, Rashawn,** and **Rayshawn; Tyshawn.**

DION(TE): (m) multiple origins; Dion has a long history, being a diminutive of Dionysius or a similar name (see Chapter 5). It appears for a character in Shakespeare's *A Winter's Tale.* In the 19th century it became particularly popular in the African American community and thus fed into the fashion for invented names. Several coined names alternate the endings "-on" and "-onte." Dion has been on the popularity charts since the '60s but Deonte belongs largely to the '90s and later. Well-known bearers include doo-wop singer Dion DiMucci, football star Deion Sanders, and R&B musician DeAnte Duckett. Dion may have inspired Keion, although there is also a Scottish surname McKeon "son of Ewan" that could have contributed. Keon, the most popular spelling, appears as early as the '80s, but the main use of this name has been relatively recent. Bearers include basketball players Keyon Dooling and Keon Clark. Variants: **Deante, Deion, Deonta, Deontae, Deon,** and **Deonte.** Related names: **Keion, Keyon,** and **Keon.**

DOREEN: (f) multiple origins; possibly this is sometimes from the Gaelic name Doireann, of uncertain meaning, but it is more often likely to be a blend of DOROTHY (Chapter 8) and the suffix "-ene," similarly to Charlene. This name appears in the late 19th century as the title of a novel and was most popular in the mid–20th century. One bearer is children's author Doreen Rappaport. Variants: **Dorene** and **Dorine.**

ENOLA: (f) coined; an anagram of the word "alone." It was briefly popular around the turn of the 20th century but has been somewhat spoilt as an attractive name by being used for the Enola Gay, the plane that dropped the bomb on Hiroshima. (The plane was named after the pilot's mother.)

JADEN: (f, m) multiple origins; there is a Biblical name Jadon meaning "he will judge" or "he will plead," however the many spelling variants here point to another fashion in coined names. The general pattern starts with either d, j, k, or t, has a middle sound of d, l, r, or v, and ends with n. Between these consonants, the vowels are almost entirely free to vary, except that names in this group ending in "-yn" are almost always feminine and names ending in "-on" are almost always masculine. For other coined names with this pattern, see JALEN, JAREN, and TAVON in the current chapter, but some of the popularity and variety of names like DEVON, DARREN, and even KAREN (all Chapter 10) may echo this same fashion. One way in which names can be coined is seen in the choice of Jaden by actors Will and Jada Smith for their son, echoing his mother's name. Variants: (both) **Jadyn, Jaiden,** and **Jayden;** (f) **Jaidyn;** (m) **Jadon, Jaeden,** and **Jaydon.**

JAKAYLA: (f) coined; a blend of "Ja-" with the name Mikayla, a variant of MICHAELA (Chapter 10). This name has only been hitting the charts in the last few years, after the peak of Mikayla's popularity. Jayla may be a short form. Variant: **Jayla.**

JAMAR: (m) coined; it's possible that the ending "-mar" was taken from surnames like DelMar, or it may be a short form of Marcus, as in Jamarcus. One bearer of this name is football player Jamar Fletcher. Variants: **Jamarcus, Jamari,** and **Jomar.**

JAVON(TE): (m) multiple origins; Javon fits the fashion for "three-consonant" names like Jaren and Jalen. Jovanni may sometimes be a variant of Giovanni, an Italian form of JOHN (Chapter 8) while Jevon can be a Welsh form of JOHN. There is also an Old Testament figure Javan, said to have been the ancestor of the Greeks, but this name doesn't seem to have had much influence. People using this name group include clothing designer Jovani, musician Javon Jackson, and basketball player Juwan Howard. Variants: **Javen, Javion, Jovan, Jevon, Jovani, Jovanny, Jovany,** and **Juwan.**

JALEN: (f, m) coined; this is a name built in the "three-consonant" fashion to resemble Jaden, Jaren, and so on. Some of the feminine variants may be compounds, such as Jay + Lynn, or blends, such as Jaylene blending Jay and some name like Arlene. These names are only recently popular, although Jalen has risen rapidly for boys, and Jayla similarly for girls. Some bearers include basketball player Jalen Rose on the male side and paleontologist Jaelyn Eberle on the female side. Variants: (both) **Jaylin;** (f) **Jaelyn, Jailene, Jailyn, Jalyn, Jalynn, Jaylene, Jaylyn,** and **Jaylynn;** (m) **Jalon, Jaylan, Jaylen,** and **Jaylon.**

JALIYAH: (f) coined?; the name Jaliyah looks as if it ought to be Arabic, and there is an Arabic word *jaliyah* meaning "community" (although it doesn't appear as a name), but this might be a coincidence of sound. Jaliyah has shown up on the charts only in the last couple of years.

JAREN: (m) multiple origins; in addition to matching the fashion for "three-consonant" names, there is also an obscure Biblical name Jaron meaning "to cry or sing in rejoicing." The name appears on the charts in the '80s. Jaron Lanier was a pioneer in the field of virtual reality. Variant: **Jaron.**

JAZLYN: (f) coined; this is most likely a blending of JASMINE (Chapter 12) and LYNN (Chapter 14). Jazlyn J. is the main character in a series of children's books, and may be responsible for its recent popularity.

KIANA: (f) coined; this name is possibly taken from DIANA (Chapter 5), similarly to Deandre and Keandre. A similar name is Tiana, which appears somewhat earlier, borne for example by Australian actress Tianna Sansbury. Variants: **Keanna, Kianna,** and **Quiana.** Related names: **Tiana,** and **Tianna.**

LADONNA: (f) Italian or Spanish; the lady. This comes from a nickname, possibly originally taken from an epithet of the Virgin. This name was somewhat popular for a number of decades in the mid–20th century and is borne by Native American politician and activist LaDonna Harris.

LAKEISHA, KEISHA: (f) coined; some consider Keisha a short form of Lakeisha, but Keisha was more common than the longer form when they first showed up and appears to be the original. This would undermine derivations of LaKeisha from an African name. Both names have been relatively popular in the '70s and '80s. Bearers include basketball player LaKeisha Taylor and actress Keisha Castle-Hughes, the star of *Whale Rider.* Variants: **Keesha, Keishla, Kesha, Keshia, Kisha; Lakesha, Lakeshia,** and **Lakisha.**

LAMAR: (m) French; the sea; the lake. This surname began being used as a given name in the 19th century and helped inspire the sound-pattern of coined names. One bearer is Texas congressman Lamar Smith.

LAQUITA: (f) coined; this name is popular on the early edge of the fashion for coined names, in the '70s and '80s. It may be a blend of the beginning "La-" with the Spanish endearment *chiquita.* The name is borne by historian Laquita M. Higgs.

LARUE: (f) French; the street. From a surname meaning "one who lives on a street." This name was popular during the early part of the 20th century and is one of the traditional names that inspired the recent fashion.

LASHAWN: (f, m) coined; this name is constructed similarly to DeShawn, although you should probably distinguish between Lashawn, where the female use is a borrowing of the male name, and the names ending in "-da" which appear to be exclusively female names. Female bearers include author LaShonda K. Barnett and economist Lashawn Richburg Hayes. Variants: (f) **Lashanda** and **Lashonda.**

LATASHA: (f) coined; this is a blend of "La-" with the independent name Tasha (see NATALIE in Chapter 13). Tasha became suddenly popular in the '70s and LaTasha shot up out of nowhere in the '80s, right on its heels. This name is borne by track star LaTasha Colander-Richardson. Variant: **Latosha.**

LATISHA: (f) Latin?; possibly a variant of LETICIA (Chapter 8). Laisha may be a variant, or may have been coined independently — compare it with Daisha and Tyesha. Laisha has only been on the charts recently but has been around long enough to be borne by Canadian poet and writer Laisha Rosnau. Variant: **Laisha.**

LATONIA: (f) coined; like LaTasha, this name prefixes "La-" to an independent name that was hitting its own peak of popularity at the same time in the '70s (that is TONIA, see Chapter 10). One bearer is actress LaTanya Richardson. Variants: **Latanya** and **Latonya.**

LATOYA, TOYA: (f) coined; LaToya appears to be the original name and Toya a less popular derivative. The origins of LaToya itself are obscure unless it is a variant of LaTonya. The most famous bearer of this name is probably singer LaToya Jackson.

LATRELL: (m) coined?; this name is possibly an adaptation of the English surname Luttrell meaning "otter," but is treated as a coined name today. Borne by basketball player Latrell Sprewell.

LATRICIA: (f) coined; this is a blend of "La-" with the name Patricia. This name shows up on the charts during the '70s and '80s when Tricia or Trisha was at its peak of popularity. It is found for journalist Latricia Ransom. Variant: **Latrice.**

LAVADA, LAVEDA: (f) multiple origins?; there is a traditional given name Lavada or Laveda that has been in use at least since the 19th century. The origin is unclear: suggestions include a Hebrew name or a Latin word meaning "washed, purified." The name comes into the coined names fashion by spelling, as it is commonly used today as LaVada or LaVeda.

LAVERNE: (f, m) French; place of the alder trees. Today the name may also be used as a variant of the feminine name Verna, either from a Latin word meaning "Spring" or used as a feminine form of VERNON (Chapter 13), from a similar origin. It's familiar from TV character Laverne De Fazio of the show *Laverne and Shirley.* Variants: (both) **Lavern;** (f) **Lavera, Laverna,** and **Verna.**

LAVON: (f) coined; possibly this may be used today as a blend of "La-" with the name IVONNE (Chapter 19) — but compare it with Davon, Javon, and Tavon. This name was primarily popular in the first half of the 20th century, and at that time it most likely comes from a French surname. Variant: **Lavonne.**

LAWANDA: (f) coined; this is sometimes a blend of "La-" with the independent name WANDA (Chapter 10) but this name has been popular twice: once in the '70s as a coined name, and earlier in the '30s when it appears as a variant of Louanda, possibly in turn a variant of LUCINDA (Chapter 9) (Lucinda itself is a coined name blending Lucy and Linda.) This group of names reminds us that the fashion for cutting and pasting name parts together is hardly a modern phenomenon. Today the name is borne by actress LaWanda Page. The same ending is found for Shawanda and Tawanda. Although there is a masculine name Tawanda found in Africa, e.g., for Zimbabwean sculptor Tawanda Ngandu, the American use of this as a feminine name appears to be an independent invention. In the book and movie *Fried Green Tomatoes,* the character Evelyn Couch shouts, "Tawanda!" as her battle cry. Variant: **Louanda.** Related names: **Shawanda, Tawana, Tawanda,** and **Tawanna.**

LEROY: (m) French; the king (a nickname). This name has been quite popular since the 19th century and is one of the inspirations for this group of coined names. Alain LeRoy Locke was one of the leaders of the Harlem renaissance in the '20s. Another bearer is astronaut Leroy Chiao Variants: **Leeroy.**

LEATRICE: (f) coined; this is a blend of the names LEE (Chapter 14) and BEATRICE (Chapter 8). This name was most popular around the '20s and is borne by actress Leatrice Joy and graphic artist Leatrice Eiseman.

LINA: (f) multiple origins; this name can be a diminutive of any of various names ending in "-lina," such as Angelina or Carolina. One familiar bearer is film director Lina Wertmuller.

LITZY: (f) coined; this is possibly a blend of initial "L" with the name Mitzy. This is the sole name of Mexican pop singer Litzy, who may be responsible for the recent fashion for the name.

MAC: (m) Gaelic; son. This is a nickname taken from any of many Gaelic surnames of the form Mac X, meaning "son of X." Like Lina and Van this name partakes only of the "cut" part of the "cut and paste" category. One bearer is early movie slapstick comedian Mack Sennett. Variant: **Mack.**

MALISSA: (f) multiple origins?; possibly this is a blend of Melissa with some other name. In general, the prefix "Ma-" isn't used to create new names. One bearer of this name is R&B singer Malissa Noble.

MELINDA: (f) coined; this is a blend of LINDA (Chapter 10) perhaps with MELANIE (Chapter 7). The name BELINDA (Chapter 6) may also be an influence. Malinda and Melinda may have been created independently, as the first peaks around the turn of the 20th century while the second is most popular in mid century. Malinda Blalock served in the American Civil War alongside her husband, while disguised as a man. A current bearer is philanthropist Melinda Gates. Variant: **Malinda.**

MINDY: (f) coined; this is a blend of CINDY (Chapter 5) with initial "M-," possibly influenced by Minnie or some similar name. This name started hitting the charts in the '50s and has only gone out of fashion within the last decade. One bearer is jazz singer Mindi Abair but the name may be most familiar from the title character of the TV show *Mork and Mindy.* Variant: **Mindi.**

MYRA: (f) multiple origins; in some cases this is an anagram of MARY (Chapter 8), but Saint Nicholas was the bishop of Myra, and that may be another source of the name. It appears in the 16th century as a pseudonym for the lady that Fulke Grenville addressed poetry to, and as a character in Theodore Dreiser's 1925 novel *An American Tragedy.* Myra Bradwell was the first American woman admitted to the bar to practice law.

SHAMAR: (m) coined; a compound of "Sha-" with "-mar" similarly to Jamar and Lamar. Shamar is also the title of a line of Tibetan Bhuddist teachers, but this is unlikely to have contributed to the American name. This name has only shown up on the charts in the last decade. Variant: **Shemar.**

SHANDA: (f) coined; this is possibly a shortening of some name like Sharonda, or simply a substitution of "Sh-" in Rhonda, but another possible origin is from Shawn, similarly to Glenda and Glen. Variant: **Shonda.**

SHANELL: (f) French?; possibly this is a variant of Chanel, "a channel, a ditch," which became a surname familiar from clothing and perfume designer Coco Chanel. Shanell appears at a time when Chanel is most popular as a given name (in the '90s), which supports this conclusion. If so, this is a case where an existing name has been respelled to make it fit into the pattern of coined names. Bearers include actress Shanelle Workman of the soap opera *One Life to Live.* Variants: **Shanelle; Chanel,** and **Chanelle.**

SHANICE: (f) coined; this name is possibly a variant of Janice, or a blend of that with Shanika. The name has mostly been popular in the last decade, but an earlier bearer is R&B singer Shanice Wilson. Variant: **Shaniece.**

SHANIKA: (f) coined; this is a compound of the prefix "Sha-" with the ending "-nika," as in Tanika. Nika may be from a diminutive of Nicolette. This name has primarily been popular in the '80s and '90s. Tanika may be a related creation, although there also appears to be an identical Indian name, as borne by playwright Tanika Gupta. Variants: **Shanequa** and **Shaniqua.** Related name: **Tanika.**

SHANITA: (f) coined; this was perhaps originally a variant of Shanika, as Shanita appears when that name is most popular. The name Shanta may be yet another variant, but there is also a Sanskrit name Shanta meaning "calm." These names were most popular in the '80s. Variants: **Shanta** and **Shante.**

SHARONDA: (f) coined; a compound of the prefix "Sha-" with the independent name RHONDA (Chapter 17). This was popular mostly in the '70s and '80s. Shalonda may be a variant of this, as for basketball player Shalonda Enis. Related name: **Shalonda.**

SHAYLEE: (f) coined?; possibly this is from a compound of "Sha-" with LEE (Chapter 14), but equally possible it may be a variant of Shelly or some similar name. This name has only become popular in the last few years.

TAMATHA: (f) coined; this may be a variant blend of "T-" with SAMANTHA, perhaps also influenced by TABITHA (see those two names in Chapter 16). All three first appear on the charts in the '60s.

TAMELA: (f) coined; this is a blend of initial "T-" with the name PAMELA (Chapter 6). The name was popular in the '60s and '70s.

TAMIKA: (f) coined; the latter half of the name may possibly come originally from some form of Michael, but it may simply be chosen for the sound. This name was primarily popular in the '70s and '80s and is borne by basketball player Tamika Catchings. The similar name Shamika was briefly popular in the '80s. Variants: **Tameka, Tomeka,** and **Tomika.** Related names: **Shameka** and **Shamika.**

TANGELA: (f) coined; this is a blend of the independent name ANGELA (Chapter 10) with initial "T-." This name hit the charts briefly in the '70s and is borne by basketball player Tangela Smith.

TAVON: (m) coined; this name is constructed similarly to Davon, Javon, Lavon, and so on. Unlike the feminine names beginning with "Ta-," this name has only hit the charts within the last decade. Compare this name also with the "three consonant" pattern, as for Jalen, Jaren, Javon. Variants: **Tavian** and **Tavion.**

TEAGAN: (f) multiple origins; as a girl's name this is likely to be a blend of the name MEGAN (Chapter 10) with initial "T-," although it can also be a borrowing of the Gaelic masculine name Tadhgan, usually translated as "poet." Another possible blend is with the name Reagan, which can be used as a girl's name. This name has become popular only very recently.

TRAVON: (m) coined; this name most likely belongs to the same construction pattern as Davon, Javon, Tavon, and so on, but if so it is the only name with the prefix "Tra-" to have hit the popularity charts. Travon itself has been around since the '80s, while the other variants are much more recent. The prefix may be inspired by the name TREY (Chapter 13). Variants: **Trayvon, Trevin, Trevion,** and **Treyvon.**

TYREE: (m) multiple origins; this may be a short form of TYREESE, but there is also an English surname of French origin that can appear as Tyree. This name has appeared on the popularity charts since the '70s which argues against the connection with Tyreese, which only appears later.

TYREESE: (m) coined; this is presumably a compound of the prefix "Ty-" with the independent name RHYS (Chapter 18). This name has hit the charts only in the last half decade, but an earlier bearer is R&B singer Tyrese Darnell Gibson. Variant: **Tyrese.**

TYRELL: (m) English a variant of TERRELL (Chapter 19). Tyrell is a traditional name, not a coined one, however its appearance on the popularity charts only in the '80s suggests that the renewed interest in it may be influenced by the fashion for coined names. Variant: **Tyrel.**

TYRIK: (m) coined; this name may be inspired by the Arabic name TARIQ (Chapter 15), and has primarily been popular in the last decade. Variants: **Tyreek, Tyrek, Tyreke, Tyriq,** and **Tyrique.**

TYRONE: (m) Gaelic; Owen's land. This became a surname and then was picked up as a given name in the '30s when it was popularized by the father and son actors named Tyrone Power. It increased in popularity until the '70s but has fallen off somewhat since then. This name almost certainly supplied the prefix "Ty-" for other coined names. The diminutive Ty has been increasing in popularity over the last half century, in many cases used in honor of baseball great Ty Cobb. The name LaRon may be inspired from this name, but it could be a compound of "La-" with the independent name Ron. The name is borne by performing storyteller LaRon Williams. Variants: **Tyron** and **Tyrin**. Diminutive: **Ty**. Related name: **Laron**.

VAN: (m) coined; from; originating from. This is a short nickname taken from any number of Dutch surnames of the form "Van X," in other words, "from X." Like MAC (above), this was originally a nickname used by someone with one of the relevant surnames but was picked up for use as an independent given name. One prominent bearer is actor Van Johnson. A German variant, Von, is also found. This name has been mildly popular for most of the last century but has fallen somewhat out of fashion in the last few decades. Variant: **Von**.

Part IV

Describing the World: Names of Quality, Character, and Location

The 5th Wave   By Rich Tennant

"Of course I respect your work at a pharmaceutical company. Little Dristan and Bactine here should be proof of that."

In this part . . .

At some point in life, everyone will ask, "What does my name mean?" With only a few exceptions, if you dig far enough back, every name means something. The chapters in this section explore some of the common types of meaning that have produced names, from virtues and descriptions, to locations and forces of nature. Meaning can also come from the associations a name brings, and this section covers names associated with particular cultures.

Chapter 12

Re-using Rubies, Roses, and Robins: Names from the Natural World

Most people figure that flower, bird, and gem names are a product of Victorian sentimentality, but the full story is more complicated. Some of these names, like Viola, Jacinto, or Diamond date back to the Medieval period or earlier. Others, such as Sage, Jasmine, and Raven are very recent fashions for names that we've forgotten were used long ago. And some that you consider obvious — like Rose and Garnet — had entirely different origins, even though you think of them now as flowers and jewels. Often the same name may be given to boys as a traditional surname and to girls as a descriptive name, such as Ruby or Holly.

Flowers and Gems

For the most part, flower and gem names are either relatively recent adoptions or derive from surnames. The exceptions are usually of Greek or Latin origin and often come with colorful stories about how the flower (or person) got its name.

AMBER: (f) English; a soft golden stone made from fossilized resin. The name really took off in the '60s, spurred on by the popularity of Kathleen Winsor's historic novel *Forever Amber* and its film version. It reached a peak in the '80s, a time when amber jewelry also starts to see great popularity. Lately you may associate it with actress Tiffani-Amber Thiessen and the "Amber Alert" system for tracking down abducted children (named after an abductee).

BERYL: (f, m) English; a family of gemstones that includes emerald and aquamarine. The name is taken directly from the gemstone, so its surprising to find it used for men as well as women starting in the late 19th century. Prominent bearers all seem to have been women, including early aviator Beryl Markham and novelist Beryl Bainbridge.

CORAL: (f) English; a precious material, usually red or pink, that is the skeleton of a colony of microscopic sea creatures. This Victorian name fell out of popularity early in the 20th century, but is echoed in names like Coralie and Coraline (although these actually derive from Greek *kore* "maiden"). Variants: **Coralie** and **Coraline.**

DAISY: (f) English; any of various flowers with a circle of elongated petals radiating from a round center. This was one of the earliest of the flower names, but was probably inspired by a translation of French *Marguerite* (which, incidentally, can also mean "pearl"). Daisy can be as down to earth as the addressee of the song *A Bicycle Built for Two* or as patrician as F. Scott Fitzgerald's heroine in *The Great Gatsby.* The name has been continuously popular since its coinage, although it fell somewhat in the mid–20th century.

DALIA: (f) coined; as with many New World flowers, the common name of the dahlia comes from the name of a botonist, in this case Andre Dahl of Sweden. The spelling Dalia has started appearing in the last couple of decades. Presumably the parents who choose it are *not* thinking of the gruesome "Black Dahlia" murder case of the late '40s.

DIAMOND: (f, m) English; the hardest known gemstone and a symbol of wealth and elegance. This name has recently been used for both boys and girls, although it is more popular for the latter as you may expect for a jewel name. But boys may look to "Diamond Jim" Brady, a late 19th-century financier with a rags-to-riches history, or actor Lou Diamond Phillips.

EBONY: (f) English; a hard black wood often used for musical instruments or fine furniture. The name sees a sudden popularity in the '70s. Variant: **Eboni.**

ESMERALDA: (f) Spanish; a green gem, the emerald. This is the name of the gypsy heroine of Victor Hugo's *The Hunchback of Notre Dame,* although it was her nickname not her given name. It has seen a great increase in popularity over the second half of the 20th century, and recently the English form Emerald is also found. Variant: **Emerald.**

FERN: (f) English; a nonflowering plant with curled fronds. Another Victorian coinage that slowly fell out of favor in the last century. It's surprising that heroine of E.B. White's children's book *Charlotte's Web* (that is, the human heroine rather than the spider) didn't give it a further boost in the '50s. Variant: **Ferne.**

FLORENCE: (f, m) Italian; from the city of Florence, Italy, or from an old Roman family name. But the city name, and the other related names, all derive originally from Latin *flos* "flower." The Roman goddess Flora represented the abundance of the flowering world, and the state of Florida was named after its vegetation. Both male and female names in this group have been popular since Roman times, although by the early 20th century Florence was coming to be seen exclusively as a girl's name, perhaps partly from the fame of nursing pioneer Florence Nightengale. More recently you have track star Florence Griffith Joyner. Variants: (f) **Flor, Flora,** and **Florida;** (m) **Florencio, Florentino,** and **Florian.** Diminutive: (f) **Flo.**

FOREST, FORREST: (m) English; forest, woods. Given name use is taken from the surname, with popularity deriving from people like Confederate general Nathan Bedford Forrest and continued by actors like Forrest Tucker and DeForest Kelly. Variant: **DeForest.**

GARNET, GARNETT: (f, m) English; a blood-red gemstone. Girls have most likely been named for the jewel and boys for the unrelated surname. In both cases, the name became rare in the early 20th century, although for recent examples you can look to Canadian folk singer Garnet Rogers (brother of the better-known Stan).

HAZEL: (f, m) English; the hazel tree (also known as filbert). This name is more popular among girls than boys, and in both cases has declined in use through the 20th century. The TV series *Hazel* about a maid may have associated the name too much with the title character's occupation for it to remain fashionable. Variant: **Hazle.**

HEATH: (m) English; not a specific plant, but a class of low scrubby mountain vegetation. The surge of popularity of this name in the '60s probably comes from Lee Majors' early role in the TV western *The Big Valley.*

HEATHER: (f) English; a shrub with small purple flowers, often associated with Scotland. Used occasionally by the Victorians, the name took off like a rocket in the '70s to make it all the way to number 8. It has become almost synonymous with blonde actresses such as Heather Locklear and Heather Graham, although the "Heathers" in the movie of the same name are less than stellar recommendations.

HOLLY: (f, m) English; an evergreen tree with red berries associated with Christmas. Like *Heather,* this name sees a surge of popularity centered on the '70s. Male examples early in the century are probably from the surname, although still originating with the tree. Variants: (f) **Hollie** and **Holli.**

HYACINTH: (m) Greek; a spring bulb with a spike of small flowers, usually purple. In Greek mythology, Hyacinth was a beautiful boy doomed by a god's jealousy, who turned at death into the flower that bears his name. The modern use is due to an early Christian martyr who bore the name. The Spanish version Jacinto appeared occasionally in the early 20th century. Variant: **Jacinto.**

IRIS: (f) Greek; the iris flower, named after the Greek goddess of the rainbow. The name has had a relatively steady popularity. The recent movie *Iris* tells the story of poet Iris Murdoch. In Greek mythology, Iris is the messenger of the gods on Olympus.

IVY: (f, m) English; a clinging vine. Despite the name's association with "ivy-covered halls," it has been in relatively constant popularity as a girls' name since its introduction by the Victorians. As usual, the occasional use for boys is probably inspired by the family name, coming from an unrelated place name. Variant: **Ivey.**

JADE: (f, m) English; a hard green stone popular in Asian art. The name has become popular for both boys and girls only recently. (It wouldn't have been used as a name in Victorian times as the word had negative connotations implying a slovenly woman or one with a bad reputation.) Jada may be a variant, as seen for actress Jada Pinkett-Smith. Variants: (f) **Jada** and **Jayde.**

JASMINE, YASMIN: (f) Persian; a small strongly-scented flower sometimes used in tea. The name has long been popular in the Middle East, and the recent popularity of variants starting with the letter "Y-" as for actress Yasmine Bleeth are probably due to a general interest in Islamic culture. The English form Jasmine probably stems originally from a character in James Elroy Flecker's play *Hassan,* but shot up drastically in popularity in the '90s probably due to the character in Disney's animated *Aladdin.* Another variant is seen for author Jessamine West. Variants: **Jasmin, Jasmyn, Jazmin, Jazmine, Jazmyn, Jazmyne, Jessamine, Jessamyn, Yasmeen, Yasmin, Yasmine,** and **Yazmin.**

JEWEL, JEWELL: (f, m) English; a gem, a precious stone. This Victorian name fell from popularity but has recently shown new interest. Singer Jewel considers the name distinctive enough to use all by itself. See also poet and writer Jewel Gomez. As a boy's name, it may be from the surname, originally indicating the profession of jeweler, but it faded from popularity over the first half of the 20th century.

LAUREL: (f, m) Latin; the laurel tree, symbol of poetry and victory. As a girl's name, this is probably a diminutive of LAURA (Chapter 6), while as a boy's name it's more likely to be from the surname (for example, comedian Stan Laurel), but since both derive originally from the tree, we're safe in including them. The name shifts from male to female use around the '20s. The laurel has long been a symbol of victory and accomplishment in the form of a wreath of the leaves.

MAGNOLIA: (f) coined; a tree with large white flowers named for French botanist Pierre Magnol. The magnolia flower has been a metaphor of feminine beauty in the American South, as in the movie *Steel Magnolias.* As a name, however, it fell largely out of favor in the early 20th century.

MYRTLE: (f) Greek; an ornamental shrub. A Latin form of the name, Myrtilla, shows up in ancient times and was revived in the 19th century about the same time that Myrtle became popular. Like many of the flower names, it fell from popularity in the first half of the 20th century. Diminutive: **Myrtie.**

NARCISSUS, NARCISO: (m) Greek; a member of the daffodil family whose name is commonly associated with a root meaning "numbness" from a medical property of some types of the flower. Given that the legendary Greek Narcissus ended up drowning in a pond (and then being memorialized as a flower) because he was so in love with himself that he dove in after his own reflection, it seems an inauspicious name, and yet there are scattered examples of it in use. Narciso is an Italian form and showed up occasionally in the early 20th century.

OLIVE: (f) Latin; the olive tree. The olive branch or wreath has been a symbol of peace. The Latin form Olivia has been popular since classical times and features as the heroine of Shakespeare's *Twelfth Night.* While Olive declined in popularity, Olivia shot up in the last few decades to reach as high as number 5. Among the bearers are singer Olivia Newton-John and actress Olivia de Havilland. Intriguing Olives include 19th-century South African feminist writer Olive Schreiner. A diminutive of this name is borne by actresses Liv Ullman and Liv Tyler. Variants: **Alivia** and **Olivia.** Diminutives: **Liv** and **Ollie.**

OPAL: (f) Greek; a soft iridescent gemstone. Opal fell out of favor somewhat in the first half of the 20th century.

PANSY: (f) English; a small garden flower also known as hearts-ease. This was never a particularly popular name, but there is a Pansy in Henry James' novel *Portrait of a Lady.*

PEARL: (f, m) English; a gem formed by oysters or other shellfish to protect against an irritation. The name may have been partly inspired by one of the meanings of the name Margaret. Pearl is the heroine's daughter in Nathaniel Hawthorne's *The Scarlet Letter* and has been kept in mind by women such as author Pearl S. Buck and singer Pearl Bailey. It fell out of use as a man's name in the early 20th century, derived most likely from the surname (but also referring to the gemstone). Variants: (f) **Pearle, Pearlie, Perline,** and **Pearla.**

RUBY: (f, m) English; a red gemstone. The male name may be a nickname for Reuben or possibly from a surname. As a girl's name it remains relatively popular from the Victorian era to the present day. Bearers include dancer Ruby Keeler and Ruby Bridges, one of the child-heros of school integration, immortalized in Norman Rockwell's painting on the topic. Variants: (f) **Rubi, Rubie,** and **Rubye.**

SAGE: (f, m) English; an aromatic herb used in cooking. Sage had a brief popularity as a girl's name in the 16th to 17th century, more likely as a virtue name meaning "wise" than in reference to the plant. It has become somewhat popular for both boys and girls in the last couple of decades, this time most likely from the plant. Sage is considered a cleansing influence and often used as incense. Variant: (f) **Saige.**

SYLVIA (f), **SYLVAN** (m), **SYLVESTER** (m): Latin; forest, of the forest. The Roman god Silvanus was protector of the forests, while Sylvester came into popularity via several early saints and popes. Today you have actor and director Sylvester Stallone, although he may lose the recognition contest to an animated cat with a fondness for tweety birds. An early example of this name is the nickname of Rhea Silvia, mother of Romulus and Remus the legendary founders of Rome. Shakespeare's use of it in *Two Gentlemen of Verona* brought it into popularity in England, and it has continued to be relatively popular through the 20th century. Poet Sylvia Plath, financial expert Sylvia Porter, and harpist Sylvia Woods show the name's continuing popularity. Variant: (f) **Silvia;** (m) **Sylvio.**

VIOLA, VIOLET, VIOLETTE: (f) Latin; the violet flower. This is one of the handful of flower names with ancient roots. The French form *Violette* is found in the Middle Ages, and the popularity of *Viola* begins with the heroine of Shakespeare's *Twelfth Night.* Violet features in the 19th century novel *The Sea-Captain* by Lord Lytton, as well as muralist Violet Oakley and Edwardian socialite Violet Trefusis. The Italian *Violetta* appears in Giuseppe Verdi's opeta *La Traviata.* Most of these names fell into disuse in the mid–20th century, but *Violet* has seen a sudden resurgence lately.

Animals and Birds

The practice of naming people after birds and animals has ancient origins, most likely inspired by animals sacred to a particular tribe or family. The oldest names tend to be taken from creatures that still have strong symbolic associations: eagles, lions, bears, and ravens.

AQUILA: (m) Latin; eagle. Latin texts of the Bible mention an Aquila who was host to St. Paul at Corinth, although this seems to be a substitution for a Greek original *Akula* which may have meant "acorn" instead. But Aquila was a familiar Latin name in any case. It was revived along with other Biblical names in the Reformation, when it's also found as a woman's name, probably due to the "a" ending misleading people into thinking it should be feminine.

ARIEL: (f, m) Hebrew; lion of God, or God is a Lion. The name occurs in the Bible both for a man and as a symbolic name for Jerusalem. But when Shakespeare used it for his "airy spirit" in *The Tempest,* he was clearly punning off the English word "air," and that meaning seems to have entirely inspired the feminine use, popularized most recently by Disney's cartoon version of *The Little Mermaid.* The boy's name has had some slight popularity in the later 20th century. Famous bearers include Israeli prime minister Ariel Sharon.

BROCK: (m) English; a badger. This name progressed from a nickname to a surname and then to a given name. It has been growing in popularity in the later part of the 20th century, possibly because it matches both the fashion for names beginning in "Br-" from the later century and the fashion for "hard" one-syllable names from mid century. One bearer is actor Brock Peters.

COLUMBUS: (m) Latin; a dove. A group of Latin names derive from this root, and from them come the masculine Gaelic names Colm and Malcolm, and Columbina, the name of a female character in Commedia del' Arte. The popularity of the name Columbus comes from the famous explorer, but has declined somewhat in the later 20th century. Variants: **Colm** and **Malcom.**

DOVIE: (f) English; a diminutive of dove. The name probably originated in an endearing nickname, although the name Dove appeared rarely in the Middle Ages as a man's name. Dovie was mildly popular in the early part of the 20th century.

DRAKE: (m) English; either "a male duck" or "a dragon." Taken from the surname, this is probably rarely chosen for the original meaning. Bearers of the surname include famous explorer (or pirate, depending on your point of view) Sir Francis Drake. Today you have Erle Stanley Gardner's detective Paul Drake and actor Drake Hogestyn. The name has enjoyed a sharp rise in popularity lately.

LEO: (m) Latin; a lion. This was a popular name among early Popes, resulting in its general popularity, although more recently it has been popularized more through Jewish use. The diminutive Lionel also dates back to the Middle Ages. Leo and Leon have been quite popular, although declining somewhat in the later 20th century. Lionel has been somewhat less popular but is used steadily. The various forms are found for guitarist Leo Kotke, novelists Leo Tolstoy and Leon Uris, singer Lionel Richie, and actor Lionel Barrymore. Variants: **Leon, Leonel,** and **Lionel.**

MERLE: (f, m) French; a blackbird. The association with the French bird name may be after-the-fact, and the name may instead have various origins including the surname Merrill, the given name MURIEL (Chapter 18), and perhaps even a nickname from MERLIN (Chapter 6). As a boy's name it is relatively popular in the early part of the 20th century, with more recent bearers such as singers Merle Travis and Merle Haggard. As a girl's name it began somewhat earlier and fell out of popularity rather suddenly around the '40s. Bearers include actress Merle Oberon. Variants: **Mearl, Merl, Murl, Myrl,** and **Myrle;** and **Merrill.**

PALOMA: (f) Spanish; a dove. Doves seem to be a popular type of bird name, perhaps because of their Christian symbolism (the dove that returned to Noah's ark and the dove used in art to represent the Holy Spirit). Bearers include famous daughter and designer Paloma Picasso and ballerina Paloma Herrera. The name has seen some increase in popularity in the last few decades.

PHOENIX: (m) Greek; a mythical bird that is reborn from its own funeral pyre. The original meaning of the word was "a Phoenician." This name has become suddenly popular in the last decade, possibly directly from the bird, but possibly from the city in Arizona. The family of acting brothers River, Rain, and Joaquin Phoenix adopted the surname as a symbol of new beginnings.

RAVEN: (f, m) English; a large member of the crow family. The name has seen a very sudden surge of popularity starting in the '80s. The female title character of TV's *That's So Raven* is one example. Interestingly, it's hitting the charts today only as a girl's name while historically the name was masculine. Hrafn was an ancient Norse form, and the English version is found in the early Medieval period. The Latin equivalent *corvus* produced the surnames Corbett, Corby, and Corbin, of which the last is enjoying a recent surge in popularity for boys. The connection between the two sets of names was exploited in the soap opera *Love of Life* in the '50s for character Paul Raven's alter ego Matt Corby. Variants: (m) **Corbett, Corby, Corbin,** and **Korbin.**

RONAN: (m) Gaelic; a seal. Seals figure prominently in Irish folklore, and the ancient origins of this name suggest it may have been a totem animal. The name has only started showing up in significant numbers in the U.S. in the last decade but has always enjoyed some small popularity in Ireland.

TAUREAN: (m) Latin; bull-like, someone born under the sign of Taurus the bull. This is something of an odd name, but perhaps is part of a long tradition of naming children for the circumstances of their birth (see Chapter 13). This name pops up on the radar around the '80s, and has already produced a few celebrities such as actor Taurean Blacque.

TODD, TOD: (m) English; a fox. Current usage comes from the surname, and only perusers of baby-name books are likely to know the original meaning. The name soars to popularity coming into the '60s. Bearers include golfer Todd Hamilton and 9/11 hero Todd Beamer.

Finding False Flora and Fauna: Flower and Bird Names That Really Aren't

What's more important when you choose a name for its meaning: the original derivation of the name, or the meaning it has to you today? Both can be important, as it doesn't matter that you *know* a name means "great conquering hero" if it *sounds* like it means "little wiggly worm." (Not that there's any name with this particular problem.) Over the centuries, old meanings may wear away and new meanings may be more immediate in your mind. The following names look as if they refer to plants, gems, animals, or birds . . . but they didn't start out that way.

BASIL: (m) Greek; a king. The cooking herb was originally named to mean something like "the king's herb" (and any pesto-lover may agree). But the name *Basil* means a king, not a spice. St. Basil gave rise to the early popularity of the name, especially in the Eastern Orthodox Church but also in the west throughout the Medieval period and later. It has fallen somewhat in popularity in the second half of the 20th century but the late actor Basil Rathbone is still memorable. Variant: **Vasili** (Russian).

CRYSTALL: (f, m) multiple origins; modernly, from the English word "crystal," meaning a clear gemstone, but historically a Scottish nickname for CHRISTOPHER (Chapter 8). Medieval examples are clearly the latter, but when the name shows up as a girl's name in the later 20th century, it is most likely a novel coinage meaning the gemstone. Bearers include Linda Evans' character Krystal Carrington in *Dynasty,* and Chrystal, the title character of a recent Billy Bob Thornton movie. Variants: **Christal, Christel, Chrystal, Cristal, Kristal, Krystal,** and **Krystle.**

DELPHINE: (f) Greek; this is not the Flipper-type dolphin or even the less familiar dolphin fish, but "having to do with Delphi," the Greek location of a famous ancient oracle. An unrelated Medieval masculine name Dolfinn has Norse origins. This name appears for the heroine of Madame de Staël's epistolary novel *Delphine,* as well as the name of French actress Delphine Seyrig. Variants: **Delfina,** as well as the less fishy **Delphia** and **Delpha.**

GRIFFIN: (m) Welsh; probably "strong lord," but the meaning is not entirely certain. When the Welsh name Gruffudd was put into Latin, it was changed into Griffinus to follow the rules of Latin pronunciation. This caused people to associate the name with the legendary gryphon, a monster with the hindquarters of a lion and the foreparts of an eagle. (A fair number of Medieval Gruffudds chose a gryphon for their coats of arms.) It's a rare name in America, brought by Welsh colonists, but it's had a sudden surge of popularity since the '80s. Bearers include actor and director Griffin Dunne and TV host Merv Griffin.

IVORY: (f, m) English; the teeth, usually of elephants or walruses, used as a gemstone. Ivory, as a man's name, is more likely to be taken either from the French place name Ivry, or from a surname deriving from the Norse name Ivar. It fell off in popularity in the early part of the 20th century, but the variant Ivor is relatively common in Britain, where famous bearers have included actor and songwriter Ivor Novello (who shows up as a character in the movie *Gosford Park*). Variant: **Ivor.**

JASPER: (m) uncertain; one possible origin is a Persian word meaning "treasure holder." Medieval tradition names the Biblical "three wise men" as Caspar, Balthazar, and Melchior. Caspar in turn became Gaspar and then Jasper, matching the gemstone by coincidence. All variants of the name have had some continuous popularity. Jasper has been a popular literary name starting at least as early as Francis Beaumont's 17th century play *The Knight of the Burning Pestle,* and continuing through an assortment of 19th century romantic novels, including those of James Fennimore Cooper, William Makepeace Thackeray, and Thomas Hardy. Outside literature you have artist Jasper Johns. Caspar has been less popular, but recently you have politician Caspar Weinberger. Variants: **Caspar** and **Gaspar.**

KITTY: (f) English; a pet form of KATHERINE (see Chapter 8), not a cat. As a nickname, this has been popular since the Middle Ages, although it has declined somewhat in the later 20th century. Borne by TV personality Kitty Carlisle, celebrity biographer Kitty Kelley, and country singer Kitty Wells. Variants: **Kat, Kit,** and **Kittie.**

LILY, LILLY: (f) English; originally a diminutive of ELIZABETH (see Chapter 8), although probably given today for the flower. It has been popular among actresses from Lily Langtry to Lily Tomlin. The name has often been popular among Asian immigrants to translate similar flower names, and this may be the case for Malaysian-born Canadian author Lily Chow. After falling somewhat out of popularity, Lily has shot up in the last few decades. See also LIL-LIAN (Chapter 9). Variants: **Lilia, Lilla,** and **Lillie.**

MARLIN: (m) origins complex; most likely a variant of MERLIN (Chapter 6). Unsurprisingly you haven't seen that many fish names becoming popular, and the marlin fish has nothing to do with this name. For that matter, the name Merlin comes not from the falcon of that name, but from a Latin form of the Welsh name Myrddin, itself a mistaken interpretation of the place name *Caerfyrddin* which means "sea fortress." This type of name origin can make simple explanations very difficult. The name is borne by TV nature-show host Marlin Perkins and diplomat Marlin Fitzwater. Another variant was popularized almost single-handedly by actor Marlon Brando. Variants: **Marlon** and **Marlyn.**

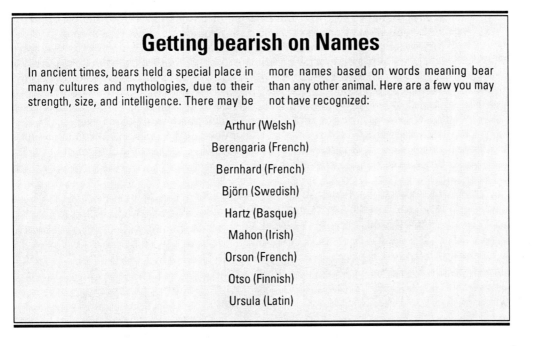

Getting bearish on Names

In ancient times, bears held a special place in many cultures and mythologies, due to their strength, size, and intelligence. There may be more names based on words meaning bear than any other animal. Here are a few you may not have recognized:

Arthur (Welsh)

Berengaria (French)

Bernhard (French)

Björn (Swedish)

Hartz (Basque)

Mahon (Irish)

Orson (French)

Otso (Finnish)

Ursula (Latin)

MARTIN: (m) Latin; associated with the Roman war-god Mars, rather than the small barnyard bird. (See Chapter 8.)

REED: (m) English; red-colored. Given the number of boys names you see taken from place names, it wouldn't be entirely surprising to see a name like Reed being similar to Forest or Heath, but instead you see an older pronunciation of the color word. The name has only been mildly popular, used by baseball player Reed Johnson and comic book hero Reed Richards. Variant: **Reid.**

ROBIN: (f, m) English; a nickname for Robert. The connection with the bird is real: The English robin was given this nickname just as the wren was nicknamed Jenny. (The American robin is related only by resemblance in having a reddish breast.) Originally, the name was masculine, borne by celebrities from the legendary hero Robin Hood up through comedian Robin Williams. But because bird names are generally thought to be feminine, it started being given to girls as an independent name, probably sometime in the 19th century. Women with the name have included feminist Robin Morgan, actress Robin Wright, and linguist Robin Tolmach Lakoff. Both male and female uses of the name rise to a peak in the mid–20th century. Variants: (f) **Robyn** and **Robbin.**

ROSE, ROSA: (f) multiple origins; in some cases from the flower, but historically more often from a Germanic root meaning "horse." Rosa is used in Spanish and some other Romance languages. Very early on, this name in all its forms became associated with the rose, sometimes called the "queen of flowers." The rose, in turn, was often associated symbolically with the Virgin Mary, which fed the popularity of the names. With the Victorian fashion for flower names, Rose became quite popular. The simple form of the name has been borne by presidential mother Rose Kennedy and country singer Rose Maddox. Rosa brings to mind civil rights activist Rosa Parks. Variants: **Rosia, Rosie, Rosina, Rosita, Rossie.** There are also a large number of compound names involving Rose (see Chapter 11).

TALON: (m) French; a variant of the Old French name Talo, rather than an animal's claw. The name has had some small popularity lately, most likely for its sound rather than its meaning.

Chapter 13

Advertising Attributes

· ·

In This Chapter

▶ Finding names that fit physical attributes

▶ Using names that define personal qualities

▶ Choosing a name that fits the birth

▶ Checking out names that describe occupations

· ·

*W*hile almost all names have some sort of meaning, it's rare for traditional given names to describe something personal about the bearer. After all, when you're bestowing a name on a newborn baby, it's difficult to tell if she will be tall (Alta) or he will be bald (Calvin). Names that describe a person's appearance, personality, or occupation generally begin as personal nicknames, turn into family surnames, and only then return as given names. In some cases, a name will appear to be descriptive but will actually have an entirely different origin. I've included a few of those here when the apparent meaning is particularly interesting.

Looking in the Mirror

People have always been obsessed with looks, and many descriptive names originally commented on appearance, for good or ill. This section discusses names that describe general attractiveness (Belle "beautiful"), general descriptions (Rufus "red"), and specific peculiarities (Cameron "crooked nose").

ALBA: (f) Latin; white. This is rare as a given name, although often found as a surname.

ALGERNON: (m) French; with a moustache. Originally this was a nickname of William de Percy, founder of the Percy family. It was turned into a given name in the 15th century and has remained in occasional use since then.

ALTA: (f) Spanish; high, tall. The name was moderately popular from the Victorian era through the early 20th century. It isn't clear whether Altha is a variant of this name or of Althea. Both names were popular at the time it appears. Variant: **Altha.**

BELLE (f), **BEAU** (m): French; beautiful, handsome. Belle is sometimes also a diminutive of Isabelle. The feminine names in this group were primarily popular in the 19th century, trailing over into the early 20th, while the masculine names only really hit the charts in the later 20th century. An early example of Beau is the nickname for Regency-era dandy Beau Brummel, but despite the meaning it is also associated with rugged figures like the title character of the movie *Beau Geste* and actor Beau Bridges. Another variant is seen for rhythm and blues musician Bo Diddley. On the women's side, you have politician Bella Abzug and notorious outlaw Belle Starr. Variants: **Bell** and **Bella**; (m) **Bo.**

BLAKE: (f, m) English; black (probably referring to hair color). Use of this as a given name comes from the surname. As a boy's name, it has been increasing strongly in popularity through the later 20th century. It's only hit the charts as a girl's name in the last decade. TV character Blake Carrington (on *Dynasty*) shares this name with writer and director Blake Edwards.

BLAINE: (m) English; with a blemish or swelling. The name may sometimes refer to the landscape, for example, a hill. As for most names taken from surnames, this has come in as a boy's name but is a good candidate for crossover. Gymnast Blaine Wilson is one bearer. Variant: **Blane.**

BONNIE: (f, m) English; beautiful (from the French *bonne* "good"). As an ordinary word, Bonnie is associated with Scottish dialects, and the name tended to arise originally in families with Scottish connections. Well-known bearers include country singer Bonnie Raitt and Olympic speed skater Bonnie Blair. The name enjoyed its greatest popularity in the mid–20th century. The Spanish name Bonita is related linguistically, but is not a direct variant of this name. Variants: **Bonita** and **Bonny.**

BROWN: (m) English; brown, brown haired. This is a rather rare name, from the surname. More common than the English name Brown is a German or Italian version, Bruno, which was established as a given name in Medieval times. This name is found for the title character of Iris Murdoch's novel *Bruno's Dream*. It was popular in the early 20th century but declined after that. Variant: **Bruno.**

CALVIN: (m) Latin; bald. This was originally a surname, and is often used in honor of Protestant reformer John Calvin. It only began to be seen as a given name in the 18th century. The name has been consistently popular throughout the 20th century. Bearers have ranged from U.S. president Calvin Coolidge to fashion designer Calvin Klein, to the comic-strip character in *Calvin and Hobbes*. Variant: **Kalvin.**

CAMERON: (f, m) Gaelic; crooked nose. Originally a personal nickname, this became the name of a Scottish clan and so became more generally popular during the 19the-century fad for all things Scottish. The name has been growing in popularity for both boys and girls in the later part of the 20th century. Female use has been rising sharply but so far the boys are holding their own. The popularity of actresses like Cameron Diaz and Camryn Manheim may tip the balance. Variants: (f) **Camryn, Kemeron,** and **Kamryn;** (m) **Camren, Camron, Kameron, Kamren,** and **Kamron.**

CHIQUITA: (f) Spanish; little one; an endearment. The name was mildly popular around the '70s.

CIARA (f), **CIARAN** (m): Gaelic; black. The feminine name has probably become merged and confused with variant spellings and pronunciations of SIERRA (Chapter 14), as well as matching coined names like Tiara. All the names in this group have become popular primarily in the last few decades. Variants: (f) **Keara, Kiara, Kiarra, Kiera, Kierra,** and **Kyara;** (m) **Kieran.**

COLE, COLEMAN: (m) English; black as coal. Coleman is sometimes an occupational surname for a charcoal burner, and in other cases is a variant of the given name Columbanus. Coleman follows the usual pattern for names taken from surnames: popular in the later 19th century and declining after that. But Cole has been becoming popular in the later 20th century, probably following the fashion for strong, one-syllable names. Variant: **Kole.**

DEXTER: (m) Latin; right, right handed. Historically, Dexter derives more commonly from an occupational name meaning "dyer, one who dyes cloth". It has been only mildly popular, but more so in the mid–20th century. It was the name of saxophonist Dexter Gordon.

DIMPLE: (f) English; a person with dimples. This is a curious name that pops up in the '20s and is almost certainly unrelated to the name Dimple found today in India.

DUANE: (m) Gaelic; black, black haired. The spelling Dwayne has probably been influenced by the unrelated names Wayne and Dwight. Somewhat unusually for a boy's name, there are a wide variety of spellings for this name, mostly appearing on the charts when the name was most popular in the mid–20th century. Well-known bearers include guitarist Duane Eddy and actor Dwayne Hickman. Variants: **Dewayne, Duwayne, Dwain, Dwaine, Dwane,** and **Dwayne.**

GINGER: (f) English; a diminutive of VIRGINIA (Chapter 14), but it can also mean "ginger-haired, red-haired". The most famous bearer is probably actress and dancer Ginger Rogers. Another well-known example was the character Ginger on the TV show *Gilligan's Island.* The name was quite popular in the mid–20th century but has fallen out of fashion.

GOLDEN: (f, m) English; golden, golden haired. This is most likely taken from the surname. The form Golden fell out of use at the beginning of the 20th century. Goldie is much more popular in the mid century, as for actress and comedian Goldie Hawn. Israeli Prime Minister Golda Meir bore another variant. Variants: (f) **Golda, Goldia,** and **Goldie.**

GRANT: (m) French; large, tall. The name has been consistently popular throughout the 20th century, although much of the popularity may come from surname examples, such as U.S. president Ulysses S. Grant and actor Cary Grant.

GREEN: (m) English; sometimes "green" in the sense of "young, immature", but more often a place name "living at the village green". This is found rarely as a given name around the turn of the 20th century.

GWEN (f), **GWYN** (m): Welsh; white, fair. These names have been more popular in Britain than the U.S. Gwen is often short for GWENDOLEN (Chapter 6) and was mildly popular in the mid–20th century. One bearer is actress Gwen Verdon.

LLOYD: (m) Welsh; brown, gray, usually referring to hair. The beginning sound of the Welsh name doesn't exist in English, which is why you sometimes find spellings like Floyd that try to approximate it. Both Lloyd and Floyd were quite popular in the later 19th century and into the early 20th. Well-known bearers include actor Lloyd Bridges and Texas senator Lloyd Bentsen. Variants: **Floyd** and **Loyd.**

MAGNUS: (m) Latin; great, large. This became a given name in Scandinavia in the Medieval period, and its rare use in the early 20th century may be due to immigrants from that region.

PINKIE: (f) English; most likely a nickname for someone fond of wearing pink. A rare name in the early 20th century.

RUFUS: (m) Latin; red, red haired. This became a personal name very early on — there are two men named Rufus mentioned in the New Testament — but it was still being used as a nickname for a red-haired person during the Middle Ages. It was quite popular in the early 20th century but has declined since then. One well-known bearer is musician Rufus Wainwright.

RUSSEL: (m) French; reddish-brown (of hair). Although modern use of this name is most likely taken from the surname, it can be found as a given name in the Medieval period. It saw a significant revival in the late 19th century along with other aristocratic-sounding surnames. It is known today from Australian actor Russell Crowe. Variant: **Russell.** Diminutive: **Russ.**

RUSTY: (m) English; red-haired. This was originally a nickname, but became popular as a given name in the mid–20th century. One bearer is Olympic speed skater Rusty Smith.

SHAYNA: (f) Yiddish; beautiful. Sometimes this name may be a variant of SEAN (Chapter 10) instead. The name started hitting the charts only in the last few decades. Variant: **Shaina.**

SULLIVAN: (m) Gaelic; dark-eyed (or at least something-eyed, opinions differ on the adjective). From the surname O'Sullivan. It has only very recently been used as a given name.

VIRIDIANA: (f) Latin; green. It's unclear what this name would be describing, and it may simply be an exotic-sounding "fancy name," perhaps influenced by the popularity of DIANA (Chapter 5). This shows up for the title character of a rather lurid Spanish movie in the '60s, but because the name hits the popularity charts only briefly in the early '90s a direct connection is unlikely.

Acting It Out

Nicknames may also comment on personality or habits. The names that have survived generally indicate positive ones: Curtis "courteous," Felix "happy," and Desiree "desired." Some of these have been created directly from the descriptive words, but others took the surname route to their current use.

BLYTHE: (f) English; happy, carefree. This is a rare name, seen for actress Blythe Danner.

CHANCE: (m) English; fortunate, lucky. This may sometimes be a diminutive of Chauncey, from a French place name. The name has risen sharply in popularity in the last several decades.

CHARISMA: (f) Greek; the power to attract followers. It is a rare name, taken directly from the ordinary word. TV actress Charisma Carpenter is one bearer.

CURTIS: (m) English; courteous, polite. When it first became a name, the word courteous meant "suitable to be a courtier" rather than the more general meaning it has today. Both Curtis and Kurt were quite popular in the mid–20th century and the name has had strong staying power. Bearers include musician Curtis Mayfield, novelist Kurt Vonnegut, and rocker Kurt Cobain. Variants: **Curt, Curtiss, Kirt, Kurt,** and **Kurtis.**

DESIREE: (f) French; desired one. Sometimes the English word *desire* is found as a name as well and seems to have developed as a "virtue name" (see Chapter 9) without sexual connotations. One famous bearer was Desiree Clary, one-time love of Napoleon Bonaparte who ended up becoming queen of Sweden instead. The name has been quite popular in the last several decades. Variant: **Desirae.**

ESSENCE: (f) English; true nature, essence. An unusual name that has hit the charts only in the last couple of decades.

FELIX: (m) Latin; happy. (See also the feminine forms FELICIA and FELICITY in Chapter 16.) The name has retained a fairly steady popularity for centuries, starting with several early popes and picking up an odd assortment of well-known bearers including composer Felix Mendelssohn, cartoon character Felix the cat, and fastidious TV bachelor Felix Ungar of *The Odd Couple.*

FIDEL: (m) Latin; faithful. The name has had a low but steady popularity through the 20th century. The most famous bearer is probably Cuba's ruler, Fidel Castro.

GAY: (f) English or French; happy, joyful. The name was fairly popular in the mid–20th century but has fallen out of fashion, at least partly due to the increasing use of "gay" as an informal word for homosexual. It never really hit the charts as a male name, although the use is familiar from journalist Gay Talese. Variant: **Gaye.**

HAVEN: (f) English; a safe place, a harbor. The name has shown up in use only recently.

JOLIE: (f) English or French; happy, jolly. This is a rare name, popular only in the last decade, possibly inspired by the surname of actress Angelina Jolie.

JOY: (f, m) English; happiness, joy. The name Joyce is often mistakenly connected with this one, and instead derives from the same Germanic root as JOSCELYN (Chapter 8). Advice columnist Dr. Joyce Brothers is one famous bearer and another is zoologist Joy Adamson (author of *Born Free*). Variant: **Joyce.**

LIBERTY: (f) English; freedom, liberty. This is another name only popularized in the last decade. Most likely it is taken directly from the ordinary word.

LOYAL: (m) English; faithful, loyal. Possibly the given name is taken from a surname, as it is primarily popular in the early 20th century. Loy may be a diminutive. Variant: **Loy.**

MIRACLE: (f) English; a miracle, a wondrous event. This may sometimes be a translation of the Spanish name MILAGROS (Chapter 15). The name has shot up in popularity over the last couple decades.

MODESTO: (m) Spanish; modest, bashful. The name was mildly popular in the earlier 20th century, but has fallen out of fashion.

NADIA: (f) Russian; hope. The name was popularized in the 20th century by Russian immigrants. One famous bearer is Romanian "perfect 10" gymnast Nadia Comaneci, and her influence may be at work in the name's sudden popularity starting in the '70s. The variant Nadine has been popular for even longer, as for South African novelist Nadine Gordimer. Variant: **Nadine.**

NOBLE: (m) English; well-born, noble. This name was popular primarily in the early 20th century, and so it's likely to have been taken from the surname.

NOLAN: (m) Gaelic; acclaimed, famous. The name has had a consistent mild popularity for the last century but has recently been rising in the charts. One bearer is pitcher Nolan Ryan.

NOVA: (f) Latin or Spanish; new. This was occasionally used in the early part of the 20th century. Variant: **Novella.**

REILLY: (f, m) Gaelic; valiant, brave. As Riley, this has been fairly popular throughout the last century. The spelling variants, as well as use as a girl's name, are much more recent developments. Variants: (both) **Riley** and **Rylee;** (f) **Ryleigh** and **Rylie;** (m) **Ryley.**

RENEE (f), **RENE** (m): French; re-born, born again. The name commemorates the resurrection of Christ. Historically, An unrelated Germanic name Rainer may also have contributed to the use of this name. Famous bearers have included mathematician René Descartes, artist René Magritte, and actress Renée Zellweger. Variants: (f) **Renae, Renata, Rene, Renea,** and **Renita.**

ROYAL: (m) English; kingly, noble, royal. The name was mildly popular in the first half of the 20th century and is probably taken from a surname.

SANTA (f), **SANTOS** (m) Spanish; blessed, saintly. This group of names was mildly popular in the early part of the 20th century. The one exception is Santana (usually a contraction of Santa Ana, that is, "Saint Anne") which hits the charts only in the '80s. There may be some influence from musician Carlos Santana, although the spelling of the name has led people to treat it as feminine. Variants; (f) **Santana, Santina,** and **Santos;** (m) **Santino, Santo.**

SINCERE: (m) English; sincere, having true intentions. The name is almost certainly taken directly from the ordinary word, so it's unusual that it shows up as a boy's name rather than a girl's. It has been popular only in the last decade.

SOLEDAD: (f) Spanish; solitary, lonely, from an epithet of the Virgin Mary. This is a very rare name, perhaps because of its meaning, or perhaps because of the famous prison of that name.

STAR: (f) English; a star, an excellent person. This is probably a translation of the Latin name Stella, which began as a poetic name in the Renaissance. Stella was quite popular in the later 19th century, although it has declined steadily since then. Starr enjoyed only a brief popularity in the '90s. One well-known bearer is TV personality Star Jones (whose name is actually short for Starlet). Variants: (f) **Starr, Starla,** and **Stella.**

STORMY (f), **STORM** (m): English; a storm, a tempest. As a nickname, it indicates someone with a stormy temper, although today it may be used simply as a nature-related name. It is a rare name for both boys and girls in the last couple of decades.

SUNNY: (f) English; happy, bright, sunny. These names show up on the charts briefly in the '70s, suggesting that the stereotype of them as being "hippie names" may not be far off. Variant: **Sunshine.**

TRUMAN: (m) English; a faithful or trusty person. The name is taken from a surname and had a consistent mild popularity in the early part of the 20th century when it is found for author Truman Capote.

UNIQUE: (f) English; one-of-a-kind, unique. Given that this name has been hitting the popularity charts in the '90s, it clearly doesn't fulfill its literal meaning.

Celebrating the Circumstances of Birth

Some nicknames describe attributes that *are* known at birth: the day or season of the birth, or the culture of origin. Many of these names started out as given names, and today it's rare for them to have literal meaning. Several names of African origin discussed in Chapter 15 also fall in this category.

APRIL: (f) Latin; (born in) the month of April. This is one of the few apparent month names that comes primarily from the calendar, rather than the resemblance being coincidental. The name has been popular in the later part of the 20th century. Variant: **Abril.**

AUTUMN: (f) English; the season of autumn. This name has shot up the popularity charts in recent decades and seems to be newly adopted as a given name.

BRITTON: (m) English; a Breton, someone from Britany. Historically, this generally would not have meant "someone from Britain." The name shows up occasionally in the '90s, probably as part of the fashion for names starting with "Br-."

CREOLA: (f) English; a Creole woman. This is a rare name, appearing in the early 20th century.

DOMINIC: (m) Latin; Sunday, someone born on a Sunday. (For the equivalent feminine name, see Chapter 19.) This is a very popular name in Catholic regions, although it is probably not often given with its original meaning these days. It may also be given in honor of St. Dominic, the founder of the Dominican order. Several variants have been on the popularity charts throughout the 20th century, especially Dominic, as for British actor Dominic Monaghan (featured in *The Lord of the Rings*). Dominique is sometimes considered a specifically feminine form of the name, but it is found for basketball player Dominique Wilkins. Variants: **Domenic, Domenick, Domenico, Domingo, Dominic, Dominick, Dominik, Dominique, Dominque,** and **Domonique.**

EASTER: (f) English; someone born on Easter. The name has occasionally become confused with ESTHER (Chapter 4) and both had a peak of popularity in the early 20th century.

EPIPHANY: (m) Latin; the feast of Epiphany, celebrating the visit of the Magi to the newborn Christ. This name has the same meaning as TIFFANY or Theophania (Chapter 8), but the male name Epiphany shows up in the mid–20th century while the female name has seen its greatest recent popularity in the last few decades of the century. Variant: **Epifanio.**

GAETANO: (m) Italian; from the region of Gaete in Italy. The name may sometimes be confused with Gitano, "gipsy." This was a rare name in the early part of the 20th century.

GERMAINE: (f, m) French; German. This has been a given name since the Middle Ages. Through the 20th century the most popular forms have been masculine German and feminine Germaine. Although Germaine originated as a feminine form, it is found for both boys and girls, especially at its peak of popularity in the '70s, while Jermaine seems to be primarily masculine. Pop singer Jermaine Jackson was one of the brothers forming the Jackson Five. Also familiar is Australian feminist author Germaine Greer. Variants: (m) **German, Jermain,** and **Jermaine.**

JUNIOR: (m) Latin; younger, usually indicating a son who bears the same name as his father. This name has shown up consistently, if not commonly, through most of the 20th century.

MAJOR: (m) Latin; bigger, larger. The name may come more immediately from the military rank.

MAY: (f) Latin; the month of May, named after the Roman goddess Maia. Another source for this name is as a diminutive of MARY (Chapter 8), and this probably contributed to its popularity in compounds, especially in the form Mae. One bearer is poet Maya Angelou, although her use of the name is said to have an entirely different origin. Variants: **Mai, Maya, Maye, Maia,** and **Maiya.**

NATALIE: (f) Latin; birthday, specifically, Christ's birthday, Christmas. Names commemorating Christmas are the most common of the holiday-related names. This name became popular in the later 19th century, and a Russian diminutive, Natasha, was introduced only slightly later. Both reached their peak of popularity in the '80s. The name has been borne by actresses Natalie Wood and Natalie Portman, singer Natalie Cole, and Olympic swimming champion Natalie Coughlin. One of the several diminutives is used by actress Talia Shire. Variants: **Natalia, Nataly, Natalya, Nathalia, Nathalie, Nathaly, Natasha,** and **Natosha.** Diminutives: **Talia, Taliyah, Tatiana, Tatyana, Tasha,** and **Tosha.**

NATIVIDAD: (f) Spanish; the nativity, that is, Christmas. This is yet another Christmas-related name that had mild popularity in the early part of the 20th century.

NOELLE (f), **NOEL** (m) French; this name has the same derivation and meaning as NATALIE (see earlier in this chapter). The masculine forms of the name have generally been more common, as for playwright Noël Coward. The distinction of using Noelle for girls and Noel for boys is in the process of being lost, but Noelle has always been the most common spelling for the feminine name. Variant: (f) **Noelia.**

NORMAN: (m) English; Northman, a man from Normandy. This developed into a given name very early on, although modern use is often by way of the surname. Novelist Norman Mailer is one well-known bearer. Variant: **Normand.**

OCTAVIA (f), **OCTAVIO** (m) Latin; eighth, eighth-born child. Compare this name with QUENTIN (later in this chapter). Other names of this type that never quite caught on are Secunda (2nd), Tertia (3rd), and Decimus (10th). The Roman emperor known as Augustus began life as Octavius and this Latin form is sometimes still used as a scholarly form. Variant: **Octavius.**

PASQUALE: (m) Spanish; Easter, a child born at Easter. The name was mildly popular in the early part of the 20th century. Variant: **Pascual.**

QUENTIN: (m) Latin; fifth, fifth-born child. The ancient Romans could be very unimaginative in their given names, and eventually they gave up on the older given names entirely and turned their nicknames into given names. This one stuck around but was no longer given based on birth order. Medieval use of this name was often in honor of an early saint. Any time there was a revival of interest in old Roman names, Quentin was likely to see a resurgence. One of these revivals came in the 19th century when the name was used for the title character of Sir Walter Scott's *Quentin Durward.* The name Quincy is from the same source, but via a French place name taken from the personal name. In the TV medical detective show *Quincy,* the title is taken from the main character's surname. Variants: **Quentin, Quincy, Quintin,** and **Quinton.**

SCOTT: (m) English; a person from Scotland. This could be taken from a family name or be a personal nickname for someone with Scottish ancestry, turned into a given name. The name became extremely popular in the mid to late 20th century, so there is no lack of namesakes, including actors Scott Glenn and Scott Baio, Olympic skater Scott Hamilton, and basketball player Scottie Pippen. Variants: **Scot, Scottie,** and **Scotty.**

SIXTO: (m) Latin; sixth, sixth-born child. See QUENTIN and OCTAVIO (earlier in this chapter for both) for similar names. This name shows up rarely in the mid–20th century.

SPRING: (f) English; the springtime of the year. The name may sometimes be from a surname, originally meaning "a lively person." This is a rare name, only hitting the charts briefly in the '70s.

SUMMER: (f) English; summertime. There is also a surname Summer that may be a variant of Sumpter, referring to someone who cares for pack horses. In the case of both Spring and Summer, their use today is primarily for girls, suggesting that the seasonal meaning is being considered, rather than simply being the use of a family surname. Summer has been increasing significantly in popularity in the later part of the 20th century. Variant: **Sommer.**

TREY: (m) French; three, third. This seems to have come from a nickname for someone who was the third of their name (for example, Robert Williams III may be nicknamed Trey). The name has had a mild popularity in the last several decades. Variants: **Trae** and **Tre.**

VAUGHAN: (m) Welsh; small, junior. Originally, this was sometimes used in the same way as Junior, for a man who had the same name as his father. Modern use is taken from the surname and has held relatively steady in popularity through the last century. One well-known bearer is composer Vaughan Williams. This name may be the source of one set of recently coined names, given the spelling Devaughn as a clue (see Chapter 11). Variant: **Vaughn.**

VERNON: (m) French; spring, springtime. The meaning comes by a roundabout route: The French surname comes from a place name based on an old Roman given name Vernus, whose root means "Spring." The form Vern may be a diminutive, or may be directly from the French surname of similar origin. Vernon was quite popular during the early 20th century, with Vern somewhat less so. The name most calls to mind early science fiction writer Jules Verne, who bore it as a surname. Variants: **Vern** and **Verne.**

WALLACE: (m) English; foreigner, Welsh person. Originally this term was used by the Anglo-Saxons to describe any of the foreigners on their borders, including the Welsh, Cornish, and Scots. The Scottish hero William Wallace (of *Braveheart* fame) has led many to consider the name primarily Scottish.

Keeping Occupied

We're currently seeing a revived fashion for names that originally described a person's occupation or station in life. The recent interest in names like Taylor, Tyler, and Hunter seems to be based more on sound than meaning, but jobs have always been a popular source for family names. This section also includes surnames taken from titles, like Earl or Regina, but these were originally nicknames, not a sign that the family was noble. Although they are hardly ordinary occupations, this section also lists names referring to supernatural and heavenly occupations, like angels.

AMIR: (m) Arabic; prince, governor. The ordinary word is often seen as "emir." This name has been increasing rapidly in popularity in the last several decades.

ANGEL: (f, m) Greek; messenger of god, angel. As a male name, Angel is primarily found in the Hispanic community, although other variants are more widespread. One bearer is jockey Angel Cordero, Jr. The male names have held steady at a moderately high popularity over the last century. Girls have more commonly used one of the variants such as ANGELA (Chapter 10), ANGELICA, or ANGELINA (Chapter 18), but the simple form Angel has become more popular in recent decades. Variants; (m) **Angelo, Dangelo.**

BARON: (m) French or English; a baron, a nobleman. A rare name, popular mostly in the mid–20th century. Variant: **Barron.**

BISHOP: (m) English; a bishop, a church leader. As with many of the title-derived names, this is rather rare. Despite being taken from an ordinary surname, when used as a given name, it has a tendency to make the name sound like a title.

BRIDGER: (m) English; someone who builds bridges (or simply lives at a bridge). This is a recent adoption as a given name, and is taken from the surname.

CARTER: (m) English; someone who drives a cart or makes deliveries using a cart. Despite the ordinariness of the occupation, this name has achieved a certain amount of popularity due to the prominence of several families bearing it. It has increased significantly in popularity in the last couple of decades, which may partly be out of admiration for U.S. president Jimmy Carter.

DEACON: (m) English; a deacon, one of the lay offices in some churches. It has been a rare name. Football star Deacon Jones picked it up originally as a nickname.

DUKE: (m) English; a duke, a nobleman (from Latin *dux* "leader"). It may also sometimes be a nickname for Marmaduke. Duke is familiar as the nickname of actor John Wayne, for whom the occasional examples in the '50s and '60s may have been given. For Jazz musician Duke Ellington it was also originally a nickname, but he came to use it as a given name.

EARLINE (f), **EARL** (m) English; an earl, a nobleman. This has been popular enough as a given name to have given rise to a set of feminine variants using the suffix "-ine" and is by far the most popular of the title-based names. Prominent examples are supreme court chief justice Earl Warren and mystery novelist Erle Stanley Gardner. Variants: (f) **Earlene** and **Erlene**; (m) **Earle, Earlie, Early,** and **Erle.**

ELROY: (m) Spanish; the king. This is the same name as French LEROY, taken from a nickname for someone who acted kingly. The name enjoyed moderate popularity through much of the 20th century.

FAIRY: (f) English; a fairy, a supernatural sprite. One may expect this to be something of a New Age name, found in recent decades, but instead you see the brief fashion for it falling in the '20s.

FLETCHER: (m) English; someone who makes arrows. It came into use as a given name in the 19th century and declined in popularity only in the mid–20th century. Those familiar with a book or movie version of *Mutiny on the Bounty* may associate it with mutineer Fletcher Christian. Another example is fantasy novelist Fletcher Pratt.

FOSTER: (m) English; a forester, someone who guards and takes care of a forest. Like most surname-derived names, this was popular in the later 19th century but declined in the early part of the 20th.

FRANKLIN: (m) English; a free landowner. The name has been extremely popular since the 19th century, peaking in the '30s. Early use of it is likely to have been in honor of Benjamin Franklin. One prominent bearer was U.S. president Franklin Delano Roosevelt. Frank may be used as a diminutive of this name, although it is more commonly from Francis. Variant: **Franklyn.**

FREEMAN: (m) English; a free man, originally a social class rather than a personal description. The name was mildly popular in the first half of the 20th century. One famous bearer is physicist Freeman Dyson.

GARDNER: (m) English; a gardener, someone who takes care of a garden. This is rarer than most of the occupational given names.

GENERAL: (m) English; a general, a high military rank. (See also MAJOR earlier in this chapter.) This has been used rarely in the early 20th century.

HARPER: (m) English; someone who plays the harp. The name is quite rare and rather confusingly the best known bearer is female: Harper Lee, author of *To Kill a Mockingbird.*

HAYWARD: (m) English; someone responsible for protecting the hay fields. This name is found occasionally through the early part of the 20th century.

HUNTER: (f, m) English; a hunter, someone who hunts game (originally, for a living rather than for sport). As a boy's name it has been mildly popular through much of the 20th century and began climbing the charts steeply in the '80s, after which it became popular for girls as well. One well-known bearer is writer Hunter S. Thompson for whom the description "gonzo journalism" was invented.

JUDGE: (m) English; a judge, someone who presides over a court. This is rare, like most of the very transparent occupational names.

KING: (m) English; a king, a ruler. Although not as popular as EARL (see earlier in this chapter), this is more common than most title-based names. Movie director King Vidor is one example of the name.

MALIK: (m) Arabic; a king. This name has been shooting up the charts in the last few decades. One bearer is actor Malik Yoba. Variants: **Malique.**

MARQUIS: (m) French; a marquis, a nobleman. This name has only appeared on the popularity charts in the last several decades, and somewhat surprisingly a variety of spellings all show up at the same time. Variants: **Marques, Marquez,** and **Marquise.**

MARSHAL: (m) French; someone who cares for horses, although later it came by extension to mean a military officer. The name has held a steady high popularity through the last century. One bearer is Canadian writer Marshall McLuhan. Variant: **Marshall.**

MASON: (m) English; a builder in brick and stone. The name has also acquired strong connections to the fraternal group known as the Masonic Order. It has been moderately popular throughout the last century, and has jumped significantly up the charts in recent decades. One bearer is character actor Mason Adams.

MILLER: (m) English; a miller, someone who grinds grain into flour. This was a rare name in the early part of the 20th century, although it is quite common as a surname, as for orchestra leader Glenn Miller.

PALMER: (m) English; a pilgrim, taken from the palm branch used as a symbol of the pilgrimage to Jerusalem. Mildly popular for the first half of the 20th century. The name is borne by movie producer Palmer West.

PARKER: (f, m) English; someone who cares for a park. After following the usual pattern for surname-based given names, Parker has been seeing a revival in recent decades, when it is also found for girls. An example of the latter use is actress Parker Posey.

PORTER: (m) English; someone who caries or transports goods. This is another occupational name that has been seeing a recent revival.

PRINCESS (f), **PRINCE** (m): English; a noble rank, often indicating the child of a king or queen. Both the male and female names have been moderately popular in recent decades. The best known male example is the musician known solely as Prince (when he isn't using an unpronounceable glyph).

QUEEN: (f) English; a queen, a noblewoman. The word originally meant simply "woman," and this helps account for its use as a given name in Medieval times. Current popularity is from its use as a nickname rather than a continuous tradition. One bearer is blues singer Queenie Watts. More recently, singer Queen Latifah uses it more as a nickname than a given name. Variant: **Queenie.**

REGINA (f), **REX** (m) Latin; a queen/king. This nickname can also be found in the French forms Reine and Roy, although Roy may sometimes come instead from a Gaelic nickname meaning "red." The French form can also be found in the name LEROY "the king" (Chapter 11). The possessive form of Rex, Regis "belonging to the king," may also be found. This group of names is somewhat more common than most title-based names, largely because the literal meaning is disguised somewhat. For the most part, these names hit their peak in the mid–20th century. Bearers include actor Rex Harrison, TV host Regis Philbin, and actress Regina Taylor. Variants: (f) **Raina, Reine, Rayna, Reina, Rena,** and **Reyna;** (m) **Regis, Rey, Reyes,** and **Roy.**

RYDER: (m) English; a rider, a horseman, a knight. This name has become suddenly popular in the last decade.

SAWYER: (m) English; someone who runs a sawmill. It is quite common as a surname, but only recently has been used as a given name.

SERAPHINA: (f) Hebrew; a type of angel. This name may be compared with ANGELINA but has never become quite as popular. There was a Medieval saint of this name.

SMITH: (m) English; someone who works with metal, typically a blacksmith. This is a fairly rare name, found mostly in the early 20th century.

TANNER: (m) English; someone who tans hides into leather. It's another of the occupational names that has seen recent interest. This recent fashion seems to be driven more by sound than meaning, which would explain the sudden interest in Tanner, Taylor, and Tyler. you can probably expect to see Tanner starting to be used for girls as well, like the other two.

TAYLOR: (f, m) English; a maker of clothing. As a male name, this has seen a relatively steady popularity with some recent increase, but female use has shot up astoundingly from not even making the charts in the '70s to number 9 in the '90s. One possible source for this is the surname of actress Elizabeth Taylor, but other forces may be at work. Variant: **Tayler.**

TYLER: (f, m) English; a tiler, someone who lays tiles. Along with Taylor, this is the success story of the occupational names. In this case, it's the boys who took the name to number 9 in the '90s. Variant: **Tylor.**

WEBSTER: (m) English; a weaver, someone who weaves cloth. This was a rare name in the early 20th century, but a more recent example is for the title character of the TV series *Webster.*

Pointing out virtues and flaws

Different cultures have had different ideas about what to describe in a nickname. Some praise virtues, others consider this unlucky and comment on defects. Some are preoccupied with physical appearance, others focus on actions. But there are some meanings and types of descriptions that are found across a wide variety of languages.

Color:

✔ Black: Blake, Ciara, Cole, Duane, Kieran, Melanie, and Nigel

✔ Red: Gough, Rowan, Roy, Rufus, Russel, and Rusty

✔ White, fair: Alba, Blanche, Candide, Finn, and Gwen

Size:

✔ Large: Alta, Grant, and Magnus

✔ Small: Paul and Vaughn

Royalty:

✔ King: Brendan, Elroy, King, Leroy, Malik, and Rex

✔ Queen: Queen, Regina, and Reyna

Chapter 14

Moving In: When Place Names and Natural Features Become First Names

. . . .

In This Chapter

▶ Looking at naming patterns

▶ Finding names from places

▶ Getting name ideas from natural features

. . . .

*G*iven names and names of places have a long history of cross-fertilization. Places have been named after the people who lived there, and people in turn may be named (or at least nicknamed) after the places they live. Some names in this chapter have cycled through the process more than once!

Taking a Peek at the Naming Patterns

Given names taken from place names or the names of natural features turn the usual naming pattern on its head. Instead of girls getting all the fun, this group of names are more often given to boys. The reason is simple: Most of these names first turned into family surnames, and the practice of turning surnames into given names has traditionally benefited boys more than girls.

There are exceptions to this pattern. Names of countries are often considered feminine (or at least often look feminine). So names like *India* and *China* tend to skip the surname step and go straight to being girls' names. Even when the name doesn't end with that telltale "a," a country name like Brittany is more likely to enter the field as a girl's name.

Names from descriptions of natural features like *Cliff, Rock,* or *Glen* may be taken from surnames, but just as often they may be given for the image of strength and ruggedness they project.

More recent place-name borrowings may follow more than one rule. *Sierra* (mountain) may be given to boys as a natural feature and be given to girls following the "final-a" rule.

In some cases, a given name may be identical to a place name without having a direct connection. *Paris,* as a girl's name, is most likely inspired by the glamorous city, but as a boy's name it connects historically with the Paris of Greek legend. Florence (whether for boys or girls) comes from an old Roman family name rather than from the city.

Taking Your Proper Places

Proper names of places usually refer to a specific location. Generally they start out as surnames for families that lived in those places and only later are taken up as given names. In some cases, though, these names started out as personal names that were later used to name locations.

ALFORD: (m) English; multiple origins: ford of alder trees, ford by a temple, or Ealdgyth's ford. It declined in popularity in the early 20th century.

ALTON: (m) English; various origins such as "old town," or "Alf's town". The name is not well known, although it enjoyed a rather steady mild popularity throughout the early part of the 20th century. Alton Locke is the hero of Charles Kingsley's novel by that name.

AMERICA (f), **AMERICO** (m) Italian; a variant of HENRY (Chapter 8). Although sometimes debated, an accepted theory is that the place name America came from the name of Italian cartographer Amerigo Vespucci. There are also Medieval examples of America and Americus as Latinized forms of the English name Almeric, although there is no reason to believe that those names had any influence on the place name. Both America and Americo enjoyed a brief popularity in the early 20th century, presumably among enthusiastic recent immigrants. America has seen a sudden resurgence in the last decade and time will tell whether it stays the course.

ASHLEY: (f, m) English; ash wood, forest of ash trees. This could be the model for gender issues in modern name fashions. In the spelling Ashley (and only in that one spelling) it became popular as a boy's name starting around the mid–20th century and reached its peak of popularity in the '70s and '80s.

It started hitting the charts as a girl's name in the '60s in the same spelling and quickly shot up to be number 4 in the '80s. This was the kiss of death for its use as a boy's name, and by the '90s that use had nearly disappeared. In contrast, when feminine use hit its peak (number 1 in the '90s) it had inspired at least six popular variants. The timing of the male popularity suggests it was due to the character Ashley Wilkes in Margaret Mitchell's *Gone With The Wind*. Female use seems to have grown simply as a self-supported fashion, although there is a general trend of names ending in "-ley" becoming girls' names. Singer Ashley Judd is a part of the trend, not a cause of it, although designer Laura Ashley may have been an early influence. Variants (f): **Ashely, Ashlee, Ashleigh, Ashli, Ashlie,** and **Ashly.**

ASHLYN, ASHLYNN (f) English; ash tree hill. There are other possibilities for the origin of this name. Some people prefer to associate it with the Medieval French given name Ascelin. There is also a rare Irish name Aisling (meaning "dream, vision") that can be intermingled with this name. The girl's name has had a sudden popularity in recent decades, perhaps partly influenced by Ashley. There is a line of baby furniture with the brand name Ashlynn which may have influenced susceptible parents-to-be!

ASHTON: (f, m) English; ash tree town. The name became suddenly popular for both boys and girls in equal numbers starting in the '80s, but in an unusual twist, the male popularity continued rising while the female use has dropped (perhaps diverted to ASHLEY and ASHLYN). Just as there is a general pattern of names ending in "-ley" becoming girls' names, names ending in "-ton" (or in "n" in general) seem to be associated more with boys. Bearers include actor Ashton Kutcher and early horror fiction writer Clark Ashton Smith. Variant: (f) **Ashtyn.**

ASIA: (f) Greek; East, where the sun rises. Continent names are rare as given names, despite the fact that continents have always been personified as female (as in the Greek legend of Europa and the bull). This name has become popular in the last couple of decades. Bearers include Italian actress Asia Argento.

BARTON: (m) English; barley town. The name enjoyed a mild popularity in the early 20th century. If it were appearing as a girl's name it would be tempting to credit the fame of Clara Barton, founder of the American Red Cross. But there seem to be no famous male Bartons to have inspired the interest. Barton Fink is the title character of a Coen brothers film.

BENTON: (m) English; town where bent-grass grows, or possibly bean town. This is a popular place name in the U.S. but use as a given name mostly fell off in the mid–20th century.

BETHANY: (f) Hebrew; meaning uncertain; This is the village east of Jerusalem where Jesus is said to have raised Lazarus from the dead. The resemblance to the BETH (see Chapter 10) group of nicknames for Elizabeth no doubt contributed to its popularity. It has appeared mostly in the later 20th century, peaking in the '80s. Variant: **Bethanie.**

BEVERLEY: (f) English; beaver stream. In the 19th century, it was found primarily as a man's name (for example, British writer Beverley Nichols). Its popularity as a woman's name may have been sparked by the title character of G.B. McCutcheon's novel *Beverly of Graustark.* In addition to bearers such as children's writer Beverly Cleary and operatic singer Beverly Sills, the glamorous associations of film capitol Beverly Hills helped propel it to popularity in the mid–20th century. Variants: **Beverlee** and **Beverly.**

BLAIR: (f, m) Gaelic; a plain, a field. Unlike many place names, this increases in popularity for boys through the 20th century. The feminine name has had some small popularity in recent decades. The timing isn't right for the horror film *The Blair Witch Project* to be responsible, but a character of this name on the TV show *The Facts of Life* is more likely.

BRADFORD: (m) English; broad ford, wide river-crossing. It was moderately popular through the mid–20th century, perhaps sometimes used in honor of William Bradford, first governor of Plymouth Massachusetts.

BRADLEY: (m) English; broad meadow. Like most place-based surnames, this began with occasional use in the 19th century. Charles Dickens gave the name to the character Bradley Headstone in *Our Mutual Friend.* The significant boost of popularity the name saw in the '50s and later may have been partly in honor of World War II general Omar N. Bradley, but the name was also swept up in the general fashion for boys' names beginning with "Br-" and continues in high popularity through the end of the century. Variant: **Bradly.** Diminutive: **Brad.**

BRADY: (m) English; broad island. The name has increased steadily in popularity through the 20th century, riding the coattails of the fashion for names starting in "Br-."

BRIGHAM: (m) English; farm by a bridge. It is rarely used, generally in honor of Mormon founder Brigham Young.

BRITTANY: (f) English; the English name for the region of Brittany in northern France. The origin is the same as the name Britain. The name first hits the charts in the '70s and explodes in popularity, reaching number 6 in the '90s. Pop singer Britney Spears rides the wave but doesn't seem to have caused it. Like the other popular late-century names starting with "Br-" this seems to have been the right sound at the right time. Variants: **Britany, Britney, Britni, Britny, Brittaney, Brittani, Brittanie, Brittany, Brittnee, Brittney, Brittni, Brittnie,** and **Brittny.**

BROOKLYN: (f) Dutch; marshy watercourse. The original Dutch form of the name is Breukelen. The name has had a sudden recent popularity. Its use as a girl's name, contrary to the default for place names is probably due to the "-lyn" ending, which resembles many traditional feminine names. Variant: **Brooklynn.**

BUFORD: (m) French; beautiful fortress. The original French form is Beaufort, and this can also be found as a given name. It was popular in the late 19th and early 20th century, at least partly in honor of Civil War general John Buford. Tennessee sheriff Buford Pusser was the inspiration for the movie *Walking Tall.* Variant: **Beaufort.**

CARMEL: (f, m) Hebrew; garden. The name comes from the biblical Mount Carmel and gave its name to the Carmelite order of nuns. It was popular beginning in the late 19th century and up through the mid 20th. Carmela Soprano is a character in the popular *Sopranos* TV series. See also CARMEN (Chapter 17). Variants: (f) **Carmela, Carmella, Carmilla,** and **Carmelita;** (m) **Carmelo.**

CAROLINA: (f) English; belonging to Charles. The states of North and South Carolina were named in honor of Charles I of England. But Carolina is also an independent feminine name deriving from Carlo, an Italian form of Charles. Today there's no telling in any particular case whether the name is used as a traditional name or in honor of the state. It has been growing in popularity for the last several decades although it hasn't ever truly gone out of fashion since the 17th century. See also CAROLINE (Chapter 9), CAROLYN (Chapter 10).

CHELSEA: (f) English; landing place for chalk or limestone. See Chapter 17.

CHESTER: (m) English; the city of Chester, England. The name derives originally from Latin *castrum* "a castle." The name was quite popular around the turn of the 20th century but has declined somewhat since then. Chester A. Arthur became president of the United States in 1881 at the death of Garfield.

CHINA: (f) no specific language; the English name for the country derives from the name of the Qin dynasty. This has been used occasionally very recently as a name. The variant Chyna is used by a professional wrestler as a stage name. Variants: **Chyna** and **Chynna.**

CLAYTON: (m) English; town in clay soil. The name has had a startlingly steady popularity over the last century. Actor Clayton Moore became synonymous with his TV role as the Lone Ranger. Diminutive: **Clay.**

CLEVELAND: (m) English; land with cliffs. It declined in popularity somewhat in the later part of the 20th century. Some of the interest in this name may be in honor of President Grover Cleveland. Cleve Backster's research may be single-handedly responsible for the idea of talking to your houseplants. Diminutive: **Cleve.**

CLIFFORD: (m) English; river-crossing by a cliff. Starting in the late 19th century — perhaps inspired by the character of Clifford Pyncheon in Nathanial Hawthorne's *The House of the Seven Gables* — this name continued to be quite popular throughout most of the 20th century, but has been in sudden decline in the last couple of decades. Currently, those in pre-school circles will be most familiar with this as the name of a big red dog.

CLIFTON: (m) English; town on a cliff or hill. The name had a steady mild popularity through much of the 20th century. Actor Clifton Webb is one well-known bearer.

CLINTON: (m) English; town with an enclosed fence. It has been relatively popular throughout the 20th century, although declining somewhat in the last decade. The diminutive Clint has had regular ups and downs, reaching its peak in the '50s and '60s corresponding to (if not necessarily caused by) the early career of actor Clint Eastwood. It's probably too soon to tell whether former president Bill Clinton will have an effect on the name's popularity. Diminutive: **Clint.**

CLYDE: (m) various origins; either from the river Clyde in Scotland or the river Clwyd in Wales. This name became popular in the U.S. in the later 19th century (for women as well as men), evidently directly from the place name, rather than through a surname. It has declined significantly only in the last couple of decades. Among bearers, you should probably call Clyde Barrow (of Bonnie and Clyde) notorious rather than famous. Astronomer Clyde Tombaugh discovered the planet Pluto. Variant: **Cloyd** (probably influenced by Floyd).

COLBY: (m) English; Cole's village. The name is perhaps best known as a variety of cheese (and a college in Maine), but has been rising recently in popularity as a given name. Variant: **Kolby.**

DAKOTA: (f, m) Dakota; the name of the (Native American) Dakota people. See Chapter 15.

DALLAS: (m) English; meaning uncertain, but probably involving "dale" (valley). The name has enjoyed a fairly steady mild popularity, relatively unaffected in the '80s by the popular TV show of this name (although that decade saw a brief fashion for Dallas as a girl's name).

DALTON: (m) English; town in a valley (dale). The name was somewhat uncommon for most of the 20th century, but rises a bit in the last couple of decades. Actor Timothy Dalton has been one of a succession of James Bonds. Somewhat less familiar is Hollywood writer Dalton Trumbo. Variants: **Daulton** and **Delton.**

DAYTON: (m) English; meaning uncertain, but the last part is the familiar "town."

DELMER: (m) French; from the sea. The name was popular mainly in the early 20th century. Variant: **Delmar.**

DENVER: (m) English; place where the Danes passed. It has never been particularly common, but has been used fairly consistently throughout the 20th century. Character actor Denver Pyle was a staple of classic TV.

DESMOND: (m) Gaelic; South Munster (Ireland). The name was mostly popular in the later 20th century, but has been popular in Britain for quite some time. Desmond Morris has written a number of popular books on animal behavior.

DEVON: (f, m) Brythonic; from the ancient tribal name *Dumnonia.* See Chapter 10.

DIXIE: (f) English; a poetic name for the American South whose origins are unclear. It was popularized by the 1858 song of that name. The name had a peak of popularity in the '30s and '40s but has declined somewhat since then.

DOUGLAS: (m) Gaelic; dark blue (originally a river name). This is consistently popular throughout the 20th century, especially midcentury. Two generations of Douglas Fairbanks thrilled us on the silver screen. Another source of midcentury popularity may have been General Douglas MacArthur. Curiously, the earliest use of Douglas as a given name (in the 16th century) was for women as often as for men, but feminine use has entirely disappeared. Variant: **Douglass.** Diminutive: **Doug.**

ELBA: (f) Latin; belonging to the Ligurians (an ancient nationality). The isle of Elba off the coast of Italy is best known as the place of Napoleon's first exile. (The given name may instead be a short form of some name like Elberta.) It had a moderate popularity for several decades in the mid–20th century.

ELDON: (m) English; Ella's hill. As is usual with place-based surnames, this was most popular in the 19th century and sees a slow decline in the early 20th. Elden and Alden may be variants, but they have other possible origins. Variants: **Alden** and **Elden.**

ELWOOD: (m) English; possibly elm wood. The name was somewhat popular through the first half of the 20th century. Variant: **Ellwood.**

ERIN: (f) Gaelic; belonging to Ireland. See Chapter 5.

FELTON: (m) English; town in a field. The name was mildly popular in the early 20th century.

GARFIELD: (m) English; meaning uncertain, possibly "a triangular field." It is sometimes used in honor of U.S. president James A. Garfield but was fading in popularity through the early 20th century.

GARLAND: (m) English; a triangular piece of land (or a maker of garlands). This name retained its popularity later than many of the other place names popularized in the 19th century. It is best known as the surname of actress Judy Garland.

GENEVA: (f) Gaulish?; meaning uncertain. The name's popularity has trailed off somewhat since the earlier part of the 20th century.

GORDON: (m) English; meaning uncertain. Due to the Scottish location of the place, some theories make the name of Gaelic origin. It has been quite popular through much of the 20th century, although this has fallen off lately. Famous bearers include millionaire Gordon Getty and Canadian songwriter and singer Gordon Lightfoot.

GRAHAM: (m) English; Gray house. The name is strongly associated with Scotland. It has risen in popularity somewhat in recent decades. This name is shared by inventor Alexander Graham Bell, prolific novelist Graham Greene, and rock musician Graham Nash of Crosby, Stills, Nash, and Young. Variant: **Graeme.**

GRANVILLE: (m) French; big town. Writer and critic Granville Hicks bore this name at the height of its popularity in the early 20th century.

HAILEY: (f) English; hay meadow. See Chapter 18.

HAMILTON: (m) English; meaning uncertain, possibly "cut-off hill." It has never been particularly popular, although Charles Dickens used it for a character in *Our Mutual Friend,* and it may sometimes be used in honor of early U.S. statesman Alexander Hamilton.

HARLEY: (f, m) English; Hare's wood. This has maintained a fairly steady popularity as a boy's name throughout the 20th century, and even risen somewhat lately, when it is also found for girls. Some small part of its popularity may come from the mystique of Harley-Davidson motorcycles.

HAYDEN: (f, m) English; Hay valley. Perhaps it comes sometimes from the German surname Haydn, as for composer Joseph Haydn. The name has enjoyed an enormous surge in popularity for boys in the last couple decades, shooting from number 983 in the '80s to number 85 in 2003, when it is also found occasionally as a girl's name. Some of this popularity may be attributable to actor Hayden Christensen (starring in the *Star Wars* movie *Attack of the Clones*), but this name also benefits from a recent fashion for names with this rhyme pattern (for example, Aidan, Caden, and Bradon).

HEAVEN: (f) English; the heavens, either in the sense of "sky" or of "paradise." The name has only appeared in the last couple of decades, but is rising swiftly in popularity. There's an unusual variant Nevaeh, formed by spelling the name backwards, that has shot up to high popularity in the last decade. Variant: **Nevaeh.**

HOUSTON: (m) English; Hugo's town. The name has had rare, but consistent, popularity through the last century. It is probably given as often in honor of early Texan Sam Houston as for the city named after him. Variant: **Huston.**

INDIA: (f) no specific language; the English name for the country of India derives from the same root as *Hindu,* one of the principal ethnic groups in the region. There's a sudden interest in the name in recent decades, but it also appears rarely ever since the late 19th century. Some interest in the name may have been due to the character of India Wilkes in the book and movie *Gone With the Wind,* but a more recent model is R&B singer India Arie. Variant: **Indiana.**

IONA: (f) Gaelic; possibly "place of yew trees," but this is not certain. Other theories derive the given name from a variant of JOAN (Chapter 8). It has appeared rarely since the late 19th century, but declined significantly after the mid 20th. A variant of the name is borne by British actress Ione Skye. Variant: **Ione.**

JORDAN: (f, m) Hebrew; flowing down — the name of a river. It has been popular as a male name since the Middle Ages, although it became confused with an unrelated German name Jordanes. The name has risen sharply in popularity since the '70s both for boys and now for girls as well. Well-known bearers include basketball superstar Michael Jordan and the title character of the TV show *Crossing Jordan.* Variants: (m) **Jorden, Jordon;** (both) **Jordyn;** Diminutives: **Jordi** and **Jordy.**

KEATON: (m) English; a river name, possibly from an ancient tribal name. It has enjoyed a sudden popularity in recent decades, perhaps more for the sound pattern than for any specific associations. As a surname, it is familiar from actor Buster Keaton.

KELLY: (f, m) multiple origins; rarely this name may be from a Welsh word meaning "grove," but most often it is from the Irish surname Ó Ceallaigh, from a root meaning "one who lives in a monastic cell." It has been used as a male name since the late 19th century and increased in popularity starting in the

'50s when it also started appearing for girls. Female use rapidly outstripped male use and it reached as high as number 14 on the girls' charts in the '70s. Well-known bearers of the name include TV host Kelly Ripa and science-fiction artist Frank Kelly Freas. Variants: (both) **Kelley**; (f) **Kelli, Kellie.**

KELVIN: (m) Gaelic; narrow water (a river name). The name may also sometimes be a blend of CALVIN (Chapter 13) and MELVIN (Chapter 18). The most famous bearer had this as a title: William Thomson, Baron Kelvin, who gave his name to the Kelvin temperature scale. It has been mildly popular for the last half century or so.

KENDALL: (f, m) English; the valley of the river Kent. The river name comes from a Brythonic root of uncertain meaning. The name has been increasingly popular for boys through the later 20th century, and has enjoyed a suddenly popularity for girls in recent decades. Variants: **Kendal** and **Kendell.**

KENT: (m) Brythonic; probably "border" or "edge, coast." The name reached its peak of popularity in the mid–20th century but has declined significantly since then. The most famous Kent may be Clark Kent, alter-ego of Superman, but a more down-to-earth bearer is North Dakota senator Kent Conrad.

KIMBERLEY: (f, m) English; various origins, all involving an Anglo-Saxon personal name plus "meadow." The name was first adopted as a male name in the early 20th century, commemorating the town of Kimberley in South Africa. It shifted abruptly to being a girl's name around the '50s and today is considered only that. Kimberly shot up rapidly to number 5 and held that place for two decades in the '60s and '70s. The usual diminutive is Kim, as for actress Kim Basinger. Kim can also be found as a male name, but from a different source (see Chapter 6). Variants: **Kimberlee, Kimberli,** and **Kimberly;** Diminutive: **Kim.**

KIRBY: (m) English; village with a church. Kirby had a mild popularity in the mid–20th century but is otherwise rare. Bearers include baseball Hall of Famer Kirby Puckett and comic book artist Jack Kirby.

LANDON: (m) English; meaning uncertain. The recent burst of popularity of this name may be a combination of the fashion for names ending in "n" for boys, and an interest in honoring actor and director Michael Landon. Variant: **Landen.**

LESLEY: (f, m) Brythonic; meaning uncertain, possibly "court of the holly tree." See Chapter 6.

LINCOLN: (m) Brythonic + Latin; from the Latin *Lindum Colonia* "settlement at Lindum," where *Lindum* is a Brythonic word meaning "lake." Lincoln has had mild but consistent popularity throughout the 20th century. Most current use is in honor of U.S. president Abraham Lincoln.

LINDSAY, LINDSEY: (f, m) English; island in the Lincoln district. There was a slight fashion for this as a boy's name in the mid–20th century, but it suddenly shifted to female use in the '70s and shot up in popularity. Actress Lindsey Wagner, best known for the TV series *The Bionic Woman,* may have had some part in promoting the name. Variants: (f) **Linsey, Lyndsay, Lyndsey,** and **Lynsey.**

LONDON: (f, m) English; the city of London, originally *Londinium* (of uncertain meaning). Interest in the name is too recent to find famous given name bearers, but actress Julie London has it as a surname.

LORRAINE: (f) French; Lothar's kingdom, named after an early ruler. The popularity of the name may be due to its similarity to LAURA (Chapter 6), and the name may sometimes come from a compound Laura-Anne. It was most popular in the early 20th century. Lorraine Hansberry wrote the play (later movie) *A Raisin in the Sun.* Variants: **Laraine** and **Loraine.**

LYNDON: (m) English; hill of linden trees. The name was briefly fashionable in the mid–20th century, particularly in the '60s. The most famous bearer of the name was President Lyndon B. Johnson.

MILAN: (m) Gaulish; middle of the plain. The name occurs rarely through the early 20th century.

MILTON: (m) English; either "middle town" or "mill town." It was quite popular through the first half of the 20th century but has been declining somewhat since then. The name immediately brings to mind 17th-century poet John Milton (writer of *Paradise Lost*). More recently it is found for board-game inventor Milton Bradley and economist Milton Friedman.

MISSOURI: (f) Algonquian; from the Native American tribal name, meaning "place of large canoes." This is a very rare name, used around the turn of the 20th century and most likely inspired by Missouri's admission to statehood.

MONSERRATE: (f) Spanish; jagged mountain range. The name comes from a Benedictine monastery near Barcelona, which became popular as a place of pilgrimage due to visions of the Virgin seen there. It was mildly popular through the first half of the 20th century. Variant: **Monserrat.**

MONTANA: (f, m) Spanish; mountainous region. Although found only in the last couple of decades, it's been equally popular for both genders, despite the "-a" ending. A famous bearer is football star Joe Montana.

MONTE, MONTY: (m) French; a mountain. Sometimes it is used as a short form of Montgomery (a French place name). The short forms have enjoyed a mild popularity mostly in the mid–20th century, the only time when Montgomery itself hits the charts at all (perhaps partly in honor of the World War II general). Variant: **Montgomery.**

MORTON: (m) English; town by a marsh. It has been mildly popular through the first half of the 20th century. Musical Mortons include composer Morton Feldman and jazz musician Jelly Roll Morton.

NEWTON: (m) English; new town. Best known as the surname of early physicist and mathematician Sir Isaac Newton. The name declined in popularity through the first half of the 20th century.

ODESSA: (f) multiple origins; a city in Ukraine (and Texas), or sometimes a feminine form of Odyseus. The name declined in popularity through the early 20th century.

PARIS: (f, m) Gaulish; as a place name, from the Gaulish tribal name *Parisi,* but see Chapter 5.

PAYTON, PEYTON: (f, m) English; various origins: Pacca's ridge or Paega's town. The name sees a sudden popularity, equally for boys and girls, starting in the '90s. The location that comes instantly to mind is *Peyton Place,* the archetypal prime-time soap opera. Male bearers include football player Peyton Manning. The female Paytons may still be too young to be famous.

PRESTON: (m) English; priest's town. One bearer is playwright Preston Jones. Somewhat unusually, this name has been increasing steadily in popularity throughout the 20th century.

RALEIGH: (m) English; red meadow. The name is best known, perhaps, as the surname of Elizabethan courtier Sir Walter Raleigh, the namesake of Raleigh, North Carolina. It was mildly popular during the early 20th century.

RHONDA: (f) Welsh; noisy, babbling (a river name). See Chapter 17.

ROCHELLE: (f) French; little rock. There is a French sea-side resort named La Rochelle. In most cases, however, this name is likely to be a variant of RACHEL (Chapter 4).

ROMA: (f) Italian; Rome, named after its legendary founder Romulus. The name enjoyed a moderate popularity in the first half of the 20th century.

ROSS: (m) Welsh; Moor, heath. The best known Ross is located in Scotland, though. This name has had consistent popularity through the last century. Bearers include mystery writer Ross Macdonald and TV character Ross Geller of *Friends.*

SAVANNAH: (f) Arawakan via Spanish; a treeless plain. The name was popular in the late 19th century then dropped out of use until revived in the '80s when it shot up the charts again. One up-and-coming bearer is actress Savannah Haske (seen in the TV show *Third Watch*). Variants: **Savana, Savanah,** and **Savanna.**

SHELBY: (f, m) English; possibly "farm on a plateau." The boy's name has been consistently popular, despite competition from the girls ever since the '30s, although the girls look to be winning out. Variants: (f) **Shelbi** and **Shelbie.**

SHELDON: (m) English; flat-topped hill. The name has had a constant mild popularity, especially in the mid–20th century. Sheldon Corthell is the central character of Frank Norris's 1903 novel *The Pit.* Science fiction author Alice Sheldon is better known by her pen name James Tiptree. Variant: **Shelton.**

SHIRLEY: (f, m) English; meadow belonging to the shire. See Chapter 18.

SIENNA: (f) Italian; the city was originally *Sena Julia* from the personal name *Senius* (according to legend). It is now best known as an artist's pigment made from the reddish brown earth in the area. The name has started showing up only recently.

SKYE: (f) Gaelic; possibly "a wing" for the shape of the island. The name is seen in the last couple of decades. The most common spelling suggests that it is the island people are thinking of, rather than the ordinary word "sky." Variant: **Sky.**

STANFORD: (m) English; stony river crossing. The name appears rarely through most of the 20th century. Stan may be a diminutive of Stanford, but more often it comes from STANLEY (see below). The fame of Stanford University (named in memory of the son of railroad magnate Leland Stanford) may overwhelm other associations.

STANLEY: (m) English; stony meadow. See Chapter 10.

TRENT: (m) Brythonic; a river name from roots meaning "through" and "road, journey." (So if you're talking about the Trent, it's certainly true that "a river runs through it.") The name is seen with increasing frequency through the second half of the 20th century. Recent bearers include Mississippi senator Trent Lott. The river name also occurs in Trenton, which has become popular in recent decades. Variant: **Trenton.**

TREVOR: (m) Welsh; large town. The name has been quite popular ever since the '60s. There are many famous Trevors in the entertainment industry, including British character actor Trevor Howard, film composer Trevor Jones, and director Trevor Nunn. Variant: **Trever.**

TROY: (m) French; from Troyes, France, although sometimes the name may be given because of the literary location of the Trojan war. The name has been quite popular throughout the 20th century, peaking in the '60s. It may be no coincidence that this coincides with Troy Donoghue's career as a movie idol.

VERONA: (f) Italian; a city in northern Italy, of uncertain origin. The name had some popularity around the turn of the 20th century.

VIRGINIA: (f) Latin; belonging to the virgin (in this case, Elizabeth I, known as "the virgin queen"). There is also a Roman legendary character by this name, but more recent popularity seems tied to the state. Virginia Dare was the first child born in the New World to English parents, named after the Virginia colony. The name became extremely popular in the later 19th century and on into the early part of the 20th and has only declined a little since then. Other famous bearers include novelist Virginia Woolf and the dancer better known as Ginger Rogers. Diminutives: **Vergie, Virgie, Ginger,** and **Ginny.**

WALTON: (m) English; multiple origins: town of the foreigners, town in a wood, town by a wall, and others. It was popular in the early 20th century, but has fallen out of use more recently. The popularity of the TV show *The Waltons* failed to revive it significantly.

WESLEY: (m) English; western meadow. The name has had a very steady moderate popularity throughout the 20th century. General Wesley Clark, once supreme commander of NATO, recently tried his hand at running for president. Actor Wesley Snipes specializes in action films like *Blade* and *U.S. Marshalls.* Variant: **Westley;** Diminutive: **Wes.**

WESTON: (m) English; western town. Weston has become somewhat popular in the later part of the 20th century.

WILTON: (m) English; multiple origins: "willow town," "town with a well," or "town on the river Wylye." The name had a steady popularity in the first half of the 20th century but has fallen out of use. Wilton was the full name of Wilt "the Stilt" Chamberlain, one of the early superstars in basketball.

WINFIELD: (m) English; meaning uncertain, but the second part is the word "field." The name was somewhat popular in the early 20th century.

WINSTON: (m) English; town of a man named Wine. The name has been consistently used but never more than mildly popular. Not even World War II British Prime Minister Winston Churchill could give it much of a boost. Variant: **Winton.**

XAVIER: (m) Basque; new house. Another form of the same name, Etcheverry or Etcheberry, is found as a surname but not a given name. It was popularized as the surname of St. Francis Xavier, and taken up as a given name in its own right. The name has seen increasing popularity in the second half of the 20th century, perhaps partly as a result of growing Hispanic use. Variant: **Javier, Xzavier,** and **Zavier.**

ZION: (m) Hebrew; a name for Israel. It has seen a sudden major popularity in the last decade.

Touring the world through names

Note: All the names listed below can be found within this chapter.

If you start at the SIERRAs and head east through DENVER you can go north to pick up MONTANA and the DAKOTAs before seeing the midwestern cities of DAYTON and CLEVELAND. Then you swing back to Texas to pick up DALLAS and HOUSTON before a leisurely tour through DIXIE, enjoying SAVANNAH, the CAROLINAs, and VIRGINIA. You depart AMERICA from BROOKLYN, crossing the Atlantic to the emerald shores of ERIN. In England you pass through LINCOLN and KENT then cross the channel. From BRITTANY it's a short drive to PARIS, then across the Alps to GENEVA and down the Italian peninsula to see MILAN and ROMA. Having crossed the Mediterranean, you pass through JORDAN and pick up the old Spice Road to INDIA and CHINA in ASIA. After that, you may still look forward to ending your journey in HEAVEN.

Featuring the Natural World in Names

While proper place names usually refer to a specific location, words for natural features are more generic and refer to an entire class of locations. As surnames, they often arose to distinguish neighbors: John who lives at the ford rather than John who lives by the meadow. But these given names may also be taken directly from the ordinary words, rather than from surnames.

BROOK, BROOKE: (f) English; a stream. This seems to be part of the fashion for names starting with "Br-" that began around the '70s, but Brooke has increased significantly in popularity, no doubt partly by inspiration of model and actress Brooke Shields.

BROOKS: (m) English; streams. This name has seen a steady low popularity throughout the 20th century.

BRYN: (f, m) Welsh; hill. See Chapter 17.

CHANTAL: (f) French; a stone, a rock. The name probably became popular as the surname of the 17th-century French saint Jeanne de Chantal. It's had a brief recent popularity, centered around the '80s Variants: **Chantel, Chantelle, Shantel,** and **Shantell.**

CLIFF: (m) English; a cliff, a precipice. Sometimes a short form of CLIFFORD (see earlier in this chapter). Cliff has been mildly popular in the mid–20th century. The name is known from pop singer Cliff Richard and actor Cliff Edwards.

CRAIG: (m) Gaelic or Welsh; a rock. Craig rose steadily to a high popularity just after the mid–20th century but has since fallen mostly out of use again. For a variety of Craigs, you have food writer Craig Claiborne and New Hampshire governor Craig Benson. Variant: **Kraig.**

DALE: (f, m) English; a valley. The name was quite popular through the middle part of the 20th century for boys and always much less popular for girls, despite the influence of actress Dale Evans, wife and co-star of cowboy actor Roy Rogers.

DELL: (m) English; a valley (the same root as DALE). There was a brief rare interest in this name in the mid–20th century. The variant Del is more likely a short form of Delbert.

DELTA: (f) Greek; a place where a river widens entering the sea; named for its triangular shape resembling the Greek letter delta. The name occurs rarely around 1900 but some interest may be revived by actress Delta Burke, best known for *Designing Women.*

FORD: (m) English; a river crossing. Ford had a slight popularity around the beginning of the 20th century, possibly in honor of automotive pioneer Henry Ford.

GARTH: (m) English; an enclosed yard. The name has had a consistent but low popularity through much of the 20th century. Country singer Garth Brooks is one well-known bearer.

GLENNA (f), **GLEN** (m): Gaelic, Welsh; a valley; *glen* is the Gaelic word while *glyn* is the related Welsh word. Glen(n) has always been more popular than Glyn(n)for the male name, fading from a rather high popularity only in the last few decades. There are several well-known musical Glens, including band leader Glenn Miller and country singer Glen Campbell. For women, Glenna starts out as the more popular form, but the coined variant Glenda surpasses it in the '40s. The latter is most familiar from actress Glenda Jackson. Actress Glenn Close bears a form more usually considered male. Early TV actress Glynis Johns bears another variant. Variants: (m) **Glenn, Glyn,** and **Glynn;** (f) **Glenda, Glennie,** and **Glynis.**

LANE: (f, m) English; a road, a lane. The given name is taken from the surname, but has been popular mostly in the later 20th century. On the female side, Layne Beachley is an Australian surfing champion. Variant: **Layne.**

LEE, LEIGH: (f, m) English; either "a wood" or "a clearing, a meadow." In the spelling "Lee" the name became quite popular for men (and only slightly less so for women) in the later 19th century, largely in honor of Civil War general Robert E. Lee. As the specific association faded, the name spread more generally but has remained high in popularity. The spelling "Leigh" starts hitting the charts for both men and women around the '40s, but the men rapidly concede the field to the ladies, and there has been a parallel shift away from female use of Lee. (For this reason, when the sound "lee" at the end of a name is spelled "leigh," it will almost always be used as a girl's name.) Leigh Brackett may have benefited from the gender ambiguity of the name when she started her career as a science fiction writer in the '40s — a time when it was generally opined that women couldn't write in that field. Variant: (f) **Lea.**

LOMA: (f) Spanish; hill. The name may also be a short form of PALOMA (Chapter 12). It was a rare name in the early 20th century.

LYNN: (f, m) Brythonic; a lake. Originally this was much more popular for men than women in the later 19th century, but the numbers switched around the '30s and it has since been primarily a female name. Influenced by this, most names ending in "-lyn" have migrated to the female side. Actress Lynn Redgrave is a famous representative of the name. Variant: (both) **Lyn,** (f) **Linnea** and **Lynne.** Diminutive: (f) **Linnie.**

MEADOW: (f) English; a meadow, a grassy field. The name has begun being used as a given name only recently.

RIDGE: (m) English; a ridge, a line of sharp hills. The name has shown up very rarely in the last decade or so. This and the following RIVER (see later in this chapter) may be rare cases of taking boy's names directly from ordinary words.

RIVER: (m) English; a river, a water-course. The name has had increasing popularity only in the last couple of decades. One likely source of inspiration has been actor River Phoenix.

ROCK: (m) English; a rock, a stone. This name may be in the current category under false pretenses and instead be an Englishing of the Italian name Rocco. Both Rock and Rocky became popular just as Rocco faded in the mid–20th century. The name of movie star Rock Hudson was direct from the stone, however, being one of those Hollywood publicist's inventions. Variant: **Rocco** and **Rocky.**

SIERRA: (f) Spanish; a mountain range. This name shows up abruptly in the '80s and climbs the charts rapidly. Sierra has a strong outdoorsy feel, not simply from the meaning, but from association with the environmentalist Sierra Club. Variants: **Ciarra, Ciera,** and **Cierra.**

STONE: (m) English; a rock, a stone. This has been a rare name in the last couple of decades, suggesting that it may be a new coinage rather than the use of a surname. News anchor Stone Phillips is one bearer of this name. Variant: **Stoney.**

WADE: (m) English; a ford, a place where you can wade. The name has been consistently popular throughout the 20th century. There is a minor character in *Gone With the Wind* named Wade, where it is said he was named after the surname of his father's commanding officer.

WARREN: (m) French; a river name (Varenne). The name has fallen off somewhat in popularity from the earlier part of the 20th century but has never become rare. President Warren G. Harding and actor Warren Beatty are two famous bearers of the name.

WORTH: (m) English; an enclosure, a homestead. It may also be attractive for its ordinary meaning, "value, quality." It was a rare name around the turn of the 20th century at a time when the House of Worth was a leading clothing designer.

Chapter 15

Exploring the World of Names

As a nation of immigrants, the name pool is drawn from the entire world. Historic forces have emphasized the names of Europe, but whether names are carried in on a tide of immigration or sought out by people researching their family heritage, our culture is enriched by a myriad of cultures. European names are covered in many chapters of this book, but this chapter focuses on names taken from, or popular in, other parts of the world that have either been in common use in the U.S. or have well-known American bearers who may inspire further use.

Names from the Americas: Natives and Newcomers

A handful of names from Native American languages have come into general use, in some cases via place or tribal names, such as Dakota, in other cases because they have been popularized by a famous bearer, such as Shania. A much larger New World influence on the name pool comes from names made popular in the various Hispanic cultures of the Americas. While most of these are Spanish in origin, the fashions and names involved are often distinct from those of Spain.

ANAHI: (f) Guarani; meaning uncertain, said to be the name of a type of tree. The name comes from a delightful (if probably apocryphal) story associated with the Anahi mine in Bolivia. The mine was said to come as the dowry of an Indian princess named Anahi who married a Spanish conquistador. The name has become quite popular in Central and South America and has hit the charts in the U.S. in the last decade. One bearer is single-name Mexican actress and singer Anahi.

ARACELI: (f) Spanish; altar of heaven. The name is popular in Spain as well as the Americas, borne by Spanish mountain climber Araceli Segarra. It has become popular in the U.S. in recent decades. Variant: **Aracely.**

BELEN: (f) Spanish; Bethlehem. The place name Belén was applied to a number of places in the New World, including a Brazilian city in the heart of the Amazon. Use as a girl's name may be from any of these places or directly from the Biblical place name. The name has only hit the popularity charts very recently.

BRISA: (f) Spanish; breeze. A popular element in place names, and the use as a girl's name may come from these rather than directly from the ordinary word. Mildly popular in the last decade.

CHEYENNE: (f) Dakota; unintelligible speaker. There is something of a world-wide tradition of groups of people being named by their neighbors with something meaning "those people over there who talk funny." (See BARBARA in Chapter 7.) In this case, the common name for this Algonquian tribe comes from their neighbors, the Dakota (or Sioux, as they were called by *their* neighbors). Cheyenne has been a popular commercial product name, evoking images of the rugged Wild West. Use as a feminine given name may partly be influenced by the chance resemblance to ANNE (Chapter 8), as seen in some of the spelling variants. It has been quite popular in the last couple of decades. Variants: **Cheyanne, Chianne, Chyann,** and **Shyanne.**

CONCEPCION: (f) Spanish; conception, from a reference to the Immaculate Conception. It is also popular as a place name in South America. A somewhat old-fashioned name these days, it was fairly popular in the early part of the 20th century. Variant: **Concetta.**

CONSUELO: (f) Spanish; consolation, from an epithet of the Virgin Mary, *Nuestra Señora del Consuelo,* "Our Lady of Consolation." The name is interesting for being grammatically masculine (ending in "-o") but used for girls. Mildly popular in the earlier part of the 20th century, but less so in recent decades. One bearer is federal appeals court justice Consuelo Maria Callahan.

CRUZ: (f, m) Spanish; a cross, a crucifix. The name has been popular for both boys and girls, although recently the male use has won out. One prominent bearer is Californian politician Cruz Bustamante.

DAKOTA: (f, m) Dakota; friends, allies. The Siouxan name for themselves, commemorated in the names of two states covering their historic territory. It has been used for both boys and girls in recent decades, although somewhat unusually the boys are using more spelling variants. One bearer is child-actress Dakota Fanning. Variants: (m) **Dakoda** and **Dakotah.**

DIEGO: (m) Spanish; meaning uncertain. Often mistakenly believed to come from a re-interpretation of Sant-iago (Saint James) as San-tiago/San-diego. This is, instead, from an entirely different saint whose name derives from the Latin Didacus. The 15th-century Saint Diego of Alcala was the namesake of the mission that grew into the city of San Diego in southern California, but the name has been quite popular since before the life of that saint. One famous bearer is Mexican artist Diego Rivera and the name has been increasing steadily in popularity over the last half century.

DOLORES: (f) Spanish; sorrows, from an epithet of the Virgin, *Maria de Dolores* "Mary of Sorrows." It was quite popular in the '20s and '30s and has only seriously fallen out of fashion in the last couple of decades. One bearer is labor activist Delores Huerta. Variants: **Delores, Deloris,** and **Doloris.**

GUADALUPE: (f, m) Spanish; valley of the wolf. A Spanish place name of mixed Arabic and Spanish origin. It became popular as a given name via the Virgin of Guadalupe, who became the patroness of Mexico after appearing in a vision in the early 16th century. The connection of a Spanish place name with the story is hard to interpret, and the original may have been a native name that sounded like the familiar Guadalupe. The name has been consistently popular for both boys and girls. Diminutive: **Lupe.**

INEZ: (f) Spanish; a variant of AGNES (see Chapter 8). The name had been popular even outside the Hispanic community in the early part of the 20th century, but has fallen out of fashion more recently. Variant: **Ines.**

ITZEL: (f) uncertain; some sources suggest a Mayan origin, but the roots of the name are unclear other than that it is popular in the Hispanic community. It has been increasing sharply in popularity in the last couple of decades.

LUZ: (f) Spanish; light, from yet another epithet of the Virgin. Perhaps sometimes used as a variant of LUCY (see Chapter 16). It has been consistently popular, especially in the mid–20th century.

MILAGROS: (f) Spanish; miracles, from an epithet of Mary. Mildly popular through the mid–20th century, but out of fashion in recent decades, perhaps partly because the name is grammatically masculine. One bearer is Venezuelan tennis player Milagros Sequera.

NAKIA: (f, m) Navajo; Mexican, apparently a variant of the word *nakai.* The sudden and brief popularity of this name can almost certainly be traced to a short-running 1974 TV detective show titled *Nakia* after the main character, a Navajo policeman.

NAYELI: (f) uncertain; claimed by some sources to be Zapotec for "I love you." It has become popular only in the last decade or so. Variant: **Nayely.**

PILAR: (f) Spanish; pillar, from a vision seen by Saint Iago of Compostella of "Our Lady of the pillar." The name has been rare enough that it only hit the popularity charts briefly in the '20s. One bearer is Mexican singer and TV actress Pilar Montenegro.

RAMIRO: (m) Spanish; from Germanic roots meaning "famous advice." The name has been popular in Spain since the time of the Visigoths and gave rise to the surname Ramirez. It has been mildly popular in the U.S. through most of the 20th century. One bearer is former Panamanian baseball player Ramiro Mendoza.

SHANIA: (f) Ojibway; I'm on the way. Singer Shania Twain chose this stage name to honor her late stepfather. Perhaps thanks to her influence, this name has shot up the charts starting in the '90s. It's possible that some uses of the name Shania are independently coined, blending the popular first syllable "Sha-" with a name like Tania or Sonia. Variant: **Shaniya.**

SHASTA: (f) unknown native Californian language; meaning uncertain. The name of an extremely picturesque mountain and lake in northern California, as well as the surrounding county. Briefly popular in the '80s.

SHAWNEE: (f) Algonquian; southerners; a tribal name. One of several names of Native American tribes that have become used as given names. It has been only briefly popular within the last decade. Variant: **Shani.**

TRINIDAD: (f, m) Spanish; trinity. This religious-inspired name has been popular as a place name, one good example being the island of Trinidad that forms part of the country of Trinidad and Tobago. It showed up occasionally as both a male and female name in the early part of the 20th century. The use of the English form Trinity, which has shot up to a very high popularity in the last decade, is most likely independent, rather than being taken from the Spanish name. Variant: **Trinity.**

WINONA: (f) Dakota; first-born daughter, eldest daughter. One may expect this name to have become popular only recently, inspired by singer Wynona Judd and actress Winona Ryder, but in fact they represent the tail end of a fashion centered in the early part of the 20th century. The name has an interesting history. The story of one Dakota woman of this name was immortalized and romanticized in an 1881 poem *Winona* by H. L. Gordon, and towns scattered across several midwestern states adopted the name. Use as a given name outside the Dakota community derives primarily from the place names and the literary use. Variant: **Wynona.**

YAHIR: (m) uncertain; meaning uncertain, but see YAJAIRA, (see later in this chapter). This name has suddenly become quite popular in the last couple of years. One possible inspiration is pop singer Yahir Othón Parra.

YAJAIRA: (f) uncertain; meaning uncertain. The name was popularized by a character in the Spanish-language soap opera *Esmeralda* in the '70s, and origins in various native Central and South American languages have been proposed. Variant: **Yahaira.**

Names from Africa and the Middle East

Starting around the '70s, there has been a strong interest in the African American community for names used in, or associated with, Africa. Due to the historic association of Islam with much of northern Africa, the same impulses have led to an interest in Arabic names, even among non-Muslims. In addition to the popularity of specific names, the sound structure of these names has been one influence on African American fashions in coined names (see Chapter 11).

ALI: (m) Arabic; sublime, exalted. Often used in honor of Ali ibn Abi Talib, a cousin of Muhammad and the 4th caliph. The name has been moderately popular for the last several decades.

AMINA: (f) Arabic; faithful, honest. The name of Tunisian pop singer Amina Annabi. It has become somewhat popular in the last decade.

ASHA: (f) Arabic; life. Relatively simple names like this often coincidentally exist in more than one language, and the name of Indian singer Asha Bhosle is most likely an unrelated Sanskrit name meaning "wish, desire."

ASHANTI: (f) Ashanti; the name of the Ashanti people in Ghana. It has been showing up as a girl's name in the last couple of decades and has been increasing sharply in popularity in the last couple of years, perhaps inspired by R&B singer Ashanti.

BARACK: (m) Arabic; blessing. In the case of Illinois senator Barack Obama, the Arabic name had been borrowed into Swahili.

CHAYA (f), **CHAIM** (m): Hebrew; life. While many Hebrew names are of scriptural origin, these are taken from ordinary words. Chaim has been in use since Medieval times, and Chaya may be of similar antiquity. Both names have connections to the popular musical *Fiddler on the Roof.* One of the daughters in the story is named Chaya, and Chaim is the first name of the actor Topol who played the main character on both stage and screen. Both names have seen some popularity in recent decades.

HAMZA: (m) Arabic; strong. Most often used in honor of an uncle of Muhammad who was an early convert to Islam. It has seen some recent popularity.

ISIS: (f) Egyptian; meaning uncertain. Isis is the Greek form of the name of the goddess Aset, who governed both fertility and funerals. Her name also appears in ISIDORE (see Chapter 8). Isis has jumped into popularity in the last decade.

JELANI: (m) Ibo, a language of Nigeria; mighty, strong. The name has just barely made the popularity charts within the last decade.

KENYA: (f, m) Kikuyu; white mountain. The country of Kenya is named after Mount Kenya, whose name in Kikuyu is more properly Kere-Nyaga. At first, Kenya appeared as both a male and female name, no doubt inspired by Kenyan independence in the mid '60s, but it rapidly became used for girls only due to the "-a" ending.

KENYATTA: (f, m) Kikuyu; meaning uncertain, but including the country name Kenya. There was a brief fashion among both boys and girls for this name in the '70s in honor of Jomo Kenyatta, the first president of Kenya.

KHALIL: (m) Arabic; friend; best friend. The name is familiar from the poet Khalil Gibran. It enjoyed a brief popularity in the '90s. Variant: **Kahlil.**

KOFI: (m) Twi, a language of Ghana; born on Friday. It is common in some African cultures to be given multiple names including one describing the circumstances of birth. This name is familiar from United Nations Secretary-General Kofi Annan.

KWAME: (m) Akan, a language of Ghana; born on Saturday. As with KOFI (see earlier in this chapter), this may be given as one of several names. Civil rights leader Ralph Abernathy named his youngest child Kwame Luthuli, most likely in honor of Ghana's first president Kwame Nkrumah and South Africa's Nobel Peace Prize winner Albert Luthuli. The name is rare, but hit the popularity charts in the '90s.

LATIFA: (f) Arabic; gentle. The name is familiar from rap star Queen Latifah and has had some slight popularity in the last decade. Variant: **Latifah.**

MUSTAFA: (m) Arabic; chosen, selected. This was the name of Turkish general Mustafa Kamal, better known by the name Atatürk, which he adopted after becoming the first president of the modern Turkish republic. Mustafa has been seeing a slight popularity in the last decade.

NAJEE: (m) Arabic; saved, rescued. A rare name in recent years. It is the lone stage name of Jazz saxophonist Najee.

OMAR: (m) Arabic; flourishing. The name was first popularized in Islam by the second caliph, Umar ibn al-Khattab. It is more generally familiar in the U.S. than many Arabic names, thanks to actor Omar Sharif and poet Omar Khayyam. Variants: **Omari** and **Omer.**

RAKEEM: (m) Arabic; meaning uncertain, possibly "judicious." The name has had some slight popularity in the last decade.

SAMIRA: (f) Arabic; a lively conversationalist. The name has only recently become popular.

SYED: (m) Arabic; happy. The name has been mildly popular in recent decades. One prominent bearer was Sir Syed Ahmad Khan, a significant figure in the development of the modern state of India.

TANISHA: (f) Hausa, a language of Nigeria; born on Monday. Another one of the birth day names popular in some African cultures. Compare this name with the sound patterns found in some popular constructed names (see Chapter 11). Variant: **Tanesha** and **Tenisha.**

TARIQ: (m) Arabic; one who knocks (on the door). The Arabic name for the morning star. The name of the rock of Gibraltar (Jebel Tariq) commemorates the 8th-century governor of Tangier, Tariq ibn Ziyad. It has been slightly popular in recent decades. Variant: **Tarik.**

YADIRA: (f) Hebrew; friend. Mildly popular in recent decades.

ZAIRE: (m) uncertain; possibly taken from Nzadi, "the river," one local name for the Congo river. The country once known as Zaire has now returned to a variant on its older name of Congo, in both cases referring to the major river that defines the region. It has only become popular as a personal name in the last decade.

Names from Asia and the Pacific

The 20th century has seen a vast increase in the influence of Asia and the Pacific region on American culture. But there has been great variability in how much the names of these cultures have made their way into the larger society. Relatively few given names from Japan, China, or Korea have made it into general use, despite the size of those communities, partially due to the custom of adopting "American names" for public use. In contrast, Indian immigrants are more likely to continue using traditional names, even in later generations, and a general interest in Indian culture and religion starting in the '60s have encouraged the use of Indian names. A sprinkling of other cultures have provided names that hit the American charts at some time.

ADITYA: (m) Hindi; sun. The recent popularity of this name may be related to the Indian business group Aditya Birla, named after its founder.

AKIRA: (f) Japanese; intelligent. Although this name is masculine in Japanese, as for famous filmmaker Akira Kurusawa, it seems to have been taken up in American use as a feminine name, due to the "-a" ending.

ANANDA: (f) Sanskrit; happiness, joy. A popular name associated with meditation centers, which may account for its occasional use in the U.S.

ANIYA: (f) Japanese?; meaning uncertain. This name may have multiple origins, but some examples are clearly Japanese. It has had a sudden popularity in the last couple of decades. Variant: **Aniyah.**

ANJALI: (f) Hindi; joining hands. There has been some very recent interest in this name.

CHANDRA: (f) Sanskrit; the moon; shining. The name was suddenly popular in the '70s for unclear reasons, perhaps simply a growing interest in Indian culture. One bearer is professional tennis player Chandra Rubin. Variant: **Chanda.**

KALI: (f) multiple origins; possibly for the Hindu goddess of destruction, but another Pacific connection is a Hawaiian volcano goddess of this name. The name is also simple enough in form that it may come from other sources coincidentally. Whatever the origin, the name has been moderately popular in the last couple of decades.

KALPANA: (f) Hindi; imagination. Kalpana Chawla was an astronaut on the ill-fated final flight of the Columbia shuttle.

KARMA: (f) Sanskrit; fate, destiny. The Carma that appears on the popularity charts in the '30s is unlikely to be of Indian origin, however. Variant: **Carma.**

KEANU: (m) Hawaiian; possibly "cool breeze." Actor Keanu Reeves has given a variety of translations for his name, and it isn't clear that they are all intended seriously. The recent interest in Keanu can probably be chalked up to his influence, though.

KOBE: (m) Japanese; the name of a city in Japan. In all likelihood, this name actually derives from a short-form of the surname Jacoby, as seen in spellings like Coby. But when used in the spelling Kobe, the Japanese connection comes strongly to mind, and it is the most popular form, no doubt due to the influence of basketball star Kobe Bryant. Variants: **Coby** and **Koby.**

LEILANIL: (f) Hawaiian; heavenly garland. The popularity of this name is entirely due to the Harry Owens song *Sweet Leilani,* popularized by Bing Crosby in the movie *Waikiki Wedding,* which won the 1937 Oscar for best song. It has appeared occasionally since the '40s and rose sharply in popularity in the last decade, possibly related to the 1996 album of the same title by Dennis Pavao.

MOHINI: (f) Sanskrit; enchanting. This name has recently become familiar from Olympic gymnast Mohini Bhardwaj.

PARMINDER: (f) Sanskrit; supreme goddess. Actress Parminder Nagra has been bringing this name to more general attention since she joined the TV show *ER.*

PRANAV: (m) Sanskrit; the name of the sacred syllable "om." This name has become somewhat popular in the last decade.

TAJ: (m) Sanskrit; crown. The name is familiar in part from the place name Taj Mahal, the great mausoleum for the empress Mumtaz Mahal, but it's also a common Indian name that has hit the popularity charts in the last few years. Variant: **Tahj.**

TAMIKO: (f) Japanese; people-child. Alternately, this may be a variant of the coined name TAMIKA (see Chapter 11).

YOKO: (f) Japanese; multiple possible readings: four, positive, side. Popularized by artist Yoko Ono, widow of ex-Beatle John Lennon.

YOSHIKO: (f) Japanese; good child. The popularity charts show this name appearing in the U.S. in the 1910s. This is rather surprising, as Japanese immigration (especially of women) was not very high yet at that time, but it would be hard to find a better explanation for the name's origin.

Part V
Seeking the Stars: Names from Popular Culture

The 5th Wave   By Rich Tennant

"I really think it's a boy. Why else would I turn off 'Masterpiece Theater' to hog the remote through a two-hour 'Wrestlemania'?"

In this part . . .

Name fashions arise from the names we hear, and those names that more people hear are more likely to become fashionable. So it isn't surprising that TV and film stars, characters on the big or small screens, and nationally known sports heroes have had a disproportionate influence on which names become popular. Even popular songs have produced fashionable names.

Chapter 16

Sitcoms, Soaps, and Serials: Names from TV Land

In This Chapter

▶ Checking out TV's early years for possible names

▶ Discovering the latest names from TV land

Movie stars may be more glamorous, but television actors and characters are right there in your living room, day in and day out. Naming characters after them may sometimes feel more like honoring a close friend than reaching out to touch a star.

Searching the Early Years

In the golden age of television, popular shows created a common American mythos, shaping and reflecting your idea of who we are as a society. So it's no surprise that the names of TV actors and their characters have also shaped and reflected the naming fashions. Here are some names that people may associate closely with classic TV shows up through the '60s.

ANISSA: (f) coined?; possibly a blending of ANNE (Chapter 8) and LISA (Chapter 10). There is, however, a name Annys that is a Medieval variant of AGNES (Chapter 8). Child actress Anissa Jones played "Buffy," the young sister in the series *A Family Affair* in the '60s. That same decade is when the name first appears on the popularity charts, which is unlikely to be a coincidence. It has had a very mild popularity since then.

ALTHEA: (f) Greek; healing; making wholesome. (A non-Greek origin with unknown meaning is also possible.) In Greek mythology Althaea was the mother of Meleagar who was fated to die when a particular log was burnt in the fire. Althaea preserved the log safely for many years, but when she heard that her son, Meleagar, had killed her brothers in a fight over a girl, she threw the log back on the fire and he died. There's some lesson in there about not making your mother mad. The name was revived in 17th-century poetry, such as that of Richard Lovelace. For some unknown reason, Althea has been a favorite name for soap opera characters, being found for Dr. Althea Davis in *The Doctors*, Althea Dennis in *The Brighter Day*, and Althea Raven in *Love of Life*. Another more recent TV character connection is Althea Tibbs, the wife of Virgil Tibbs in the series *In the Heat of the Night*. In contrast with the name's television popularity, it was declining in real-life use at the same time and is quite rare today, although it can be found for tennis pro Althea Gibson.

ARTEMAS: (m) Greek; presumably derived from Artemis, the goddess of the hunt. (See ARTEMISIA, Chapter 18.) This name is mentioned in the New Testament, guaranteeing it a chance of revival despite the pagan association. In the Latin form Artemus it was used as a pen name by 19th-century humorist Charles Farrar Browne. The main character of the tongue-in-cheek western series *Wild Wild West* was named Artemus Gordon. Variant: **Artemus.**

AUDREY: (f) English; noble strength. From the Old English name Etheldreda. The 7th-century Queen Etheldreda of Northumbria became a saint, starting an unfortunate chain of events for her name, as the cheap trinkets sold in later ages at her festival were described as "Saint Awdry's" or "Tawdry." (Fortunately, girls named Audrey today rarely need to worry that their classmates will know this piece of trivia.) The name gradually declined in popularity up through the 17th century but was revived in the late 19th as part of the fashion for things Medieval. It was already at a peak of popularity in the mid–20th century when actress Audrey Hepburn put the seal of glamour on the name. The television connection comes from the variant Audra, borne by the character Audra Barkely in the western series *The Big Valley*. Variant: **Audra.**

BEN: (m) Hebrew; a diminutive of BENJAMIN (Chapter 4). This short form has been used as an independent name since at least as early as the 19th century. It came into the 20th century at a very high popularity and only declined since then in favor of the full form, Benjamin. On television it became associated with strong but somewhat avuncular men, such as Dr. Ben Casey, from the series of the same name, and Ben Cartwright, in *Bonanza*. Another theatrical connection is actor Ben Kingsley.

BRETT: (f, m) English; a Breton, someone from Brittany. Taken from the surname, most likely during the 19th century. An early bearer was 19th-century writer Bret Harte. The hero of the TV series *Maverick* (and its later revival as *Bret Maverick*) was one of a horde of video cowboys. Interestingly the character and his brothers heralded the coming fashion for names of the "Br-" pattern, being named Bret, Bart, and Brent. Bret suddenly pops up high on the charts in the decade when this series first appeared, and you can consider it a solid cause and effect. On the female side, you have comedian Brett Butler, star of the more recent series *Grace Under Fire*. Britt can sometimes be a variant of this same name, but in the case of actress Britt Ekland it is more likely to be a diminutive of Brigitte. Variants: **Bret** and **Britt.**

CHET: (m) English; a diminutive of the surname Chester or Chesley. News anchor Chet Huntley formed half the team of Huntley and Brinkley, who were a byword for dependable news and analysis in the '50s and '60s. It may be a tribute to Huntley's influence that the name Chet briefly hit the popularity charts in that time.

DESI: (m) Spanish; a diminutive of Desiderio, "desired one." Cuban-born musician Desi Arnaz found a second career in comedy, teamed with his wife Lucille Ball, through a series of TV shows. The name has never become generally popular, however.

EPHRAIM: (m) uncertain; meaning uncertain. In the Old Testament, the name of a grandson of Jacob; some sources suggest that it may be Hebrew meaning "very fruitful" but this is taken largely from an offhand comment in the passage where the name appears. It was revived in the 18th century, especially in New England, and for some unknown reason became a nickname for the grizzly bear. Actor Efrem Zimbalist, Jr. starred in the early true-crime series *The F.B.I.* Variants: **Efrain, Efrem,** and **Efren.**

GOMER: (m) Hebrew; ember. The name of one of Noah's grandsons. It also appears elsewhere as a woman's name, but does not appear to have been revived in this use. The Jim Nabors character Gomer Pyle appeared first in *The Andy Griffith Show* and later spun off *Gomer Pyle, U.S.M.C.* The somewhat goofy nature of the character made it unlikely that this name would become fashionable as a result.

JADA: (f) uncertain; possibly a variant of the gem name JADE (Chapter 12). An early bearer of this name is actress Jada Rowland in the soap opera *The Secret Storm.* More recently it has been made popular by actress Jada Pinkett-Smith Variants: **Jaida** and **Jayda.**

JAY: (m) English; chatterer, from the bird "jay." Sometimes a diminutive of James, or simply standing for the initial "J" from any name with that spelling. Actor Jay Silverheels elevated the role of "faithful Indian sidekick" above the usual sterotypes in the TV series *The Lone Ranger.* A more recent television connection is talk-show host Jay Leno.

LUCY: (f) Latin; light. The original name is Lucia and was greatly popularized by a 4th-century martyred saint. The variant Lucilla, later Lucille, was borne by another early saint. The names are related in origin to the masculine names LUKE (Chapter 4), LUCIUS (Chapter 7), and LUCIAN (Chapter 17). Like many saints' names, Lucy fell out of popularity during the Reformation, but was revived in the 19th century. Both Lucy and Lucille were quite popular coming into the 20th century and have only gradually fallen off. In the early years of television, Lucille Ball was the queen of comedy, starring in a succession of popular series and variety shows, such as *I Love Lucy.* More recent TV Lucys have been New Zealand actress Lucy Lawless in *Xena, Warrior Princess* and Lucy Liu in *Ally McBeal.* The name was given a uniquely '60s spin in the psychedelic Beatles song *Lucy in the Sky with Diamonds.* Variants: **Lucie, Lucienne, Lucila, Lucile, Lucilla, Lucille,** and **Lue.**

MARLO: (f) multiple origins; in some cases a diminutive of Mary or Margaret, although there is also a Spanish surname Marlo that is unlikely to have contributed to the given name. Actress Marlo Thomas of *That Girl* is probably responsible for the bump in popularity seen for the name in the '60s and '70s. Variant: **Marla.**

MAVERICK: (m) English; a loner, a rogue, especially of cattle who stray from the herd. The surname of TV cowboy Bret Maverick represents him as a loner and individualist. Maverick is not a traditional surname, so the recent fashion for the name can either be attributed to the TV character or the ordinary word.

MAXWELL: (m) English; the well or pool of Maccus (a personal name). Like many other surnames, this was revived as a given name in the 19th century and slowly declined in popularity over the 20th. It has suddenly picked up again since the '80s. This is somewhat late to be connected with the career of bumbling secret agent Maxwell Smart in the TV series *Get Smart.*

MAYNARD: (m) French; from Germanic roots meaning "strong and hardy." A moderately popular name in the early 20th century, most likely taken more directly from the surname. It fell out of fashion after the '60s. Maynard Krebs was the beatnik sidekick (played by Bob Denver) of the title character of *The Lives of Dobie Gillis.*

SAMANTHA: (f) coined; apparently a blend of SAMUEL (Chapter 4) with some name like Anthea. The name first came to attention in a series of comic novels by Marietta Holley in the late 19th century, and then was made glamorous by the character of Tracy Samantha Lord in the movie *High Society.* But the name exploded onto the charts in the '60s with the appearance of the character Samantha Stevens in the TV show *Bewitched.* The fashion for Samantha was no flash in the pan; it continued rising until it hit number 5 in the '90s. Another bearer is actress Samantha Eggar. Variant: **Samatha.**

TABITHA: (f) Aramaic; a deer, an antelope. The name evokes a sense of grace and beauty. In the New Testament, when a woman named Tabitha is briefly mentioned, the text notes that her name in Greek would be DORCAS (Chapter 4). Like Samantha, Tabitha showed up with sudden popularity in the '60s, after it was used for a character in the popular TV fantasy *Bewitched.* Variant: **Tabatha.**

WARD: (m) English; a watchman. Taken into use from the surname in the 19th century, it came into the 20th century at a relatively high level of popularity. Oddly, the popularity of the series *Leave it to Beaver,* featuring paterfamilias Ward Cleaver coincided with (if it did not actually cause) the final decline of the name's popularity.

WYATT: (m) English; from Guyot, a diminutive of the French name GUY (Chapter 8). The name had been mildly popular in the 19th century, taken from the surname, but revived again in the mid–20th century in the wake of the first of a series of TV shows and movies about the life and legend of western lawman Wyatt Earp.

Noting the Neilsen Newcomers

With the rise of cable stations and the fading influence of the "big three" networks, you no longer have a sense that we're all watching the same shows. At the same time, the boundary between the worlds of television, movies, and live theater have become less rigid. So the influence of more recent TV actors and characters on naming can be harder to identify. This section explores some names familiar from TV shows of the last few decades — the ones that you new parents are likely to have grown up watching.

AINSLEY: (f) English; either "An's meadow" or "meadow with a hermitage." This shows up only in the last several years on the popularity charts as a girl's name and doesn't seem to have followed the usual pattern for names taken from surnames in that it wasn't taken up in the 19th century and wasn't used first for boys. Today, names ending in "-ley" or "-leigh" are generally treated as girls' names, so this seems to have been a very recent adoption. One possible inspiration is the character of Ainsley Hayes on the TV show *The West Wing.* Variant: **Ansley.**

ALEXIS: (f, m) Greek; helper, defender. Sometimes used as a diminutive of ALEXANDER (Chapter 6), but this is also an independent name. It came into English use via French and Russian use and often keeps those associations. It has become quite popular for both boys and girls in the last half century, although only the girls have brought it into the top ten. This is likely to be due, in part, to the inspiration of the character Alexis Carrington on the show *Dynasty.* Another diminutive of Alexandra that pops up on TV is Lexie, as for the character on the Scottish TV series *Monarch of the Glen.* Variants: (f) **Alexus** and **Alexys.** Diminutives: (f) **Lexi, Lexie, Lexis,** and **Lexus.**

ALLY: (f) English; usually a diminutive of ALISON (Chapter 8). The variant Allie was somewhat popular in the early part of the 20th century and then was revived again in the '90s, possibly inspired by the TV series *Kate and Allie,* while Ally hits the charts right on the heels of the debut of *Ally McBeal.* As a woman's name, Ali is a variant of this, rather than being related to the masculine Ali, which is from Arabic. Variants: **Ali** and **Allie.**

AMY: (f) French; friend, beloved. The name was popular in the Middle Ages and then was revived again by 19th-century romantics. With a few ups and downs, it made it all the way up to number 2 in the '70s, a popularity wave that presidential daughter Amy Carter was riding. Currently, Amy is borne by both actress Amy Brenneman and her title character on the show *Judging Amy.* Variants: **Aimee, Ami,** and **Amie.**

ARSENIO: (m) Italian; possibly "man from Arsinna"; from an old Roman name. An early Saint Arsenius gave this name some small popularity. Today it is borne by talk show host Arsenio Hall.

AVERY: (f, m) English; a variant of ALFRED (Chapter 9). This surname came into use as a masculine given name in the 19th century and has recently enjoyed a further increase in popularity, as well as beginning to be used for girls, too. One bearer is actor Avery Brooks, star of the series *Star Trek: Deep Space Nine.*

BAILEY: (f, m) English; a bailiff, a sheriff. This name has become popular for both boys and girls in the last several decades, with the girls enjoying more spelling variants. This popularity has been reflected on the screen with characters such as Bailey Salinger in *Party of Five.* Variants: (f) **Bailee** and **Baylee.**

BARNABAS: (m) Hebrew; son of Exhortation. Barnaby is another variant, sometimes shortened to Barney. The name appears in the New Testament and was becoming popular during the early settlement of New England. Barnabas has a bit of a stiff, formal feel, suited to Barnabas Collins, the undead central character of the serial *Dark Shadows.* Barnaby is a bit more informal and folksy, as for the title character of the detective show *Barnaby Jones.* But Barney is the only version that seriously hits the recent popularity charts, although even it has declined by the mid–20th century. Examples include the title character of the humorous police drama *Barney Miller* as well as stone-age cartoon character Barney Rubble. Variants: **Barnaby** and **Barney.**

BLOSSOM: (f) English; a flower, a blossom. This doesn't seem to have been among the popular Victorian flower names, but it did appear occasionally in the early 20th century. The free-spirited title character of the TV show *Blossom* gives it more of a '70s twist.

BUFFY: (f) English; a diminutive of ELIZABETH (Chapter 8), from a baby-talk version of Bethie. The name became associated with the "Valley girl" stereotype and was picked for that reason for the title character of the movie *Buffy the Vampire Slayer* and the spin-off TV series of the same name. The fictional Buffy would have been born in the only decade when this name shows up on the popularity charts. A very different image of the name comes from folksinger Buffy Sainte-Marie.

CALLISTA: (f) Greek; most beautiful. In Greek mythology, Callisto was turned into a bear because of Hera's jealousy, and then put in the stars as the Great Bear. The name was used in its original form for a deliciously evil villainess in *Xena: Warrior Princess,* but modern use has generally preferred an "a" at the end. Actress Calista Flockhart starred in the comic law drama *Ally McBeal,* and the appearance of this form of the name on the charts in the last decade can be attributed to her. Variants: **Calista** and **Callisto.**

CHANDLER: (f, m) English; originally, a candle maker; later, one who sells supplies to ships. This is part of the more recent fashion for adopting occupational surnames as given names, rather than being part of the 19th-century fashion for surnames in general. The creators of the popular TV show *Friends* must have noticed the growing fashion for this name when they named the character Chandler Bing, but the show clearly gave the name a major boost.

Use as a girl's name has lagged slightly, but given common patterns, it's possible that Chandler will some day be considered primarily a girl's name. The Spanish or Italian form Candelario appeared rarely in the early 20th century. Variant: (m) **Candelario.**

CHRISSY: (f) English; a diminutive of CHRISTIAN (Chapter 8). This hit the charts briefly as an independent name in the '70s, perhaps not by coincidence at the same time as the character Chrissy Snow featured in the "dumb blonde" role in *Three's Company.* Variant: **Crissy.**

CONSTANCE: (f) Latin; constant, steady. From an old Roman family name *Constantius* or *Constantinus.* The name was popular in the Middle Ages and — treated as a virtue name — continued in use after the Reformation. It was given literary treatment by Chaucer in his *Canterbury Tales.* Early in the mid–20th century, the diminutive Connie surpassed the original name. Pop singer Connie Francis made the name cozy and familiar, while actress Connie Sellecca has given it a more sophisticated air in series like *Hotel.* Diminutive: **Connie.**

DANA: (f, m) English; either "valley" or "a Dane, someone from Denmark." In some cases it may be used as a diminutive of DANIEL (Chapter 4). In feminine use, it may sometimes be a shortening of DIANA (Chapter 5), but the variant Danae could also be from the character in Greek mythology, the mother of the hero Perseus. In the later 19th century, Dana was primarily a boy's name, but the "-a" ending has led parents to prefer using it for girls in the last half century. One current exception is *Saturday Night Live* regular, comedian Dana Carvey. Variants: (f) **Danae, Dania, Danna,** and **Dayna;** (m) **Dane** and **Dayne.**

DAWSON: (m) English; son of David. (Daw is a Medieval diminutive of David.) It's often the case that a movie or TV show taps into a name fashion early enough in its rise to appear to have entirely caused it. The name Dawson started creeping up the popularity charts four years before the debut of the TV show *Dawson's Creek,* but the year that show appeared, it jumped 500 places up the charts.

DELLA: (f) English; a diminutive of ADELE (Chapter 9), perhaps influenced by names such as Ella and Delia. It started showing up in the late 19th century and was quite popular at the turn of the century. One bearer is Della Reese, one of the stars of the series *Touched by an Angel.* Variant: **Dell.**

DIRK: (m) Dutch; a variant of DERICK (Chapter 9) and so of THEODORIC (Chapter 7). Given its resemblance to the name of a type of dagger, Dirk seems nicely fitted to be the name of a dashing leading man. Two bearers in that category are British actor Dirk Bogarde, and American actor Dirk Benedict, perhaps best known for his character on *Battlestar Galactica.*

ERICA: (f) Norse; a feminine form of ERIC (see Chapter 5). This name followed a similar popularity curve to the male name, showing up around the '70s and most popular in the '80s and '90s. (Erica is also the Latin name of the plant known in English as heather, and it's possible that it is sometimes used as a flower name, but that word has a different origin.) Famous bearers include Erica Jong, author of *Fear of Flying,* long-running soap opera character Erica Kane in *All My Children,* and singer Eryka Badu. Variants: **Eric, Ericka, Erika, Eryka,** and **Erykah.**

FALLON: (f) Gaelic; ruler. From the surname O'Fallon. This had a very brief popularity in the '80s, after the character of Fallon Carrington Colby in the prime time soap opera *Dynasty.*

FARRAH: (f) English?; possibly a variant of the surname Ferrer "smith, iron-worker," but there is also an Arabic name Farah meaning "joy, cheerfulness." Actress Farrah Fawcett inspired a brief fashion for this name in the '70s when she co-starred in *Charlie's Angels.*

FELICIA: (f) Latin; happy. A feminine equivalent of FELIX (Chapter 13). The TV show *Felicity* inspired an immediate fashion for that variant of the name beginning in 1999. Some spelling variants seem to be influenced by Phyllis, as for actress Phylicia Rashad of *The Cosby Show.* The more usual spelling Felicia has been quite popular in the later 20th century. Variants: **Felecia, Felicita, Felisha,** and **Phylicia.**

FRASIER: (m) complex origin; from the French place name Frisselle, possibly meaning "place of ash trees," but influenced by "fraise," a heraldic term for a strawberry flower, adopted as the badge of the Scottish Frasiers. Most recently, this name has been made visible by Frasier Crane, title character of the TV show *Frasier.*

GERAINT: (m) Welsh; a variant of the Latin name Gerontius, "old man." The name has been popular in Wales since the Middle Ages, featured in Arthurian legend, but has not managed significant cross-over to more general use. Welsh-Canadian actor Geraint Wyn Davies has made the name more familiar to American audiences in shows such as *Forever Knight.*

HUDSON: (f, m) English; son of Hudd, a diminutive of HUGH (Chapter 8). The sudden popularity of Hudson as a boy's name, starting in the mid '90s is not immediately explainable. The surname of Rock Hudson doesn't seem to have made any inroads during his lifetime, and there's no direct connection to the 1991 movie *Hudson Hawk.* On the female side, you have actress Hudson Leick, with a recurring role on *Xena, Warrior Princess.*

JOSIAH: (m) Hebrew; God supports. The name has been revived during various fashions for Biblical names. More recently, it seems to be part of a specific fashion for reviving lesser-used Biblical names starting with "J," such as Jacob, Joshua, and Jonathan. The creators of the TV series *The West Wing* tapped into that fashion when they named their fictional president Josiah Bartlet.

KELSEY: (f, m) English; meaning uncertain, but the ending is "island." The name has become popular for both boys and girls in the last several decades, although actor Kelsey Grammer of *Frasier* predates the recent fashion. Variants: (f) **Kelcie, Kelsea, Kelsi,** and **Kelsie.**

KERMIT: (m) Gaelic; son of Dermot. From the surname MacDhiarmait (pronounced "Mac Kermit"). The name was mildly popular through the earlier parts of the 20th century, but the fame of the puppet-character Kermit the Frog on the children's show *Sesame Street* beginning in 1969 seems to have taken it out of ordinary use.

LACY: (f, m) French; a surname from a French place name. Lacy began the 20th century as a boy's name, taken from the surname, declining from a mild popularity to fall out of fashion in the '60s. But in the '70s it suddenly started showing up as a girl's name, perhaps inspired by the image of lace and frills. Actress Lacey Chabert was part of this fashion, starting her career as a child in *All My Children.* It was the surname of one of the title characters of the police drama *Cagney and Lacey.*

LEVAR: (m) French?; possibly a variant of Levre, "a hare, one who hunts hares," but perhaps instead a coined name. The name had a brief fashion in the '70s inspired by actor LeVar Burton on the mini-series *Roots.*

LORNE: (m) English; a variant of Lauren, from LAURENCE (Chapter 8). For a related feminine name, see LAUREN (Chapter 17). It's unusual for a traditional male name to have as many variants as this one does. One of the more unusual spellings is Lorne, as borne by actor Lorne Green who popularized this form briefly in the '60s when he starred in the TV western *Bonanza.* Loren has consistently been the most popular of the variants over the last century. Variants: **Lauren, Loran, Loren,** and **Lorin.**

LONA: (f) multiple origins; in some cases, a feminine borrowing of Lonnie and its variants (see Chapter 9 under ALONZO), but in other cases possibly a version of LANA (Chapter 18). One variant is borne by actress Loni Anderson, perhaps best known for her role on *WKRP in Cincinnati.* Variants: **Loni, Lonie, Lonna,** and **Lonnie.**

MALLORY: (f) French; unfortunate, unlucky. This name burst onto the charts in the '80s in response to the Mallory Keaton, the sister of Michael J. Fox's character on *Family Ties.* In a larger context, this is one of a number of not-previously-used surnames that have become popular for girls in recent decades.

MARGO: (f) French; a diminutive of MARGARET (Chapter 8). An older spelling of the name is borne by actress Margot Kidder, who played Lois Lane to Christopher Reeves' *Superman.* The form Margo has replaced it in popularity in the later part of the 20th century. Variant: **Margot.**

MATT: (m) English; a diminutive of MATTHEW (Chapter 8). The short, solid sound of Matt has worked well for the image of actors such as Matt Damon, Matt LeBlanc, and Matt Dillon. Another Matt Dillon was the central character of the long-running western *Gunsmoke.*

MAYIM: (f) Hebrew; water. Actress Mayim Bialik starred on the TV show *Blossom,* but unlike her character's name, hers has never quite made it onto the popularity charts.

MELINA: (f) Greek; yellow, yellow-haired. The name may sometimes instead be a short form of some name like Emmaline, but the prominent bearers all seem to have strong Greek connections, such as actress Melina Kanakaredes of the eclectic drama *Providence.*

NERO: (m) Latin; strong. An old Roman family name used in the Claudian family. The Roman emperor known by this name gave it much to live down, being notorious (not entirely fairly) for having persecuted early Christians and fiddling while Rome burned. Perhaps for this reason the name has never been generally popular, but it has been redeemed somewhat by fictional detective Nero Wolfe, created by Rex Stout and dramatized in a succession of TV versions.

NEVE: (f) multiple origins; in the case of actress Neve Campbell of *Party of Five,* this was her Dutch mother's maiden name, originally meaning "nephew." But the form Neva, popular in the early part of the 20th century, may instead be from a Spanish or Italian word for "snow." Variant: **Neva.**

NIA: (f) multiple origins; sometimes a Welsh variant of Gaelic Niamh "radiance," but sometimes a diminutive of various names ending in "-nia." In the case of writer and actress Nia Vardalos *(My Big Fat Greek Wedding),* it is short for Antonia. It has become rather popular in the last few years, possibly partly in her honor. Variants: **Nya** and **Nyah.**

NIKITA: (f) Russian; a diminutive of NICHOLE (Chapter 8). In Russian, it can be a male name, as for Soviet premier Nikita Kruschev. Recently it has been borne by the title character of the movie and TV series *La Femme Nikita,* although the name has been mildly popular since the '70s.

RADAMES: (m) Greek; meaning uncertain. Radames or Rhadames is the name of the tenor (heroic) role in Verdi's opera *Aida.* (Although the character is Egyptian, the name is clearly Greek.) It enjoyed a somewhat surprising, if minor, popularity in the '40s and '50s and seems to be rather popular in Central and South America. Actor Radames Pera played the young Kwai Chang Caine on the TV series *Kung Fu.*

REMINGTON: (m) English; town on the Riming brook. The recent mild popularity of this name seems entirely due to the TV detective show *Remington Steele,* where the title character begins as the fictitious boss of the agency, named from a typewriter brand. (Then Pierce Brosnan's character moves into the fictional role and the action takes off.)

RHODA: (f) Greek; rose. This shows up as a New Testament name and may sometimes have been used for that reason, but it never seriously challenged Rose in popularity. The name was fairly popular around the turn of the 20th century but has since fallen out of fashion. Rhoda Morgenstern was the best friend of Mary Tyler Moore's character Mary Richards on *The Mary Tyler Moore Show.*

SABRINA: (f) Brythonic; meaning uncertain. The earliest name of the Severn river. The name first became popular in the '60s, jumping out of nowhere halfway up the charts. This initial boost was most likely due to the title character of the Audrey Hepburn movie *Sabrina,* for although the comic book precursor to TV's *Sabrina the Teenage Witch* first appeared in the early '60s, she took a long time to catch on. Another advertisement for the name was the character of Sabrina Duncan on *Charlie's Angels.*

TAMARA: (f) Hebrew; palm tree. There were several Biblical women with the name Tamar but it never seems to have caught on during any of the Biblical revivals. In modern use, Tamara is likely to be from an entirely different origin, possibly Slavic, but in any case via Russian use. It was most popular around the middle of the 20th century. An early use of the name was for the character Tamyra in George Chapman's 1604 *Bussy D'Ambois.* Actress Tamera Mowry and her twin sister Tia starred in the sitcom *Sister Sister.* Another variant of the name, Tamala, may be a blend with some name like Pamela. Variants: **Tamera, Tamra, Tamyra,** and **Tamala.**

TELLY: (m) Greek; a diminutive of Aristotle, the name of an ancient Greek philosopher. Actor Telly Savalas is of Greek origin and made this name briefly popular in the '70s when he starred in the detective series *Kojak.*

TYNE: (f) English; the river Tyne, used as a surname. The name has never been particularly popular, but is familiar from actress Tyne Daly of the police drama *Cagney and Lacey* and more recently in *Judging Amy.*

VALENE: (f) coined; a blend of VALERIE (Chapter 10) with the common feminine ending "-ine." The name of *Dallas,* and later *Knot's Landing,* character Valene Ewing Gibson Waleska. And speaking of which . . .

WALESKA: (f) multiple origins; a Polish surname, which is probably the source of the surname of *Knot's Landing* character Valene Ewing Gibson Waleska. The show correlates with the brief appearance of this name on the popularity charts in the '70s, but the connection seems unlikely. There is also a town of Waleska in Georgia that claims to be named after a Native American woman, Warluskee. Whether the story has historical validity is another question.

WILLOW: (f) English; a willow tree. While a number of tree names have been taken up as given names, both in the Victorian era and in the later 20th century, the appearance of Willow on the popularity charts abruptly in the last half dozen years seems entirely creditable to the continuing character of that name on the show *Buffy the Vampire Slayer*.

XANDER: (m) Greek; a diminutive of ALEXANDER (Chapter 6). This may be another beneficiary of the popular TV show *Buffy the Vampire Slayer*. The appearance of Xander and Zander on the charts corresponds closely with the timing of the show, although the names have been in rare use for some time. Variant: **Zander.**

XENA: (f) Greek; foreigner. An appropriate meaning for the name of the title character of *Xena, Warrior Princess*. The show doesn't seem to have sparked any significant interest in the name, though, although Zena appeared occasionally around the turn of the 20th century. Variant: **Zena.**

Naming babies after celebrities and celebrity babies

If there were a patron saint for the children of celebrities who have been saddled with peculiar names, a good candidate would be the son of ill-fated Medieval lovers Abelard and Heloise, who was christened with the name Astrolabe. (An astrolabe is a type of navigational instrument — think of it as the equivalent of being named "Global-positioning-system.") To be fair, for the most part, celebrities name their children the same sorts of things that everyone else does. But when they pick unusual names, you all hear about it. Before you think about using one of these names for your child, consider that these kids can afford therapists for any name-related emotional trauma!

✔ Apple — Gwyneth Paltrow's daughter.

✔ Chastity — daughter of Sonny Bono and Cher (this one is starting to sound rather tame, in context).

✔ Dweezil and Moon Unit — Frank Zappa had another daughter named Diva.

✔ Heavenly Hiraani Tiger Lily — daughter of late TV personality Paula Yates; and one suspects you can also lay the blame on Yates for the names of her three children with Bob Geldof: Fifi-Trixibelle, Peaches, and Pixie.

✔ Ireland — Kim Bassinger's daughter.

✔ Lourdes — Madonna's daughter doesn't actually have that unusual a name; Lourdes has been on the popularity charts for the last half century.

✔ Prince Michael — the son of pop singer Michael Jackson.

✔ Sailor Lee — daughter of model Christie Brinkley.

✔ Zowie — the son of rock star David Bowie (yeah, "Zowie Bowie").

Chapter 17

Tuning In to Musical Names

*L*ike most celebrities, singers and songwriters have often been the inspiration for fashionable names. In the competitive world of music, an eye-catching name can be an asset, so you often find unusual forms of names, catchy spellings, or interesting nicknames coming from this source. Of course, musical inspiration isn't limited to the performers: Musicians often write songs specifically addressed to someone by name, and it isn't unusual for a name to become more popular after being featured in a song. Imagine growing up having your very own song! (It can cut both ways, of course. Not all popular songs are suitably addressed to a young child.)

This chapter focuses on names that are closely associated with a particular musician or tune, or those that have clearly been popularized through song. Naturally, in the section, "Lyrical Names," the balance is heavier towards girls, as more love songs are addressed to girls than guys.

Getting Down with Singers and Songwriters

Some singers have either chosen, or been lucky enough to have been given, names so unusual that a single name is enough to identify them — people like Donovan, Enya, or Selena. Some musicians, like Elvis or Aretha have taken ordinary names and turned them into their own trademarks.

AALIYAH: (f) Arabic; exalted, outstanding. The name has only been generally popular since the '90s, and following the rise of rock singer Aaliyah, this name has risen as high as number 91. It is independently quite popular in the Muslim community. Variants: **Alia, Aliya, Aliyah,** and **Aleah.**

ALANIS: (f) Greek?; the meaning for this name is uncertain. According to most sources, the father of Alanis Morissette wanted to give her some version of his name, Alan, but didn't like the available options until he spotted Alanis in a Greek newspaper. There's no guarantee the name is Greek (Greek newspapers mention non-Greeks, after all), or even that it started out as a name. If Greek, it certainly isn't related linguistically to the name ALAN (Chapter 8), and yet given the name's inspiration, it's clearly being used as a creative variant of that name. See what fun you can have confounding future scholars with just a little inventiveness?

ANNIE: (f) English; a diminutive of ANNE (see Chapter 8). Annie is quite popular in the early part of 20th century but declines somewhat after that. Singer Annie Lennox of the Eurhythmics is only one of a large number of famous Annies, including Old West sharpshooter Annie Oakley, educator Annie Sullivan, and the title character of the comic strip-inspired musical *Annie*. The version of the name borne by independent recording artist Ani DiFranco has not yet hit the popularity charts. Variant: **Ani.**

ARETHA: (f) Greek; virtue. The name's brief popularity in the '60s and '70s parallels the rising career of the "queen of soul," Aretha Franklin, so it seems safe to attribute the name's popularity entirely to her. Variant: **Areta.**

ARLO: (m) uncertain; there seems to be little agreement on the origin and meaning of the name Arlo. Some sources suggest a Spanish origin meaning "bayberry," others suggest an English origin meaning "hill," presumably deriving it as a variant of the surname Harlow. (A more literal meaning would be "tribal hill.") The latter seems more likely, given the name's popularity in the early part of the 20th century. After falling out of favor, it got a brief lift in the '70s with the fame of Arlo Guthrie's classic story-ballad *Alice's Restaurant*.

BENNY: (m) English; diminutive of either BENJAMIN (Chapter 4) or BENEDICT (Chapter 8). Benny Goodman led one of the great big bands of the early mid–20th century as well as being a wizard on the clarinet. Another musical Bennie is the fictional rock singer in Elton John's song *Bennie and the Jets*. Variant: **Bennie.**

BEYONCE: (f) French?; meaning uncertain. Singer Beyoncé Knowles (of the group Destiny's Child) received her name from her mother's maiden name. In 2001 when she won the ASCAP Pop Singer of the Year Award, enough parents named their daughters after her for the name to hit the charts briefly.

BRUCE: (m) English; from a French place name Braose or Brieuse. The surname is most famous from the medieval Scottish king Robert de Bruce. It was taken up as a given name in the 19th century and has been relatively popular throughout the last century, peaking in the '50s. Rock singer and songwriter Bruce Springsteen was born during that boom.

BRYN: (f, m) Welsh; a hill. Welsh operatic singer Bryn Terfel has joined the ranks of classical singers who put a toe over the line into pop stardom. The name Bryn is uncommon, but is used in the U.S. by both boys and girls. (A feminine connection may come from the Pennsylvanian women's college Bryn Mawr, whose Welsh name means "big hill.") Variant: **Brynn.**

BUDDY: (m) English; friend. From a baby-talk version of "brother." Early rock star Buddy Holly was famous for bouncy upbeat songs like *Peggy Sue* (another musical name, although not featured in this book). The name is shared by character actor Buddy Ebsen. Both Bud and Buddy have been mildly popular through much of the early 20th century. Variant: **Buddie.** Diminutive: **Bud.**

CAROL, CARLY: (f) English; feminine forms of Charles "a man." Before I make the musical connection, this seems a good place to tease apart all the names in this group. The earliest feminine form of Charles to enter English use was probably CHARLOTTE in the 17th century (see Chapter 9), followed closely by CAROLINE (Chapter 14) in the 18th. (See below in "Lyrical Names.") Caroline shortened eventually to CAROL, often re-interpreted as referring to a song, and in the mid–20th century developed into CAROLYN (see Chapter 10). The German form of the man's name (Carl) gave rise in the mid–20th century to CARLA (see Chapter 10) and the diminutive CARLY. Carol deserves a place among musical names all on its own, but the connection is strengthened by singer-songwriter Carole King. The explosion of popularity for variants of Carly in the '80s and later suggests you may trace much of the interest in this name to the career of Carly Simon. Variants: (for Carol) **Carole, Karol, Caryl, Carrol,** and **Carroll;** (for Carly) **Carlee, Carley, Carli, Carlie, Carolee, Karlee, Karley, Karli, Karlie,** and **Karly.**

CELINE: (f) multiple origins; either a French diminutive of Marceline or a spelling variant of SELENA (see later in this chapter for this name's entry). Given Céline Dion's French-Canadian origins, you'd want to bet on the former in her case. She may be best known for the *Titanic* theme song, *My Heart Will Go On.* The name has only become somewhat popular in the last decade, making it likely that Céline Dion is a major source. Variant: **Celina.**

CHUCK: (m) English; a diminutive of CHARLES (see Chapter 9). This name has been used as an informal diminutive for some time but appeared as an independent name only in the mid–20th century, Rock and Roll Hall of Famer Chuck Berry may have helped inspire this use although he himself was born Charles rather than Chuck.

DEAN: (m) English; either "a valley" or "(the occupation of) dean." In the case of classic crooner Dean Martin, this name is a translation of the Italian Dino. The name has been consistently popular, peaking slightly in the mid–20th century. Variant: **Deane,** and **Dino.**

DOLLY: (f) English; a diminutive of DOROTHY (see Chapter 8). "Dolly" may seem an odd thing to name a living girl until you realize that the toy took the name from the girl instead of the other way around. Flamboyant country singer Dolly Parton shares the name with the title character of the musical *Hello Dolly!* This nickname has been around at least since Shakespeare's time, when it is found for the comic character Doll Tearsheet in *Henry IV, Part 2,* but in recent decades it has fallen out of use. Variants: **Doll** and **Dollie.**

DONNA, MADONNA: (f) Italian; lady (*madonna,* meaning my lady, in other words, the Virgin Mary). Donna is a title rather than a name in the original Italian, but became quite fashionable in the U.S., working its way up to number 8 in the '60s. Singer Donna Summer became the icon of the disco craze. The name is also a favorite in lyrics, including *Donna Donna* (recorded by Donovan, among others) and *Donna* by Richie Valens. The somewhat startled reaction to the name of one-name musical star Madonna is unfair: The name was mildly popular through most of the first half of the 20th century. Variants: **Dona, Donnie,** and **Donita.**

DONOVAN: (m) Gaelic; dark brown. There is something about being a pop singing sensation that seems to call for going by a single name (witness Cher, Madonna, Sting, and so on). Donovan was an early leader in this fashion, falling on the border between folk and rock. The name has become popular enough since the '60s to have variants on the charts — somewhat unusual for a male name. Variant: **Donavan** and **Donavon.**

DORSEY: (m) French; from the town of Orsay. This appears as a given name in the 19th century but was falling out of popularity by the mid–20th century when the big band musicians Tommy and Jimmy Dorsey made the name a household word.

DUSTY: (f, m) English; as a male name, a diminutive of DUSTIN (see Chapter 18). Ordinarily the name conjures up images of gritty cowboys, as in Garrison Keillor's radio-play characters Dusty and Lefty. Female use is primarily after British singer Dusty Springfield (born Mary O'Brien).

DYLAN: (m) Welsh; see Chapter 5.

ELLA: (f) Latin; a diminutive of various names ending in "-ella," such as Isabella, Marcella, or Gabriella. Today the name is nearly synonymous with jazz singer Ella Fitzgerald, but it has declined from its popularity in the early 20th century and has only recently began to regain ground.

ELTON: (m) English; multiple origins: usually "Ælla's town" but sometimes "eel town." The name is most familiar from rock singer-songwriter Elton John, although his popularity doesn't seem to have given the name a boost, as it has been steadily declining since the mid–20th century.

ELVIS: (m) English; meaning uncertain. The name has been consistently popular since the late 19th century, but it seems to have been given only a mild boost by "the King," Elvis Presley. Music seems to attract men named Elvis, another being New Wave rocker Elvis Costello. Variant: **Alvis.**

ENYA: (f) Gaelic; either radiance, splendor, or possibly "kernal". Enya is an English phonetic version of the Irish names Áine or Eithne, both of which may also sometimes be found. Both names are borne by Irish folk musicians: the single-named Enya (whose Irish name is Eithne Ní Bhraonáin), and harpist Aine Minogue.

ETTA: (f) English; a diminutive of any name ending in "-etta," for example, Henrietta, Coretta, and Pauletta. Blues singer Etta James is one well-known bearer. The name was quite popular through the early 20th century but has fallen off somewhat since then. Variant: **Ettie.**

FABIAN: (m) Latin; bean farmer, or possibly, man from Fabiae. There was an early pope by this name and Shakespeare uses it for a minor character in *Twelfth Night.* In his day, pop singer Fabian set many a teen heart fluttering. Although he gave the name its start in the '50s, there may be other forces at work as it has been growing steadily in popularity ever since.

GLORIA: (f) Latin; glory. First popularized in the late 19th century by a character in George Bernard Shaw's play *You Never Can Tell,* the name rose swiftly to high popularity in the mid–20th century. Latin pop singer Gloria Estefan and disco singer Gloria Gaynor carry this name, and it is enshrined in the Van Morrison song *Gloria* (as well as the refrains to innumerable Christmas carols).

JAGGER: (m) German; hunter. The surname of Rolling Stones singer Mick Jagger has only started appearing on the popularity charts in the last few years, which is rather late in his career for there to be a direct connection.

JANIS, JANICE: (f) English; a diminutive of JANET, which is originally from JOHN (see Chapter 8). The name first appeared for the title character of the 1899 novel *Janice Meredith* by Paul Leicester Ford. Janice was extremely popular through the mid–20th century and this is when the variant Janis appeared as well. The latter seems to be the more musical form, belonging to singer-songwriters Janis Joplin and Janis Ian. Variant: **Janessa** and **Jannice.**

JETHRO: (m) Hebrew; abundance. The name of heavy metal band Jethro Tull is taken from a 17th century agriculturalist of that name. The name has never been particularly popular, perhaps due to a certain backwoods air.

KYLIE: (f) uncertain; a popular derivation offered for this name is from a word in one of the native Australian languages meaning "a curved stick, a boomerang"; however, the appearance of the name at a time when KELLY (Chapter 14) had shot up to number 17 suggests a less exotic origin. Variants of this name also blend into the KAY+LEE group of compound names (see Chapter 11). The popularity of the Australian explanation for the name may be partly due to Australian pop singer Kylie Minogue. Variants: **Kylee** and **Kyleigh.**

LENA: (f) various languages; a diminutive of either MAGDALENA (Chapter 8) or HELENA (Chapter 5). Actress and singer Lena Horne made this name elegant and sultry. It declined somewhat in the later part of the 20th century, but has been in steady use. Variants: **Lenna, Lennie,** and **Lina.**

LAUREN: (f) Latin; see Chapter 16 for the male use of this name, which is generally as a short form of LAURENCE. The female name may be either derived from LAURA (Chapter 6) or taken directly as a feminine version of LAURENCE (Chapter 8). The name has an abundance of variants and several of them are borne by musicians, including folk singer Loreena McKennitt and R&B musician Lauryn Hill. Variants: **Lorena, Lorene, Loren, Lauryn, Laurine, Laureen,** and **Lorine.** See also LAURA (Chapter 6), LORRAINE (Chapter 14), and LAUREL (Chapter 12).

LUCIAN: (m) Latin; light. Operatic tenor Luciano Pavarotti may be responsible for a recent resurgence in his name, after it had fallen out of favor earlier in the 20th century along with other immigrant names. Variant: **Lucien.**

LYLE: (m) English; island. The earliest sighting as a given name is in an early 19th century novel *Olive* by Mrs. Craik. It has remained steady in mild popularity through the 20th century. Country-western singer Lyle Lovett puts an alliterative twist on the name.

MARIAH: (f) Latin; a spelling variant of the name MARIA which has picked up a different pronunciation from the root name. R&B artist Mariah Carey bears it and you will find varying opinions on whether the song from the musical *Paint Your Wagon* should be written *They Call the Wind Mariah* or *Maria.* (In any event, in the song it's pronounced like Mariah.) The name saw its biggest spike in popularity in the '90s, corresponding with Mariah Carey's career. Variant: **Moriah.**

MELBA: (f) coined; taken from the name of the city of Melbourne, Australia. Soprano Nellie Melba took a stage name inspired by that of her hometown and she in turn became famous enough to pass the name on to Melba toast and Peach Melba (a dish created in her honor). The name was moderately popular as a given name around the turn of the 20th century, at the height of her career.

MILES: (m) various origins; the name is often from German Milo, of uncertain meaning, or a nickname from MICHAEL (Chapter 8), but it may sometimes be from Latin *miles,* meaning "a soldier." Musical bearers include jazz artist Miles Davis. The name has been rising slightly in popularity in recent decades. Variants: **Myles** and **Milo.**

NAT: (f, m) Hebrew; a diminutive of NATHANIEL (Chapter 9), but it may also be short for other names beginning with "Nat-" such as NATHAN (Chapter 9) or the girl's name NATALIE (Chapter 13). you see a connection being made in the names of crooner Nat King Cole and his daughter Natalie. As an independent name, Nat fell somewhat out of use in the early 20th century.

NORA: (f) various origins; a short form of names ending in "-nora" such as HONORA (see Chapter 9) or ELEANORA (see Chapter 8). Jazz and blues musician Norah Jones uses a variant spelling of this name. It has been slipping down the list for most of the 20th century. Variant: **Norah.**

ODETTA, ODETTE: (f) French; homeland. A variant of an old German name Odille. Sometimes also used as a diminutive of Otto. Blues and folk singer Odetta is another of those one-name celebrities. Odette seems to be an inherently musical name, as there have been any number of singers who bear it, including folk singer Odette Michell and opera singer Odette Beaupré, to say nothing of the heroine of the ballet *Swan Lake.* Variants: **Odille, Otilia, Ottie,** and **Ottile.**

OTIS: (m) English; riches. A variant of Otto. Otis Redding specializes in soulful ballads like *Dock of the Bay.* The name has been consistently popular through the last century, only dropping off somewhat in the last couple decades. Variant: **Ottis.**

OZZY: (m) English; a diminutive of Osborne, a Norse-origin name meaning "divine bear." It would be hard to find a clearer contrast in namesakes than heavy metal rocker Ozzy Osbourne and '50s TV icon Ozzie Nelson of *Ozzie & Harriet.* Variant: **Osborne** and **Ozzie.**

PATSY: (f, m) English; a diminutive of PATRICIA (see Chapter 10) or PATRICK (see Chapter 10). Patsy began the 20th century as a man's name, but when female use shot up on the charts in the '30s, men abandoned the field. Patsy Cline was known as the "Queen of Country" for songs like *Crazy.*

RAY: (m) English; a diminutive of Raymond, although other origins are possible. Ray Charles' performance of *Georgia on my Mind* helped convince the state of Georgia to adopt it as an official song.

ROD: (m) English; a diminutive of any of various names beginning in "Rod-," such as Roderick, Rodney. British rocker Rod Stewart gives the name a vibrant aura, but failed to save it from sliding out of use in the '70s

SELINA, SELENA: (f) Greek; the moon, goddess of the moon. Tejano singing star Selena (and the movie made about her all-too-short life) should have given this name a boost, but you only see it affect the variant Selina in the '90s. A beautiful name that deserves another look. Variants: **Celena, Salena, Salina,** and **Selene.**

SINEAD: (f) Gaelic; an Irish borrowing of JANET (see Chapter 8). Given the general popularity of Irish names (and the startling variety of forms of Sean that have come into use) you may expect the name borne by Irish singer Sinead O'Connor to get more use. But the contrast between the spelling and the pronunciation ("shin-AID") may trip people up.

TAMMY: (f) English; a diminutive of TAMARA (Chapter 16). Perhaps sometimes used as a variant of other names starting with "Tam-," such as Tamsin or Tamika. This name picks up a sweet, somewhat wistful air from bearers like country music singer Tammy Wynette and the song *Tammy,* popularized by Debbie Reynolds in the movie *Tammy and the Bachelor.* Variants: **Tami, Tamie, Tammi,** and **Tammie.**

TENNILLE: (f) French?; meaning uncertain. This name showed up briefly on the popularity charts in the '70s corresponding to when the pop duo The Captain and Tennille appeared on the scene with a Grammy-winning album. In that case, it was singer Toni Tennille's surname. Variant: **Tenille.**

TORI (f), **TORY** (m): English; the feminine name is most often short for VICTORIA (Chapter 9). The masculine name is from a surname, most commonly deriving from Theodoric. Eclectic singer-songwriter Tori Amos bears this name, as does actress Tori Spelling (whose birth name is Victoria). Variants: (m) **Torey** and **Torrey.**

TRAVIS: (m) English; a variant of Traverse, a surname for someone who collected tolls at a bridge crossing. Like many surnames, it was taken up as a given name in the 19th century. This name has been steadily increasing in use through the last century and has been quite popular since the '70s, Some of that recent popularity can be attributed to country singers Randy Travis and Travis Tritt.

WAYLON: (m) multiple origins, either from an Anglo-Saxon personal name or from a place name meaning "land by the road." The personal name belonged in legend to an Anglo-Saxon god of blacksmithing. Waylon has had a sporadic mild popularity especially in the '70s and '80s which corresponds with the career peak of country singer Waylon Jennings. Variant: **Wayland.**

WHITNEY: (f, m) English; white island. Originally a surname, this was taken up for both boys and girls starting around the '60s. Although singer Whitney Houston didn't start the trend (rather, she was born right at the start of it), her 1985 Grammy award does correspond with a sudden increase in popular for the name among girls. As a boy's name it has never been more than mildly popular.

WOODY: (m) English; a nickname for any of various names beginning with "Wood-," such as, Woodrow, Woodford, and Woodville. Songwriter Woody Guthrie, who chronicled the Dustbowl and Depression experiences, was born Woodrow Wilson Guthrie named after U.S. president Woodrow Wilson. In the case of director and actor Woody Allen, it's a short form of Heywood. Woody had a brief popularity in the '40s and '50s, when Woodrow had been on the decline for some time, suggesting that it may have been used after the singer. Variant: **Woodrow.**

Looking at Lyrical Names

The ability of songs to popularize certain names can be seen in the response to works like the Beatles' *Michelle* or Joni Mitchell's *Chelsea Morning*. The names of characters in musicals or operas may also become popular, such as Norma and Aida. And ordinary words that evoke music, such as Harmony or Melody, have also become popular as names.

AIDA: (f) uncertain; the name of an Ethiopian princess in Giuseppe Verdi's opera of the same name. It seems unlikely that Verdi researched ancient Ethiopian names for the purpose, although the Egyptian names in the opera are mostly historic. Aida rose to a peak of popularity in the '30s.

ANGIE: (f) English; a diminutive of ANGELA (Chapter 10) or various related names. The Rolling Stones' *Angie* is a fairly straightforward angst-ridden love song, but Helen Reddy's *Angie Baby* makes you think more of a late-night *Twilight Zone* episode. Actress Angie Dickenson may be more responsible for the increase in popularity the name saw in the '60s and '70s.

ARIA: (f) Italian; a song, an air, especially an operatic solo. The name has become mildly popular in the last few years, perhaps inspired in part by model and actress Aria Giovanni.

BERNADETTE: (f) French; a feminine form of BERNARD (Chapter 8) "brave bear." This is the name of a hit song by the Four Tops, but use of the name is more strongly associated with St. Bernadette (born Marie Bernarde Soubirous) who had a vision of the Virgin Mary at Lourdes. The name saw some boost in ratings after the saint's canonization in 1933, but it had always enjoyed some popularity.

BRANDY: (f) English; a distilled liquor made from wine (originally from a Dutch word meaning "burnt wine"). If this had first shown up as a man's name, you'd expect Brandy to be a diminutive of BRANDON (Chapter 10) or some name in that group, but that doesn't seem to be the case here. Alternately, it may have been inspired by a combination of Randy and the oncoming fad for names starting with "Br-' in the '70s. The band Looking Glass released the song *Brandy (You're a Fine Girl)* in the early '70s, just when the name took off. Another musical connection is actress and singer Brandy Norwood, who generally goes by plain Brandy. Variants: **Brandi, Brandie,** and **Brandee.**

CADENCE: (f) English; in music, a series of chords or intervals that ends a phrase or tune. This name has had a sudden, if mild, popularity in the last couple of years. It may simply be part of a fashion for musical related terms used as names.

CANDIDA (f), **CANDIDE** (m): Latin; white, bright. The feminine name is featured in the Tony Orlando and Dawn song *Candida,* who are probably responsible for briefly rescuing the name in the '70s, although it had been used earlier in the century. The title character of Voltaire's *Candide,* turned into an opera by Leonard Bernstein, is male, and in its Italian form Candido the name was mildly popular during the first half of the 20th century.

CARMEN: (f) Spanish; a Spanish form of CARMEL (see Chapter 14), but soon reinterpreted as a Spanish word meaning "song." Georges Bizet's opera *Carmen* features a Spanish gypsy of the name. Actress Carmen Electra also bears it. The name has always been fairly popular, but reached its peak in the '40s.

CAROLINE: (f) Italian; a feminine form of CHARLES (Chapter 9) "a man" — see the discussion under CAROL earlier in this chapter. Neil Diamond's lush *Sweet Caroline* is an excellent advertisement for this name.

CECILIA: (f) Latin; blind. From an old Roman family name. St. Cecilia is the patroness of musicians, giving this name an extra connection. Simon and Garfunkel's *Cecilia* gives the name a catchy beat (if not the best of reputations). Variant: **Celia, Cecelia, Cecile,** and **Cecily.**

CHELSEA: (f) English; a landing place for chalk or limestone. Joni Mitchell's song *Chelsea Morning* was the inspiration for presidential daughter Chelsea Clinton's name, and given the timing of the sudden appearance of the name, she wasn't the only one. Variants: **Chellsie, Chelsey, Chelsi, Chelsie,** and **Chelsy.**

CHERISH, CHERIE, SHERRY: (f) French; beloved, cherished one. This group of names has an embarrassment of musical namesakes: *Cherish* performed by The Association, *Sherry* by the Four Seasons, *Ma Cherie Amour* by various singers, including Stevie Wonder. This group of names has been popular mostly around the mid–20th century and after. The first of the variants to hit the name charts was Cherry, and the reinterpretation of this as the fruit may explain the appearance of Cherise (a blend of *cherry* and the French word for cherry, *cerise*). Variants: **Cheri, Cherri, Cherry,** and **Cherise; Shari, Sherrie, Sherri, Sherie, Sheri, Sheree,** and **Sherita.**

DAWN: (f) English; the dawn, morning. The name may sometimes be a variant of DONNA (see earlier in this chapter). Dawn was popular long before the Four Seasons' song of that title came out, but it was given a little boost of popularity around that time. Variant: **Dawna.**

DELIA: (f) Greek; from the isle of Delos, a nickname of the goddess Artemis, who was born there. Sometimes also a short form of CORDELIA (Chapter 6) , Fidelia, or similar names. The name has been moderately popular throughout the 20th century, although it's fallen somewhat in recent decades. Johnny Cash's song *Delia's Gone* does not, unfortunately, make it sound like fun to be a Delia. (Being a typical Johnny Cash song, it involves murder, regret, and prison.)

GEORGIA: (f) Greek; a farmer (feminine form of GEORGE, Chapter 9). The lyrics of the song *Georgia on My Mind* are vague enough that you aren't sure whether the singer is pining for a girlfriend or the state he left behind. (The state of Georgia has decided on the latter and adopted it as their official state song.)

HARMONY: (f) English; a pleasant combination of sounds, the conjunction of two or more notes in a pleasing way. This appeared on the charts briefly in the '70s and has returned slightly more commonly in the last decade. Harmony might be thought of as a continuation in the fashion for "virtue names," similarly to CHARITY and PRUDENCE (Chapter 9).

IRENE: (f) Greek; peace. Although this name was common in classical times, it only came into English use in the mid–19th century. The Weavers made *Goodnight, Irene* one of their signature songs. Variant: **Irena.**

JULIA: (f) Latin; meaning uncertain. From an old Roman family name which the Romans claimed meant "downy or bearded" but which may instead be related to the divine name Jove. Related names are JULIANA (see Chapter 8) and JULIET (see Chapter 6). The Beatles had a hit song about *Julia*. Another musical connection is superstar vocalist Julie Andrews. Variants: **Julie** and **Juli.** Diminutive: **Lia** (perhaps).

LAYLA: (f) Arabic; night. The name was first brought into English use when Lord Byron used it in his poem *The Giaour,* and it was repeatedly used in romantic Orientalist literature after that. Derek & the Dominos had a hit song with *Layla.* The popularity of the name declined somewhat in the first half of the 20th century, but has recently seen a new interest. Variants: **Leila, Lela,** and **Lelah.**

LOLA: (f) Spanish; a diminutive of DOLORES (see Chapter 15). The further diminutive Lolita has fallen out of use, perhaps poisoned by Vladimir Nabokov's novel and character of that name. The song *Lola* by the Kinks gave the name an interesting spin. Earlier it was featured for a somewhat brassier character in *Whatever Lola Wants* in the musical *Damn Yankees.* Variant: **Lolita.**

LYRIC: (f) English; the words to a song, or more technically a song of no defined length or meter. Like several other names taken from musically related words this is a very recent adoption and has enjoyed a slight popularity only in the last decade.

MAYBELLENE: (f) English; a variant of Mable, originally from Latin Amabilis "lovable." The spelling variant Mabelle is sometimes reinterpreted as French "my beautiful one." The influence of Chuck Berry's energetic *Maybellene* may have been countered somewhat by the association of the name with the Maybelline cosmetics company. Mable has been the most popular of this group of names, but all have fallen out of fashion in the second half of the 20th century. Variants: **Amabilis, Mabel, Mabelle, Mable, Maybell,** and **Maybelle.**

MAGGIE: (f) English; a diminutive of MARGARET (see Chapter 8). Maggie has had its ups and downs. In addition to Rod Stewart's *Maggie May,* the name is associated with the character of "Maggie the cat" in Tennessee Williams' *Cat on a Hot Tin Roof.* British actress Maggie Smith is another famous bearer. Variant: **Madge.**

MANDY: (f, m) English; as a girl's name, a diminutive of AMANDA (see Chapter 6). The most recent chart-topping lyrical tribute to the name is Barry Manilow's *Mandy,* but earlier songs have included another *Mandy* by Irving Berlin for the Ziegfeld Follies and a late 19th-century song *Mandy Lee.* The origin of its use as a male name (as for actor Mandy Patinkin) is more of a mystery. Variant: **Mandi.**

MELODY: (f) English; a tune, a melody. This has become popular as a name in the later 20th century. Famous Melodys are a trifle thin on the ground, but you can point to daytime TV actress Melody Thomas Scott and Alaska historian Melody Webb. Variant: **Melodie.**

MICHELLE: (f) French; a feminine form of MICHAEL (see Chapter 8). One of the classic examples of a song influencing name popularity is the Beatles *Michelle.* The name had been around for a while, but with the hit song in 1965, the name shot up to number 9 and continued rising, along with multiple spelling variants. Other bearers include actresses Michelle Pfeiffer and Sarah Michelle Gellar. Variants: **Michele, Machelle, Mechelle, Michelina,** and **Michell.**

NORMA: (f) Italian; perhaps from Latin *norma* "a rule, precept, or pattern." The name was popularized (if not, in fact, created) for Bellini's 1831 opera of the name. It was quite popular in the first half of the 20th century, but has fallen off somewhat since then. The name has remained in mind lately through the movie *Norma Rae.* Perhaps the most famous person to *not* use the name Norma was Norma Jean Baker who became Marilyn Monroe.

RHIANNON: (f) Welsh; great queen. The name's appearance ever since the '70s can certainly be attributed to the haunting 1975 Fleetwood Mac song of this name. The song has only a loose connection with the Rhiannon of medieval Welsh legend who was something of a supernatural figure associated with magical horses and birds. (The legendary Rhiannon is also notable for her sarcasm and for getting all the best lines in the story.)

RHONDA: (f) Welsh; noisy, babbling (a river name). Most familiar from the Beach Boys' paean to *Help Me Rhonda.* Also familiar may be actress Rhonda Fleming. Variant: **Ronda.**

SUSANNAH, SUSAN, SUSIE: (f) Hebrew; a lily. Variants of Susan have been so popular in song, you can cover all the major variants of the name here. The name originally appears in biblical apocrypha in the story of Susannah being spied on in her bath by the elders, which inspired a great deal of Medieval art (perhaps for the excuse to paint a little soft porn). But although the motif was popular, the name didn't really come into widespread use until the

Reformation. The name was popular in America in the 18th century but had come to be considered old-fashioned by the end of the 19th. But with the turn of the century it saw another upsurge, and by the '50s Susan stood at number 4 with Suzanne the next most common variant along with the short form Sue. In general, the variants ending in "-a" have been less popular than the other spellings. you can start your lyrical tour in the mid–19th century with Stephen Foster's *O Susanna!* The Everly Brothers chime in with a bouncy rendition of *Wake Up, Little Suzie,* followed by the somewhat more dreamy (or perhaps trippy) *Suzanne* by Leonard Cohen. Variants: **Susann, Susanne, Suzan, Suzann, Suzanna, Suzanne, Susana, Susanna,** and **Suzette.** Diminutives: **Sue** and **Suzy.**

WINDY: (f) English; breezy, windy. The name may also be influenced by WENDY (see Chapter 6) which was at its peak of popularity in the '70s when The Association came out with *Windy.*

Chapter 18

Going Hollywood: Names from Cinema and the Arts

In This Chapter

▶ Making your mark with names of movie characters

▶ Projecting an image with actors' names

▶ Finding unusual names from studio artists

*I*n every age, there has been some group with special status whose names have been given to children in hopes of transferring some of that status to them. At one time, that group may have been patron saints; at another time, members of the ruling classes. Since the rise of the motion picture industry, movie actors and the characters they play have carried this kind of magic and glamour. Parents who choose a name from Hollywood are giving their children entire epics, not just names.

Savoring Names from the Silver Screen

Life in the movies is more intense, more beautiful, more dramatic, more everything than real life. It shouldn't surprise you that some people hope to give some of that intensity and drama as a gift to their children when they choose to give the name of a movie character. Only a very few names come specifically from characters on the silver screen, but a good handful are so closely associated with particular characters that their stories will always trail after them.

ARIEL: (f) Hebrew; lion of God. (See Chapter 12 for the male name.) If anyone doubts the influence of movie characters on naming, note that the year after Disney's animated version of *The Little Mermaid* aired, the name Ariel showed up in 98th place for girls, when it hadn't even made the charts a few years before. It is unclear how the mermaid came by this name. (She is unnamed in the original story by Hans Christian Andersen.) The airy sprite of Shakespeare's *The Tempest* may be a nearer source than the Hebrew name. Variant: **Arielle.**

BUTCH: (m) English; a nickname for a tough person, originally from the occupation of butcher. The famous outlaw Butch Cassidy (as portrayed in *Butch Cassidy and the Sundance Kid*) had, in fact, been a butcher, which may have been the source for his nickname. There was a brief fashion for this name in the mid–20th century but in general it has been a personal nickname rather than a given name.

DUNCAN: (m) Gaelic; brown headed or brown lord. The name Duncan has been popular since the Middle Ages, but lately in certain circles it's hard to hear the name without hearing the ringing statement, "My name is Duncan MacLeod of the Clan MacLeod and I am immortal." Okay, so that's from the TV series *Highlander* and not from the original sequence of movies by the same name, but the movies are where it all started. And while it's possible that the jump Duncan took several hundred places up the popularity charts in the early '90s just coincidentally happened when the TV series aired, it's not the way to bet.

ELIZA: (f) English; a diminutive of ELIZABETH (Chapter 8). This form of the name has been around since the 18th century, but with George Bernard Shaw's play *Pygmalion* and the film version of the musical *My Fair Lady,* it has become associated with the character of Eliza Doolittle, the Cockney flower girl who turns into a lady by the magic of linguistics. Variants: **Elisa, Elise, Elisha, Elissa, Elyse,** and **Elyssa.**

GIA: (f) Italian; a diminutive of various names like Giovanna (Johanna). There has been a general interest in names in this group in the last couple of decades, so it may be that the 1998 movie *Gia* about the wild and tragic life of model Gia Carangi was not the primary influence on its popularity. Variants: **Giana, Gianna,** and **Giovanna.**

GIGI: (f) French; a diminutive, possibly of various names, but in one case of Gilberte, a feminine version of Gilbert. In Colette's novel about a young girl in training for life as a courtesan, the pet name Gigi is said to substitute for Gilberte. In the movie version of the story, this never seems to be made clear, and she is known only by the diminutive.

GILDA: (f) Italian; a diminutive of a name taken from Germanic roots meaning "sacrifice." It may have first been popularized in English through Giuseppe Verdi's opera *Rigoletto,* and Agatha Christie uses it for a character in her short story "The Man in the Mist," but it became much more familiar through the 1946 movie *Gilda* starring Rita Hayworth, although that familiarity doesn't seem to have translated into a boost in usage.

GLINDA: (f) coined; possibly created as a variant of Glenda (see GLEN in Chapter 14), although there is no evidence that that name had been coined yet when L. Frank Baum published *The Wizard of Oz* in 1900. But the brief flash of popularity for Glinda as a given name corresponds precisely with the release of the film version of this story starring Judy Garland, in 1939, and so you can take the connection as a given. Variant: **Glynda.**

HERMIONE: (f) Greek; belonging to the god Hermes. In Greek legend, this was the name of a minor character in the *Illiad.* It shows up as a literary name, for example in Shakespeare's *A Winter's Tale.* A few variants of the name were popular in the early 20th century, especially Herminia. Although Hermione itself has not currently made the charts, it seems safe to predict that the major character by this name in the *Harry Potter* books and movies will change that situation in the near future. Another well-known bearer is actress Hermione Gingold. Variants: **Hermina, Hermine,** and **Herminia.**

IRMA: (f) German; a diminutive of various names like Ermengard or Ermentrude, where it derives from an element meaning "whole." The name has been moderately popular through much of the 20th century and featured as the title character in two movies: *My Friend Irma* in 1949 and *Irma la Douce* in 1963 starring Shirley MacLaine (although in the latter the character is a prostitute, which may not recommend the name to parents). Variant: **Erma.**

LOGAN: (f, m) Gaelic; little hollow. A surname from the Scottish place name, taken into use as a given name. It came into use in the 19th century along with many other surnames transferred into use as given names. But the 1976 sci-fi movie *Logan's Run* correlates with the return of this as a boy's name. Feminine use trails after by a couple of decades and isn't quite as strong. Another recent movie influence may be the character named Logan in the *X-Men* movies, better known by his nickname Wolverine.

LOIS: (f) English; either from a Greek name mentioned in the Bible, or a variant of LOUISE (Chapter 9). The name shows up rarely in the 17th century and was revived in the early 20th century. Although she seems to have had little influence on the name's popularity, the character Lois Lane, from the movies, TV shows, and comic books about *Superman* is probably the best known example. Another bearer is actress Lois Smith.

MILDRED: (f) English; mild power. The name survived the Norman Conquest partly due to a saint who bore it, but eventually it fell out of fashion only to be revived in the Romantic movement of the 19th century. Coming into the 20th century it was in the top-ten most popular women's names, and so little credit for its popularity can be given to either James M. Cain's 1941 novel *Mildred Pierce* or the movie made from it. And yet, with the name falling out of fashion, the movie is still a strong association.

RHETT: (m) uncertain; possibly a variant of BRETT (Chapter 16) or possibly related to the Greek *rhetor* "orator." In any event, the name seems to have been coined by Margaret Mitchell for her scoundrel hero in *Gone With the Wind* and its appearance in the '60s can be laid to her account.

SCARLETT: (f) English; red, scarlet. Like Rhett, a name popularized directly by Margaret Mitchell's *Gone With the Wind* and not found in use before that. Today it is also found for actress Scarlett Johansson.

TARA: (f) Gaelic; eminence; a possessive form of the place name Teamhair, the traditional seat of the high kings of Ireland. This name completes the *Gone With the Wind* trilogy, for it was the name of the estate belonging to Scarlett's family, named after their Irish heritage. Like the other names in this group, it is not found in use before the release of the move. Recent bearers include actress Tara Martin Brent and ice skater Tara Lipinski. Variants: **Tarah** and **Tera.**

THELMA: (f) coined; perhaps taken from Greek *thelema* "will, wish," but in any event coined by writer Marie Corelli for her novel of the name. It was quite popular around the turn of the 20th century and has declined gradually since then. It does not yet seem to have seen a revival from the popularity of the movie *Thelma and Louise,* but the current rarity of the name makes the association fairly strong.

Searching the Back Lot for Actors' Names

One reason that actors' names have such a noticeable effect on name fashions is that they are often carefully crafted "brand names" that are distinctly different from the names of ordinary folk. At the height of the Hollywood studio system, it was rare to find a screen credit that matched the name an actor's parents had given him. Screen names were chosen to project an image: the rugged masculinity of leading men, the exotic sophistication of leading ladies. And the success of those images is seen in the names that were snapped up by an adoring public and passed on to their own children.

ALEC: (m) Greek; a diminutive of ALEXANDER (Chapter 6). This version has been in use since the 19th century and has the appeal of being short and sharp-edged. British actor Sir Alec Guinness gave this name a certain cachet. Other notable theatrical bearers include Alec Baldwin. Variant: **Alek.**

ANGELICA: (f) Latin; like an angel. A related name with similar meaning is Angelina. Actress Anjelica Huston bears an unusual spelling of this name; unusual enough that the brief appearance of Anjelica on the popularity charts in the '90s may be due to her influence. Another popular actress from this group is Angelina Jolie. Variants: **Angelique** and **Anjelica; Angelina** and **Angeline; Angelita.**

ANNETTE: (f) French; a diminutive of ANNE (Chapter 8). French versions of names such as this generally came into popularity in the 18th or 19th century. In this case the name's peak of popularity falls in the '60s and it's extremely tempting to connect this with the career of Annette Funicello, the "it girl" of teen-oriented movies in that period. Another more recent Hollywood bearer is Annette Benning. Variant: **Annetta.**

BETTE: (f) English; a diminutive of ELIZABETH (Chapter 8). This spelling is somewhat of two minds as regards pronunciation. For actress Bette Davis, it is said the same as Betty, while actress and singer Bette Midler pronounces it like another variant, Bet. The name's major popularity in the '20s predates the career of Bette Davis by a decade, so she cannot be credited with it, although the association is very strong today. Variant: **Bet.**

BRONSON: (m) English; the meaning is not, as it may seem, "Bron's son," but from the place name Bronteston, possibly "Brand's town." The given name only begins appearing in significant numbers in the '70s, around the time that Charles Bronson had moved from playing bad-guy roles to something more resembling heroic parts.

BURL: (m) English; a variant of "butler." The name of actor and singer Burl Ives follows the more usual pattern for surnames turned into given names, coming into use in the 19th century and falling out of fashion in the early 20th.

BURTON: (m) English; multiple origins, but primarily "town with a fortification." Despite the popularity of British actor Richard Burton (who deserves to be remembered for far more than being the on-again-off-again husband of Elizabeth Taylor), the popularity of the name dates to the 19th century and not to his influence. Its diminutive, Burt, fared somewhat better, being given a clear, if minor, boost from the career of Burt Lancaster, starting in the '50s. Diminutive: **Burt.**

BUSTER: (m) English; a nickname for a strong person, perhaps one who "busts" things. Actor Buster Keaton took it as a screen name at a time when it was only starting to be an independent name, and there is a clear bump in the numbers corresponding to his early career. Another bearer was swimmer and actor Buster Crabbe for whom it was also an adopted screen name.

CARY: (m) Brythonic; a place name from an ancient river name meaning "loved." Cary Grant took it as a screen name and may well be responsible for the boost given to the name in the '40s, when his career was in full swing. Variant: **Carey.**

CHARLIZE: (f) uncertain; possibly a variant of CHARLES (Chapter 9). Actress Charlize Theron was born in South Africa, so the origin of her name is hard to track down through the usual sources. On the other hand, given the name's rarity, if her name is picked up and made fashionable, it will be easy to identify the cause.

CHARLTON: (m) English; not "Charles' town" but from the older meaning of *carl* "a peasant, a free farmer," thus "town of the peasants." The name of Charlton Heston is, perhaps, too distinctive to have become popular in ordinary use, for he certainly meets the fame requirements.

CLARK: (m) English; a clerk, a learned man. This has been a very popular name since the 19th century, perhaps too popular for any influence from the glamorous Clark Gable to show up well in the statistics.

CLAUDETTE: (f) French; a feminine form of CLAUDE (Chapter 10). Actress Claudette Colbert is clearly the source of this name's popularity beginning in the '30s as the French name is not seen in the U.S. popularity charts before that.

CORNELL: (m) multiple origins; several names have merged, all of them place names, including "crane well," "corn hill," and Cornwall from the tribal name *Cornavia*. The name's popularity starting around the '30s slightly predates the career of actor Cornel Wilde, although he may be responsible for some of its rise in the ranks. It's quite possible that some of the popularity of the name may be credited to Cornell University (founded in the late 19th century by one Ezra Cornell).

DEMI: (f) coined; a diminutive of DEMETRIA (Chapter 5). The name of actress Demi Moore made the popularity charts briefly in the '90s, corresponding with her most prominent roles. Her birth name, Demetria, came on the leading edge of the recent fashion for that name, but she can hardly be credited for that aspect.

DENZEL: (m) English; a diminutive of DENIS (Chapter 5). This is a surname popular in Cornwall that came into use as a given name in the late 19th century. It jumped from obscurity to a relatively high popularity in the '90s, matching the significant rise of the career of actor Denzel Washington. Variants: **Denzell** and **Denzil.**

DERMOT: (m) Gaelic; meaning uncertain. The name has been quite popular in Ireland since early Medieval times but has been rare in the U.S. Actor Dermot Mulroney clearly brings the name in from an Irish heritage but no one has yet given the name enough of a boost to hit the charts.

DUDLEY: (m) English; Dudda's meadow. The place name became the surname of a prominent English family and was taken up for general use in the mid–19th century, primarily by influence of a prominent family of that name in early Massachusetts. As the name fell out of fashion in the mid–20th century, it is primarily associated with a few bearers born before that, such as actor Dudley Moore.

DUSTIN: (m) English; most likely "dusty town." The place name is originally Duston and this given name may be blended somewhat with names like Austin. It rises very steeply in popularity from the '70s through '90s, corresponding fairly well with the career of Dustin Hoffman, suggesting that he may take some of the credit for this name.

ERROL: (m) uncertain; a Scottish place name of uncertain origin and meaning. It is not clear whether actor Errol Flynn was named for the Scottish location and surname or whether his name is a variant on EARL (Chapter 13). But the rise of the name starting in the '30s corresponds so closely to his career that you can be certain of the relationship.

ETHAN: (m) Hebrew; ancient. The name was brought into use very occasionally during the Reformation and is seen for Revolutionary War figure Ethan Allen. It had been out of fashion for the first half of the 20th century, but rose steadily in the latter part to hit number 7 in 2003. The career of Ethan Hawke matches only the last small part of this rise, so you must consider him to have been swept up in the tide rather than driving it. Variant: **Ethen.**

EUGENE: (m) Greek; well-born. This name may have come into English use from Germany in the 18th century but became significantly popular in the late 19th century and well into the 20th. Although the full form is found for playwright Eugene O'Neill, Hollywood seems to have been more fond of the diminutive Gene, as for actors Gene Kelly and Gene Hackman, and producer Gene Roddenberry. Variant: **Eugenio.** Diminutive: **Gene.**

EWAN: (m) Gaelic; born of the yew (tree). This name is sometimes considered to correspond with EUGENE (see above). The name has been popular in Britain but has never quite made the grade in America. If anyone can change this, it may be actor Ewan McGregor, featured in the most recent series of *Star Wars* movies, among others.

FAY: (f, m) uncertain; possibly a diminutive of FAITH (Chapter 9), but this is unclear. It may also be influenced by the use of *fay* in the meaning "fairy." Neither of these explain its use as a male name. The name was relatively popular for both men and women in the early part of the 20th century but has fallen somewhat out of fashion, leaving the field to well-known bearers such as actresses Fay Wray and Faye Dunaway and novelist Fay Weldon. Male bearers tend to get lost in the shuffle and the name is primarily thought of as feminine, to the extent that it is still used.

FONDA: (f) Spanish; from a place name meaning base or foundation. The name is familiar as the surname of the acting dynasty of Henry, Jane, Peter, and Bridget Fonda, Fonda appears briefly on the charts as a feminine name in the '60s, and the timing suggests a possible influence from the career of Jane Fonda.

FRED: (m) English; a diminutive of FREDERICK (Chapter 9). The shorter forms of Frederick seem to have been popular as stage names. you see an entire array of bearers such as Freddie Bartholomew and Fred Astaire. With such a popular name, it is impossible to identify the influence of any particular bearer, though, and these names have been consistently popular throughout the last century. Variants: **Freddie, Freddy, Fredy,** and **Fritz.**

GARRISON: (m) English; son of GERARD (Chapter 8). This surname was not previously popular, but the beginnings of a fashion for this name seen starting in the '90s may possibly be attributable to the popularity of radio personality Garrison Keillor.

GARY: (m) English; multiple origins. The stage name of Gary Cooper was taken from the city of Gary, Indiana, which in turn was named after its founder Elmer Gary. His surname may have had various origins, but GERARD or GEROLD (Chapter 8) are strong candidates. In fact, Gary had been in use as a given name since the late 19th century, but it was certainly Cooper's popularity that caused it to shoot up from occasional use to the top twenty, beginning in the '20s. Variant: **Garry.**

GINA: (f) coined; a diminutive of various names, including GEORGINA (Chapter 9)and REGINA (Chapter 13). If anyone is to be credited with the name's rise in the ranks, it may be Gina Lollobrigida, whose career corresponds with the early part of the rise. More recently it has been borne by talented women such as Gina Gershon and Geena Davis. Variant: **Geena, Gena,** and **Gene.**

GWYNETH: (f) Welsh; origins uncertain, although it may sometimes be from the place name Gwynedd as a surname, in other cases from a word meaning "happiness." It has been primarily in Welsh use since its origin in the 19th century, but actress Gwyneth Paltrow has a chance of bringing it into wider use, as it combines a pleasant exoticness with a notable example.

HAILEY: (f, m) English; multiple origins; in many cases from the surname, taken from a place name meaning "hay meadow," but it may also sometimes by a diminutive from Harry or Harriet, by way of the same "r" to "l" substitution seen in Sally and Molly. Certainly Hal is found as a derivative of Harry, but in this case you'd expect to see the name becoming popular in the later 19th century carrying over somewhat into the next. Only the form Hallie appears in the early part of the 20th century, and is quite rare appearing only for boys. The explosion of interest in this name begins in the '70s and follows the career of child actress Hayley Mills. Actress Halle Berry has another variant of the name. In an unusual turnabout, the gender-neutral sound of the name, combined with its high profile, has caused it to leak over into male use, as for another child actor, Haley Joel Osment. Variants: (both) **Haley** and **Hallie;** (f) **Hailee, Hailie, Haleigh, Hali, Halie, Halle, Haylee, Hayleigh, Hayley,** and **Haylie.**

HILTON: (m) English; town on a hill. From the surname, made famous by the Hilton hotel chain. The name has been popular from the late 19th century through the early part of the 20th. Actor Hilton McRae came on the tail end of the primary fashion for this name, and if it revives, it's equally likely that surname examples such as for Paris Hilton will bring it back as a feminine name instead.

HOYT: (m) English; a long stick, a nickname for a tall man. The name comes from the surname and follows the usual pattern for surnames, coming into use in the 19th century and trailing off in the mid 20th. Actor Hoyt Axton was born towards the tail end of this fashion.

HUMPHREY: (m) English; from a Germanic root meaning "peaceful Hun," an oxymoron if ever there were one. It became popular in the Middle Ages and fell somewhat into disuse, although never entirely out of fashion. Somewhat surprisingly, actor Humphrey Bogart failed to spark a new interest in this name.

IDA: (f) English; from a Germanic root meaning "work, labor." The name was occasionally used in Medieval times, but fell almost entirely out of use until revived in the 19th century. It came into the 20th century relatively popular but fell out of fashion again around the '70s, failing to revive under the influence of actress Ida Lupino.

INGRID: (f) Swedish; a compound of Ingir, a personal name, and an element meaning "ride." The name was popular in the early 20th century primarily among immigrants, but instead of following the usual pattern for immigrant names, it revived to even higher popularity in the '40s, at the height of Ingrid Bergman's career.

IVETTE: (f) French; a feminine diminutive of Ivo, from a Germanic root meaning "yew tree." This name does not seem to have become popular in parallel with other French diminutives in the 18th and 19th centuries, but only begins to appear in the early 20th century. This is much too early to be a consequence of the popularity of actress Yvette Mimieux, but she may still be one of the more memorable bearers. Variant: **Yvette.**

JOAQUIN: (m) Spanish; a variant of Joachim, a Hebrew name meaning "may God exalt" that is given in the Apocrypha as the name of the Virgin Mary's father. It has come into American use primarily through the Hispanic community, hence the Spanish version is popular rather than the original. The name was quite familiar in 19th-century California from both poet Joaquin Miller and bandit (or folk hero, depending on your point of view) Joaquin Murieta. It has been relatively steady in popularity throughout the last century, but has risen somewhat in the last decade, possibly in part under the influence of actor Joaquin Phoenix.

JODY: (f) uncertain; possibly a variant of JUDY, but the masculine version is usually from JOSEPH (Chapter 4) or perhaps JUDE (Chapter 4). The connection with Judy is plausible, as Jody begins appearing as a girl's name at the time of Judy's greatest popularity in the '40s. Jody, in turn, had its greatest popularity in the '70s, when actress Jodie Foster was beginning her career. Variants: **Jodi** and **Jodie.**

JUDY: (f) English; a diminutive of JUDITH (see Chapter 4). The proliferation of Judys in entertainment is more an effect than a cause of the name's great popularity throughout the mid–20th century. Judy Collins is a leading light of the folk music movement. Judy Garland was both an icon and a victim of the Hollywood movie machine. And British actress Judi Dench has recently been coming to the attention of American audiences. Variants: **Judie** and **Judi.**

KEENAN: (m) Gaelic; multiple origins, from surnames derived from given names, meaning variously "white, fair" or "ancient." Actor Keenan Wynn has had a long career, so it can't be ruled out that he had an influence on this name appearing on the charts in the '60s, but a direct connection is hard to trace. Another recent Hollywood connection is Keenan Ivory Wayans. Variants: **Keenen** and **Kenan.**

KIEFER: (m) German; cooper, barrel-maker. The name hits the charts briefly in the early '90s, which correlates enough with the career of Kiefer Sutherland to suspect a possible connection. He, in turn, was named after Warren Kiefer, the writer and director of his father's first film. Variant: **Keifer.**

KEIRA: (f) uncertain; the most likely origin is the Scottish place name Keir, from a Brythonic root meaning "fortress," which was taken up as the male name Keir in the 19th century. Keira has only appeared on the scene in the last several years, suggesting a strong connection with the career of up and coming actress Keira Knightley.

KIRSTEN: (f) Danish or Norwegian; a variant of CHRISTIANA (Chapter 8). This group of variants became popular beginning around the '60s, coming on to the scene very suddenly. That crop of girls is now hitting the screen, including Kirsten Dunst and Kirstie Alley. Variants: **Kiersten, Kirstin,** and **Kirstie.**

KYRA: (f) Greek; lady; a feminine equivalent of CYRIL (Chapter 10). The name became suddenly popular around the '90s with no apparent previous use in the U.S. This correlates fairly well with the career of Kyra Sedgwick, although occasional use predates her. Variant: **Kira.**

LANA: (f) coined; either a variant of the rare name Alana or entirely invented. While it was used occasionally from the '20s, it springs suddenly high up on the popularity charts in the '40s, corresponding well with the career of Lana Turner. Given the obscure origins of the name, this correlation seems fairly conclusive.

LIAM: (m) Gaelic; a diminutive of WILLIAM (Chapter 8). The name is popular in Ireland but not much seen in the U.S. before the '70s. It shoots up even more rapidly in the '90s, corresponding precisely with the point when the career of Liam Neeson took off.

LIZA: (f) English; a diminutive of ELIZABETH (Chapter 8). In this group you see variants that have become icons in their own right: Liza for "Liza with a Z" Minelli, and Liz, closely identified with Elizabeth Taylor. The popularity of the various versions correspond somewhat, although not perfectly, with these actresses, but at the very least the association is strong. Variants: **Liz** and **Lizzie.**

LORETTA: (f) Italian; a variant of LAURA (Chapter 6). The name held a very consistently high popularity through the first half of the 20th century, making it difficult to identify specific influences. At the very least, it has been borne by a number of talented performers, including actresses Loretta Young and Loretta Swit, and singer Loretta Lynn. Variants: **Lauretta** and **Laurette.**

LIV: (f) multiple origins; in some cases, possibly a Norse name meaning "life," but in others a diminutive of OLIVIA (Chapter 12). It is a recorded fact that actress Liv Tyler was named after Liv Ullman, but further influence on naming fashions is unknown as this name has not yet made the popularity charts.

MACAULAY: (m) Gaelic; son of Olaf. While Gaelic surnames beginning with "O'" usually drop that element as a given name (for example, Sullivan rather than O'Sullivan), there has been a growing fashion for adopting "Mac" surnames in their full form as given names. Mackenzie is probably the best known. Child star Macaulay Culkin hasn't yet led this name onto the popularity charts, but there is the potential for a general "Mac" fashion here. Variant: **Macauly.**

MARCEL: (m) Latin; a diminutive of MARK (Chapter 4) used as an independent name since classical times. The feminine form is MARCELLA (Chapter 9). Marcel has always retained a somewhat foreign air and has never been more than mildly popular, although it shows up fairly consistently. Many of the best known bearers of this name group are not American in origin, for example mime Marcel Marceau and actor Marcello Mastroianni. Variants: **Marcelino, Marcellus, Marcello, Marcelo,** and **Marcial.**

MARILYN: (f) coined; a compound of MARY and LYNN. (See Chapter 11 for compounds of this type in general.) At the time this was chosen for the screen name of Marilyn Monroe, the name was already at the peak of its popularity It spent several decades riding high in the '30s and '40s and has only declined slowly since then. Variants: **Marilynn, Marlyn, Marylin, Marylyn,** and **Merilyn.**

MARLENE: (f) coined; a compound of MARY and HELENA (see Chapter 11). Even more than Marilyn, the fate of Marlene can be chalked up to a single bearer: actress Marlene Dietrich. The name first shows up in the '20s and shoots to the top of the charts in the '30s, declining only slowly and still mildly popular today. Variants: **Marlena, Maryellen, Merlene,** and **Marlen.**

MEKHI: (m) unknown; uncertain meaning. To determine the origins of this name, one may have to ask the parents of actor Mekhi Phifer, as the recent fashion for it seems to follow his career.

MELVIN: (m) English; bad town; a variant of MELVILLE (see Chapter 9). The full form of this name may carry a certain inherent unfashionableness, for all the well-known bearers seem to prefer the diminutive Mel instead. These include director Mel Brooks, actor Mel Gibson, and the character of Mel on the TV show *Alice.* Variant: **Melvyn.** Diminutive: **Mel.**

MEREDITH: (f, m) Welsh; meaning uncertain, but part of the name means "lord." In Wales where the name has been continuously in use since the Medieval period, this is purely a male name, and it tends to remain so in British use in general, although an early female example appears in Enid Bagnold's 1935 novel *National Velvet.* Female use grew slowly in popularity from the '10s until its peak in the '70s, when it was supported by examples such as Meredith Lord Wolek and Meredith Baxter-Birney. The rare male use in America dropped off abruptly in the '40s despite examples like composer Meredith Willson. For the most part, it is now establish as a purely feminine name in the U.S.

MITZI: (f) German; a diminutive of MARY (Chapter 8). This rather informal diminutive is closely associated with actress Mitzi Gaynor, and its sudden appearance in the '50s can be chalked up to her popularity.

MONTEL: (m) French; mountain, from various places of this name. A very mild fashion for this name in the early '90s may reasonably be connected with the popularity of talk show host Montel Williams.

MURIEL: (f) Gaelic; possibly: sea-bright. Although Irish in origin, this name had been taken up in England already in the Medieval period. After a long lapse, it was revived in the later 19th century along with other romantic-sounding names and was quite popular in the early 20th. Actress Meryl Streep bears a variant of the name, although that particular spelling has not caught on seriously. The recently popular variant Mariel may sometimes be from other sources, such as MARY with the French ending "-elle." Variants: **Mariel, Mariela,** and **Meryl.**

MYRNA: (f) Gaelic; an Anglicized form of Muirne "spirited, festive." The rise of this name to a peak of popularity in the '30s can plausibly be associated with the career of actress Myrna Loy. A more recent Hollywood bearer is Myrna Clegg.

PIPER: (f) English; a piper, a flute player. This occupational surname seems not to have been taken up in use during the usual fashion for such names in the 19th century. There has been a recent interest in some more unusual occupational names, and that general fashion combined with the inspiration of actress Piper Laurie may have led to it hitting the charts with a bang in the last decade.

PRICE: (m) Welsh; son of RHYS (see below). It comes not, as one may think, from the English word "price," but as a condensed form of the phrase *ap Rhys.* It follows the usual pattern for surname-based given names, coming into use in the late 19th century and then falling rapidly out of fashion.

RHYS: (f, m) Welsh; meaning uncertain. A very old name, popular in the Middle Ages. It has continued to be used in Wales to the present, but has made its way into American use mostly via the surname derived from it. As such, it was used rarely in the early part of the 20th century but has become extremely fashionable again in the last couple of decades. For the most part, it has remained a masculine name in American use, but the prominence of actress Reese Witherspoon has rapidly brought female use up to the same level as male use in recent years. For a truly exotic take on this name, use the original spelling: Rhys. Variants: **Reece** and **Reese.**

RITA: (f) Italian, Spanish; a diminutive of Margarita, a form of MARGARET (Chapter 8). Like many actresses, Rita Hayworth found that a short nickname can be more striking and memorable than the original name when the original is overly popular. This name was extremely popular for the first half of the 20th century, though, so she can't take all the credit.

RODNEY: (m) English; a place name of uncertain meaning. Comedian Rodney Dangerfield may have gotten no respect, but he got a name that only increased in popularity for most of his career. It's hard to know whether he played any major role in the trend.

ROMAN: (m) Latin; someone from Rome. This turned from a nickname to a given name at a very early date but has only been used in English since the 19th century. It has held a steady mild popularity through the last century, featuring bearers such as director Roman Polanski.

RUPERT: (m) German; bright fame; in origin, the same name as ROBERT (Chapter 8). This name came into some use in English in the 17th century in honor of Prince Rupert of the Rhine, who supported his uncle Charles I during the English Civil War. It has been less popular in America, although it appears regularly through the early part of the 20th century. you may expect to see some revival of it inspired by young actor Rupert Grint, one of the stars of the *Harry Potter* movies.

SHIRLEY: (f, m) English; Shire glade. Taken from a surname based on the place name. It had already become more popular for women than men by the turn of the 20th century, influenced by the title character of Charlotte Brönte's 1849 novel *Shirley.* But the nails were put in the coffin of male Shirleys when child actress Shirley Temple came on the scene in the '30s and the name hit number 4 on the girl's lists. Shelley is sometimes a variant of this name, although it may sometimes be used as a diminutive of Michelle. Between them, the names in this group have covered a long string of talented actresses including Shirley Jones, Shirley MacLaine, Shelley Winter, and Shelley Long. Variants: (f) **Shelley, Shelli, Shellie, Shelly, Shirlee,** and **Shirlene.**

SIGOURNEY: (f) uncertain; perhaps involving the element "victory." The name appears to be from a Norse root, passed through French spelling, which explains some of the confusion in the reference works discussing it. Actress Sigourney Weaver chose her screen name by one of those fascinating chains of connection: from the character of Sigourney Howard in F. Scott Fitzgerald's novel *The Great Gatsby,* while Fitzgerald in turn seems to have borrowed the name from that of author Lydia Howard Sigourney. The name has yet to become popular, but when it does you can add more links to the chain.

SISSY: (f) English; a diminutive of CECILIA (Chapter 7). The name may have a second origin in a baby-talk nickname for "sister," just as Buddy comes from "brother." Actress Sissy Spacek has not yet managed to push the name onto the popularity charts.

STERLING: (m) English; starling (a type of bird), a nickname. Modern use comes from the surname, and can evoke the sense of the (unrelated) ordinary word, as in "a sterling character." The name has been moderately popular throughout the last century, with actor Sterling Hayden being one example; another is auto racer Sterling Marlin.

TALLULAH: (f) Gaelic; lady of abundance; the Gaelic form is the rather more daunting Tailefhlaith. Although the name has been used occasionally in English in the last century or two, it is so closely tied in the modern imagination to Tallulah Bankhead that the connection may be a hindrance rather than a help to its popularity.

TATUM: (f) English; village of a man named Tata. Child actress Tatum O'Neal, the daughter of actor Ryan O'Neal, was the youngest person ever to win an Oscar for her work in *Paper Moon.* The name has been rising sharply in the popularity charts but only in the last decade, so it seems unlikely to be attributable directly to her career.

THEDA: (f) English; a diminutive of THEODORA (Chapter 7) or other names beginning in "Theo-." This has been used occasionally over the last century and achieved a moderate popularity in the early 20th century following hard on the heels of the silent film career of Theda Bara, who was born Theodosia.

TIA: (f) multiple origins; unlikely, in most cases, to be the Spanish word *tia* "aunt," but rather a diminutive of any of several names ending in "-tia," or sometimes simply a coined name. The origin of Téa is similarly obscure. Some sources suggest a meaning of "goddess," suggesting that it's a diminutive of various Greek names beginning in "Thea-." Tia has been mildly popular since the '70s — too early to be a product of the careers of either Tia Carrere or Tia Mowry — while Téa has yet to appear in significant numbers. Variant: **Téa.**

Using one-name titles

When a TV show's or movie's title consists of a single name, it can create a powerful association for people. The following shows may come immediately to mind when people hear these names.

Alfie

Alice

Amélie

Anastasia

Angie

Annie

Arthur

Benson

Carrie

Casper

Charly

Columbo

Dave

Ellen

Emma

Flo

Frances

Frasier

Frida

Gigi

Gilda

Gloria

Hannibal

Harvey

Hazel

Iris

Jesse

Julia

Laura

Lili

Lolita

Mannix

Marty

Matlock

Maude

Newhart

Oliver

Phyllis

Rebecca

Rhoda

Rocky

Roseanne

Roxanne

Sabrina

Seinfeld

Shane

Tommy

Valerie

Webster

TONY: (m) English; a diminutive of ANTHONY (Chapter 7). Always fairly popular, this name has been given most often in the mid–20th century, corresponding with the rise of stars like Tony Bennett and Tony Curtis. Variant: **Toney.**

TRACY: (f, m) multiple origins; the male name is from the surname, originally from a French place name. In feminine use, it may either be a borrowing of the male name or a diminutive of THERESA (Chapter 10). Male use began rising in the '30s saw its greatest peak around the '40s and '50s, which makes it tempting to link the fashion, not with a given name this time, but with the surname of long-time leading man Spencer Tracy. Female use doesn't get seriously started until the '50s but shoots up very quickly, and this can to some extent be traced to the character of Tracy Lord in the 1956 movie *High Society,* played by Grace Kelly. More recent bearers include comedian Tracey Ullman and singer Tracy Chapman. Variants: (both) **Tracey;** (f) **Traci** and **Tracie;** (m) **Trace.**

VALENTINA (f), **VALENTINE** (f, m): Latin; healthy, strong. The name is closely associated with Saint Valentine and so with romance in general. This was certainly an association for early silent actor Rudolph Valentino (for whom it was a legitimate variant of his original surname, not simply a screen name). But male use of the name fell out of fashion around the mid–20th century, except for the diminutive Val, as used by actor Val Kilmer. The feminine name, while rare, has seen a revival lately and is borne by actress Valentina Cortesee. Variant: (m) **Valentin.** Diminutive: (m) **Val.**

WAYNE: (m) English; a wagon; a surname for someone who makes or delivers goods with a wagon. The name has been moderately popular since the later 19th century, but it became much more so in the mid–20th century in parallel with the career of archetypal western actor John Wayne. A more recent bearer is hockey star Wayne Gretzky.

Creating a Stir: Names of Studio Artists

Performing artists are very much in the public eye in our culture; studio artists, less so. Studio artists are also less likely to adopt unusual or eye-catching professional names. Most people will recognize the names of a handful of famous painters and sculptors, but we're only likely to associate the name primarily with that artist if the name is unusual (for example, Michelangelo). Here are a few names where the artistic associations of the names are likely to be prominent.

ARTEMISIA: (f) Greek; belonging to Artemis, goddess of the hunt. This was occasionally used in the 19th century. The most famous historic bearer is probably the brilliant Italian Renaissance painter Artemisia Gentileschi.

AUBREY: (f, m) French; from Germanic roots meaning "powerful elf." The name has been used occasionally since the Middle Ages, but is much more common since the 19th century, perhaps as part of the romantic revival. Artist Aubrey Beardsley worked with many of the same romantic and historic themes, but in a more sophisticated and self-conscious style, with a streak of eroticism that his Victorian predecessors worked in more subtly. Female use has only become significant in the last several decades. Variants: (f) **Aubree** and **Aubrie.**

DANTE: (m) Italian; enduring, obstinate. This is familiar as the name of the great Medieval Italian poet Dante Alighieri, and is often used in honor of him since then. Another artistic bearer was pre-Raphaelite painter Dante Gabriel Rossetti. Recently it has been increasing significantly in popularity, but this is likely to be from a simple fashion for the sound, as you see a number of variants appearing. Variants: **Daunte, Donta, Dontae,** and **Donte.**

FRIDA: (f) Spanish; a feminine diminutive of FREDERICK (Chapter 9). Mexican artist Frida Kahlo has recently seen a revival of interest in her work, crowned by a film treatment of her life starring Salma Hayek, and this has produced a revival of this form of the name. Other variants were popular mostly in the earlier part of the century. Variants: **Freda, Freeda, Freida** and **Frieda.**

HANS: (m) German; a diminutive of Johannes, in other words JOHN (Chapter 8). This form of the name is closely associated with Renaissance court painter Hans Holbein, especially known for his portraits of the court of Henry VIII. In the 20th century, the name has fared much better than many immigrant names and did not seriously fall out of fashion until the last couple of decades. The diminutive Hansel is quite rare and has probably suffered from too close an association with its use in the fairy tale *Hansel and Gretel.* Diminutive: **Hansel.**

LEONARDO: (m) Italian; from Germanic roots meaning "bold as a lion." Renaissance artist and inventor Leonardo da Vinci forever set his stamp upon this name. The English form Leonard has been significantly more popular, though, holding a steadily high position on the charts over the last century. The name's diminutives were mostly popular around midcentury. Other more recent bearers include actor Leonardo DiCaprio, songwriter Leonard Cohen, and swimmer Lenny Krayzelburg. Variants: **Lenard** and **Leonard.** Diminutives: **Len, Lennie,** and **Lenny.**

MICHELANGELO: (m) Italian; a compound of MICHAEL (Chapter 8) and ANGELO (Chapter 13). Italy was the earliest place where double names like this became fashionable and by the Renaissance they were fairly common. (See Chapter 11 for compound names of this type.) The Italian version has never made the U.S. popularity charts, but the Spanish version Miguelangel has been flirting with the bottom of the charts in recent years. Variant: **Miguelangel.**

MYRON: (m) Greek; sweet-smelling oil. The earliest known Myron was a Greek sculptor of the 5th century B.C., famous especially for his bronze figures of athletes, of which copies of his "discus-thrower" still survive. But it was an early Christian saint and martyr by this name that most likely popularized it. The name had a consistent, if mild, popularity through the first half of the 20th century but has declined since then. Famous bearers include Nobel Prize–winning economist Myron Scholes and Myron was the original given name of television interviewer Mike Wallace.

RAPHAEL: (m) Hebrew; God has healed. This is the name of one of the archangels in the Bible. It came into use in the Middle Ages and was borne by a famous Italian painter during that period. It has held a very consistent popularity over the last century, more so in the Spanish form Rafael. There is also a feminine form **Rafaela** that was mildly popular in the early part of the 20th century. Variant: **Rafael.**

SALVADOR: (m) Spanish; savior. This is a short form of the epithet San Salvador "the holy savior." Spanish surrealist painter Salvador Dali is probably the best known bearer of this name. The usual diminutive is borne by actor Sal Mineo. Variant: **Salvatore.** Diminutive: **Sal.**

TWYLA: (f) coined; the meaning, if any, is uncertain. There is no clear origin for this name. It began appearing around the turn of the 20th century and reached its greatest popularity in the '30s. The name immediately brings to mind choreographer Twyla Tharp. Variant: **Twila.**

VINCENT: (m) Latin; conquering, victorious. This was the name of several early saints, guaranteeing its Medieval popularity. That popularity has been relatively stable and it has enjoyed a high ranking throughout the last century. One very notable bearer was impressionist artist Vincent van Gogh, but the popularity of the name gives it many other associations such as film director Vincent Minnelli, actor Vincent Price, and legendary football coach Vince Lombardi. Variants: **Vicente** and **Vincenzo.** Diminutives: **Vince** and **Vinson.**

Chapter 19

Playing the Field: Names from the Sports World

. . . .

In This Chapter

▶ Finding a winning name from a list of athletes

▶ Taking names that say, "Champion"

▶ Discovering the meanings behind the names of athletic stars

. . . .

*T*he world of sports creates its own type of celebrity. Hollywood can seem far removed from your lives, but every child in a schoolyard can realistically dream of having the moves to make the big time in sports. No wonder the field is a regular source of inspiration for names.

Taking the Gold: Athletes with Distinctive Names

Actors and actresses often have unusual or colorful names by design, having chosen a distinctive stage name. In contrast, the vast majority of sports stars have relatively ordinary names. In fact, when you run down the lists of MVPs in popular sports, you see a lot of short, common names like Joe, Bob, Ted, and so forth. Distinctive names tend to be nicknames, like Red or Leftey.

But sprinkled among the Joes and Teds there are names that are unusual enough to stick in the memory. The names in this section may not be typical for athletes, but it's the athletes who bear them that you tend to think of first when you hear the name.

ANJANETTE: (f) coined; a compound of ANNE (Chapter 8) and Jeanette, derived from JOHANNA (Chapter 8). Like many coined names, this hasn't picked up a major following. There was a brief, slight fashion for it in the '70s, too early for it to have been caused by track star Anjanette Kirkland.

ANNIKA: (f) Swedish; a diminutive of ANNE (Chapter 8); one of the many local variants of the immensely popular name Anne. This one has shot up the popularity charts in the last two decades. One bearer is golfer Annika Sorenstam, although given the low profile of all but a few professional golfers, you probably can't credit her with having started the fashion.

APOLLO: (m) Greek; a god of many things, including art, music, medicine, prophecy, and with solar associations. Although some derivatives of this name, such as Apollonius, have been used in previous ages, the simple form hasn't seen much use. Olympic speed skater Apolo Anton Ohno brought the name to people's attention during the 2002 games, and set the sort of example that may create interest in it. Variant: **Apolo.**

BABE: (f) English; baby, an endearment used as a nickname. Once or twice in a generation, an athlete comes along who has such all-around excellence that nearly everything they turn to is golden. Today the specialists are so far ahead of the pack that it takes a Michael Jordan to be taken seriously when crossing over. But earlier in the 20th century, you could see people like Babe Didrikson Zaharias take the track world by storm and then "retire" to dominate another field, in her case, golf. Despite the fame of baseball great Babe Ruth, it would be hard to recommend Babe as a boy's name today.

BARRY: (m) multiple origins; most typically connected with the Irish *Ó Beargha,* from a root meaning "spear," but even the Irish surname is more commonly from an Anglo-Norman place-name meaning "rampart." There may be other independent origins; politician Barry Goldwater's name may have been a nickname from his father's rather unusual given name Baron. Barry's use as a given name was given a boost in the mid 19th century by Thackeray's novel *The Luck of Barry Lyndon.* Its popularity grew to a peak in the middle of the 20th century, and today baseball slugger Barry Bonds is likely to keep the name in the spotlight with his pursuit of the lifetime home run records of Hank Aaron and Babe Ruth. Variant: **Berry.**

BORIS: (m) Russian; fight, struggle (although other origins are possible). A rare name, although it sometimes makes the lower end of the popularity charts. During the Cold War, such a thoroughly Russian name as Boris might have been a hard sell, but today you can look to examples such as tennis great Boris Becker, novelist Boris Pasternak, actor Boris Karloff, and even perhaps Russian president Boris Yeltsin.

CAL: (m) multiple origins; a diminutive of various names, especially CALVIN (Chapter 13). Cal isn't usually used as an independent name, but it has been made famous by people like baseball legend Cal Ripken, Jr.

CASEY: (f, m) Gaelic; vigilant in war. The name may sometimes be an initialism from the letters K.C. (see Chapter 11). The most famous sporting Casey may be the fictional "Might Casey" of Ernest Lawrence Thayer's poem *Casey at the Bat.* The name holds a firm place in American folklore, with another reference being the ill-fated railroad engineer Casey Jones. It comes from the Irish surname O'Casey, and has been extremely popular both inside the Irish-American community and out. Masculine use rose rapidly beginning around the mid–20th century and peaked in the '80s, about the time when girls started bearing it in significant numbers. Since that time, usage has been roughly equal and the name may succeed in becoming a truly unisex name (although the girls get more spelling variants to play with). As a feminine name, it may have other origins than simply a borrowing of the male name. In some cases it may be a variant of Cassie (from CASSANDRA, Chapter 5), or from other less common sources, such as the plant name Acacia. Variants: (f) **Casie, Kacey, Kaci, Kacie, Kacy, Kasey, Kasie,** and **Kecia;** (m) **Kasey.**

CHAMIQUE: (f) coined; a variant of SHAMIKA (Chapter 11), spelled to look French. Women's professional basketball has only begun to achieve the public prominence that could make players like Chamique Holdsclaw a household word. This name is an excellent example of how creative spelling can add multiple layers to a name's meaning.

CHRIS: (f) Latin; usually a diminutive of CHRISTINA (Chapter 9), but it can be from any name beginning with "Chris-." For male use of CHRIS see Chapter 8. The short, energetic form Chris fits such superb athletes as tennis player Chris Evert Lloyd. Another diminutive in this group is borne by ice skater Kristi Yamaguchi. These names have been extremely popular during the second half of the 20th century. Variant: **Christi, Christie, Christy, Cristy, Kris, Kristi, Kristie,** and **Kristy.**

DAGNY: (f) Norwegian; new day. Popular in Scandinavia since the Middle Ages, this name only appeared briefly in America around the turn of the 20th century, which you can attribute to immigrant use. The rise of women's professional soccer in the U.S. has been attracting top players from all over the world, like Norways's Dagny Mellgren (although she returned to the Norwegian national team for the Olympics). Another connection with the sports world is Dagny Scott Barrios, a writer on women and long-distance running.

DARA: (f) Hebrew; wisdom. It may also be a feminization of names such as Darryl or Darren. Olympic swimmer Dara Torres has been bringing this name to people's attention, although it has been moderately popular for several decades now on its own.

DEMPSEY: (m) Gaelic; proud. This enjoyed a brief popularity in the '20s and '30s as a given name which can probably be connected with the career of boxer Jack Dempsey in the early '20s.

DOMINIQUE: (f) French; Sunday, born on a Sunday. (For the masculine version, see Chapter 13.) Gymnast Dominique Dawes has been a mainstay of world-class competition for the U.S. for quite some time, although she has not enjoyed the same superstardom as some of her colleagues. The more French-sounding variants of this name have become popular mostly in recent decades, while the Spanish versions such as Dominga were more popular in the early part of the century. Variants: **Domenica, Dominga, Dominque,** and **Domonique.**

ELGIN: (m) Gaelic?; a Scottish place name of uncertain meaning. Popularized by the title of Lord Elgin, especially the seventh of that name who brought the "Elgin marbles" from the Parthenon in Greece to England. Like many surname-based names, its main popularity was in the late 19th century, but it can be found today for basketball player Elgin Baylor.

EVANDER: (m) Greek; good man. In Greek legend, one of the survivors of the Trojan war, who founded a city in a location near where Rome would later stand. Not a particularly common name, although boxer Evander Holyfield demonstrates that sometimes the name means not simply "good" but "great."

GALE: (f, m) multiple origins; as a masculine name, most likely from the surname, which can derive either from a personal name Gualo, a nickname meaning "light, merry," or an occupational name meaning "jail, jailor." As a feminine name, usually a diminutive of ABIGAIL (Chapter 4). The story of football star Gale Sayers was featured in the movie *Brian's Song,* along with that of his friend and teammate Brian Piccolo. Female athletes with this name include track star Gail Devers. Variants: (both) **Gail** and **Gayle;** (f) **Gayla;** (m) **Gael.**

IVONNE: (f) French; a diminutive of Ivo, from a Germanic root meaning "yew tree." The root name, Ivo, was popular in France in the Medieval period and gave rise to a variety of diminutives for both men and women, but it is primarily the women's names that have come into American use. A variant spelling of this name is used by Australian tennis great Evonne Goolagong. Variants: **Evon, Evonne,** and **Yvonne.**

JERRY: (f, m) English; a diminutive of GERALD (Chapter 8) or GERARD (Chapter 8) or sometimes of JEREMY (Chapter 10). There is usually no connection between the spelling (Jerry or Gerry) and which original name it stands for. The most popular spelling for men has been Jerry, which made it into the top-20 names in the '40s and has been consistently popular over the last century. For women, it is generally short for GERALDINE (Chapter 9) and has had a more limited period of popularity, but again centered in the mid–20th century. Men in a wide range of athletic endeavors have borne this name, including boxer Gerrie Coetzee, jockey Jerry Bailey, basketball player Jerry West, and football star Jerry Rice. Variants: (both) **Gerry;** (f) **Jeri, Jerri,** and **Jerrie;** (m) **Geary, Gerrie,** and **Jere.**

JESSE: (f, m) Hebrew; God is, God exists. In some cases, this can be an initial-ism from the letters J.C. (see Chapter 11), as is the case for Olympic track star Jesse Owens. As a feminine name, it can be a diminutive of JESSICA (Chapter 6). As a male name it has been consistently popular through the last century, while female use has been declining slightly since the late 19th century. Variants: (f) **Jessi** and **Jessie**; (m) **Jess, Jessie**, and **Jessy.**

KIP: (m) multiple origins; from various surnames in several languages, including English "a pointed hill," German "a cliff," and Dutch "chicken" (perhaps for someone who raises poultry). The name enjoyed a slight popularity in the mid–20th century and is found for speed skater Kip Carpenter.

LANCE: (m) English; land; a diminutive of Lancelot. This diminutive returns the name Lancelot to its roots, as it began as a diminutive of the Germanic name Lanzo. And while Lancelot itself has perhaps been considered a bit too fancy to become popular in ordinary use, Lance has been fairly common in the later 20th century, familiar from superstar cyclist Lance Armstrong. Variant: **Lancelot.**

LENNOX: (m) Gaelic; place with elm trees. A surname taken from a Scottish place name. The name has never been particularly common but brings to mind boxing champion Lennox Lewis.

MARIO: (m) Spanish or Italian; from Latin Marius "belonging to Mars, the god of war." Some of the best known bearers have Italian family connections, as for auto racer Mario Andretti and novelist Mario Puzo, but the name has come into more general use, as for hockey player Mario Lemieux. It has held a consistently high popularity for most of the last century.

MARTINA: (f) Latin; belonging to Mars, the god of war, a feminine variant of MARTIN (Chapter 8). The name has consistently had a mild popularity in recent years, although it has never made it near the top of the charts. Borne by tennis great Martina Navratilova, as well as more recent tennis star Martina Hingis who was named after her.

MIA: (f) multiple origins; usually a diminutive of MARY (Chapter 8) in various Scandinavian languages, but sometimes used for the sense "mine, my own" as an endearment in Italian. It may also be an independent coinage in some cases. The explosion of interest in this name in the last decade can almost certainly be attributed to soccer star Mia Hamm. Other bearers have included actress Mia Farrow. Variants: **Miah, Mie, Miya, Mya,** and **Myah.**

MICKEY: (f, m) English; a diminutive of MICHAEL (Chapter 8). The popularity of this name, as might be expected, has followed that of Michael, shadowing it for most of the 20th century. The particular interest in Mickey in the '40s and '50s starts a little too early to be associated entirely with the career of baseball great Mickey Mantle, but he no doubt contributed. (Another famous

Mickey — the mouse — wouldn't necessarily be expected to give the name a boost.) Other bearers include actor Mickey Rooney, and on the female side, golfer Mickey Wright. Variants: (f) **Mickie.**

MING: (m) Chinese; light. It is unusual for Chinese names to cross over into general use in the U.S., but one good candidate for the process may be that of basketball star Yao Ming — assuming that people can keep track that "Yao" is his family surname and "Ming" is the given name.

ORAL: (m) multiple origins; one major source is a Yiddish diminutive of AARON (Chapter 4), but there are several other origins. This name was borne by baseball pitcher Orel Hershiser. Variant: **Orel.**

PELE: (m) coined; despite some rather dubious stories about how soccer great Pelé was given the nickname he is generally known by, the origin can probably be considered unknown. He was originally christened Edson.

PICABO: (f) Shoshone; shining water. The parents of Olympic skier Picabo Street encouraged self-reliance by, among other things, letting them pick their own names. Picabo chose hers at age three from the name of a local creek. This is not necessarily recommended as a method of naming children, although in this case it gave her the sort of distinctive name that gets her remembered.

REGINALD: (m) French; from two Germanic elements both meaning "force, power." The name was popular in the Middle Ages and then fell out of use, being revived around the mid–19th century. It has been moderately popular in the U.S., especially in the mid–20th century, which is too early for the fashion to have been driven by the fame of baseball slugger Reggie Jackson or defensive lineman Reggie White. Variant: **Reginal.** Diminutive: **Reggie.**

RIDDICK: (m) English; farm where reeds grow. A rare name, taken from surname use. It is familiar from boxer Riddick Bowe, but more recently from the title character of the movie *The Chronicles of Riddick* (where it is the character's surname).

ROOSEVELT: (m) Dutch; rose field. While this name is most famous as the surname of two U.S. presidents, Theodore Roosevelt and Franklin Delano Roosevelt (who were fifth cousins), it came into use as a given name mostly later, in honor especially of FDR. In this use, the most famous bearer may be football star Roosevelt "Rosie" Brown. Variant: **Rosevelt.**

SERENA: (f) Latin; calm, serene. The name has been used occasionally since the 18th century, and earlier was a literary name in Spenser's *The Faerie Queen.* It fell out of use for most of the early 20th century, but has been increasing steadily in popularity since the '60s, and especially in the last decade or so when it may be given in honor of tennis great Serena Williams. Variants: **Serina** and **Serenity.**

SHAQUILLE: (m) Arabic; handsome. A more usual spelling of the name is Shakil; the variant used by basket ball superstar Shaquille O'Neal has been spelled to look French. The name enjoyed a brief popularity in the '90s in his honor.

SHEA: (f, m) Gaelic; hawklike. Use of Shea as a given name comes by way of the Irish surname O'Shea. Not all famous names in sports belong to athletes. New York's Shea Stadium was named after attorney William Shea who helped bring the Mets to that city. Shea has been used occasionally by both boys and girls since the '80s. Variant: **Shay.**

SONNY: (m) English; son; from an affectionate nickname. This has had only mild popularity, being primarily a nickname rather than a given name. This was the case for both singer turned congressman Sonny Bono and controversial boxer Sonny Liston.

TERRELL: (m) French; one who pulls; perhaps a nickname for a stubborn person. The name has been popular primarily in the later 20th century, including for football player Terrell Davis. Variant: **Terrill.**

TIGER: (m) English; a tiger, often a nickname for an energetic person. Golf superstar Tiger Woods was nicknamed this in honor of his father's wartime friend, Nguyen Phong, nicknamed "Tiger" for his bravery. Tiger's birth name is Eldrick. This is the sort of connection that could easily turn Tiger into a given name for its own sake.

TYSON: (m) French; firebrand. Not, as it might seem, from a surname meaning "son of Tye," although there is also a surname Tye with an entirely different origin. The name Tyson sprang suddenly onto the popularity charts at a fairly high level in the '70s, but that's too early for the surname of boxer Mike Tyson to have had any hand in things. The timing is better for an influence from the surname of actress Cicely Tyson.

VENUS: (f) Latin; the goddess of love. The name was used rarely in the mid–20th century and later, but you may expect to see a new crop named in honor of tennis star Venus Williams.

WILMA: (f) German; a diminutive of Wilhelmina, a feminine form of WILLIAM (Chapter 8). This was a relatively popular name in the early 20th century but has fallen out of fashion in recent decades. Track star Wilma Rudolph's accomplishments are even more impressive given that she spent much of her childhood recovering from the effects of polio.

Proclaiming Victory: Names that Describe Athletes

People in past ages had the same interest in physical achievement that you have today. Nicknames from well-know sports became surnames and surnames became given names. Some of the activities described here were more in earnest at the time — such as archer or sailor — but today are more often pursued for entertainment.

ARCHER: (m) English; an archer, a bowman. Originally this would have been a military occupation, but today archery is a sport — whether shooting at targets or at game. This is rare as a given name.

ARMSTRONG: (m) English; someone with strong arms. you can imagine early bearers of this name to have been weight lifters or wrestlers. The name has additional sporting associations from bicycle racer Lance Armstrong.

CHASE: (f, m) English; one who runs after something, originally a hunting term. Chase has become quite popular for boys since the '80s, while girls flirted with the name very lightly in the late '90s. There are both male and female examples among soap opera actors, including Chase Parker and Chase Sanders.

DARBY: (f, m) English; a variant of the place name Derby meaning "deer village". This name comes from the site of the most famous horse race in England. It just barely skims the bottom of the popularity charts in the '70s for boys and in the '90s for girls.

FAULKNER: (m) English; a falconer; someone who hunts with hawks or falcons. In the Middle Ages, falconry was not only an extremely popular sport (among those who were rich enough to indulge in it) but was a way of putting meat on the table. It's still practiced today although participation is restricted, not by wealth, but by the large amount of care the birds require. Novelist William Faulkner makes this name familiar.

FISHER: (m) English; someone who catches fish. This name is borne by actor Fisher Stevens but may be more familiar as a surname from people like chess champion Bobby Fischer.

HURLEY: (m) English; generally from a place name indicating a meadow in the hills but hurley is also a game in the same family as field hockey (but rather more aggressive). It may also sometimes be from the Irish surname O'Hurley. This name was briefly on the charts as a given name in the '30s.

MORIARTY: (m) Gaelic; sailor, sea-farer. People in past centuries are less likely to have thought of sailing as a sport than as a livelihood or a way to get from one place to another. But in the age of engines, sail-power has largely been relegated to the realm of leisure. Moriarty is relatively common as a surname, with the most famous bearer being the fictional nemesis of detective Sherlock Holmes.

NAUTICA: (f) Greek; having to do with the sea; a sailor. The occasional use of this name in the late '90s seems to be inspired more by the clothing brand name than by an interest in ships.

RACE: (m) multiple origins; sometimes from a French nickname meaning "clean-shaven", other times from an old English given name of uncertain meaning. This may also be used as a diminutive for HORACE (see Chapter 9). It is borne by actor Race Gentry, although those of a certain generation may connect it more closely with cartoon adventurer Race Bannon of *Johnny Quest.*

WALKER: (m) English; a fuller of cloth — because this was done by walking over the fabric. This surname became mildly popular as a given name in the late 19th century and then fell slowly out of use. Starting in the '90s it has seen a resurgence, perhaps as part of the general fashion for occupational names, similarly to Taylor.

Part VI
The Part of Tens

The 5th Wave   By Rich Tennant

"Your first name really Fenderbutt? I think I call you Kemosabe."

In this part . . .

This section presents additional resources and reviews as well as some important considerations in choosing a name.

Chapter 20

Ten Practices to Avoid

In This Chapter
▶ Discovering how to avoid picking a name you'll regret
▶ Ensuring your child doesn't hate his name

Some common problems in choosing names are only problems because everyone does them. Other problems come from taking too narrow a view of what you are doing: only thinking about one part of the process, or thinking of your child only as a child and not as a future adult. Here are some of the stumbling blocks that come up again and again when parents set out to choose a name.

Start Browsing at the Front of the Alphabet

Have you ever seen a random list of names where it looked like half of them started with A, B, or C? Most name books are arranged alphabetically, and if you start browsing without any firm ideas of what you're looking for, you'll tend to stop after you've found a few names you like. If you started at the front of the book, those names are likely to be at the front of the alphabet. Now imagine everyone doing the same thing . . . It's hard to have a distinctive name when all anyone can remember is that it's one of all those "A" names.

Don't Check the Name's Popularity

I've lost count of the number of times a parent has told me, "We didn't have any idea that Emily (or some other popular name) was in the top ten when we picked it. We just heard the name and liked it. And now there are four

Emilys in her preschool class." Even though they don't remember being aware of the name being popular, chances are, one of the reasons they liked the name — and certainly one of the reasons they heard the name — was that very popularity. The names in the top ranks of popularity will work their way into your subconscious. Don't assume that you would automatically know if the name you've fallen in love with is one that half the rest of the world has also fallen in love with this year. I've never heard a parent say, "Oh, how I wish I'd picked a name for my child that was higher on the popularity charts!" But I've heard plenty wish that they'd worked a little harder to know where their proposed names stood in the rankings before settling on one.

Don't Ask Anyone Else's Opinion

We all have our blind spots. It's like that optical illusion that can either look like a vase or a pair of faces: If you're a florist, you may never see the faces at all. Remember that your child will be meeting a lot of different people, and you should get a sense of how those other people may react to the name you've picked.

Don't Research the Name's Meaning

Meaning is probably over-emphasized in the search for the perfect name, but even if you base your choice entirely on sound or association, it's a good idea to know what the name's meaning is — if any. For one thing, at some point, your child will want to know and you should have a good answer. I've always been puzzled by parents who ask, "I named my child <name> — what does it mean?" After you've already bestowed the name, it's a bit late to worry about the meaning.

Choose a Cute or Funny Name

How many jokes or amusing stories do you know that are still funny the tenth time you hear it? How about the thousandth time? If you choose a name that prompts hearers to giggle or say, "Aww!" try to imagine the ten thousandth time your child hears that response. In the extreme case, this is a good way to encourage your child to put in for a name change in adulthood.

Choose a Name that Suits a Baby

You want a name that will be perfectly fitted to your little bundle of joy. So many names are just so stuffy and overly dignified, right? However much you want to prolong the time when your child is a cute and cuddly infant, babies inevitably grow up. And a grown-up needs a grown-up name. Resist the urge to think only in the short term.

Wait Until the Last Minute

Few important decisions are improved by being made in an instant and the best flashes of inspiration have been simmering on a back burner for a while. You don't need to decide on a name six months in advance, but at least start thinking about it some time before entering the delivery room. Even if you want to wait to see if your child "looks like" a particular name, you need to fill your head with a lot of potential names so that you have a wide selection to test for the right "look."

Pick a Random Foreign Word

There has been an interesting fad in Japan for wearing clothing embellished with random English words. These aren't brand names or slogans, just random words — fashionable because they are exotic and sound pleasant. If you discover that the pretty word on your t-shirt means something unfortunate, you can change clothes. It's harder to change names. That doesn't mean you have to go as far as the Exxon company did to choose a name that doesn't exist as a word in *any* language, but keep in mind that if you borrow a word from another culture, you may be borrowing an unknown amount of baggage that comes along with the word.

Pick a Random English Word

All sorts of words have become popular names. If Rock and Destiny can become names, why not Bookshelf or Idiosyncrasy? If you just giggled, you've answered the question. If your child is the first person people encounter who is using a particular ordinary word as a name, there will be a lot of "that's not a name!" reactions to get past. Maybe it will be worth it for this particular name, but it had better be a really good one.

Insist on Calling Your Child by a Version of His Name that He Hates

It's so cute when he insists on using Rick, but he's always been your little Dickie bird and that's what he'll always be. There's no point in asking you to change after all these years, right? Wrong. Children work hard to establish their own identities and to take control over their lives. Let them take ownership of what form of their names to use. Save your stubbornness for the really important stuff. And if, at some point, your child seriously wants to change his name to something entirely different from what you chose, take the desire seriously and respect it even if you disagree.

Chapter 21

Ten Types of Resources to Consider

In This Chapter

▶ Finding resources for particular types of names

▶ Using reference works

▶ Checking out resources on the World Wide Web

*I*t would be delightful if you could find everything you need for naming your baby in the present work, but no book can be exhaustive. You may be interested in a particular type of name mentioned here but want to see a broader selection within that type. Or you may want to discover more information about a name or the past bearers of a name than can be included in a work of the present type. Here are some ideas of resources you may find useful if you want further information. We start with further information on particular classes of names and then look at groups of reference works that can be useful when choosing names. This is followed by several on-line resources that may be of particular use. The books mentioned in this chapter are the sort that you should be able to find in even a relatively small library.

Resources on Biblical Names

There are several types of resources available if you're interested in Biblical names. *Strong's Exhaustive Concordance of the Bible* is an index of all the words and names included in the Bible, giving the chapter and verse where they appear. If you want to know more information about the stories behind the names, then there are several works of the "who's who in the Bible" variety that explain the histories and relationships between the various Biblical figures.

Resources on Saints' Names

There are many reference works on saints. *Butler's Lives of the Saints* is a classic work and provides traditional biographies of many of the most important saints. *The Oxford Dictionary of Saints* has listings for both popular and obscure saints and includes an index of who is patron saint of what. Another work with similar coverage is *The Penguin Dictionary of Saints*.

Geographic and Biographic Dictionaries

If you want to find some of the connections for your name, or are trying to track down its origins, you may find some answers in biographical or geographical dictionaries. (Your local library is likely to have works of this sort.) If you suspect that a name that you're interested in may be a place name — or if you want to browse interesting place names for ideas for given names — a book such as *Webster's Geographical Dictionary* will give you short descriptions of the places named, as well as telling you where to find them on a map. More detailed information on place name meanings can be found in works like *The Concise Oxford Dictionary of English Place Names* and similar works for other languages. Biographical dictionaries will only be useful if you are looking at surnames, but if you're interested in a name that started out as a surname then works of this type can give you examples of people who bore the name and a brief synopsis of their lives.

Reference Works on Surnames

Whether you want to research variants of surnames in your family or you want to look up the meaning and origins of a name you believe to have originated as a surname, you will find a number of extensive reference works on surnames. Generally, they will cover only the surnames of a particular country, such as *The Dictionary of English Surnames* by Reaney and Wilson or *The Surnames of Scotland* by George F. Black. There are also works that cover the most common American surnames, of whatever national origin.

Your Library Genealogy Section

Most libraries will have a good selection of reference books for people trying to research their family history or the origin of their surnames and these books can also be great sources of name ideas. (The above-mentioned reference works on names will often be kept in this section.)

Other Reference Books

If you want to find a name with an interesting story behind it, consider look-ing in works such as *Brewer's Dictionary of Phrase and Fable,* which gives the stories behind proverbs as well as synopses of many myths and legends, or *Chambers Dictionary of Literary Characters,* which briefly gives the stories behind many familiar names in literature.

The Medieval Names Archive

Find an unusual name or simply an unusual spelling from lists of historic sources at www.s-gabriel.org/names/. These are articles aimed at people doing historic re-enactment who need to choose names for the historic char-acters they are creating — a task with many of the same problems as choos-ing a name for a baby. You will find many names here that you've never heard of before but that may have been wildly popular in their own day.

Social Security Administration Web Site

The Social Security Administration's Web site has information on name popu-larity over the last century: www.socialsecurity.gov/OACT/babynames/. This is the site used for information on name popularity over the last century that is discussed in the present book. People have been known to spend hours at this site tracing the popularity of all their friends' names!

Web Search Engines

Run your chosen name through a search engine, such as www.google.com, to see what associations it turns up, for good or ill. It can be particularly fun to search for the entire name you are considering (put the name in quotes in the search field) to see if anyone else in the world is using the exact same name you are planning to give your child. Another invaluable use for Web searches comes if you are considering an unusual name or an unusual spelling of a name. Searching on the name can alert you to potential connections that you were not aware of.

Online Parenting Discussion Groups

Whether you want feedback on names you're considering or need to be reminded how silly *other* people's choices can be, online groups give you the benefit of many voices with the ability to ignore them when you completely disagree. Web sites and discussion groups can be ephemeral, so a list of specific sites can become dated very quickly, but using a Web search engine to search on the keyword "parenting" will lead you to a wide variety of useful resources.

General Index

Baby Names Index

Jaron, 204
Jarred, 182
Jarrell, 127
Jarret, 127
Jarrett, 127
Jarrod, 182
Jase, 74, 199
Jasen, 74
Jasmin, 216
Jasmine, 216
Jasmyn, 216
Jason, 74
Jasper, 222
Javen, 204
Javier, 254
Javion, 204
Javon(te), 204
Jay, 273
Jayce, 199
Jaycee, 199
Jaycie, 199
Jayda, 273
Jayde, 216
Jayden, 203
Jaydon, 203
Jayla, 203
Jaylan, 204
Jaylen, 204
Jaylene, 204
Jaylin, 204
Jaylon, 204
Jaylyn, 204
Jaylynn, 204
Jayme, 154
Jayne, 177
Jayson, 74
Jazlyn, 204
Jazmin, 216
Jazmine, 216
Jazmyn, 216
Jazmyne, 216
Jean, 129
Jeana, 129
Jeane, 129
Jeanette, 129
Jeanie, 129
Jeanine, 154
Jeanna, 129
Jeanne, 129
Jeannette, 129
Jeannie, 129
Jeannine, 154
Jed, 146

Jedediah, 146
Jedidiah, 146
Jeff, 126
Jefferey, 126
Jefferson, 126
Jeffery, 126
Jeffrey, 126
Jeffry, 126
Jelani, 264
Jena, 129
Jenelle, 129
Jenifer, 182
Jenna, 182
Jennie, 182
Jennifer, 182
Jenny, 129, 182
Jerad, 182
Jerald, 127
Jeraldine, 153
Jeramie, 183
Jeramy, 183
Jere, 320
Jered, 182
Jerel, 127
Jeremey, 183
Jeremiah, 146
Jeremie, 183
Jeremy, 183
Jeri, 320
Jerilyn, 194
Jerline, 194
Jermain, 233
Jermaine, 233
Jermey, 183
Jerod, 182
Jerold, 127
Jerome, 164–165
Jeromy, 183
Jerrell, 127
Jerri, 320
Jerrie, 320
Jerrod, 182
Jerrold, 127
Jerry, 320
Jesica, 92
Jess, 321
Jessamine, 216
Jessamyn, 216
Jesse, 321
Jessi, 321
Jessica, 92
Jessie, 321
Jessika, 92

Jessy, 321
Jesus, 61
Jethro, 288
Jevon, 204
Jewel, 216
Jewell, 216
Jill, 188
Jillian, 188
Jim, 176
Jimena, 92
Jimi, 176
Jimmie, 176
Jimmy, 176
Jo, 177
Joachim, 61
Joan, 128–129
Joana, 129
Joanie, 165
Joann, 129, 194
Joanna, 129, 194
Joanne, 129, 194
Joaquin, 306
Jocelyn, 139
Jocelyne, 139
Jodi, 306
Jodie, 183, 306
Jody, 183, 306
Joe, 62
Joel, 54
Joellen, 194
Joetta, 155
Joey, 62
Johan, 129
Johana, 129
Johann, 129
Johanna, 129
Johathan, 54
John, 128–129
Johnathan, 54
Johnathon, 54
Johnie, 165
Johnna, 129
Johnnie, 165
Johnny, 165
Johnpaul, 194
Jolene, 194
Jolie, 230
Jomar, 203
Jon, 54
Jonah, 54
Jonas, 54
Jonatan, 54
Jonathan, 54

Joni, 165
Jonna, 129
Jonnie, 165
Jordan, 249
Jorden, 249
Jordi, 249
Jordon, 249
Jordy, 249
Jordyn, 249
Jorge, 153
Jose, 62
Josef, 62
Josefa, 155
Josefina, 155
Joselyn, 139
Joseph, 62
Josephine, 154–155
Josette, 155
Josh, 183
Joshua, 183
Joshuah, 183
Josiah, 278
Josie, 155
Joslyn, 139
Josue, 183
Jovan, 204
Jovani, 204
Jovanny, 204
Jovany, 204
Joy, 230
Joycelyn, 139
Juan, 129
Juana, 129
Juancarlos, 194
Juanita, 129
Judah, 54
Judas, 54
Judd, 62
Jude, 54, 62
Judge, 238
Judi, 306
Judie, 306
Judith, 55
Judson, 165
Judy, 306
Jules, 111
Juli, 294
Julia, 294
Julian, 111
Juliana, 129
Juliann, 129
Julianna, 129
Julianne, 129

BUSINESS, CAREERS & PERSONAL FINANCE

Grant Writing For Dummies
0-7645-5307-0

Home Buying For Dummies
0-7645-5331-3 *†

Also available:

- Accounting For Dummies †
  0-7645-5314-3
- Business Plans Kit For Dummies †
  0-7645-5365-8
- Cover Letters For Dummies
  0-7645-5224-4
- Frugal Living For Dummies
  0-7645-5403-4
- Leadership For Dummies
  0-7645-5176-0
- Managing For Dummies
  0-7645-1771-6

- Marketing For Dummies
  0-7645-5600-2
- Personal Finance For Dummies *
  0-7645-2590-5
- Project Management For Dummies
  0-7645-5283-X
- Resumes For Dummies †
  0-7645-5471-9
- Selling For Dummies
  0-7645-5363-1
- Small Business Kit For Dummies *†
  0-7645-5093-4

HOME & BUSINESS COMPUTER BASICS

Windows XP For Dummies
0-7645-4074-2

Excel 2003 For Dummies
0-7645-3758-X

Also available:

- ACT! 6 For Dummies
  0-7645-2645-6
- iLife '04 All-in-One Desk Reference
  For Dummies
  0-7645-7347-0
- iPAQ For Dummies
  0-7645-6769-1
- Mac OS X Panther Timesaving
  Techniques For Dummies
  0-7645-5812-9
- Macs For Dummies
  0-7645-5656-8

- Microsoft Money 2004 For Dummies
  0-7645-4195-1
- Office 2003 All-in-One Desk Reference
  For Dummies
  0-7645-3883-7
- Outlook 2003 For Dummies
  0-7645-3759-8
- PCs For Dummies
  0-7645-4074-2
- TiVo For Dummies
  0-7645-6923-6
- Upgrading and Fixing PCs For Dummies
  0-7645-1665-5
- Windows XP Timesaving Techniques
  For Dummies
  0-7645-3748-2

FOOD, HOME, GARDEN, HOBBIES, MUSIC & PETS

Feng Shui For Dummies
0-7645-5295-3

Poker For Dummies
0-7645-5232-5

Also available:

- Bass Guitar For Dummies
  0-7645-2487-9
- Diabetes Cookbook For Dummies
  0-7645-5230-9
- Gardening For Dummies *
  0-7645-5130-2
- Guitar For Dummies
  0-7645-5106-X
- Holiday Decorating For Dummies
  0-7645-2570-0
- Home Improvement All-in-One
  For Dummies
  0-7645-5680-0

- Knitting For Dummies
  0-7645-5395-X
- Piano For Dummies
  0-7645-5105-1
- Puppies For Dummies
  0-7645-5255-4
- Scrapbooking For Dummies
  0-7645-7208-3
- Senior Dogs For Dummies
  0-7645-5818-8
- Singing For Dummies
  0-7645-2475-5
- 30-Minute Meals For Dummies
  0-7645-2589-1

INTERNET & DIGITAL MEDIA

Digital Photography For Dummies
0-7645-1664-7

Starting an eBay Business For Dummies
0-7645-6924-4

Also available:

- 2005 Online Shopping Directory
  For Dummies
  0-7645-7495-7
- CD & DVD Recording For Dummies
  0-7645-5956-7
- eBay For Dummies
  0-7645-5654-1
- Fighting Spam For Dummies
  0-7645-5965-6
- Genealogy Online For Dummies
  0-7645-5964-8
- Google For Dummies
  0-7645-4420-9

- Home Recording For Musicians
  For Dummies
  0-7645-1634-5
- The Internet For Dummies
  0-7645-4173-0
- iPod & iTunes For Dummies
  0-7645-7772-7
- Preventing Identity Theft For Dummies
  0-7645-7336-5
- Pro Tools All-in-One Desk Reference
  For Dummies
  0-7645-5714-9
- Roxio Easy Media Creator For Dummies
  0-7645-7131-1

* Separate Canadian edition also available
† Separate U.K. edition also available

Available wherever books are sold. For more information or to order direct: U.S. customers visit www.dummies.com or call 1-877-762-2974.
U.K. customers visit www.wileyeurope.com or call 0800 243407. Canadian customers visit www.wiley.ca or call 1-800-567-4797.

WILEY

SPORTS, FITNESS, PARENTING, RELIGION & SPIRITUALITY

0-7645-5146-9

0-7645-5418-2

Also available:
- Adoption For Dummies
  0-7645-5488-3
- Basketball For Dummies
  0-7645-5248-1
- The Bible For Dummies
  0-7645-5296-1
- Buddhism For Dummies
  0-7645-5359-3
- Catholicism For Dummies
  0-7645-5391-7
- Hockey For Dummies
  0-7645-5228-7
- Judaism For Dummies
  0-7645-5299-6
- Martial Arts For Dummies
  0-7645-5358-5
- Pilates For Dummies
  0-7645-5397-6
- Religion For Dummies
  0-7645-5264-3
- Teaching Kids to Read For Dummies
  0-7645-4043-2
- Weight Training For Dummies
  0-7645-5168-X
- Yoga For Dummies
  0-7645-5117-5

TRAVEL

0-7645-5438-7

0-7645-5453-0

Also available:
- Alaska For Dummies
  0-7645-1761-9
- Arizona For Dummies
  0-7645-6938-4
- Cancún and the Yucatán For Dummies
  0-7645-2437-2
- Cruise Vacations For Dummies
  0-7645-6941-4
- Europe For Dummies
  0-7645-5456-5
- Ireland For Dummies
  0-7645-5455-7
- Las Vegas For Dummies
  0-7645-5448-4
- London For Dummies
  0-7645-4277-X
- New York City For Dummies
  0-7645-6945-7
- Paris For Dummies
  0-7645-5494-8
- RV Vacations For Dummies
  0-7645-5443-3
- Walt Disney World & Orlando For Dummies
  0-7645-6943-0

GRAPHICS, DESIGN & WEB DEVELOPMENT

0-7645-4345-8

0-7645-5589-8

Also available:
- Adobe Acrobat 6 PDF For Dummies
  0-7645-3760-1
- Building a Web Site For Dummies
  0-7645-7144-3
- Dreamweaver MX 2004 For Dummies
  0-7645-4342-3
- FrontPage 2003 For Dummies
  0-7645-3882-9
- HTML 4 For Dummies
  0-7645-1995-6
- Illustrator CS For Dummies
  0-7645-4084-X
- Macromedia Flash MX 2004 For Dummies
  0-7645-4358-X
- Photoshop 7 All-in-One Desk Reference For Dummies
  0-7645-1667-1
- Photoshop CS Timesaving Techniques For Dummies
  0-7645-6782-9
- PHP 5 For Dummies
  0-7645-4166-8
- PowerPoint 2003 For Dummies
  0-7645-3908-6
- QuarkXPress 6 For Dummies
  0-7645-2593-X

NETWORKING, SECURITY, PROGRAMMING & DATABASES

0-7645-6852-3

0-7645-5784-X

Also available:
- A+ Certification For Dummies
  0-7645-4187-0
- Access 2003 All-in-One Desk Reference For Dummies
  0-7645-3988-4
- Beginning Programming For Dummies
  0-7645-4997-9
- C For Dummies
  0-7645-7068-4
- Firewalls For Dummies
  0-7645-4048-3
- Home Networking For Dummies
  0-7645-42796
- Network Security For Dummies
  0-7645-1679-5
- Networking For Dummies
  0-7645-1677-9
- TCP/IP For Dummies
  0-7645-1760-0
- VBA For Dummies
  0-7645-3989-2
- Wireless All In-One Desk Reference For Dummies
  0-7645-7496-5
- Wireless Home Networking For Dummies
  0-7645-3910-8

LaVergne, TN USA
21 April 2010
180073LV00005B/168/P

For Dummies

BESTSELLING
BOOK SERIES

Baby Names For Dummies®

MAY   2010

Cheat Sheet

Finding a Type of Name You Like

Although you may not know the exact name you want to give your child, you can figure out what kinds of names you like, which can guide you into choosing a name that best fits your preferences. Try this simple exercise: List names of people you don't know and rate the names on a scale of one to five. Listing the names of people you don't know means you can be more objective because you won't be prejudiced by how you feel about the person the name reminds you of. Then look for the following — if you find that some of the names share some similarities from the following characteristics, you can discover the type(s) of name(s) that you particularly like:

- ✔ Look for similar patterns.
- ✔ Look for similar sounds.
- ✔ Look for similar length.
- ✔ Look for similar rhythms.
- ✔ Look for similar types — traditional, colorful, and so on.

Working with or without Nicknames

Some people look forward to having nicknames for their children; others simply want their children to go by one name and one name only. Although you can't guarantee that your child won't be given a nickname by someone, you can reduce the chance that a nickname can be derived from your child's given name. On the other hand, if you do want nicknames, you can increase the chance that your child will have one. Whichever your preference, check out the following ideas to find ways to work with or around nicknames:

- ✔ **Use a one-syllable name.** If you want to reduce the chance of your child getting a nickname, consider naming your child with a one-syllable name — nicknames are often formed by using the syllable with the most stress (as in, Will or Willy, for William).
- ✔ **Use an "old standard."** If you want your child to have a nickname, use a name that's been around for a long time — those often have a vast array of nicknames associated with them.
- ✔ **Use a nickname as a first name.** If you want your child to go by just one name, you can use Meg or Maggie instead of Margaret or Tom or Tommy instead of Thomas. However, be aware that you and your child will someday want the name to fit all occasions so choosing a nickname that sounds more like it belongs on a 12-year-old may not be helpful if your Tommy is shooting for a VP position one of these days.

Baby Names For Dummies®

Putting the Name to the Test

Once you've found a name you like, an important step to take before declaring, "This is it!" is to test the name. Don't make the mistake of not testing the name on the following list of individuals — you want to be sure you get a well-rounded perspective on the name you've chosen:

- **Ask a friend.** Write the name out and have a friend try to pronounce it first. You can get a good idea of how often you may have to correct the pronunciation from this test. Plus, friends can let you know if it's hard to understand, if the rhythm doesn't sound right, and so on.

- **Ask a child.** If you want an honest opinion of what kind of nicknames children may derive from the name you've chosen, ask a group of children what kind of nicknames they can come up with.

- **Ask the world.** Plug your favorite name (and all of its spelling variants) into an Internet search engine and see what type of people have the same name and what kind of associations (good or bad) that name may have with brand names, businesses, and famous faces.

- **Ask yourself.** Write the name out in several variations and post it somewhere where you have to look at it every day — how do you feel about it after a week or a month?

Choosing a Name That Fits All Occasions

You definitely want to choose a name that your child can live with . . . forever. So think about the following when choosing a name for your child:

- **Imagine everyday contexts.** Imagine how you may be addressing or talking to your child, such as announcing dinnertime or getting your child's attention across a crowded store. Say it out loud and see how it sounds — you won't get far if you try to sternly scold your child with his or her full formal name and you burst out giggling every time you say it.

- **Imagine important milestones — especially as an adult.** Imagine a play-by-play announcement on the sports field, names read out at a graduation, a wedding invitation, and so on. Make sure the name sounds appropriate for an adult; otherwise, your child may end up the laughing stock of the world when the Nobel Prize Committee announces his or her name. (Okay, maybe we need to scale the fantasies back a little.)

- **Imagine a wide range of contexts.** Make sure the name has the flexibility to be both formal and familiar and that it sounds like it can play as well as preside over meetings.

Wiley, the Wiley Publishing logo, For Dummies, the Dummies Man logo, the For Dummies Bestselling Book Series logo and all related trade dress are trademarks or registered trademarks of John Wiley & Sons, Inc. and/or its affiliates. All other trademarks are property of their respective owners.

For Dummies: Bestselling Book Series for Beginners